# THE MODERN
## CRITICAL
## SPECTRUM

PRENTICE-HALL ENGLISH LITERATURE SERIES

Maynard Mack, *editor*

PRENTICE-HALL INTERNATIONAL, INC.
*London • Tokyo • Sydney • Paris*
PRENTICE-HALL OF CANADA, LTD.
PRENTICE-HALL DE MEXICO, S.A.

# THE MODERN CRITICAL SPECTRUM

*Edited by*   GERALD JAY GOLDBERG
NANCY MARMER GOLDBERG

PRENTICE-HALL, INC.   ENGLEWOOD CLIFFS, N.J.   1962

*for* R O B B I E

# PREFACE

"Clea, my dear" I said. . . . "I have been actually meditating a book of criticism."
"Criticism!" she echoed sharply, as if the word were an insult. And she smacked
me full across the mouth—a stinging blow which brought tears to my eyes and cut
the inside of my lip against my teeth.

Lawrence Durrell, Clea

Though the critic's lot in fiction during the twentieth century has been
a hard one, in the real world he has never had it better. His eye is clear, his
appetite sharp, and his calling respected and respectable, despite the caviling
of those few diehards and new romantics who feel that he has arrogated too
much power to himself. The prestige of criticism in our age may have been
paralleled in other periods, but the over-all quantity, diversity, and quality
of the work has probably not been equalled.

For the student of modern literary criticism, the prodigious output of our
century may seem patternless and confusing. It is the main purpose of this
book to "impose cosmos on chaos" by clarifying and categorizing the dominant critical tendencies of our age. Rather than present a chronological history of twentieth-century criticism or a compilation of the major work of sem-
inal figures, we have organized our material to reveal the principal kinds of
criticism extant today. It is not our intention to suggest that each critic be
identified exclusively with the method which his particular essay represents or
to propound the simplistic idea that any critic can be neatly fitted into one
niche; few good critics confine themselves to a single mode of apprehending
literature and in practice the various methods used may overlap, even in single essays. Though the reader will detect such overlapping in many instances
(Trilling's use of the materials of biography in an essentially socio-cultural
discussion of *The Princess Casamassima* is an obvious example), our attempt
has been to choose works which illustrate as clearly and exclusively as possible a particular method of interpretation. Our emphasis throughout has
been on the criticism rather than the critic. Nevertheless, as is apparent from
the table of contents, the writers we have selected are, by and large, the
major critical figures, and among the articles included are some of the most
significant critical statements of our age. Other essays, less well known and
not easily accessible elsewhere in book form, we have reprinted on the basis
of their merit and illustrative value. All the literary genres are touched
upon, and among the principal figures discussed are Shakespeare, Shaw,
Johnson, Austen, George Eliot, Melville, James, Flaubert, Bellow, Donne,

Herbert, Milton, Pope, Coleridge, Wordsworth, Keats, and Hart Crane. Because of our emphasis on the various *methods* of criticism and the wide range of primary sources treated, this book should be as relevant for the student first learning how to analyze literature as for the specialist in the history of literary criticism.

Each division of this book contains two parts. In every instance the first essay is a theoretical statement of the particular method of criticism or approach to literature employed in that division. The second part consists of practical applications of the theory. When a division contains more than one example of applied criticism, it is because we have attempted to synthesize different, but related, critical methods under a single rubric. So, for instance, Herbert Read's theoretical statement of the function of psychological criticism is illustrated by Ernst Kris's Freudian analysis of Prince Hal's relationship to Henry IV and to Falstaff, as well as Maud Bodkin's Jungian concern with archetypical images in Coleridge's "The Ancient Mariner." David Daiches' essay on the importance to the critic of the relationship between fiction and the society which produces it is indicative of the concerns of socio-cultural criticism, but does not necessarily reflect the particular bias of its practitioners, e.g. Leslie Fiedler's treatment of Saul Bellow in terms of his "Urban-Jewish-American" heritage, Edmund Wilson's stress on the politics of Flaubert, Christopher Caudwell's Marxist interpretation of Shaw's failings, or Lionel Trilling's emphasis on the background and "social texture" of a novel by Henry James.

The largest single division of this book is given over to the uses of formal analysis, and not without cause. Even the most casual observer of the modern scene is aware that close textual reading and concern with form have been the chief critical obsessions of our time. During the past forty years, the "New Criticism" has focused its attention on such means of literary art as tension, ambiguity, structure, diction, imagery, wit, irony, and paradox. Some of these aspects of literature are defined within the section of "practical" essays, and we have tried here to include a representative sampling of the differing modes of analysis prevalent within the formalist's methodology —a sampling which should help to familiarize the student with concepts and terminology basic to much criticism today. Allen Tate's discussion of tension in poetry and Mark Schorer's comments on the importance of form —or *"achieved* content"—in fiction are perhaps the two best known essays in this section; we reprint them here as excellent and useful examples of the "New Critical" approach. Robert Heilman's suggestive analysis of the relationship between image pattern and thematic statement in *King Lear* and Maynard Mack's precise dissection of Pope's metaphorical language demonstrate the virtues of close reading. R. P. Blackmur, in discussing the language of Hart Crane's poetry, illuminates for us the "exciting splendor of a great failure." William Empson, Kenneth Burke, and John Crowe Ransom are familiar names to the reader of modern literary criticism. Empson on complex poetic attitudes and ambiguity, Ransom on Shakespeare's Latinate language, and Burke on "symbolic action" in Keats's "Ode on a Grecian Urn," are further instances of formal criticism in practice. The theory underlying (but not necessarily confining) this type of criticism is succinctly stated by Cleanth Brooks's "The Formalist Critic."

To creative writers as well as critics, the sense of a tradition has always been indispensable; constantly changing, however, is the sense of what constitutes *the* tradition. For our age, T. S. Eliot has been Moses and his pronouncements have exercised a decisive influence on modern literary taste. The controversy stemming from Eliot's first essay on Milton in 1936, in which he condemns the poet, and his subsequent retractation eleven years later are important documents in illustrating the way a tradition is established. The essay by F. R. Leavis is one of the many elaborations, this time with reference to fiction, of the idea of a tradition in English literature.

Less susceptible to fads in critical fashion, as evidenced by the tenacious hold they have maintained even to the present, are the critical methods which bring to bear biography, moral and didactic considerations, and the techniques of historical scholarship. We include here contemporary examples of these types of critical approach, though their counterparts exist in certain earlier periods of literary history and they are in no way peculiar to the twentieth century. E. M. W. Tillyard, in his controversy with C. S. Lewis, defends the position of the biographical critic against the charge of "the personal heresy" by making a valuable distinction between literary gossip and significant biographical information which gives the critic insight into the "mental pattern" of an author. Our selection from F. O. Matthiessen's discussion of Melville demonstrates the place of biography in criticism. In his essay on the humanist position, Douglas Bush reasserts for our time the didactic, ethical role of the critic; and Irving Babbitt, who was one of the most influential leaders of the New Humanism in America, writes here about another teacher and moralist, Samuel Johnson. A. S. P. Woodhouse and Louis Martz, in the essays we have reprinted, elucidate the relevance of scholarship to understanding and appraisal. Woodhouse's theoretical statement indicates the corrective and suggestive value of scholarly information; both of these attributes are evident in the excerpt we include from *The Poetry of Meditation.*

In contrast to what seems a growing academicism among followers of the formalist strategy, mythic criticism subsists today with undiminished vitality. American critics, in particular, are discovering the applicability of mythic patterns to American literature, and R. W. B. Lewis's use of "the matter of Adam" is an example of the fruitfulness of this line of criticism. Although the essays by Lewis and Philip Wheelwright have their roots in psychological criticism, notably of the Jungian school, mythic inquiry has its own *raison d'être* and, we feel, deserves separate consideration as a method of literary criticism.

A necessary but lamentable consequence of selection is omission. We are uncomfortably aware of the number of fine essays we should have liked to include. Some, fortunately, are reproduced elsewhere and easily available. Although we might have represented here such other interesting approaches as those embodied in Neo-Aristotelian, Neo-Romantic, and Existentialist criticism, we have been obliged to limit ourselves to what we consider to be the dominant critical tendencies of the twentieth century in America and England.

We wish to acknowledge the usefulness to our work and to suggest as valuable aids to the student the studies of modern literary criticism by

Stanley Edgar Hyman (*The Armed Vision: A Study in the Method of Modern Literary Criticism.* New York: Alfred A. Knopf, Inc., 1948), William Van O'Connor (*An Age of Criticism: 1900–1950.* Chicago: Henry Regnery Co., 1952), and René Wellek and Austin Warren (*Theory of Literature.* New York: Harcourt, Brace & World, Inc., 1949).

We wish to thank David Cole of Prentice-Hall, who first encouraged us to begin this book. Maynard Mack has most graciously assisted us throughout our work on matters minor and major. An especial word of gratitude is due to Professor O'Connor, who generously consented to write the introduction to this volume and whose advice, as always, was valuable and much appreciated.

Gerald Jay Goldberg<br>Nancy Marmer Goldberg

Hanover, New Hampshire

# CONTENTS

CONTENTS

## 2. THE USES OF THE SOCIO-CULTURAL MILIEU

**the theory**

**the uses**

## 3. THE USES OF TRADITION

**the theory**

**the uses**

# 7. THE USES OF PSYCHOLOGY

# 8. THE USES OF MYTH

# APPENDIX

# INTRODUCTION

Most students of literature, if asked to say how modern criticism differs from earlier criticism, would probably reply in some such fashion as this: "Oh, you mean the so-called 'New Criticism.' Well, practitioners of it are preoccupied with the *formal* characteristics of a play, poem, or novel. They are not as concerned as earlier critics were with the writer or with the audience. In fact, citing a writer's stated intention has been called the 'intentional fallacy' and a preoccupation with audience reactions has been called the 'affective fallacy.' Modern criticism concentrates on the work of art itself."

Meyer Abrams, in *The Mirror and the Lamp,* has said that there are four approaches to critical theory. One is the theory of *mimesis.* Plato and Aristotle assumed that a play was an imitation of an action. It was not history. Literary criticism up to the eighteenth century accepted this theory without question. The second, the pragmatic theory, emphasizes the audience. For example, Aristotle's doctrine of *catharsis,* the purging of pity and fear, concerned the audience. Literary criticism throughout the Christian era stressed the audience's response to the literary work. Horace stressed both the word *beauty* and the word *utility.* The third, the expressive theory, held the largest appeal for the Romantic period. It had to do with the poet's imagination, his moral nature, and it led to such a dictum as "Style is the man." The fourth, the objective theory, emphasizes the work itself. Cleanth Brooks's doctrine of "irony," about the nature of poetic language, is objective. And Mark Schorer's dictum, "Style is the subject," implies an acceptance of the objective theory.

Mr. Abrams says the four theories collectively endeavor to explain "the total situation of a work of art." It is true that currently a great many articles are written which examine the "structure" of a play, poem, or short story; which trace patterns of imagery, or reveal the meanings of key symbols. Classroom examinations of literary texts, modeled on the famous Brooks and Warren *Understanding Poetry,* tend to take this line. A reader is encouraged to be aware of aesthetic properties, formal elements, and arrangements of a work of art. It is an approach which invites a sophisticated reading of a text.

Yet it would be an error to say, as we sometimes do, that modern literary criticism is almost exclusively objective. There is too much evidence to the contrary. All four of Mr. Abrams's critical theories are to be found in modern criticism.

The mimetic theory has been emphasized by the University of Chicago Aristotelians. Someone, however, might say that they were almost alone in emphasizing mimesis. Perhaps so. But what about our concern with myth, as we find it in studies by Ernst Cassirer, Philip Wheelwright, Richard Chase, William Troy, and others? Aristotle's mimesis emphasizes the relation of the literary work to the "universe," to "nature," and to historical actions. The study of the literary work in relation to myth is also an attempt to see it in relation to the universe. Similar scholarly and critical examinations of works in relation to a "climate of opinion," a "world picture," an "age's myth," or a "country's spirit" are simply other ways of studying mimesis.

Nowadays we are likely to hear little academic jokes about the foolishness of trying to judge poetry by our emotional response to it—if it causes our skin to turn cold, raises gooseflesh, or stiffens the bristles in one's beard. Our response emotionally and intellectually, however, is really the last court of appeal. A judicious, sophisticated and learned critical article may show that a particular poem is worthy of the highest acclaim—yet a small voice inside us may say, "I don't feel it." We listen to that voice. We also hear a good deal about the fatuousness of didactic art. We want our morals in art to be treated indirectly—but the point is we want them treated. Not only the New Humanists have been concerned with ethical questions. Every critic worth his salt has been concerned. Trying to judge a work of art apart from ethical or moral considerations is like judging a glass of whiskey without relation to its alcoholic content. Moral considerations relate to the literary work. They also relate to the audience. The ancient rhetoricians knew this. So do we.

Coleridge's doctrine of the poet's imagination, an expressive theory doctrine, is commonly admired today. Most critics, for example, I. A. Richards, Kenneth Burke, or Cleanth Brooks, refer to him with deference. Chapter XV of the *Biographia* is frequently cited. Nor have we given up the "biographical fallacy," at least not entirely. Biographies of literary figures often turn on an effort to explain a writer's "wound," his psychological hurt. Having discovered and analyzed it, the biographer then proceeds to relate it to the writer's poems or novels. There are other examples of "expressive" theories. When Eliot, in "Tradition and the Individual Talent," speaks of the poet surrendering himself "as he is at the moment to something which is more valuable," to tradition, he is an "expressionist" critic.

Not even the "objective" theorists are pure. They know that a political myth is a part of *Hamlet,* a "world picture" a part of the meaning of *Henry IV,* a seventeenth-century connotation of "soule" a part of a seventeenth-century poem's meaning. Even so "pure" an objective critic as R. P. Blackmur, in "A Burden for Critics," discusses a poet's symbols in relation to the culture he is trying to comprehend and express. The objective critic cannot ignore the universe, the author, or the audience.

The modern critical spectrum *is* different from the critical spectrums of Aristotle, Dante, Sir Philip Sidney, Boileau, Goethe, Arnold, Pater, or Croce—but not so different as we sometimes suggest. Each of these critics has a great deal in common with his fellow critics, up and down the ages. And we have a lot in common with all of them. It is a matter of emphasis. In tending to stress objective theory we are not doing anything amiss. It is the work of art that gives rise to critical theory in the first place. To put the emphasis on the work of art is as good a place as any to put it. But it is not the only place the emphasis can be put.

William Van O'Connor

# THE MODERN
## CRITICAL
## SPECTRUM

# 1. THE USES OF FORMAL ANALYSIS

## The Theory

*Cleanth Brooks*

## THE FORMALIST CRITIC

Here are some articles of faith I could subscribe to:

*That literary criticism is a description and an evaluation of its object.*

*That the primary concern of criticism is with the problem of unity—the kind of whole which the literary work forms or fails to form, and the relation of the various parts to each other in building up this whole.*

*That the formal relations in a work of literature may include, but certainly exceed, those of logic.*

*That in a successful work, form and content cannot be separated.*

*That form is meaning.*

*That literature is ultimately metaphorical and symbolic.*

*That the general and the universal are not seized upon by abstraction, but got at through the concrete and the particular.*

*That literature is not a surrogate for religion.*

*That, as Allen Tate says, "specific moral problems" are the subject matter of literature, but that the purpose of literature is not to point a moral.*

*That the principles of criticism define the area relevant to literary criticism; they do not constitute a method for carrying out the criticism.*

Such statements as these would not, however, even though greatly elaborated, serve any useful purpose here. The interested reader already knows the general nature of the critical position adumbrated—or, if he does not, he can find it set forth in writings of mine or of other critics of like sympathy. Moreover, a condensed restatement of the position here would probably beget as many misunderstandings as have past attempts to set it forth. It seems much more profitable to use the present occasion for dealing with some persistent misunderstandings and objections.

In the first place, to make the poem or the novel the central concern of criticism has appeared to mean cutting it loose from its author and from his life as a man, with his own particular hopes, fears, interests, conflicts, etc. A criticism so limited may seem bloodless and hollow. It will seem so to the typical professor of literature in the graduate school, where the study of literature is still primarily a study of the ideas and personality of the author as revealed in his letters, his diaries, and the recorded conversations of his friends. It will certainly seem so to literary gossip columnists who purvey literary chitchat. It may also seem so to the young poet or novelist, beset with his own problems of composition and with his struggles to find a subject and a style and to get a hearing for himself.

In the second place, to emphasize the work seems to involve severing it from those who actually read it, and this severance may seem drastic and therefore disastrous. After all, literature is written to be read. Wordsworth's poet was a man speaking to men. In each Sunday *Times,* Mr. J. Donald Adams points out that the hungry sheep look up and are not fed; and less strenuous moralists than Mr. Adams are bound to feel a proper revulsion against "mere aestheticism." Moreover, if we neglect the audience which reads the work, including that for which it was presumably written, the literary historian is prompt to point out that the kind of audience that Pope had did condition the kind of poetry that he wrote. The poem has its roots in history, past or present. Its place in the historical context simply cannot be ignored.

I have stated these objections as sharply as I can because I am sympathetic with the state of mind which is prone to voice them. Man's experience is indeed a seamless garment, no part of which can be separated from the rest. Yet if we urge this fact of inseparability against the drawing of distinctions, then there is no point in talking about criticism at all. I am assuming that distinctions are necessary and useful and indeed inevitable.

The formalist critic knows as well as anyone that poems and plays and novels are written by men—that they do not somehow happen—and that they are written as expressions of particular personalities and are written from all sorts of motives—for money, from a desire to express oneself, for the sake of a cause, etc. Moreover, the formalist critic knows as well as anyone that literary works are merely potential until they are read—that is, that they are recreated in the minds of actual readers, who vary enormously in their capabilities, their interests, their prejudices, their ideas. But the formalist critic is concerned primarily with the work itself. Speculation on the mental processes of the author takes the critic away from the work into biography and psychology. There is no reason, of course, why he should not turn away into biography and psychology. Such explorations are very much worth making. But they should not be confused with an account of the work. Such studies describe the process of composition, not the structure of the thing composed, and they may be performed quite as validly for the poor work as for the good one. They may be validly performed for any kind of expression—non-literary as well as literary.

On the other hand, exploration of the various readings which the work has received also takes the critic away from the work into psychology and the history of taste. The various imports of a given work may well be worth studying. I. A. Richards has put us all in his debt by demonstrating what different experiences may be derived from the same poem by an apparently homogeneous group of readers; and the scholars have pointed out, all along, how different Shakespeare appeared to an 18th Century as compared with a 19th Century audience; or how sharply divergent are the estimates of John Donne's lyrics from historical period to historical period. But such work, valuable and necessary as it may be, is to be distinguished from a criticism of the work itself. The formalist critic, because he wants to criticize the work itself, makes two assumptions: (1) he assumes that the relevant part of the author's intention is what he got actually into his work; that is, he assumes that the author's intention *as realized* is the "intention" that counts, not necessarily what he was conscious of trying to do, or what he now re-members he was then trying to do. And (2) the formalist critic assumes an ideal reader: that is, instead of focusing on the varying spectrum of possible readings, he attempts to find a central point of reference from which he can focus upon the structure of the poem or novel.

But there *is* no ideal reader, someone is prompt to point out, and he will probably add that it is sheer arrogance that allows the critic, with his own blindsides and prejudices, to put himself in the position of that ideal reader. There is no ideal reader, of course, and I suppose that the practising critic can never be too often reminded of the gap between his reading and the "true" reading of the poem. But for the purpose of focusing upon the poem rather than upon his own reactions, it is a defensible strategy. Finally, of course, it is the strategy that all critics of whatever persuasion are forced to adopt. (The alternatives are desperate: either we say that one person's reading is as good as another's and equate those readings on a basis of absolute equality and thus deny the possibility of any standard reading. Or else we take a lowest common denominator of the various readings that have been made; that is, we frankly move from literary criticism into socio-psychology. To propose taking a consensus of the opinions of "quali-fied" readers is simply to split the ideal reader into a group of ideal readers.) As consequences of the distinction just referred to, the formalist critic rejects two popular tests for literary value. The first proves the value of the work from the author's "sincerity" (or the intensity of the author's feelings as he composed it). If we heard that Mr. Guest testified that he put his heart and soul into his poems, we would not be very much impressed, though I should see no reason to doubt such a statement from Mr. Guest. It would simply be critically irrelevant. Ernest Hemingway's statement in a recent issue of *Time* magazine that he counts his last novel his best is of interest for Hemingway's biography, but most readers of *Across the River and Into the Trees* would agree that it proves nothing at all about the value of the novel—that in this case the judgment is simply pathetically inept. We dis-count also such tests for poetry as that proposed by A. E. Housman—the bristling of his beard at the reading of a good poem. The intensity of his reaction has critical significance only in proportion as we have already learned to trust him as a reader. Even so, what it tells us is something about Housman—nothing decisive about the poem.

It is unfortunate if this playing down of such responses seems to deny humanity to either writer or reader. The critic may enjoy certain works very much and may be indeed intensely moved by them. I am, and I have no embarrassment in admitting the fact; but a detailed description of my emotional state on reading certain works has little to do with indicating to an interested reader what the work is and how the parts of it are related.

Should all criticism, then, be self-effacing and analytic? I hope that the answer is implicit in what I have already written, but I shall go on to spell it out. Of course not. That will depend upon the occasion and the audience. In practice, the critic's job is rarely a purely critical one. He is much more likely to be involved in dozens of more or less related tasks, some of them trivial, some of them important. He may be trying to get a hearing for a new author, or to get the attention of the freshman sitting in the back row. He may be comparing two authors, or editing a text; writing a brief newspaper review or reading a paper before the Modern Language Association. He may even be simply talking with a friend, talking about literature for the hell of it. Parable, anecdote, epigram, metaphor—these and a hundred other devices may be thoroughly legitimate for his varying purposes. He is certainly not to be asked to suppress his personal enthusiasms or his interest in social history or in politics. Least of all is he being asked to *present* his criticisms as the close reading of a text. Tact, common sense, and uncommon sense if he has it, are all requisite if the practising critic is to do his various jobs well.

But it will do the critic no harm to have a clear idea of what his specific job as a critic is. I can sympathize with writers who are tired of reading rather drab "critical analyses," and who recommend brighter, more amateur, and more "human" criticism. As ideals, these are excellent; as recipes for improving criticism, I have my doubts. Appropriate vulgarizations of these ideals are already flourishing, and have long flourished—in the class room presided over by the college lecturer of infectious enthusiasm, in the gossipy Book-of-the-Month Club bulletins, and in the columns of the *Saturday Review of Literature*.

I have assigned the critic a modest, though I think an important, role. With reference to the help which the critic can give to the practising artist, the role is even more modest. As critic, he can give only negative help. Literature is not written by formula: he can have no formula to offer. Perhaps he can do little more than indicate whether in his opinion the work has succeeded or failed. Healthy criticism and healthy creation do tend to go hand in hand. Everything else being equal, the creative artist is better off for being in touch with a vigorous criticism. But the other considerations are never equal, the case is always special, and in a given case the proper advice *could* be: quit reading criticism altogether, or read political science or history or philosophy—or join the army, or join the church.

There is certainly no doubt that the kind of specific and positive help that someone like Ezra Pound was able to give to several writers of our time is in one sense the most important kind of criticism that there can be. I think that it is not unrelated to the kind of criticism that I have described: there is the same intense concern with the text which is being built up, the same concern with "technical problems." But many other things are involved—matters which lie outside the specific ambit of criticism altogether, among them a knowledge of the personality of the particular writer, the ability to stimulate, to make positive suggestions.

A literary work is a document and as a document can be analysed in terms of the forces that have produced it, or it may be manipulated as a force in its own right. It mirrors the past, it may influence the future. These facts it would be futile to deny, and I know of no critic who does deny them. But the reduction of a work of literature to its causes does not constitute literary criticism; nor does an estimate of its effects. Good literature is more than effective rhetoric applied to true ideas—even if we could agree upon a philosophical yardstick for measuring the truth of ideas and even if we could find some way that transcended nose-counting for determining the effectiveness of the rhetoric.

A recent essay by Lionel Trilling bears very emphatically upon this point. (I refer to him the more readily because Trilling has registered some of his objections to the critical position that I maintain.) In the essay entitled "The Meaning of a Literary Idea," Trilling discusses the debt to Freud and Spengler of four American writers, O'Neill, Dos Passos, Wolfe, and Faulkner. Very justly, as it seems to me, he chooses Faulkner as the contemporary writer who, along with Ernest Hemingway, best illustrates the power and importance of ideas in literature. Trilling is thoroughly aware that his choice will seem shocking and perhaps perverse, "because," as he writes, "Hemingway and Faulkner have insisted on their indifference to the conscious intellectual tradition of our time and have acquired the reputation of achieving their effects by means that have the least possible connection with any sort of intellectuality or even with intelligence."

Here Trilling shows not only acute discernment but an admirable honesty in electing to deal with the hard cases—with the writers who do not clearly and easily make the case for the importance of ideas. I applaud the discernment and the honesty, but I wonder whether the whole discussion in his essay does not indicate that Trilling is really much closer to the so-called "new critics" than perhaps he is aware. For Trilling, one notices, rejects any simple one-to-one relation between the truth of the idea and the value of the literary work in which it is embodied. Moreover, he does not claim that "recognizable ideas of a force or weight are 'used' in the work," or "new ideas of a certain force and weight are 'produced' by the work." He praises rather the fact that we feel that Hemingway and Faulkner are "intensely at work upon the recalcitrant stuff of life." The last point is made the matter of real importance. Whereas Dos Passos, O'Neill, and Wolfe make us "feel that *they* feel that they have said the last word," "we seldom have the sense that [Hemingway and Faulkner] . . . have misrepresented to themselves the nature and the difficulty of the matter they work on."

Trilling has chosen to state the situation in terms of the writer's activity (Faulkner is intensely at work, etc.). But this judgment is plainly an inference from the quality of Faulkner's novels—Trilling has not simply heard Faulkner say that he has had to struggle with his work. (I take it Mr. Hemingway's declaration about the effort he put into the last novel impresses Trilling as little as it impresses the rest of us.)

Suppose, then, that we tried to state Mr. Trilling's point, not in terms of the effort of the artist, but in terms of the structure of the work itself. Should we not get something very like the terms used by the formalist critics? A description in terms of "tensions," of symbolic development, of ironies and their resolution? In short, is not the formalist critic trying to describe in terms of the dynamic form of the work itself how the recalcitrancy of the material is acknowledged and dealt with?

Trilling's definition of "ideas" makes it still easier to accommodate my position to his. I have already quoted a passage in which he repudiates the notion that one has to show how recognizable ideas are "used" in the work, or new ideas are "produced" by the work. He goes on to write: "All that we need to do is account for a certain aesthetic effect as being in some important part achieved by a mental process which is not different from the process by which discursive ideas are conceived, and which is to be judged by some of the criteria by which an idea is judged." One would have to look far to find a critic "formal" enough to object to this. What some of us have been at pains to insist upon is that literature does not simply "exemplify" ideas or "produce" ideas—as Trilling acknowledges. But no one claims that the writer is an inspired idiot. He uses his mind and his reader ought to use his, in processes "not different from the process by which discursive ideas are conceived." Literature is not inimical to ideas. It thrives upon ideas, but it does not present ideas patly and neatly. It involves them with the "recalcitrant stuff of life." The literary critic's job is to deal with that involvement.

The mention of Faulkner invites a closing comment upon the critic's specific job. As I have described it, it may seem so modest that one could take its performance for granted. But consider the misreadings of Faulkner now current, some of them the work of the most brilliant critics that we have, some of them quite wrong-headed, and demonstrably so. What is true of Faulkner is only less true of many another author, including many writers of the past. Literature has many "uses"—and critics propose new uses, some of them exciting and spectacular. But all the multiform uses to which literature can be put rest finally upon our knowing what a given work "means." That knowledge is basic.

# The Uses

*R. P. Blackmur*

## NEW THRESHOLDS, NEW ANATOMIES:

### NOTES ON A TEXT OF HART CRANE

**I**

It is a striking and disheartening fact that the three most ambitious poems of our time should all have failed in similar ways: in composition, in independent objective existence, and in intelligibility of language. *The Waste Land,* the *Cantos,* and *The Bridge* all fail to hang together structurally in the sense that "Prufrock," "Envoi," and "Praise for an Urn"—lesser works in every other respect—do hang together. Each of the three poems requires of the reader that he supply from outside the poem, and with the help of clues only, the important, *controlling* part of what we may loosely call the meaning. And each again deliberately presents passages, lines, phrases, and single words which no amount of outside work can illumine. The fact is striking because, aside from other considerations of magnitude, relevance, and scope, these are not the faults we lay up typically against the great dead. The typical great poet is profoundly rational, integrating, and, excepting minor accidents of incapacity, a master of ultimate verbal clarity. Light, radiance, and wholeness remain the attributes of serious art. And the fact is disheartening because no time could have greater need than our own for rational art. No time certainly could surrender more than ours does daily, with drums beating, to fanatic politics and despotically construed emotions.

But let us desert the disheartening for the merely striking aspect, and handle the matter, as we can, within the realm of poetry, taking up other matters only tacitly and by implication. Let us say provisionally that in their more important works Eliot, Pound, and Crane lack the ultimate, if mythical, quality of aseity, that quality of completeness, of independence, so great that it seems underived and an effect of pure creation. The absence of aseity may be approached variously in a given poet; but every approach to be instructive, even to find the target at all, must employ a rational

mode and the right weapon. These notes intend to examine certain characteristic passages of Hart Crane's poems as modes of language and to determine how and to what degree the effects intended were attained. The
rationale is that of poetic language; the weapons are analysis and comparison. But there are other matters which must be taken up first before
the language itself can be approached at all familiarly.

Almost everyone who has written on Crane has found in him a central
defect, either of imagination or execution, or both. Long ago, in his Preface
to *White Buildings,* Allen Tate complained that for all his talent Crane had
not found a suitable theme. Later, in his admirable review of *The Bridge,*
Yvor Winters brought and substantiated the charge (by demonstrating the
exceptions) that even when he had found a theme Crane could not entirely
digest it and at crucial points simply was unable to express it in objective
form. These charges hold; and all that is here said is only in explication of
them from a third point of view.

Waldo Frank, in his Introduction to the *Collected Poems,* acting more
as an apologist than a critic, proffers two explanations of Crane's incom-
pleteness as a poet, to neither of which can I assent, but of which I think
both should be borne in mind. Mr. Frank believes that Crane will be understood and found whole when our culture has been restored from revolutionary collectivism to a predominant interest in the person; when the
value of expressing the personal in the terms of the cosmic shall again seem
supreme. This hypothesis would seem untenable unless it is construed as
relevant to the present examination; when it runs immediately into the
hands of the obvious but useful statement that Crane was interested in
persons rather than the class struggle. Mr. Frank's other explanation is that
Crane's poetry was based upon the mystical perception of the "organic
continuity between the self and a seemingly chaotic world." Crane "was
too virile to deny the experience of continuity; he let the world pour in;
and since his nuclear self was not disciplined to detachment from his nerves
and passions, he lived exacerbated in a constant swing between ecstasy and
exhaustion." I confess I do not understand "organic continuity" in this
context, and all my efforts to do so are defeated by the subsequent word
"detachment." Nor can I see how this particular concept of continuity
can be very useful without the addition and control of a thorough super-
naturalism. The control for mystic psychology is theology, and what is
thereby controlled is the idiosyncrasy of insight, not the technique of poetry.

What Mr. Frank says not-rationally can be usefully re-translated to
that plane on which skilled readers ordinarily read good poetry; which is a
rational plane; which is, on analysis, the plane of competent technical appreciation. Such a translation, while committing grave injustice on Mr.
Frank, comes nearer doing justice to Crane. It restores and brings home the
strictures of Tate and Winters, and it brings judgment comparatively back
to the minute particulars (Blake's phrase) which are alone apprehensible.
To compose the nuclear self and the seemingly chaotic world is to find a
suitable theme, and the inability so to compose rises as much from immaturity and indiscipline of the major poetic uses of language as from personal immaturity and indiscipline. Baudelaire only rarely reached the point
of self-discipline and Whitman never; but Baudelaire's language is both

disciplined and mature, and Whitman's sometimes so. *Les Fleurs du Mal* are a profound poetic ordering of a life disorderly, distraught, and deracinated, a life excruciated, in the semantic sense of that word, to the extreme. And Whitman, on his side, by a very different use of language, gave torrential expression to the romantic disorder of life in flux, whereas his private sensibility seems either to have been suitably well-ordered or to have felt no need of order.

Whitman and Baudelaire are not chosen with reference to Crane by accident but because they are suggestively apposite. The suggestion may be made, not as blank truth but for the light there is in it, that Crane had the sensibility typical of Baudelaire and so misunderstood himself that he attempted to write *The Bridge* as if he had the sensibility typical of Whitman. Whitman characteristically let himself go in words, in any words and by all means the handiest, until his impulse was used up. Baudelaire no less characteristically caught himself up in his words, recording, ordering, and binding together the implications and tacit meanings of his impulse until in his best poems the words he used are, as I. A. Richards would say, inexhaustible objects of meditation. Baudelaire aimed at control, Whitman at release. It is for these reasons that the influence of Whitman is an impediment to the *practice* (to be distinguished from the reading) of poetry, and that the influence of Baudelaire is re-animation itself. (It may be noted that Baudelaire had at his back a well-articulated version of the Catholic Church to control the moral aspect of his meanings, where Whitman had merely an inarticulate pantheism.)

To apply this dichotomy to Crane is not difficult if it is done tentatively, without requiring that it be too fruitful, and without requiring that it be final at all. The clue or nexus is found, aside from the poems themselves, in certain prose statements. Letters are suspect and especially letters addressed to a patron, since the aim is less conviction by argument than the persuasive dramatization of an attitude. It is therefore necessary in the following extract from a letter to Otto Kahn that the reader accomplish a reduction in the magnitude of terms.

Of the section of *The Bridge* called "The Dance" Crane wrote: "Here one is on the pure mythical and smoky soil at last! Not only do I describe the conflict between the two races in this dance—I also became identified with the Indian and his world before it is over, which is the only method possible of ever really possessing the Indian and his world as a cultural factor." Etc. I suggest that, confronted with the tight, tense, intensely personal lyric quatrains of the verse itself, verse compact with the deliberately inarticulate interfusion of the senses, Crane's statement of intention has only an *ipse dixit* pertinence; that taken otherwise, taken as a living index of substance, it only multiplies the actual confusion of the verse and impoverishes its achieved scope. Taken seriously, it puts an impossible burden on the reader: the burden of reading two poems at once, the one that appears and the "real" poem which does not appear except by an act of faith. This would be reading by legerdemain, which at the moment of achievement must always collapse, self-obfuscated.

Again, in the same letter, Crane wrote that, "The range of *The Bridge* has been called colossal by more than one critic who has seen the ms.,

and though I have found the subject to be vaster than I had at first realized,
I am still highly confident of its final articulation into a continuous and
eloquent span. . . . *The Aeneid* was not written in two years—nor in four,
and in more than one sense I feel justified in comparing the historical and
cultural scope of *The Bridge* to that great work. It is at least a symphony
with an epic theme, and a work of considerable profundity and inspiration."

The question is whether this was wishful thinking of the vague order
commonest in revery, convinced and sincere statement of intention, or an
effect of the profound duplicity—a deception in the very will of things—in
Crane's fundamental attitudes toward his work; or whether Crane merely
misunderstood the logical import of the words he used. I incline to the
notion of duplicity, since it is beneath and sanctions the other notions as
well; the very duplicity by which the talents of a Baudelaire appear to their
possessor disguised and disfigured in the themes of a Whitman, the same
fundamental duplicity of human knowledge whereby an accustomed disorder seems the order most to be cherished, or whereby a religion which at
its heart denies life enriches living. In the particular reference, if I am right,
it is possible to believe that Crane labored to perfect both the strategy and
the tactics of language so as to animate and maneuver his perceptions—and
then fought the wrong war and against an enemy that displayed, to his
weapons, no vulnerable target. He wrote in a language of which it was the
virtue to accrete, modify, and interrelate moments of emotional vision—
moments at which the sense of being gains its greatest access—moments
at which, by the felt nature of knowledge, the revealed thing is its own
meaning; and he attempted to apply his language, in his major effort, to a
theme that required a sweeping, discrete, indicative, anecdotal language, a
language in which, by force of movement, mere cataloguing can replace
and often surpass representation. He used the private lyric to write the
cultural epic; used the mode of intensive contemplation, which secures
ends, to present the mind's actions, which have no ends. The confusion of
tool and purpose not only led him astray in conceiving his themes; it obscured at crucial moments the exact character of the work he was actually
doing. At any rate we find most impenetrable and ineluctable, in certain
places, the very matters he had the genius to see and the technique to clarify:
the matters which are the substance of rare and valid emotion. The confusion, that is, led him to content himself at times with the mere cataloguing
statement, enough for him because he knew the rest, of what required completely objective embodiment.

Another, if ancillary, method of enforcing the same suggestion (of radical
confusion) is to observe the disparity between Crane's announced purpose
and the masters he studied. Poets commonly profit most where they can
borrow most, from the poets with whom by instinct, education, and accident of contact, they are most nearly unanimous. Thus poetic character
is early predicted. In Crane's case, the nature of the influences to which he
submitted himself remained similar from the beginning to the end and
were the dominant ones of his generation. It was the influence of what we
may call, with little exaggeration, the school of tortured sensibility—a
school of which we perhaps first became aware in Baudelaire's misappre-
hension of Poe, and later, in the hardly less misapprehending resurrection

of Donne. Crane benefited, and was deformed by, this influence both directly and by an assortment of indirection; but he never surmounted it. He read the modern French poets who are the result of Baudelaire, but he did not read Racine of whom Baudelaire was himself a product. He read Wallace Stevens, whose strength and serenity may in some sense be assigned to the combined influence of the French moderns and, say, Plato; but he did not, at least affectively, read Plato. He read Eliot, and through and in terms of him, the chosen Elizabethans—though more in Donne and Webster than in Jonson and Middleton; but he did not, so to speak, read the Christianity from which Eliot derives his ultimate strength, and by which he is presently transforming himself. I use the word *read* in a strong sense; there is textual evidence of reading throughout the poems. The last influence Crane exhibited is no different in character and in the use to which he put it than the earliest: the poem called "The Hurricane" derives immediately from the metric of Hopkins but not ultimately from Hopkins' integrating sensibility. Thus Crane fitted himself for the exploitation of the peculiar, the unique, the agonized and the tortured perception, and he developed language-patterns for the essentially incoherent aspects of experience: the aspects in which experience assaults rather than informs the sensibility. Yet, granting his sensibility, with his avowed epic purpose he had done better had he gone to school to Milton and Racine, and, in modern times, to Hardy and Bridges—or even Masefield—for narrative sweep.

Crane had, in short, the wrong masters for his chosen fulfillment, or he used some of the right masters in the wrong way: leeching upon them, as a poet must, but taking the wrong nourishment, taking from them not what was hardest and most substantial—what made them great poets—but taking rather what was easiest, taking what was peculiar and idiosyncratic. That is what kills so many of Crane's poems, what must have made them impervious, once they were discharged, even to himself. It is perhaps, too, what killed Crane the man—because in a profound sense, to those who use it, poetry is the only means of putting a tolerable order upon the emotions. Crane's predicament—that his means defeated his ends—was not unusual, but his case was extreme. In more normal form it is the predicament of immaturity. Crane's mind was slow and massive, a cumulus of substance; it had, to use a word of his own, the synergical quality, and with time it might have worked together, clarified, and become its own meaning. But he hastened the process and did not survive to maturity.

Certainly there is a hasty immaturity in the short essay on Modern Poetry, reprinted as an appendix to the *Collected Poems,* an immaturity both in the intellectual terms employed and in the stress with which the attitude they rehearse is held. Most of the paper tilts at windmills, and the lance is too heavy for the wielding hand. In less than five pages there is deployed more confused thinking than is to be found in all his poems put together. Poetry is not, as Crane says it is, an architectural art—or not without a good deal of qualification; it is a linear art, an art of succession, and the only art it resembles formally is plain song. Nor can Stravinsky and the cubists be compared, as Crane compares them, in the quality of their abstractions with the abstractions of mathematical physics: the aims are disparate; expression and theoretic manipulation can never exist on the same plane. Nor can psychological analyses, in literature, be distinguished in motive and quality from dramatic analyses. Again, and finally, the use of the term *psychosis* as a laudatory epithet for the substance of Whitman, represents to me the uttermost misconstruction of the nature of poetry: a psychosis is a mental derangement not due to an organic lesion or neurosis. A theory of neurosis (as, say, Aiken has held it in *Blue Voyage*) is more tenable scientifically; but neither it seems to me has other than a stultifying critical use. Yet, despite the confusion and positive irrationality of Crane's language the general tendency is sound, the aspiration sane. He wanted to write good poetry and his archetype was Dante; that is enough. But in his prose thinking he had the wrong words for his thoughts, as in his poetry he had often the wrong themes for his words.

## II

So far, if the points have been maintained at all, what I have written adds up to the suggestion that in reading Hart Crane we must make allowances for him—not historical allowances as we do for Shakespeare, religious allowances as for Dante and Milton, or philosophical as for Goethe and Lucretius—but fundamental allowances whereby we agree to supply or overlook what does not appear in the poems, and whereby we agree to forgive or guess blindly at those parts of the poems which are unintelligible. In this Crane is not an uncommon case, though the particular allowances may perhaps be unique. There are some poets where everything is allowed for the sake of isolated effects. Sedley is perhaps the supreme example in English; there is nothing in him but two lines, but these are famous and will always be worth saving. Waller is the more normal example, or King, where two or three poems are the whole gist. Crane has both poems and passages; and in fact there is hardly a poem of his which has not something in it, and a very definite something, worth saving.

The nature of that saving quality, for it saves him no less than ourselves, Crane has himself most clearly expressed in a stanza from the poem called "Wine Menagerie."

> New thresholds, new anatomies! Wine talons
> Build freedom up about me and distill
> This competence—to travel in a tear
> Sparkling alone, within another's will.

I hope to show that this stanza illustrates almost inexhaustibly, to minds at all aware, both the substance and the aspiration of Crane's poetry, the character and value of his perceptions, and his method of handling words to control them. If we accept the stanza as a sort of declaration of policy and apply it as our own provisional policy to the sum of his work, although we limit its scope we shall deepen and articulate our appreciation—a process, that of appreciation, which amounts not to wringing a few figs from thistles but to expressing the wine itself.

Paraphrase does not greatly help. We can, for the meat of it, no more be concerned with the prose sense of the words than Crane evidently was. Crane habitually re-created his words from within, developing meaning to the point of idiom; and that habit is the constant and indubitable sign of talent. The meanings themselves are the idioms and have a twist and life of their own. It is only by ourselves meditating on and *using* these idioms— it is only by emulation—that we can master them and accede to their life.

Analysis, however, does help, and in two directions. It will by itself increase our intimacy with the words as they appear; and it will as the nexus among comparisons disclose that standard of achievement, inherent in this special use of poetic language, by which alone the value of the work may be judged. (Analysis, in these uses, does not cut deep, it does not cut at all: it merely distinguishes particulars; and the particulars must be re-seen in their proper focus before the labor benefits.)

Moving in the first direction, toward intimacy, we can say that Crane employed an extreme mode of free association; that operation among words where it is the product rather than the addition that counts. There was, for example, no logical or emotional connection between thresholds and anatomies until Crane verbally juxtaposed them and tied them together with the cohesive of his meter. Yet, so associated, they modify and act upon each other mutually and produce a fresh meaning of which the parts cannot be segregated. Some latent, unsuspected part of the cumulus of meaning in each word has excited, so to speak, and affected a corresponding part in the others. It is the juxtaposition which is the agent of selection, and it is a combination of meter and the carried-over influence of the rest of the poem, plus the as yet undetermined expectations aroused, which is the agent of emphasis and identification. It should be noted that, so far as the poem is concerned, the words themselves contain and do not merely indicate the feelings which compose the meaning; the poet's job was to put the words together like bricks in a wall. In lesser poetry of the same order, and in poetry of different orders, words may only indicate or refer to or substitute for the feelings; then we have the poetry of vicarious statement, which takes the place of, often to the highest purpose, the actual complete presentation, such as we have here. Here there is nothing for the words to take the place of; they are their own life, and have an organic continuity, not with the poet's mind nor with the experience they represent, but with themselves. We see that thresholds open upon anatomies: upon things to be explored and understood and felt freshly as an adventure; and we see that the anatomies, what is to be explored, are known from a new vantage, and that the vantage is part of the anatomy. The separate meanings of the words fairly rush at each other; the right ones join and those irrelevant to the juncture are for the moment—the whole time of the poem—lost in limbo. Thus the association "New thresholds, new anatomies!" which at first inspection might seem specious or arbitrary (were we not used to reading poetry) not only does not produce a distortion but, the stress and strain being equal, turns out wholly natural and independently alive.

In the next phrase the association of the word "talons" with the context seems less significantly performed. So far as it refers back and expresses a seizing together, a clutching by a bird of prey, it is an excellent word well-chosen and spliced in. The further notion, suggested by the word "wine," of release, would also seem relevant. There is, too, an unidentifiable possibility—for Crane used words in very special senses indeed—of "talons" in the sense of cards left after the deal; and there is even, to push matters to the limit, a bare chance that some element of the etymon—ankle, heel— has been pressed into service. But the possibilities have among them none specially discriminated, and whichever you choose for use, the dead weight of the others must be provisionally carried along, which is what makes the phrase slightly fuzzy. And however you construe "wine talons" you cannot, without distorting what you have and allowing for the gap or lacuna of what you have not, make your construction fit either or both of the verbs which it governs. Talons neither build nor distill even when salvation by rhyme is in question. If Crane meant—as indeed he may have—that wines are distilled and become brandies or spirits, then he showed a poverty of technique in using the transitive instead of the intransitive form. Objection can be carried too far, when it renders itself nugatory. These remarks are meant as a kind of exploration; and if we now make the allowance for the unidentified distortion and supply with good will the lacuna in the very heart of the middle phrases, the rest of the stanza becomes as plain and vivid as poetry of this order need ever be. To complete the whole association, the reader need only remember that Crane probably had in mind, and made new use of Blake's lines:

> For a Tear is an Intellectual Thing,
> And a Sigh is the Sword of an Angel King.

It is interesting to observe that Blake was talking against war and that his primary meaning was much the same as that expressed negatively in "Auguries of Innocence" by the following couplet:

> He who shall train the Horse to War
> Shall never pass the Polar Bar.

Crane ignored the primary meaning, and extracted and emphasized what was in Blake's image a latent or secondary meaning. Or possibly he combined—made a free association of—the intellectual tear with

> Every Tear from Every Eye
> Becomes a Babe in Eternity;

only substituting the more dramatic notion of will for intellect. What is important to note is that, whatever its origin, the meaning as Crane presents it is completely transformed and subjugated to the control of the "New thresholds, new anatomies!"

The stanza we have been considering is only arbitrarily separated from the whole poem—just as the poem itself ought to be read in the context of the whole *White Buildings* section. The point is, that for appreciation— and for denigration—all of Crane should be read thoroughly, at least once, with similar attention to detail. That is the way in which Crane worked. Later readings may be more liberated and more irresponsible—as some people read the Bible for what they call its poetry or a case history for its thrill; but they never get either the poetry or the thrill without a preliminary fundamental intimacy with the rational technique involved. Here it is a question of achieving some notion of a special poetic process. The principle of association which controls this stanza resembles the notion of wine as escape, release, father of insight and seed of metamorphosis, which controls the poem; and, in its turn, the notion of extra-logical, intoxicated metamorphosis of the senses controls and innervates Crane's whole sensibility.

To illustrate the uniformity of approach, a few examples are presented, some that succeed and some that fail. In "Lachrymae Christi" consider the line

> Thy Nazarene and tinder eyes.

(Note, from the title, that we are here again concerned with tears as the vehicle-image of insight, and that, in the end, Christ is identified with Dionysus.) "Nazarene," the epithet for Christ, is here used as an adjective of quality in conjunction with the noun "tinder" also used as an adjective; an arrangement which will seem baffling only to those who underestimate the seriousness with which Crane remodeled words. The first three lines of the poem read:

> Whitely, while benzine
> Rinsings from the moon
> Dissolve all but the windows of the mills.

Benzine is a fluid, cleansing and solvent, has a characteristic tang and smart to it, and is here associated with the light of the moon, which, through the word "rinsings," is itself modified by it. It is, I think, the carried-over influence of "benzine" which gives startling aptness to "Nazarene." It is, if I am correct for any reader but myself, an example of suspended association, or telekinesis; and it is, too, an example of syllabic interpenetration or internal punning as habitually practiced in the later prose of Joyce. The influence of one word on the other reminds us that Christ the Saviour cleanses and solves and has, too, the quality of light. "Tinder" is a simpler instance of how Crane could at once isolate a word and bind it in, impregnating it with new meaning. Tinder is used to kindle fire, powder, and light; a word incipient and bristling with the action proper to its being. The association is completed when it is remembered that "tinder" is very nearly a homonym for "tender" and, *in this setting,* puns upon it.

Immediately following, in the same poem, there is a parenthesis which I have not been able to penetrate with any certainty, though the possibilities are both fascinating and exciting. The important words in it do not possess the excluding, limiting power over themselves and their relations by which alone the precise, vital element in an ambiguity is secured. What Crane may have meant privately cannot be in question—his words may have represented for him a perfect tautology; we are concerned only with how the words act upon each other—or fail to act—so as to commit an appreciable meaning. I quote the first clause of the parenthesis.

> Let sphinxes from the ripe
> Borage of death have cleared my tongue
> Once and again . . .

It is syntax rather than grammar that is obscure. I take it that "let" is here a somewhat homemade adjective and that Crane is making a direct statement, so that the problem is to construe the right meanings of the right words in the right references; which will be an admirable exercise in exegesis, but an exercise only. The applicable senses of "let" are these: neglected or weary, permitted or prevented, hired, and let in the sense that blood is let. Sphinxes are inscrutable, have secrets, propound riddles to travelers and strangle those who cannot answer. "Borage" has at least three senses: something rough (sonantly suggestive of barrage and barrier), a blue-flowered, hairy-leaved plant, and a cordial made from the plant. The Shorter Oxford Dictionary quotes this jingle from Hooker: "I Borage always bring courage." One guess is that Crane meant something to the effect that if you meditate enough on death it has the same bracing and warming effect as drinking a cordial, so that the riddles of life (or death) are answered. But something very near the contrary may have been intended; or both. In any case a guess is ultimately worthless because, with the defective syntax, the words do not verify it. Crane had a profound feeling for the hearts of words, and how they beat and cohabited, but here they overtopped him; the meanings in the words themselves are superior to the use to which he put them. The operation of selective cross-pollination not only failed but was not even rightly attempted. The language remains in the condition of that which it was intended to express: in the flux of intoxicated sense; whereas the language of the other lines of this poem here examined—the language, not the sense—is disintoxicated and candid. The point is that the quality of Crane's success is also the quality of his failure, and the distinction is perhaps by the hair of accident.

In the part of *The Bridge* called "Virginia," and in scores of places elsewhere, there is a single vivid image, of no structural importance, but of great delight as ornament: it both fits the poem and has a startling separate beauty of its own, the phrase: "Peonies with pony manes." [1] The freshness has nothing to do with accurate observation, of which it is devoid, but has its source in the arbitrary character of the association: it is created observation. Another example is contained in

> Down Wall, from girder into street noon leaks,
> A rip-tooth of the sky's acetylene;

which is no more forced than many of Crashaw's best images. It is, of course, the pyramiding associations of the word "acetylene" that create the observation: representing as it does an intolerable quality of light and a torch for cutting metal, and so on.

Similarly, again and again, both in important and in ornamental phrases, there are effects only half secured, words which are not the right words but only the nearest words. E.g.: "What eats the pattern with *ubiquity*. . . . Take this *sheaf* of dust upon your tongue. . . Preparing *penguin* flexions of the arms . . . [A tugboat] with one *galvanic* blare . . . I heard the *hush of lava wrestling* your arms." Etc. Not that the italicized words are wrong

1 Compare Marianne Moore's "the lion's ferocious chrysanthemum head."

but that they fall short of the control and precision of impact necessary to vitalize them permanently.

There remains to consider the second help of analysis (the first was to promote intimacy with particulars), namely, to disclose the standard of Crane's achievement in terms of what he actually accomplished; an effort which at once involves comparison of Crane with rendered possibilities in the same realm of language taken from other poets. For Crane was not alone; style, like knowledge, of which it is the expressive grace, is a product of collaboration; and his standard, whether consciously or not, was outside himself, in verse written in accord with his own bent: which the following, if looked at with the right eye, will exemplify.

> Sunt lacrimae rerum et mentem mortalia tangunt.——*Vergil*

> Lo giorno se n'andava, e l'aer bruno
>     toglieva gli animai, che sono in terra,
>     dalle fatiche loro.——*Dante*

> A brittle glory shineth in his face;
> As brittle as the glory is the face.——*Shakespeare*

> Adieu donc, chants du cuivre et soupirs de la flûte!
> Plaisirs, ne tentez plus un coeur sombre et boudeur!
> Le Printemps adorable a perdu son odeur!——*Baudelaire*

> But Love has pitched his mansion in
> The place of excrement;
> For nothing can be sole or whole
> That has not been rent.——*Yeats*

> She dreams a little, and she feels the dark
> Encroachment of that old catastrophe,
> As a calm darkens among water-lights.——*Stevens*

The relevant context is assumed to be present, as we have been assuming it all along with Crane. Every quotation, except that from Yeats which is recent, should be well known. They bring to mind at once, on one side, the sustaining, glory-breeding power of magnificent form joined to great intellect. Before that impact Crane's magnitude shrinks. On the other side, the side of the particulars, he shrinks no less. The significant words in each selection, and so in the lines themselves, will bear and require understanding to the limit of analysis and limitless meditation. Here, as in Crane, words are associated by the poetic process so as to produce a new and living, an idiomatic, meaning, differing from and surpassing the separate factors involved. The difference—which is where Crane falls short of his standard —is this. Crane's effects remain tricks which can only be resorted to arbitrarily. The effects in the other poets—secured by more craft rather than less—become, immediately they are understood, permanent idioms which enrich the resources of language for all who have the talent to use them. It is perhaps the difference between the immediate unbalance of the assaulted, intoxicated sensibility and the final, no less exciting, clarity of the sane, mirroring sensibility.

It is said that Crane's inchoate heart and distorted intellect only witness the disease of his generation; but I have cited two poets, if not of his generation still his contemporaries, who escaped the contagion. It is the stigma of the first order of poets (a class which includes many minor names and deletes some of the best known) that they master so much of life as they represent. In Crane the poet succumbed with the man.

What judgment flows from these strictures need not impede the appreciation of Crane's insight, observation, and intense, if confused, vision, but ought rather to help determine it. Merely because Crane is imperfect in his kind is no reason to give him up; there is no plethora of perfection, and the imperfect beauty, like life, retains its fascination. And there is about him, too—such were his gifts for the hearts of words, such the vitality of his intelligence—the distraught but exciting splendor of a great failure.

*Robert Bechtold Heilman*

# POOR NAKED WRETCHES
# AND PROUD ARRAY:
## THE CLOTHES PATTERN

*. . . The Vestural tissue, namely, of woolen or other cloth; which Man's Soul wears as its outmost wrappage and overall; . . . In all speculations they have tacitly figured man as a* Clothed Animal; *whereas he is by nature a* Naked Animal; *and only in certain circumstances, by purpose and device, masks himself in Clothes.*

.        .        .

*Happy he who can look through the Clothes of a Man . . . into the Man himself . . . .*

.        .        .

*Thus in this one pregnant subject of CLOTHES, rightly understood, is included all that men have thought, dreamed, done, and been. . . .*

Carlyle, *Sartor Resartus*

.        .        .

The problem of *seeing* human experience accurately is not one which Shakespeare oversimplifies or reduces to a formula. In fact, the whole content of the sight pattern [in *King Lear*] is resolved into the Sophoclean paradox that the blind may see better than the proudly keen-eyed. But the play also attacks the problem of seeing and understanding from another direction: it presents elaborately the obstacles which interpose between human sight and its objects. We are made fully aware that man faces obdurate materials, efforts to deceive, and his own tendency to reconstruct the objective world according to his own preconceptions. It is at least comprehensible that Lear mistakes the moral identity of Goneril, Regan, Cordelia, and Kent, and subsequently fails to suspect that his new follower is Kent: and that Gloucester likewise confuses the nature of his two sons and later does not recognize the helper of his blindness. These errors may be fatal or

Reprinted from *This Great Stage* by Robert Bechtold Heilman, by permission of Louisiana State University Press and the author. Copyright 1948 by Louisiana State University Press, Baton Rouge, Louisiana.

merely pathetic; but we are not invited merely to condemn or to sympathize. Instead we are compelled to enter fully into perceptual experiences of
distracting difficulty and hence to feel—if not to follow out to metaphysical
conclusions—oppressive problems of personal identity. When Edgar soliloquizes, "Edgar I nothing am" (II.iii, 21),[1] the lines embody a good deal of
the pathos of exile. But the effects are more poignant when Lear for the
first time runs into a double problem of identity in a world where all has
seemed secure.[2] He asks Goneril, "Are you our daughter?" (I.iv, 238), and
he continues more sharply, "Your name, fair gentlewoman?"[3] (257). But
his most anguished questions are addressed to himself:

> Doth any here know me? This is not Lear.
> Doth Lear walk thus? speak thus? Where are his eyes?
>
> .        .        .
>
> Who is it that can tell me who I am?[4] (I.iv, 246–50)

What the play gets into, then, is some preliminary speculation about
appearance and reality. In this speculation, the disguises are the larger
dramatic components of the ideological structure; it is impossible *not* to regard them as something more than necessities imposed upon the characters
by circumstance. There are two kinds of disguise in the play—the psychological and the physical; the psychological disguises, except Edgar's, conceal
unscrupulous intentions; the physical are protective. Thus there is an ironic
correspondence among all the disguised people: they cannot manage by being candidly themselves: *appearances* rule, or seem to rule, the world. Yet
that kinship only heightens the moral distinction between acquisitiveness
and survival. In dealing with Edmund, Goneril, and Regan, Shakespeare is
actually making a sardonic comment on what we today know as "success," as
"winning friends and influencing people." But if pretense and hyprocrisy
are base, it does not follow that candid integrity has an easy road in an
actual world. Cordelia and Kent suffer in their society because they are not

[1] [The line numbers are those which appear in the Kittredge edition of *King Lear*.]
[2] The painful doubts which are among the early factors in Lear's mental downfall are
parodied in the scene in which Kent, as Lear's messenger, runs into Oswald, Goneril's
messenger, before Gloucester's castle, and denounces and beats him.
> *Osw.* Why dost thou use me thus? I know thee not.
> *Kent.* Fellow, I know thee.
> *Osw.* What dost thou know me for? (II.ii, 12–14)
Kent then launches into his famous series of vituperative terms for Oswald, who comments, "Why, what a monstrous fellow art thou, thus to rail on one that's neither known
of thee nor knows thee!" (28–29) For Oswald, the problem of identity remains at the level
of introductions, and his questions are a comic version of Lear's anguished inquiries. There
are other comments on the problem of identity in Mark Van Doren's *Shakespeare* (New
York, 1939), pp. 245, 249.
[3] Note how the courteous vocative adds to the incisiveness of the irony. Lear's tense incredulity is balanced by Goneril's matter-of-fact assurance,
> This admiration, sir, is much o' th' savour
> Of other your new pranks. I do beseech you
> To understand my purposes aright. (I.iv, 258–60)
[4] In a later scene, waiting for Cornwall outside Gloucester's castle, Lear makes a tremendous effort to control his growing rage and comments,
> We are not ourselves
> When nature, being oppress'd, commands the mind
> To suffer with the body. (II.iv, 108–10)

disguised, not tempered to the prevailing winds; the Fool must cover his grasp of reality with irrelevancies; Edgar must undertake a complete negation of real personality; Kent must disguise himself even from his patron. In such a world Lear must ask what *reality* is, and he can deal with an apparently insoluble question only by departing, to all intents and purposes, from the world of reality.

Initially the play appears to commit itself to the cynical view that only appearances count in the world. As a whole, however, the drama disposes of this early hypothesis: appearance comes eventually to be understood, and properly valued. The first two lines of the last speech in the play, indeed, are more than rough-cut didacticism: they apply specifically to the theme which we are here discussing. The speaker, Edgar, says,

> The weight of this sad time we must obey,
> Speak what we feel, not what we ought to say. (V.iii, 323–24)

Here, finally, all appearances are dissolved. In the meantime, however, they have strongly influenced the action. Throughout the play there is a systematic commentary upon appearances that are misread, upon the difficulties of perceiving the world truly, upon the failure—which may itself be a spiritual affirmation—to put up a good appearance, upon, that is, naïveté, defenselessness, innocence. This commentary appears especially in the *clothes pattern,* as components of which we find, on the one hand, larger dramatic elements such as the clothing and nakedness of characters, and, on the other, the recurrent imagery of clothes.

In the center of this pattern is Edgar. Since his disguise has both psychological and physical aspects, Edgar has a place in different structural elements in the play. As a pretended lunatic he helps develop the madness pattern; as a disguised person he is the most conspicuous figure in the clothes pattern. His disguise, of course, is virtual nakedness, and it illustrates how inevitably the literal and commonplace goes over into the symbolic. This nakedness is at one level simply a technical propriety in the Bedlam beggar; but by its particular inadequacy to a cold and stormy night—the language of III.iv never permits us to forget the cold—it becomes a symbol of that defenselessness in the world which Edgar has already shown and indeed of the situation of innocent people generally, unprotected by worldliness or pretense [5] in a world swept by the storms of ambition and other uncontrolled emotions. But Edgar's nakedness is also a defense, and in terms of the play the innocent have always a defense, if not against immediate enemies, at least against ultimate corruption. The naked wretches may ultimately have a better protection than those who are proudly arrayed in what the world values. To strip oneself may be folly; but nakedness may be an aid to understanding. The clothes pattern, like the sight pattern, contains its paradoxes,[6] and thus it is woven into the main fabric of meaning. In *King Lear* deprivation is often the way to gain.

---

5 Cf. Lear's statement that his *"frank* heart gave all" (III.iv, 20).
6 Harbage has a chapter on paradoxes (Alfred Harbage, *As They Liked It* [New York, 1947], pp. 73 ff.) but makes no mention of those in this play. He does point out how misery enlarges the sympathies in *Lear* (pp. 175–76). The paradoxes of clothing and nakedness in *Lear* are similar to those in *Macbeth* which Cleanth Brooks has pointed

## LEAR

The clothes pattern makes a running commentary on the intellectual and moral problems that arise in Lear's kingdom. Edgar is driven to a nakedness that is a symbol of his defenselessness and yet itself a kind of defense. Lear finally tries to tear off his clothes to be like Edgar. But the impact upon us of that apparently deranged impulse becomes very much stronger when we are made to realize, by the language of earlier scenes, that in effect some of Lear's main actions have pointed toward the clothes-tearing scene as a climax. At the very start Lear says,

> Since now we will *divest* us both of rule,
> Interest of territory, cares of state, (I.i, 50–51)

but this *undressing* for easy sleep is also a removal of armor against the arrows of fortune; Lear himself points up the situation a minute later when he tells Goneril and Regan and their husbands,

> I do *invest* you jointly with my power,
> Pre-eminence and all the large effects
> That troop with majesty. (132–34)

Lear naïvely makes an exception: "Only we shall retain/The name and th' additions to a king" (137–38). He would retain prerogatives without responsibility, immunity without safeguards, warmth without clothes. He forgets that there are no naked kings [7] (it is just a few lines later that Kent calls him mad), and he is not yet aware in what sense he can, as he has said, "unburthen'd crawl toward death" (I.i, 42). His own words symbolize a basic mistake which initiates the whole train of tragic consequences. His withdrawal from the world of action is not only the removal of a burden; it is likewise the removal of a necessary protection.[8] He cannot be "unburthen'd" unless he is willing to be unqualifiedly unburdened. Although ideally it ought not to be so, in fact abdication means the poorhouse. The paradoxical interdependence of security and responsibility Lear does not realize; he oversimplifies the situation; some hard learning lies before him.[9]

---

out (*The Well Wrought Urn* [New York, 1947], pp. 42 ff.). A point made by Miss Spurgeon is relevant to the present discussion: "Another aspect of evil which specially interested Shakespeare, and seemed to him its most dangerous feature, was its power of disguising itself as good—. . . . This quality is pictured by him chiefly in terms of clothing and painting, and is especially frequent in his early work" (Caroline F. E. Spurgeon, *Shakespeare's Imagery and What It Tells Us* [New York and Cambridge, 1936], p. 164).

7 A sentence in Sidney's *Arcadia* comes very close to describing Lear's present situation. The king of Paphlagonia tells how he gradually lost his function to a bastard son, ". . . so that ere I was aware, I had left my selfe nothing but the name of a King" (quoted, H. H. Furness ed., *King Lear*, New Variorum Edition, 10th ed. [Philadelphia, 1880], p. 388).

8 Cf. Chapter I, pp. 35–36.

9 The problem which Lear faces suggests different metaphors to different readers. One critic has said, in a conversation, "Lear needs to be re-educated. The plot of the play is his re-education. When he learns what the images are saying, his education is complete." Another: "Lear is living in a melodrama. He has to learn to live in a tragedy." That is, he must progress from a simple blame of villains to an awareness of his own responsibility for disaster.

Oswald gives the first lesson by his insolence in I.iv; then a brilliant teacher, the Fool, begins to bring home to him the fact that he has lost the apparel of royalty. The Fool jeers, ". . . when thou gav'st them the rod and put'st down thine own breeches,"

> Then they for sudden joy did weep (I.iv, 189–91);

this is excellent: not only does it help develop the children-parents theme, but it tells us that Lear has actually reduced himself to the status of a child. The Fool exclaims, ". . . I can tell why a snail has a house. . . . Why, to put's head in; not to give it away to his daughters, and leave his horns without a case" (I.v, 30–33). To take off his crown was to lose his house. Lear's change of garb echoes in another song of the Fool's:

> Fathers that wear rags
> Do make their children blind (II.iv, 48–49)—

lines in which—an illustration of the regular coalescence of patterns in the play—both the sight and clothing symbols are at work. Lear—told that he is a child, houseless, ragged—begins to see what has happened. When Regan suggests that Lear try to make it up with Goneril, he ironically rehearses a speech for himself as suppliant: "On my knees I beg/That you'll vouch-safe me raiment, bed and food" (II.iv, 157–58)—*raiment*, a symbol of all that he has given up and can neither get back by asking nor even ask for. So when Lear runs in the storm "unbonneted" (III.i, 14), "bareheaded" (III.ii, 60; cf. III.vii, 59), his unprotectedness is more than physical and more than an accident or device of staging. There is a special ironic per-tinence in the fact that it is his *head* which is bare, for thus the experience is unmistakably connected both with his own initial decision and act and also with the madness that is to overtake him: he has specifically bared his head by giving away his crown, saying to his "beloved sons," "This coronet part betwixt you" (I.i, 141). Shakespeare seems to be consciously using the crown in his development of theme; the scepter, for instance, would not be nearly so well adapted to the symbolic structure. Now the Fool never lets Lear forget his bareheadedness or the source of it, and his repeated reference to it is a way of letting us see that it is more than a casual device for making suffering concrete. The Fool offers Lear his "coxcomb" and makes jokes about it (I.iv, 106 ff.), and finally advises him to "beg another of thy daughters" (121); then he suggests that he will break an egg and give Lear "the two crowns of the egg" to replace the two halves of the crown he gave away (171); and his bitterest comment follows Lear's first bout with the storm: "He that has a house to put's head in has a good head-piece."

> The cod-piece that will house
>   Before the head has any,
> The head and he shall louse. . . . (III.ii, 27–29)

The head is bare of its crown; the torture is in part the result of bad head-work; and at the same time bareheadedness suggests the unprotected sensi-tive mind which will soon give way. The storm beats about Lear's head in the same way in which emotional and intellectual storms batter at his mind.

In the context the efforts of Kent and Gloucester to bring Lear to shelter become more than a one-dimensional kindness; the men are trying to reduce the effect of what he has let himself in for; and their efforts are exactly comparable to Edgar's later services to Gloucester.

But if by giving up the clothes of kingship Lear has laid himself open to the buffets of the world, he has at the same time become capable of wider feelings, and wider perceptions. With the Fool's pity-by-derision is contrasted a direct expression of pity by Lear himself. The scene is on the heath, before a hovel; and Lear has told the Fool to go in first. Lear says,

> You houseless poverty—
>
> .     .     .
>
> Poor naked wretches, wheresoe'er you are,
> That bide the pelting of this pitiless storm,
> How shall your houseless heads and unfed sides,
> Your loop'd and window'd raggedness, defend you
> From seasons such as these? Oh, I have ta'en
> Too little care of this! Take physic, pomp;
> Expose thyself to feel what wretches feel. . . .
>
> (III.iv, 26–34)

*Naked, houseless* (especially conspicuous in its combination with *heads*), *raggedness,* and *expose* continue the clothes pattern and gain strength from it: they must not do all their work at the moment but can call upon habits of response, and upon associations, which their fellows have helped establish. By the same token, if the passage is at one level a statement of compassion for the materially underprivileged—and the significance of Lear's new pity, which all critics have observed, is by no means to be ignored—it is also, in the symbolic context, a recognition of the fate of the innocent in the world, the unprotected with whom Lear is now identified. If "I have ta'en too little care" gives voice to a characteristic indifference of royalty, it also suggests Lear's specific failing: his unawareness of the realities of the suffering encountered by the defenseless, his selfish passion for verbal luxuries within his own apparently impregnable stronghold, has played a part in undermining his own position. His passionate loathing of his daughters is complicated by the gradual realization of his own responsibility in the situation. Thus in the clothes pattern we find an implied commentary upon the tragic flaw.

Edgar ("poor Tom") appears a few seconds later, and for some time the stories of Edgar and Lear are almost fused, especially by means of the clothes pattern. When Lear, speaking as if Edgar had been brought to his present pass by daughters, asks, "Would'st thou give 'em all?" (III.iv, 67), the Fool wonderfully interjects, "Nay, he reserv'd a blanket, else we had all been sham'd" (68), ironically applying a standard of modesty that, when high matters of justice are at stake, is petty and irrelevant. He suggests, too, the ironic disparity between Lear and Edgar: the former has literally more clothes yet is now more seriously exposed in an inimical world. Edgar tells of his sinful past and moralizes, and from all his words the clothes imagery, although it does not have a primary position, is never absent. He says that he "wore gloves in my cap" (III.iv, 88), and he exhorts: "set not thy sweet heart on proud array" (84), "Let not the creaking of shoes nor the rustling of silks betray thy poor heart to women" (97–98), and "Keep . . . thy hand out of placket . . ." (100). The ironic unnecessariness of such injunctions is a way of emphasizing the defenselessness of this pair who now have nothing in common with the bold and worldly young man Edgar describes; at the same time we cannot help thinking that Lear, if he was not precisely a victim of the rustling of silks, did most certainly betray his poor heart to women, and that above all he did not intelligently enough devote himself to proud array—to the complex of privilege and responsibility implied by the purple. The imaginary young Tom and the actual Lear had both misconceived proud array, taking it as immunity to the ills that flesh is heir to.

Then Lear, still contemplating Edgar's "uncover'd body" (106), makes the speech which is the climax of the pattern so far, is, actually, the goal of most of what has gone before. Concluding that Edgar owes nothing to worm, beast, or sheep for clothes, Lear reasons, "Ha! here's three on's are sophisticated! Thou art the thing itself; unaccommodated man is no more but such a poor, bare, forked animal as thou art. Off, off, you lendings! come, unbutton here" (111–14). His effort to tear off his clothes is an ironic conclusion to the sequence begun in Act I, when Lear said that he would *divest* himself of rule, land, and cares. Then he acted in hope of a quiet old age; now he acts in bitter disillusionment in which, even though his mind is giving way, he carries to a mercilessly logical extreme his fierce sense of the appropriate, a sense which others have brutally violated. Tearing off clothes may be, clinically, a symptom of delirium; [10] but the scientifically accurate contributes perfectly to the symbolic pattern: in Lear's situation, nakedness alone is meaningful and clothes are a "sophistication." Edgar is right; he is at one with nature; unaccommodated in the essentials of royal life, Lear finds his remnants of "proud array" a mockery. After all this symbolic sloughing off of the externals of life by one who has undergone agonizing deprivations, "poor Tom's" tireless pitter-patter about his past echoes on—apparently aimless, but with its occasional thrusts into the heart of the present. For once, he tells us, he "had three suits to his back, six shirts to his body" (141–42). Lear, too, before his divestiture, had suits enough. Thus, by the aid of the pattern, pseudo-mad irrelevancies actually contribute to the imaginative richness of the play.

So the Lear who is in effect naked wants to be naked in fact; the passion for a harmonizing of inner and outer belongs to his bitter enlightenment. But his mind wanders; it is not yet ready for the fanatic concentration on a single theme that it is capable of in IV.vi, where the mad Lear gives his climactic description of the world. Yet there is an obsession with clothes that can show itself in word or deed; Shakespeare does not allow us to forget the problem of covering—whether it be for protection or literally for *decency*, that is, fittingness. From the impulse to strip down to nature Lear ironically goes on, the next time we see him, to criticize Edgar's meager garb as "Persian" (III.vi, 83–86)—contrary to "nature," perhaps?—and then, by the time of his next appearance (to Edgar and Gloucester, in the country

---

[10] Kittredge's note *(King Lear* [Boston, 1940], p. 182). Cf. G. Wilson Knight's discussion of this passage in *The Wheel of Fire* (Oxford, 1930), p. 201, and the connection he makes between the clothes symbolism and the nature theme.

near Dover), to put on from nature a "fantastic" garb of, in the stage directions added by different editors, "wild flowers" or "weeds" (IV.vi, 79). The immediate link with the earlier episode of Lear's stripping himself is twofold: it is Edgar, once naked, who promptly comments, "The safer sense will ne'er accommodate/His master thus" (81–82); and his very use of *accommodate* at once reminds us that Lear is still, in his own earlier words to Edgar, "unaccommodated man." Cordelia has already described Lear as

> Crown'd with rank fumiter and furrow weeds,
> With hardocks, hemlock, nettles, cuckoo flow'rs,
> Darnell, and all the idle weeds that grow
> In our sustaining corn (IV.iv, 3–6)—

plants long ago identified as "bitter, biting, poisonous, pungent, lurid, and distracting" and as emblematic of madness.[11] In Lear then is still the powerful urgency toward the appropriate, toward a correspondence of inner and outer; Cordelia's term "idle weeds," which is probably to be read as a pun, points the irony of his state, and at the same time faintly suggests the moral situation of the kingdom as a whole. It is as if some underlying sanity in Lear had driven him to a parody of himself as king, to an expression of his discovery, through his attempted exercise of prerogatives after his abdication, that all he possessed was a parody of kingship. His nakedness is covered by mock adornments. The whole sequence of experiences is emphasized by Cordelia's use of the word *crown'd*—incidentally the only authentic textual evidence of Lear's attire. For in Act I Lear took off a crown; in Act III he was bareheaded; and now he has a mock crown. Yet it is important to recognize that in this incongruity there is nothing of the ludicrous; nor is there a jeer or an easy bid for pity. In one sense, Lear has his crown of thorns—a symbol of the anguish which is the heart of the redemptive experience.[12] In another sense, he is on the way to restoration of a kind, at least to such a one as he can have—to recovery, in part, of mental balance, to a reunion with Cordelia, a realization of his own spiritual potentialities. And, considered in the immediate context, he is on the way to his final brilliant court scene in the fields near Dover (IV.iv, V.iii). I say "court scene" because there his royal quality, his personal force, and his imaginative vigor are the dominating center of all events. If not a king in fact, he is a king by nature—in this natural scene, and with a crown from nature, a crown that is a flimsy likeness of the symbol of earthly kingship, an image of grief and failure, and yet somehow an insigne of what has been kept—and of something gained.

11 For an elaborate discussion of these points see Furness, pp. 257 ff.
12 To G. Wilson Knight this meaning is central to the interpretation of *Lear* and of the tragedies generally. See *Principles of Shakespearian Production* (New York, 1936), pp. 83, 222 ff. Knight argues that each tragic hero is a "miniature Christ" (p. 231) and that the "ritualistic concept of sacrifice" dominates the tragedies. The heroes give up earthly kingship and undergo spiritual initiation. The clothes pattern which I am tracing in this chapter takes us very close to such a conclusion. Granville-Barker speaks of Lear's taking upon himself the burden of the whole world's sorrow, of his "transition from malediction to martyrdom" (Harley Granville-Barker, *Prefaces to Shakespeare* [Princeton, 1946], I, p. 289).

## TURNS OF FORTUNE'S WHEEL

In the clothes pattern we find regularly a symbolic echo of changes in circumstance. There is a hint of this in Lear's irony-laden remark to Edgar: ". . . I do not like the fashion of your garments: you will say they are Persian attire; but let them be changed" (III.vi, 84–86). Now actually the "Persian," that is, "luxurious," Edgar is on the point of giving up the nakedness which Lear has so ironically misconceived. But before Edgar is clothed, his nakedness is to be used for one more important point. After being blinded, Gloucester wanders on the heath and meets Edgar, "poor mad Tom," whom he proposes to use as guide. Almost the first thing Gloucester recalls from the meetings of the preceding night—the night of the storm— is that Tom is naked, and he says to the Old Man, ". . . bring some covering for this naked soul" (IV.i, 44). Thus through the clothes pattern we see that Gloucester, like Lear, is growing in charity, and at the same time that Gloucester is evincing what is tantamount to an ironic reversal of attitude to the Edgar whom he had stripped of privilege. Edgar, of course, he does not yet know, but Gloucester's act is directed *toward someone who reminds him of Edgar*. Of seeing "Tom" in the storm he says,

> My son
> Came then into my mind, and yet my mind
> Was then scarce friends with him. I have heard more since.
> (IV.i, 33–35)

When we next see the pair, that is, on the way to Dover cliffs, Edgar is dressed (IV.vi). The end of Edgar's nakedness coincides exactly with his dual change of status with regard to his father: he is now Gloucester's guardian, and Gloucester knows the truth about him. Both as a man upon whom are thrust the responsibilities of protector and as a son who knows that he has regained his father's love,[13] he gains strength and defenses; he is no longer the unprotected wanderer. He is no longer the unloved outlander, so to speak, the Theban, the Athenian, the Persian that Lear had taken him for; spiritually he is again at home in his native country, in his own home. At the same time this meaning of clothes—the recovery of a personal status from which he had been an outcast—is richly intertwined with another meaning discussed at the beginning of this chapter, that which arises from the problem of identity. Gloucester thinks his companion has

---

[13] Chambers, who makes *King Lear* a play about love (R. W. Chambers, *King Lear* [Glasgow, 1940], pp. 49 ff.), stresses the fact that Gloucester and Lear both die in a happy knowledge of the recovery of their children's love. It may be said that Cordelia and Edgar are equally happy to recover parental love. If, as Knight and Chambers, among others, argue, Lear and Gloucester travel through Purgatory, perhaps the same interpretation may be made of Edgar's naked wandering. This view is coherent with my earlier suggestion (see Chapter I, note 34) that at the beginning of the play, in so unquestioningly allowing himself to be put upon by Edmund, Edgar is guilty of an error comparable to the tragic flaws of the major characters who are equally deceived. Since Edgar's mistake leads him to commit no wrong and has no direct effect upon another's destiny, his purgation is comparably mild. It is, too, purgation at a nonsacramental level; he becomes less the man of spiritual than the man of practical vision.

changed, both in voice and in manner of speech. Edgar insists: "You're much deceiv'd. In nothing am I chang'd/But in my garments" (IV.vi, 9–10). Again the ironic note: once before, Edgar had not been changed, though Gloucester had thought so—and had been "deceived"; and, more widely, much that has been looked upon by both Gloucester and Lear as human change has been but in the garments, in the external semblance of people. But if Edgar has remained the same, the front which he has had to present to the world has had to change, and the clothes commentary emphasizes one more of these changes. In Act V Edgar appears to Albany disguised (V.i, after 37), and then, for the fight with Edmund, not only disguised but armed (V.iii, after 118); and after fatally wounding Edmund he reveals himself (V.iii, 169)—the first time he has appeared as himself since II.i. His dress has accurately mirrored every change from innocence in flight to competence in affairs.[14] But there is one other complication: Edgar tells how his identification of himself has caused Gloucester's death (V.iii, 192 ff.): for the second time Gloucester, upon the removal of a son's disguise, has seen too much. The removal of Edmund's psychological disguise brought the double shock of recognizing the nature of Edmund and the injustice to Edgar. These recognition scenes are ironically linked. The recognition of what Edmund is and of what Edmund has caused him to do to Edgar brings Gloucester to despair, and he seeks death; Edgar saves him from death-by-despair, and then, in revealing himself to Gloucester, paves the way for his death—a death-by-ecstasy. Edgar blames himself for having maintained his disguise. Disguise, then, is complexly treated: it may be necessary to saving life, but it can also be instrumental in death.

The clothes pattern continues its enriching commentary upon Lear on into his two climactic scenes in the latter part of the play. At the end of his passionate reason-in-madness speech Lear cries, "Pull off my boots; harder, harder, so" (IV.vi, 177). In one sense the words are an ironic resumption of the orders which were once his wont—appropriate to the powerful, commanding personality which Lear has exhibited throughout the scene; in another they tie up, as we shall see, with the first-act lines on his "retirement" from the kingship; finally they suggest the end of a journey and rest. Lear's wanderings are over, indeed, and, when next we see him, he is in his restorative sleep. "Is he arrayed?" asks Cordelia—a question which, in the context we have been describing, is more than factual. What is Lear's state? Is he naked against the buffeting of a stormy world? Is he still in his wild

---

14 The clothes symbolism also makes a skeletal commentary upon Kent's change of fortune. Kent is forced into disguise, and shortly thereafter he is placed in the stocks— "cruel garters," as the Fool calls them (II.iv, 7) (he puns on *crewel*, worsted, as all editors point out), ironically treating the materials of punishment as if they were an adornment. Later Kent tells a Gentleman that "Some dear cause/Will in concealment wrap me up awhile" (IV.iii, 53–54). Then, when things seem to be going better, Cordelia urges Kent,
> Be better suited.
> These weeds are memories of those worser hours.
> I prithee put them off. (IV.vii, 6–8)
Clothes are directly made into a symbol of condition. But the irony of it is that conditions only seem to be better. Like Edgar, Kent does not appear as himself until the final scene in the play; but his struggles, and the emotional impact of his experiences, have exhausted him, and it is clear that he will not live long (V.iii, 321–22).

garb? The Gentleman answers, "Ay, madam; in the heaviness of sleep/We put fresh garments on him" (IV.vii, 20–22). Lear gets a fresh start. The symbolism continues when Lear cannot identify "these garments" (or "where I did lodge last night") (67–68), just as he cannot tell generally what has happened and is happening to him. In the new clothes we see his return to something like normal understanding, and in the strangeness of his clothes to him, his failure to recognize, after distortions have become the regular thing, a normal world. From his early proud array to the present, his clothes, the outer surface or covering which he should present to the world, have been a problem to him. But such comforts as he now comes into are too late to save him, and, as Lear goes down, we see in the clothes pattern, precisely as we have found it in the sight pattern, a synthesizing comment on his career. Just before the final "look, look" with which he calls attention to Cordelia's face, he says, "Pray you, undo this button. Thank you, sir" (V.iii, 309)—an indication, presumably, of the physical distress which is death's messenger. But these unobtrusive words extend imaginatively way beyond the bare physiological fact which at the realistic level they denote: they are a means of pulling together a whole series of lines into an embracing system of meaning. Lear makes his last royal command, a very mild one, yet it takes us into the heart of the tragedy. For his words take us back to the *divest* of Act I, when he was preparing casually for retirement, for ease before the final sleep; to the frantic *unbutton here* of Act III, when he was attempting to make physical fact conform to the spiritual unprotectedness which he had brought about by his earlier disrobing; and to the *pull off my boots* of Act IV, when the fiercest travel in the hard world was over; and they tell us of a final freeing from clothes that can be followed by no new agony. Lear gives up prerogative and protection, throws away clothes which have no meaning, prepares to rest after a long struggle, and finally, a consequence of all that has gone before, gives up life. The king's only safe divestment is death.

So we see Lear repeatedly taking off what in a practical, normal situation he should be keeping on—and, at the same time, undergoing losses that finally include life. Yet these losses are not spiritual; indeed, they accompany an adjustment of values. If we see the movement of Lear from well-accoutered king to half-clad fugitive, from putting off of cares to giving up of life, we also observe his progress from eyeless rage to seeing beneath the surfaces that deceived him. Once a victim of angry pride, he says to Cordelia, in his next-to-last speech to her, "I'll kneel down/And ask of thee forgiveness" (V.iii, 10–11).

Not that we should ignore losses in the world. In fact, we tend to think primarily, if not exclusively, of the fact that he who does not clothe himself properly against a hard world is lost. Yet there is another side to the picture: he with too thick a sheathe in the workaday world is morally lost.

## LEAR'S DAUGHTERS

The play constantly asks that we consider the front that characters present to the world and the relationship between that front and their moral quality. Not only the disguises, but the imagery raises the subject. Speaking of

Oswald, Kent expresses anger "That such a slave as this should wear a sword,/Who wears no honesty" (II.ii, 78–79). In contrast with the physically naked, the relatively well-heeled Oswald is naked morally.[15] Only a few lines later—an ironic juxtaposition—Cornwall accuses Kent of putting on a false surface—just as Kent has accused Oswald of having a dishonest exterior: the two sets of lines make an interesting counterpoint within the scene. Cornwall says of Kent, who, having verbally cut Oswald to pieces, defends his own "plain" speech:

> This is some fellow
> Who, having been prais'd for bluntness, doth affect
> A saucy roughness, and constrains the garb
> Quite from his nature. (II.ii, 101–104)

Cornwall is wrong; plainness is Kent's regular garb. It is not a good shield in the practical world,[16] but it is an index of a saving spiritual quality. But

[15] Earlier, Kent sneers at Oswald, ". . . a tailor made thee" (II.ii, 59–60). Oswald's naïve incomprehension permits Kent to expand on his joke. Oswald's particular kind of obtuseness is given further expression in another scene when he reports to Goneril how Albany had received from him the news "Of Gloucester's treachery/And of the loyal service of his son": Albany "told me I had turn'd the wrong side out" (IV.ii, 6–9). Oswald has missed the point again. But at the same time his lines have almost a choral value, for as the clothes pattern makes clear, many characters have turned the wrong side out.

[16] Kent, though he is disguised, has his own kind of nakedness in the world. The Fool makes this point when he says that Kent should take his coxcomb. He explains, "Why? For taking one's part that's out of favour. Nay, an thou canst not smile as the wind sits, thou'lt catch cold shortly. There, take my coxcomb!" (I.iv, 111–13) The irony of Kent's being liable to "catch cold" is that his situation is his own choice, and it is obviously different from what Lear expected it to be. In exiling Kent, Lear said, "Five days we do allot thee for provision/To *shield* thee from diseases of the world" (I.i, 176–77). Kent disguised himself against Lear but could not disguise the honesty which gets him into trouble with Cornwall. In passing, we may note the possibility of a pun in *provision*. Kent did not "see for" himself in the way Lear assumed that he would. But he does see for himself morally.

Lear's grant of five days in which Kent may prepare to "shield" himself prepares an effective irony in that Kent not only shields himself but spends most of his time shielding Lear—to the extent that either can be shielded; the reversal of their roles is comparable to that in the relations of Gloucester and Edgar. *Shield,* with a rather general meaning abstracted from the original metaphor, is a convenient link between the dramatic use of clothes and that of shelter, which plays a considerable part in the drama, not only in a literal way but also at the level of implication and overtone. Lear gives up one castle, is virtually forced out of two others (cf. II.iv, 179–80, 206 ff., 291 ff.), faces a storm in the open, and finds shelter in hovel, farmhouse, and tent. His problem is pointed by the continued witticisms of the Fool on the subject of shelter (I.v, 30 ff.; II.iv, 52–53, 81–82; III.ii, 25 ff.). Edgar, Gloucester, and Kent have similar experiences. What we have is a series of symbolic statements, comparable to those made in terms of dress, about man's defenses against the world, and about what man has done to man. Yet the main problem is never the one of finding or recovering shelter: that approach belongs to the problem play. For the ambivalence which such a word as *shield* may have, see Albany's line to Goneril, "A woman's shape doth shield thee" (IV.ii, 67). Man must be shielded; but a shield may also protect evil.

We enter a special wing of the shelter problem, so to speak, in the matter of Lear's retinue and its reduction: how does one distinguish luxury from necessity? Shakespeare clearly perceives the psychological basis of the problem. But the answer made by the play—if *answer* be not taken as a simple statement of sums and quotients—comes properly under the theme of rationality and irrationality, with which we shall deal in Chapters VIII and IX.

Cornwall's words unite with Kent's words on Oswald to form a miniature word drama characteristic of the play: it briefly presents for us the whole problem of appearance and reality—and of what kind of appearance or dress really saves the human being.

Like Lear, Cordelia at the start seems to be divesting herself of an essential protective covering: she astonishes France by being able to "dismantle/ So many folds of favor" (I.i, 220–21). In one sense, the figure describes what, as we have seen, Cordelia herself has done. But Lear, uncrowned, unbonneted, beaten by the storm, has come to insight; he blames himself for Cordelia's fate. Kent tells of Lear's "sovereign shame" for "his own unkindness,/That stripp'd her from his benediction . . ." [17] (IV.iii, 44–45). At this time in the play, when the clothes pattern has been fully developed, *stripp'd* has special force.

But if Cordelia has opened herself to misfortune, she penetrates with assurance the disguise in which her sisters appear to have wooed fortune successfully:

> Time shall unfold what plighted [enfolded] cunning hides;
> Who cover faults, at last shame them derides. (I.i, 283–84)

Here is the other side of the case: in contrast with those who are stripped but save their souls we must see those who have thick clothes in the world but of whose souls there is no evidence. Ironically, even in the world these latter are not finally safe. But time is slow to unfold, and three acts, full of injury and suffering, must pass before the garments of the worldly begin to wear thin and betray the wearer. Things are at last going badly for the sisters when Albany, picking up Cordelia's word from Act I, can cry to Goneril, "Thou changed and self-cover'd thing, for shame" (IV.ii, 62); and it is appropriately Albany who closes the record of Goneril and Regan with exactly the right words, "Cover their faces" [18] (V.iii, 242). The dead must be covered, of course; but beneath this conventional meaning there lurks an ironic commentary prepared for by the clothes imagery—the final covering of the self-covered, the final removal from sight of those who had kept their true selves from Lear's sight. Time unfolds, and death covers at last. And the line is "Cover their *faces*"[19]—the hard looks and scornful eyes; clothing and sight patterns come together.

[17] Cf. Cordelia's asking Lear for his benediction and telling him he must not kneel (IV.vii, 57–59). Later he is still planning to kneel and ask her forgiveness (V.iii, 10–11). Humility in exile is the reverse of the original pride in prosperity—in both characters.

[18] Earlier in the same scene Regan uses a word which seems a deliberate choice. She speaks of Edmund as "In my rights/By me *invested*" (V.iii, 68–69)—thus echoing Lear's own word in Act I, "I do invest you jointly with my power" (I.i, 132), and repeating his process of trying to make the succession in political power conform to the emotions of the moment. But both investitures fail to achieve their end—a failure intimated immediately by means of another language pattern which the play uses, that of disease and medicine: Regan soon cries "Sick, O, sick!" (V.iii, 95), just as in the first scene Kent speaks of Lear's "foul disease" (I.i, 167).

[19] Miss Spurgeon comments that Shakespeare's interest in the human face and his use of it in indicating emotions have never been adequately noticed (*op. cit.*, p. 58).

## CHORUS

In the record which Albany closes there is one earlier entry, a speech by Lear to Regan, which in itself is powerful enough but which, when it is read in the light of the pattern, takes on the resonant force of a choral statement about human experience. In a minute Lear is to plunge bareheaded into the storm, and there to join the naked Edgar. He is delivering a passionate invective against his daughters.

> If only to go warm were gorgeous,
> Why, nature needs not what thou gorgeous wear'st
> Which scarcely keeps thee warm. (II.iv, 271–73)

Lear almost foreshadows his own effort, in Act III, to strip down to nature by this accusation that his daughter is out of harmony with nature. She wears more than she needs, but to him she applies the canon of necessity. She strips him as he had stripped Cordelia from his favor. She is overdressed, but she will not allow him a satisfactory equipage. She shows us proud array at its worst—irresponsible, selfish. Ironically, what she wears does not keep her warm; Lear now recognizes her essential coldness. Yet she is the very antithesis of the poor naked wretches of whom Lear will soon think more, and among whom he will be. For the poor naked wretches of the play, the victims of the world, will survive in spirit. The gorgeous are doomed. In proud array, Lear failed; uncrowned, half-naked, he is saved. This is a central paradox of the play.

In interpreting the play, we must place beside the vast implications of *seeing* and *not seeing* the equally extensive ones of *taking off* and *putting on*. Human beings may with ironically good intentions remove the coverings which constitute or symbolize their defense against experience; or they may be stripped of them; or they may resort to nakedness. Human beings may likewise put on new coverings, as a defense in a disordered world, or as a disguise of real intentions that must not appear openly until evil ends have been achieved or until the danger from evil forces is lessened. Some men do not see clearly enough; some see too clearly; some are not adequately clad; and some are overdressed. Further, fate does not let some dress as they will, and others cannot see the character behind the dress. The images and symbols give us an inordinately complex world. But we may say, in general, that upon the quality of his seeing and upon the quality of his dress depends man's fate in the world. The play, however, goes on to a subject beyond man's fate in the world—man's moral and spiritual fate. In that realm, paradoxically, blindness and nakedness may have their values, for they do not exclude the possibility, respectively, of man's having insight, and immunity to worldly corruption. The blind are not misled by their eyes, nor the naked by their proud array.

*Maynard Mack*

## "WIT AND POETRY AND POPE":

SOME OBSERVATIONS
ON HIS IMAGERY

I

The point of departure of this essay is the current and useful description of Pope's kind of poetry as a poetry of statement.[1] One advantage of this description is that it is general enough to apply to other poetry as well. It asks us to bear in mind—what the temper of our present sensibility often disposes us to forget—that all poetry is in some sense poetry of statement; that without statement neither the Metaphysical kind of poem, witty, intellectual, and definitive, nor the Romantic kind, fluid and as it were infinitive (to mention only two) could be articulated at all; and accordingly, that the project of discrimination we are engaged on here is one of degree and not of kind.

Still, the real merit of the phrase is that it can apply specifically to Pope: it can set the problem. On the one hand, Pope writes a poetry with striking prose affinities. It has the Augustan virtues of perspicuity and ease which, whatever their status in poetry, are among the distinguishing attributes of prose discourse. It utilizes the denotative emphasis of Augustan diction, its precision and conciseness; the logical emphasis inherent in couplet rhetoric, its parallelism and antithesis. And it honours a whole body of reticences, reserves, restraints, exemplified perhaps best in the term "correctness," which tend to subdue and generalize its feeling and its wit. On the other hand, every reader of Pope is conscious of a host of qualities that look the other way. There is the kind of thing that Mr. Eliot is apparently glancing at when he says of Dryden's poetry that it states "immensely."[2] Or Mr. Tillotson, when he remarks in Pope a "composite activity," "a combination of simultaneous effects."[3] Or what Mr. Leavis and Mr. Wimsatt have pointed to in saying that Pope reconciles correctness with a subtle complexity, offsets and complicates the abstract logical patterns of his verse with counter-patterns which are alogical, poetic.[4]

Facing this duality in its leading poet, the eighteenth century (if I may over-simplify to make the point) was usually able to read the terms as "poetry is statement" and dismiss the problem: "If Pope be not a poet, where

Reprinted from *Pope and his Contemporaries,* edited by James L. Clifford and Louis A. Landa, by permission of Oxford University Press, Inc., New York, N. Y., and the author. Copyright 1949 by Maynard Mack.

[1] The phrase probably owes its present currency to Mr. Mark Van Doren's use of it in his study of *The Poetry of John Dryden* (1920; republished in 1931 and 1946).

[2] T. S. Eliot, "John Dryden," 1922 (*Selected Essays,* 1932, p. 273).

[3] G. Tillotson, *On the Poetry of Pope* (1938), pp. 156, 141. Cf. also his *Essays in Criticism* (1942), p. 103.

[4] F. R. Leavis, *Revaluation* (1936), p. 71; W. K. Wimsatt, "Rhetoric and Poems: The Example of Pope" (in *English Institute Essays, 1948,* 1949, pp. 198 ff.).

is poetry to be found?" [5] The nineteenth century tended to re-aline the terms in an antithesis, "poetry or statement," and rested its case by denying Pope a poet's name: "Dryden and Pope are not classics of our poetry, they are classics of our prose." [6] Our own present rephrasing, in which the antithesis becomes a paradox, seems to me an improvement. It enables us to take account of both extremes; to see that if Johnson was right in his evaluation of Pope's success, Arnold was right in his perception of some of the conditions out of which the success was made. By the same token, it enables us to situate the distinctive character of Pope's achievement—and hence of the critical problem he presents—in a very special kind of reconciliation between qualities of poetry and prose, a reconciliation managed even after the maximum concessions have been made to prose.

In this essay I want to discuss some of the aspects of this reconciliation that affect Pope's imagery. We regard imagery to-day, especially metaphor, as the most essential of the means by which language achieves poetic character, whether we choose to designate this character in its totality as "iconic," "alogical," "opaque," "complex," or by any other of our present set of honorific terms. If we are right in this assumption about metaphor, it implies that a poetry of statement will be signalized not by the absence of metaphorical effects but by their use in such a way that they do not disturb a logical surface of statement. And this, I think, is true in the case of Pope. In response to the sensibility of his time (and doubtless his own sensibility, too), Pope seems to me to have evolved an amazing variety of ways of obtaining the interest, richness, or tensions of metaphor while preserving, at any rate in appearance, those prose-like simplicities without which (as he probably agreed with Swift) "no human Performance can arrive to any great Perfection." [7] My purpose here is therefore to indicate some of the general principles that govern the effect of metaphor in Pope's poetry and then proceed to several of his characteristic methods of obtaining the benefits of metaphor without being, in any of the ordinary senses, strikingly metaphoric.

## II

Probably the best place to begin an examination of this kind is with a passage from Pope's *Elegy on the Death of an Unfortunate Lady,* which has often been cited as evidence of his belonging to the Metaphysical "line of wit":

> Most souls, 'tis true, but peep out once an age,
> Dull sullen pris'ners in the body's cage:
> Dim lights of life that burn a length of years,
> Useless, unseen, as lamps in sepulchres;
> Like Eastern kings a lazy state they keep,
> And close confin'd to their own palace sleep.[8]

[5] Johnson, "Life of Pope" (*Lives of the Poets,* ed. G. B. Hill, iii. 251).
[6] Arnold, "The Study of Poetry," *Essays in Criticism, Second Series* (*Wks.,* 1903, iv. 31).
[7] *A Letter to a Young Clergyman,* 1721 ( *Wks.,* ed. Herbert Davis, ix. 68).
[8] Ll. 17–22. This passage is cited for its metaphysical character by Middleton Murry, *Countries of the Mind* (1922), p. 86, and F. R. Leavis, *op. cit.,* pp. 70 ff.

The general affinities of these lines with Metaphysical poetry certainly need no emphasis, and the opening metaphor, at least, can be traced back through Dryden's

> imprison'd in so sweet a cage
> A soul might well be pleas'd to pass an age [9]

to Donne's

> She, whose faire body no such prison was
> But that a Soule might well be pleas'd to passe
> An age in her.[10]

Since we are looking for differences, however, we must not fail to notice that Pope rarely uses these extensive collocations of witty and ingenious images, and that when he does, it is almost always to establish something that his poems intend to disvalue—here a death-in-life theme, contrasting with a life-in-death theme built up around the lady. In consequence, only certain areas in Pope's poetry show the type of imagery that most Metaphysical poems tend to show throughout, with the result that the centre of gravity in his poetry often passes to other kinds of complication. It passes, for example, to such powerful counterpointings of tone and meaning as are obtained in the *Unfortunate Lady* by modulating from lines like those quoted to those beginning "Yet shall thy grave with rising flow'rs be drest." [11] The contrast in theme and feeling that these lines offer to those above is one that Donne would have elected to obtain through a conjunction of brilliant images. Pope obtains it—not only here, but habitually in his poems—through a conjunction of styles. The implied comparison usually possesses the richness and suggestiveness of a metaphor but is not, in any strict sense, metaphorical.

We must notice also in the passage quoted that the images, witty and to some extent ingenious as they are, stem from comparisons that are at bottom traditional and familiar—the soul as prisoner, lamp, monarch, the body as cage, sepulchre, palace. This is Pope's normal practice. Except in comic poetry like the *Dunciad* (where, again, it is partly a matter of disvaluing) he rarely stresses heterogeneity in the objects he brings together. For this reason he has little occasion to expand or amplify his comparisons in the manner we associate with Donne. It has not been often enough remarked, I think, that the "extended" Metaphysical image is a simple consequence of the Metaphysical discovery of "occult resemblances in things apparently unlike." That is to say, if one sets about comparing lovers to compasses at all, or the world to a beheaded man,[12] one is bound to specify in some detail the nature of the resemblances that make the image relevant; the value of the image is, as it were, generated in the process of constructing it. But it is also spent there. If such images seem wittier than any other kind because they display their wit at length, they also have less power in reserve.

[9] *To the Duchess of Ormond*, ll. 118–19.
[10] *The Second Anniversary*, ll. 221–3.
[11] L1. 63 ff.
[12] For the second instance, see *The Second Anniversary*, ll. 9 ff.

There is nothing in Donne's compass image, handsome as it is, to tempt the imagination to keep on unfolding it beyond the point at which the poet leaves it. On the other hand, Donne's gold-leaf image in the same poem has this power. It has it because it is powerfully compressed, and it can be powerfully compressed because it does not have to generate all its own potential: it is nourished at the source by normal and traditional associations. Pope's images, as suggested above, rely heavily on such associations. They take the ordinary established relationships of, say, singing and breath and soul, flesh and oblivion and marble, sepulchre and decay, finger and flute, parent and child, body and beauty, and with a delicate readjustment, freshen and fortify their implications:

> Oft as the mounting larks their notes prepare
> They fall, and leave their little lives in air.

> Tho' cold like you, unmov'd and silent grown,
> I have not yet forgot myself to stone.

> See the sad waste of all-devouring years,
> How Rome her own sad sepulchre appears.

> Such were the notes thy once-lov'd poet sung,
> Till death untimely stopp'd his tuneful tongue.[13]

> Me, let the tender Office long engage
> To rock the Cradle of reposing Age.

> Still round and round the ghosts of beauty glide,
> And haunt the places where their honour died.[14]

Finally, we must notice that the closed couplet exercises on images a peculiarly muting or subordinating influence. When we look at Dryden's lines quoted earlier, we see that, though he has taken over in large part the very words of Donne, the image in his verse has somehow become submerged. The reason, I think, is partly that Donne has sprawled the image across a weak rhyme which calls no attention to itself, whereas Dryden has suspended it within a strong rhyme which has a meaning of its own—which suggests, in fact, a correspondence between the soul's envelopment in body and its envelopment in time. Partly, also, that the movement of Donne's lines (and this is customary in his couplet poetry) exists simply to carry the image on its back; its pattern, in so far as it has any, is determined by and coextensive with the image. Dryden's couplet, on the other hand, being closed, has an assertive pattern of its own. The coiling and uncoiling rhythmical effect that comes from alternation of inverted with normal word order works with the movement of meaning to emphasize the logical stages

---

[13] This example illustrates particularly well the way in which an unbroken logical surface can cushion and absorb a powerful or even violent image. If we were to paraphrase the image, we should have to say something like: "Death took up the instrument of Parnell's music, and fingering (stopping) it in his own (untimely) tempo, brought the music to a premature (untimely) stop." Yet the effect of the normal logical meaning of "stopp'd" is to carry us smoothly across the opposites that are being yoked here.

[14] The quotations are from *Windsor Forest*, ll. 133–4; *Eloisa to Abelard*, ll. 23–4; *To Mr. Addison*, ll. 1–2; *To Robert, Earl of Oxford*, ll. 1–2; *Epistle to Dr. Arbuthnot*, ll. 408–9; and *Moral Essays*, ii, ll. 241–2.

of the soul's acceptance ("so sweet a cage"; "might well be pleas'd"; "pleas'd to pass an age") and the climactic stage is affirmed by rhyme. The closed couplet, in other words, tends to subdue images by putting them into competition with other forms of complication.

This point can be illustrated equally well from Pope. In the lines from the *Unfortunate Lady,* certainly the wittiest and boldest image is that in the third couplet. Yet here again the interest of the comparison has to compete with other interests—the strong rhyme, the parallelism, the humorously inverted syntax in both lines, which by withholding the completion of the sense units as long as possible keeps rather a lazy state itself.[15] Or take a passage in which Pope is developing one of Donne's images. This is Donne:

> Now,
> The ladies come; As Pirates, which doe know
> That there came weak ships fraught with Cutchannel
> The men board them.[16]

This is Pope:

> Painted for sight, and essenc'd for the smell,
> Like Frigates fraught with Spice and Cochine'l,
> Sail in the Ladies: How each Pyrate eyes
> So weak a Vessel, and so rich a Prize!
> Top-gallant he, and she in all her Trim,
> He boarding her, she striking sail to him.[17]

Donne is not at his best in this case, and Pope has the advantage of maturing Donne's idea at length—about as much at length as he was ever inclined to go. Still, leaving all that aside, one can see, I think, that Pope's figure, in spite of its richer elaborations, is not the primary and exclusive focus of attention that Donne's is. Donne's, as in our earlier instance, is the sole occupant of the verse rhetoric which presents it; Pope's is jostled for *Lebensraum* by many other contenders. There is, first, the drama of the ladies' arrival, which the verse itself is at some pains to enact in the first two and a half lines. Then there is the confrontation of forces in line 3, and the double assessment of the booty in line 4, both again rhetorically enacted. Finally, in line 5 comes a brilliant chiastic *rapprochement* of male and female in their bedizenment, to be followed in line 6 by an extension and also a qualification of this *rapprochement* with respect to sex (both parties are interested in the amorous duel, but their functions differ), the former carried by the metrical parallel, the latter by the antithesis in the sense. All these effects grow out of the potentialities of couplet rhetoric, not out of the image; and though they may co-operate with imagery, as here, they have a life of their own which tends to mute it.[18]

[15] This effect is easily verified by rearranging the words in normal order.
[16] *Satyre IV,* ll. 187–90.
[17] *The Fourth Satire of Dr. John Donne, Versifyed,* ll. 226–31.
[18] See also on this point, with respect to Dryden, M. W. Prior, *The Language of Tragedy* (1947), p. 169.

## III

So far we have been discussing orthodox kinds of imagery in Pope's poetry, together with some of the modifications to which this imagery is subjected. It is time to turn now to some of his more reticent modes of imaging, which achieve metaphorical effect without using what it is customary to regard as metaphor. The first of these may be studied in his proper names.

Pope's names warrant an essay in themselves. With the possible exception of Milton, no poet has woven so many so happily into verse. And this is not simply because, as Pope said of himself,

> Whoe'er offends, at some unlucky Time,
> Slides into Verse, and hitches in a Rhyme,[19]

but because Pope saw, like Milton, the qualitative elements (including in Pope's case the humorous qualities) that could be extracted from proper names. For an effect of romance, sonority, and exoticism akin to Milton's, though much mitigated by the couplet, any passage of his translation of Homer's catalogue of ships will do:

> The Paphlagonians Pylaemenes rules,
> Where rich Henetia breeds her savage Mules,
> Where Erythinus' rising Clifts are seen,
> Thy Groves of Box, Cytorus! ever green;
> And where Aegyalus and Cromna lie,
> And lofty Sesamus invades the Sky;
> And where Parthenius, roll'd thro' Banks of Flow'rs,
> Reflects her bord'ring Palaces and Bow'rs.[20]

For a combination of romance and humour, this passage:

> First he relates, how sinking to the chin,
> Smit with his mien, the Mud-nymphs suck'd him in:
> How young Lutetia, softer than the down,
> Nigrina black, and Merdamante brown,
> Vy'd for his love in jetty bow'rs below,
> As Hylas fair was ravish'd long ago.[21]

And for pure humour:

> 'Twas chatt'ring, grinning, mouthing, jabb'ring all,
> And Noise and Norton, Brangling and Breval,
> Dennis and Dissonance, and captious Art,
> And Snip-snap short, and Interruption smart,
> And Demonstration thin, and Theses thick,
> And Major, Minor, and Conclusion quick.[22]

19 *Imit. of Hor., Sat. II*, i, ll. 77–8.
20 *Iliad*, ii, ll. 1034 ff.
21 *Dunciad* (1743), ii, ll. 331–6.
22 *Ibid.*, ll. 237–42.

It will be observed in all these passages that as the names slide into verse they tend to take on a metaphorical colouring. Those in the first and third passages are of real places and persons, but the poetry does not require, any more than Milton's, that we identify them closely. Instead they become vehicles of an aura of associations clinging to epic warriors before Troy, or else of the vulgarity of a disputatious literature, which swallows up writers as Noise, Brangling, Dissonance swallow up Norton, Breval, and Dennis. Pope is a master of this metaphorical play with names. Sometimes the names he uses are quasi-metaphorical to begin with, like those he has invented in the Lutetia passage above. Or like those which allude—Adonis, Atossa, Shylock, Balaam, Timon, Sporus. Or those which have an allegorical cast—Uxorio, Worldly, Sir Morgan, Sir Visto, Patritio, Papillia, Hippia. Or those which personify—Avarice, Profusion, Billingsgate, Sophistry, Mathesis. Pope's habit with these classes of names is to interlayer them among his real objects and real persons, so that there results an additional and peculiarly suggestive kind of metaphorical play between concrete and abstract: allegorical Sir Morgan astride his cheese; [23] allusive Adonis driving to St. James's a whole herd of swine; [24] or personified Morality, Chicane, Casuistry, and Dulness suddenly brought into incongruous union with a judge named Page:

> Morality, by her false Guardians drawn,
> Chicane in Furs, and Casuistry in Lawn,
> Gasps, as they straiten at each end the cord,
> And dies, when Dulness gives her Page the word.[25]

Unquestionably, however, Pope's best metaphorical effects with names were obtained from specific ones, as in the lines on Dennis and Dissonance above. Did a certain duchess show an indiscriminate appetite for men? How better image it than with a nice derangement of proper names, opened with a particularly felicitous "what":

> What has not fired her bosom or her brain?
> Caesar and Tall-boy, Charles, and Charlemagne.[26]

Did the vein of poetry in contemporary versifiers hardly weigh up to a gramme? Then doubtless it was an age when

> nine such Poets made a Tate.[27]

Why was philosophy at Oxford so backward, so ponderous? Because the Oxford logicians came riding whip and spur, through thin and thick,

> On German Crousaz and Dutch Burgersdyck.[28]

[23] *Moral Essays*, iii, 1. 61.
[24] *Ibid.*, ll. 73–4.
[25] *Dunciad* (1743), iv, ll. 27–30.
[26] *Moral Essays*, ii, ll. 77–8.
[27] *Epistle to Dr. Arbuthnot*, 1. 190.
[28] *Dunciad* (1743), iv, 1. 198.

Or, since the current drama was slavishly derivative, why not let the patch-work image be projected partly with syntax and partly with names—a roll-call of stately ones, a tumbling huddle of risible ones:

> A past, vamp'd, future, old reviv'd, new piece,
> Twixt Plautus, Fletcher, Shakespeare, and Corneille
> Can make a Cibber, Tibbald, or Ozell.[29]

A second restrained mode of imaging in Pope's poetry is the allusion. Not simply the kind of descriptive allusion to persons, places, events, and characters that all poets make continual use of, and of which I shall say nothing here, but a kind that is specifically evaluative, constructing its image by setting beside some present object or situation not so much an-other object or situation as another dimension, a different sphere—fre-quently for the purpose of diminishing what is present, but often, too, for the purpose of enlarging or elevating it. Familiar examples of the first use are the correspondence of Sporus to Satan in one of his more degrading disguises—"at the Ear of *Eve,* familiar Toad"; [30] or (more humorously) of Cibber to Satan, on his exalted throne, at the opening of *Dunciad,* ii. A less familiar example is the witty correspondence suggested in *Dunciad,* iv between the dunces irresistibly drawn into the gravitational field of Dul-ness—

> by sure Attraction led
> And strong impulsive gravity of Head [31]—

and the feeling Sin has in Milton's poem, after the Fall, of being pulled toward earth by "sympathy, or some connatural force,"

> Powerful at greatest distance to unite
> With secret amity things of like kind. . . .
> Nor can I miss the way, so strongly drawn
> By this new-felt attraction and instinct.[32]

As for the second use, the *Essay on Man* begins with a particularly fine example, in the "garden tempting with forbidden fruit"; [33] while *Windsor Forest* both begins and ends with one; the groves of Eden, which establish the central symbol of the poem; and the dove of Noah, also described as the dove of grace and peace, which throws around Pope's vision of England as she comes out of her continental wars all the seventeenth-century religious associations of covenant, happy rescue, and divine mission.[34]

This evaluative kind of metaphor in Pope, whether diminishing or en-larging, is usually religious, and often very powerfully so. Here are some

29 *Ibid.,* i, ll. 284–6.
30 *Epistle to Dr. Arbuthnot,* l. 319.
31 Ll. 75–6.
32 Bk. x, ll. 244 ff.
33 Ep. i, l. 8.
34 Ll. 8 and 429–30.

instances in the lighter hues (I limit myself to instances that I think have
not been recorded by Pope's editors):

> And Heav'n is won by violence of Song.[35]
>
> And Zeal for that great House which eats him up.[36]
>
> Blest be the *Great!* for those they take away.[37]
>
> And instant, fancy feels th' imputed sense.[38]

These colours are darker:

> Each does but hate his neighbour as himself.[39]
>
> What Lady's Face is not a whited Wall? [40]

And this, though light in tone, carries a scathing indictment of the perversion of religious values in a money culture. Since it admirably illustrates
the way allusion can construct a cogent metaphor without intruding on a
casual surface and is, in fact, one of the most scarifying passages Pope ever
wrote, I quote it in full:

> On some, a *Priest* succinct in Amice white,
> Attends; *all flesh is nothing in his Sight!*
> Beeves, at his touch, at once to jelly *turn,*
> And the huge Boar is shrunk into an *Urn:*
> The board with specious *miracles* he loads,
> *Turns* Hares to Larks, and Pigeons into Toads.
> Another (for in all what one can shine?)
> Explains the Seve and Verdeur of the *Vine.*
> What cannot copious *Sacrifice attone?*
> Thy Treufles, Perigord! thy Hams, Bayonne!
> With French *Libation,* and Italian Strain
> *Wash* Bladen *white,* and *expiate* Hays's stain.
> Knight lifts the head, for what are crowds undone
> To *three essential* Partridges *in one?* [41]

There are two other modes of imagery of which Pope is fond, modes
that the concision of the closed couplet encourages and almost insists on,
though no other writer of the couplet has perfected them to a like extent.
These are pun and juxtaposition. Juxtaposition operates in Pope's poetry
in several ways. One of them, as has lately been pointed out,[42] is through
zeugma, which the economy of this verse form often calls for and which can
itself be modulated either into metaphor—"Or stain her Honour, or her
new Brocade," or into pun—"And sometimes Counsel take—and sometimes
*Tea.*" [43] (In either case, the effect is ultimately metaphorical, a correspond-

35 *Imit. of Hor., Ep. II.* i, 1. 240. Cf. Matt. xi. 12.

36 *Moral Essays,* iii, 1. 208. Cf. Ps. lxix. 9.

37 *Epistle to Dr. Arbuthnot,* 1. 225. Cf. Job i. 21.

38 *Dunciad,* ii, 1. 200. Cf. the theological sense of "imputed."

39 *Moral Essays,* iii, 1. 108. Cf. Matt. xxii. 39. I have noticed this allusion elsewhere (*College English* [1946], vii. 269).

40 *The Fourth Satire of Dr. John Donne, Versifyed,* 1. 151. Cf. Matt. xxiii. 27. (The allusion is Pope's addition.)

41 *Dunciad* (1743), iv, ll. 549–62. (Italics mine.)

42 In Mr. Wimsatt's essay cited above. Cf. also Austin Warren, "The Mask of Pope" (*Rage for Order,* 1948, p. 45).

43 *Rape of the Lock,* ii, 1. 107, iii, 1. 8.

ence being suggested between Belinda's attitudes to chastity and brocade, or between Queen Anne's, and her society's, to politics and tea.)

My own concern, however, is not with zeugma, but with the metaphorical effects that can arise from simple juxtaposition. For example, from a list of items *seriatim,* with one inharmonious term:

> Puffs, Powders, Patches, Bibles, Billet-doux.[44]

Or from a simple parallel inside the line:

> Dried Butterflies, and Tomes of Casuistry.[45]

Or from a similar parallel inside the couplet:

> Now Lapdogs give themselves the rowzing Shake,
> And sleepless Lovers, just at Twelve, awake.[46]

This is a very versatile device. In the *Rape of the Lock,* from which the above examples are taken, Pope uses it to mirror in his lines and couplets the disarray of values in the society he describes, the confounding of antithetical objects like lapdogs and lovers, bibles and *billets-doux.* On the other hand, in the *Essay on Man,* this same device, redirected by the context, can be made to mirror the "equalizing" view of antithetical objects taken by the eye of God or by the god-like magnanimous man:

> A hero perish, or a sparrow fall.[47]
> As toys and empires, for a god-like mind.[48]

It is also a very sensitive device. The potential metaphor that every juxtaposition tends to carry in suspension requires only the slightest jostling to precipitate it out. Sometimes a well-placed alliteration will do it:

> The Mind, in Metaphysics at a Loss,
> May wander in a wilderness of Moss.[49]

Sometimes an inter-animation of words, as here between the "smooth" eunuch and the "eas'd" sea:

> Where, eas'd of Fleets, the Adriatic main
> Wafts the smooth Eunuch and enamour'd Swain.[50]

And sometimes a set of puns, as in this example, fusing the biologist with the object of his study:

> The most recluse, discreetly open'd, find
> Congenial matter in the Cockle-kind.[51]

[44] *Ibid.,* i, 1. 138.
[45] *Ibid.,* v, 1. 122. A particularly graceful comparison in its suggestion of a common animation, brilliance, delicacy of movement, and perishableness in the worlds of ethics and Lepidoptera.
[46] *Ibid.,* i, ll. 15–16.
[47] Ep. i, 1. 88.
[48] Ep. iv, 1. 180.
[49] *Dunciad* (1743), iv, ll. 449–50.
[50] *Ibid.,* ll. 309–10.
[51] *Ibid.,* ll. 447–8.

Pun, of course, brings before us Pope's most prolific source of imagery in his comic and satiric poetry—which is to say, in the bulk of his work. His puns in other poems—*Windsor Forest, Eloisa,* the *Essay on Man,* the *Essay on Criticism*—are deeply buried and always reticent. But in the satires and the *Dunciad,* particularly the latter, he spends them openly and recklessly, with superb effect. They cease to be in these poems ordinary puns, like those we find in Metaphysical poetry, where, because of the conceit, pun has a lesser job to do; they become instead Metaphysical conceits themselves, yoking together violently, as Mr. Leavis has noticed,[52] the most heterogeneous ideas. Moreover, when they are used together with ordinary images, the real metaphorical power is likely to be lodged in them. Thus the following figures are not especially bold themselves, but the puns inside them open out like peacocks' tails:

> Ye tinsel Insects! whom a Court maintains,
> That counts your Beauties only by your *Stains.*
>
> On others Int'rest her gay liv'ry flings,
> Int'rest that waves on *Party-colour'd* wings.
>
> At length Corruption, like a gen'ral flood,
> (So long by watchful ministers withstood)
> Shall deluge all; and Av'rice, creeping on,
> Spread like a *low-born* mist, and blot the sun.[53]

Here, then, are four classes of metaphorical effect in Pope's poetry, all of them obtained outside the normal channels of overt simile and metaphor. One of them, juxtaposition (its collateral descendant, zeugma, would make a second), stems from the structure of the closed couplet itself. Two more, allusion and pun, are encouraged to a large extent by its fixed and narrow room. And none of them, it is important to notice, calls attention to itself as metaphorical. Between them, nevertheless, without violating at all the prose conventions of the Augustan mode, they do a good deal of the work that we to-day associate with the extended metaphor and conceit.

## IV

The devices of complication touched on in the preceding sections pertain primarily to local texture: the line and couplet. I want to add to these, in conclusion, three patterns that are more pervasive; that help supply the kind of unity in Pope's poems which he is popularly not supposed to have. Actually, there is a wide variety of such patterns. There are the characteristics of the dramatic speaker of every poem, who shifts his style, manner, and quality of feeling considerably from poem to poem, as anyone will see who will compare carefully the *Essay on Criticism* with the *Essay on Man,* or the *Epistle to Dr. Arbuthnot* with that to Augustus. There is the character of the interlocutor in the poems that have dialogue, by no means a man of straw. There is the implicit theme, usually announced in a word or phrase

---

[52] *Op. cit.,* p. 99.
[53] From *Epil. to the Sats., Dial.* ii, ll. 220–1; *Dunciad* (1743), iv., ll. 537–8; and *Moral Essays,* iii, ll. 135–8. (Italics mine.)

toward the outset of the poem, and while seldom developed in recurrent imagery, as in Shakespeare, almost always developed in recurrent references and situations. There is also, often, a kind of pattern of words that reticulates through a poem, enmeshing a larger and larger field of associations—for instance, words meaning light in the *Essay on Criticism,* or the word "head" (and, of course, all terms for darkness) in the *Dunciad.* And there are a great many more such unifying agents.

The three that I shall examine briefly here are irony, the portrait, and mock-heroic. Pope's irony, fully analysed, would require a book. The point about it that is most relevant to our present topic is that it is a mode of complication closely resembling metaphor. At its most refined, in fact, as in Swift's *Modest Proposal* or Pope's praise of George II in the *Epistle to Augustus,* it asks us to lay together not two, but three, different perspectives on reality. First, the surface, and second, the intended meanings, these two corresponding roughly to vehicle and tenor in a metaphor; and then, third— to use again the Pope and Swift examples—the kind of propositions that English projectors were *usually* making about Ireland, or the poets about George II. Pervasive irony of this type—of which there is a good deal in Pope—tends to resist the presence of bold imagery, for two reasons. In the first place, because it consists already in a mutual translation, to and fro, between one kind of complex whole with all its particularities clinging to it (what is said), and a different complex whole with all its revised particularities (what is meant); a translation that profuse or striking imagery only clutters and impedes. And in the second place, because the success of the medium depends on adopting the attitudes, motives, and so far as possible even the terms of a very conventional point of view. If one is going to write an ironic love song "in the modern taste," one almost has to refer to "Cupid's purple pinions" [54]; or if a panegyric on George II, to the usual terms for kingly prowess:

> Your Country, chief, in Arms abroad defend.[55]

To find a more striking phrase would destroy the subtlety of the ironic comment (i.e., its resemblance to what a Cibber might have said); and would, of course, too, destroy the mutual translation between the arms of battle and those of Madame Walmoden.

To all this, in the *Epistle to Augustus,* is added the further layer of metaphor that results from Pope's imitation of what Horace had written about *his* Caesar. Nor is this layer confined alone to the poems which are imitations. The Roman background, it has been well observed, is a kind of universal Augustan metaphor or "myth." [56] It lies behind Pope's work, and much of Swift's and Fielding's, like a charged magnetic field, a reservoir of attitudes whose energy can be released into their own creations at a touch. Not through the Horatian or Virgilian or Ovidian tags; these are only its minor aspect; but through the imposed standard of a mighty and civilized tradition in arts, morals, government. At the same time, conveniently, it is a standard

---

54 Cf. Swift's *A Love Song, in the Modern Taste,* st. I.
55 *Imit. of Hor., Ep. II,* i, l. 3.
56 Cf. J. C. Maxwell, "Demigods and Pickpockets," *Scrutiny,* xi (1942-3), 34 ff.

that can be used two ways: for a paradigm of the great and good now lost
in the corruptions of the present, as in the comparison of George II with
Augustus Caesar; or for the headwaters of a stream down which still flow the
stable and continuing classic values:

> You show us Rome was glorious, not profuse.
> The world's just wonder, and ev'n thine, O Rome!
> Who would not weep, if Atticus were he! [57]

This last example brings us to Pope's portraits. These, again, have the
complicating characteristics of metaphors, without drawing attention to
themselves as such. They are often erroneously called "illustrations," as if
their content were exhausted in being identified with some abstraction implied or stated by the poem. But what abstractions will exhaust the characters of Atticus, Sporus, Atossa, Balaam, and a score of others? To instance
from one of the simplest portraits, so that it may be quoted entire, here is
Narcissa:

> "Odious! in woollen! 'twould a saint provoke!"
> (Were the last words that poor Narcissa spoke):
> "No, let a charming chintz, and Brussels lace
> Wrap my cold limbs, and shade my lifeless face:
> One would not, sure, look frightful when one's dead:
> And—Betty—give this cheek a little red." [58]

This, to the extent that it illustrates anything, illustrates the poem's prose
argument that our ruling passion continues to our last breath. But as a
metaphor it explores, not without considerable profundity, through the
character of one type of woman, the character of the human predicament
itself. Here we have, as her name implies, the foolish self-lover; but also—
in a wider, more inevitable, and uncensorable sense—the self-lover who
inhabits each of us by virtue of our mortal situation, the very principle of
identity refusing to be erased. Here, too, we have the foolish concern for
appearances, vastly magnified by the incongruity of its occasion; but also
the fundamental human clutching at the familiar and the known. And embracing it all is the central paradox of human feelings about death and life.
Cold limbs don't need wrapping (the conjunction of terms itself suggests that
death can be apprehended but not comprehended), nor dead faces shading;
and yet, as our own death rituals show, somehow they do. The levels of
feeling and experience startled into activity in this short passage can hardly
be more than pointed at in the clumsiness of paraphrase. The irony of
words like "saint," the ambiguities of "charming" and "shade," the tremendous compression in "frightful" of "the anguish of the marrow, The
ague of the skeleton," accumulate as one contemplates them.

All of Pope's portraits have at least the complexity of this one, and all are
equally metaphorical in effect. If they do not call attention to themselves as
metaphors, it is probably because in them the vehicle has largely absorbed
the tenor; for metaphors in general seem to take on prominence according

---

[57] From *Moral Essays*, iv, 1. 23; *Essay on Criticism*, 1. 248; *Epistle to Dr. Arbuthnot*, 1. 214.
[58] *Moral Essays*, i, ll. 246–51.

as both the tenor and the vehicle (viz. lovers as well as compasses) are insisted on at once. In any case, they behave like metaphors in Pope's poems, usually assuming, in addition to their functions locally, an important unifying role. Sometimes they define the entire structure of a poem, as in *Moral Essays,* ii, where they develop the easy-going aphorism of the opening—"Most women have no characters at all"—into a mature interpretation of what personality is. Sometimes they supply the central symbols, as with Timon in *Moral Essays,* iv, "Vice" in Dialogue ii of the *Epilogue to the Satires,* or the Man of Ross and Balaam in *Moral Essays,* iii. Likewise, in *Arbuthnot,* Atticus and Sporus appear at just the crucial phases in the argument and knit up, as it were, the two essential ganglia in the sinews of the drama that the poem acts out between the poet and his adversaries. They give us, successively, the poet analytical and judicial, who can recognize the virtues of his opponents ("Blest with each Talent and each Art to please"), whose deliberation is such that he can even mirror in his language—its subjunctives, its antitheses, the way it hangs the portrait over an individual without identifying it with him—the tentative, insinuating, never-wholly-committed hollow man who is Atticus; and then the poet roused and righteous, no longer judicial but executive, touching with Ithuriel's spear the invader in the garden, spitting from his mouth (with a concentration of sibilants and labials) the withered apple-seed. Both portraits are essential to the drama that unifies the poem.

The great pervasive metaphor of Augustan literature, however, including Pope's poetry, is the metaphor of tone: the mock-heroic. It is very closely allied, of course, to the classical or Roman myth touched on earlier and is, like that, a reservoir of strength. By its means, without the use of overt imagery at all, opposite and discordant qualities may be locked together in "a balance or reconcilement of sameness with difference, of the general with the concrete, the idea with the image, the individual with the representative, the sense of novelty and freshness with old and familiar objects"—the mock-heroic seems made on purpose to fit this definition of Coleridge's of the power of imagination. For a literature of decorums like the Augustan, it was a metaphor with every sort of value. It could be used in the large, as in *Joseph Andrews, Tom Jones, The Beggar's Opera, The Rape of the Lock, The Dunciad,* or in the small—the passage, the line. It could be set in motion by a passing allusion, not necessarily to the classics:

> Calm Temperance, whose blessings those partake,
> Who hunger, and who thirst, for scribling sake;

by a word:

> Glad chains, warm furs, broad banners, and broad faces;

even by a cadence:

> And the fresh vomit run for ever green.[59]

Moreover, it was a way of getting the local, the ephemeral, the pressure of life as it was lived, into poetry, and yet distancing it in amber:

[59] From *Dunciad* (1743), i, ll. 49–50, 88; ii, l. 156.

That live-long wig, which Gorgon's self might own,
Eternal buckle takes in Parian stone.[60]

It was also a way of qualifying an attitude, of genuinely "heroicizing" a Man of Ross, a parson Adams, a School-mistress, yet undercutting them with a more inclusive attitude:

Rise, *honest* Muse! and sing the Man of Ross.[61]

Above all—and this, I think, was its supreme advantage for Pope—it was a metaphor that could be made to look two ways. If the heroic genre and the heroic episodes lurking behind *The Rape of the Lock* diminish many of the values of this society, they also partially throw their weight behind some others. Clarissa's speech is an excellent case in point.[62] Her words represent a sad shrinkage from the epic views of Glaucus which reverberate behind them, views involving real heroism and (to adapt Mr. Eliot's phrase) the awful daring of a real surrender. Still, the effect of the contrast is not wholly minimizing. Clarissa's vision of life, worldly as it is when seen against the heroic standard, surpasses the others in the poem and points, even if obliquely, to the tragic conflict between the human lot and the human will that is common to life at every level.

This flexibility of the mock-heroic metaphor is seen in its greatest perfection in the *Dunciad*. There are, indeed, three thicknesses of metaphor in this poem: an over-all metaphor, in which the poem as a whole serves as vehicle for a tenor which is the decline of literary and human values generally; a network of local metaphor, in which this poem is especially prolific; and in between, the specifically mock-heroic metaphor which springs from holding the tone and often the circumstances of heroic poetry against the triviality of the dunces and their activities. But what is striking about this metaphor in the *Dunciad,* and indicative of its flexibility, is that it is applied quite differently from the way it is applied in the *Rape of the Lock*. There, the epic mode as vehicle either depresses the values of the actors, as with Belinda, or somewhat supports them, as with Clarissa. Here, on the contrary, one of the two lines of development (the comic) grows from allowing the actors to depress and degrade the heroic mode, its dignity and beauty. Again and again Pope builds up in the poem effects of striking epic richness, only to let them be broken down, disfigured, stained—as the word "vomit" stains the lovely movement and suggestion of the epic line quoted above. Thus the diving and other games in Book II disfigure the idea of noble emulation and suggest the befoulment of heroic values through the befoulment of the words and activities in which these values are recorded. Thus the fop's Grand Tour in IV mutilates a classical and Renaissance ideal (cf. also Virgil's Aeneas, to whose destined wanderings toward Rome the fop's are likened) of wisdom ripened by commerce with men and cities. Indeed, the lines of the whole passage are balanced between the ideal and the fop's perversions of it:

[60] *Moral Essays,* iii, ll. 294–5.
[61] *Ibid.,* l. 250. (Italics mine.) The blend of irony and praise is carefully maintained throughout the passage.
[62] Canto v, ll. 9 ff.

> A dauntless infant! never scar'd with God.
> Europe he saw, and Europe saw him too.
> Judicious drank, and greatly daring dined;

or between related ideals and what has happened to them:

> To happy Convents, bosomed deep in Vines,
> Where slumber Abbots, purple as their Wines.

or between epic resonances, the epic names, and the sorry facts:

> To where the Seine, obsequious as she runs,
> Pours at great Bourbon's feet her silken sons.[63]

This is one line of development in the *Dunciad*. The other is its converse: the epic vehicle is gradually made throughout the poem to enlarge and give a status of serious menace to all this ludicrous activity. Here the epic circumstance of a presiding goddess proved invaluable. Partly ludicrous herself, she could also become the locus of inexhaustible negation behind the movements of her trivial puppets; her force could be associated humorously, but also seriously, with the powerful names of Chaos, Night, Anti-Christ, and with perversions of favourite order symbols like the sun, monarchy, and gravitation. Here, too, the epic backgrounds as supplied by Milton could be drawn in. Mr. C. S. Lewis has remarked of *Paradise Lost* that "only those will fully understand it who see that it might have been a comic poem." [64] The *Dunciad* is one realization of that might-have-been. Over and above the flow of Miltonic echoes and allusions, or the structural resemblances like Cibber's (or Theobald's) Pisgah-vision based on Adam's, or the clustered names of dunces like those of Milton's devils, thick as the leaves that strew bad books in Grubstreet—the *Dunciad* is a version of Milton's theme in being the story of an uncreating Logos. As the poem progresses, our sense of this increases through the calling in of more and more powerful associations by the epic vehicle. The activities of the dunces and of Dulness are more and more equated with religious anti-values, culminating in the passage on the Eucharist quoted earlier. The metaphor of the coronation of the king-dunce moves always closer to and then flows into the metaphor of the Day of the Lord, the descent of the anti-Messiah, the uncreating Word. Meantime, symbols which have formerly been ludicrous—insects, for instance, or sleep—are given by this expansion in the epic vehicle a more sombre cast. The dunces thicken and become less individual, more anonymous, expressive of blind inertia—bees in swarm, or locusts blackening the land. Sleep becomes tied up with its baser physical manifestations, with drunkenness, with deception, with ignorance, with neglect of obligation, and finally with death. This is the sleep which *is* death, we realize, a *Narrendämmerung*, the twilight of the moral will. And yet, because of the ambivalence of the mock-heroic metaphor, Pope can keep to the end the tension between all these creatures as comic and ridiculous, and their destructive potentiality in being so. Certainly two of the finest puns in any

[63] *Dunciad* (1743), iv, ll. 284 ff.
[64] *A Preface to Paradise Lost* (1942), p. 93.

poetry are those with which he continues to exploit this tension at the very end of the poem, when Dulness finally *yawns* and Nature *nods.*

### V

The purpose of this essay has been to supply a few, a very few, of the materials that are requisite for giving the phrase "poetry of statement" specific content. I have tried to suggest that Pope is poetic, but not in the way that the Metaphysicals are poetic, even where he is most like them; that if the prominent metaphor is the distinctive item in their practice, this has been replaced in Pope's poetry partly by devices of greater compression, like allusion and pun, partly by devices that are more distributive, like irony and mock-heroic, and of course by a multitude of other elements—the net effect of all these being to submerge the multiplicities of poetic language just beneath the singleness of prose. Twenty-five years ago it would have been equally important to say that Pope is not poetic as the Romantics are poetic, for in this century there has always been a tendency to subsume him as far as possible under the reigning orthodoxy. It is true that in certain areas Pope's poetry faintly resembles that of the Romantics; in certain others, that of the line of wit. But the task of criticism for the future, when we are likely to be paying more and more attention to Pope as our own poetry moves in the direction suggested by Mr. Auden, and by Mr. Eliot in his *Quartets,* is not with Pope as a pre-Romantic or a post-Metaphysical, but as an Augustan poet whose peculiar accomplishment, however we may choose to rate it on the ultimate scale of values, was the successful fusion of some of the most antithetical features of verse and prose.

*John Crowe Ransom*

## ON SHAKESPEARE'S LANGUAGE

When Wordsworth declared:

*We must be free or die, who speak the tongue That Shakespeare spake,*

he was referring to the heritage of Shakespeare as an official *exemplum* to which the English national spirit, if it should ever flag, might look and renew itself. We will affirm the sentiment. But I should like to look for a moment at the literary estate of Shakespeare as a property both larger and more specific than that. Let us regard Shakespeare as a fountain of language, from which was to flow and is yet to flow our peculiar English literature. More than any other writer, he laid down poetic strategies that suited the language, and one of his practices will be my present topic. It was good in his poetry, and it has determined the practice of other poets; it is surprisingly determining today, after the centuries of revolution in every department of life; and here, on a continent he never saw.

The specific usage which I have in mind as having been so fruitful is Shakespeare's way of compounding Latinical elements with his native English. I say his way of doing it; it is commonplace to bring Latinical words into English discourse, and was in Shakespeare's time; but not to do it in Shakespeare's way. He made it his frequent way only after he had come to maturity, but there are many instances of it. Thus Macbeth has Duncan's blood upon his hand and soliloquizes:

> *Will all great Neptune's ocean wash this blood*
> *Clean from my hand? No, this my hand will rather*
> *The multitudinous seas incarnadine,*
> *Making the green one red.*

We need not attribute much conscious Latinity to the first line; probably the public of Shakespeare's time had quite assimilated their Neptune, and indicated possession by the epithet they gave him; it is a folk locution rather than a literary one. So that, if we do not stop on this line, we may say that the four lines constitute a passage in native English, almost monosyllabic, broken by that Latinical explosion in the third line. The last line is specially primitive, having three strong accented words juxtaposed with some peril to the clear syntax; for we wonder, I think, whether to take *one* as going with *green* or with *red;* but a locution like *solid red* while explicit would be mildly Latinical, and it is apparently Shakespeare's idea to follow up the Latinical third line by about half a line of primitive language even with its natural disabilities.

The two big words do not represent Shakespeare's Latinity at its best but they are impressive enough. *Multitudinous* is *multitudo* plus *-ous,* the adjective suffix used in English to denote that the noun root it attaches to is Latin, and doubtless itself an adaptation of the Latin suffix *-osus.* (The native adjective is formed of an English noun plus a *-y* or *-ish* suffix; and many poets have liked to stud their verse with homely *-y* adjectives; Keats for example.) Multitudinous has something to do with many-ness, but we cannot tell whether it means here that the seas are many, or that the seas have so many waters. A fairly synonymous word would be *innumerable,* but that is too easy, and too well assimilated into the language already. Tennyson used it in the famous line,

> *And murmuring of innumerable bees,*

but he did it, we may suppose, for the purpose of his sound-pattern. Its Latin meaning is explicit and brings nothing strange into its English context. Keats had tried for something bolder when he described the colored windowpanes of Madeline's boudoir as

> *Innumerable of stains and splendid dyes;*

where the *of*-phrase is a kind of English for what we used to call the Ablative of Specification; that is, Keats tried to restore life to a commonplace Latinical word by recovering an original Latin idiom. As for Macbeth's speech, we wonder if there may not be some idiomatic relation of *seas* to *multitudi-nous*. And *incarnadine* is one of those words from the Latin by way of the French, Latinical in the second degree. It is the French name of a pigment, here used by Shakespeare—probably for the first time—as a verb meaning to color to the shade of that pigment. But its proximity to *multitudinous* induces Latinity into our consciousness so that we stop and reflect upon its Latin meaning: to paint to the color of blood.

We can readily isolate from the later plays of Shakespeare many passages of three, four, or five lines each, having just about this architecture, and this poetic quality. They show a condensation of Latinical effect in a context of unusually pure English. And the Latinical words will seem fresh, the test being that we feel obliged to go back to the Latin to explore the full sense of them.

Everybody understands now that Shakespeare knew a good deal of Latin, and for example more than might be supposed if one banked too heavily on Jonson's reproach that he had "small Latin and less Greek." At the free grammar school in Avon he must have got just the right amount of Latin to conceive a great fondness for it, and to have its resonance always afterward going through his head, and never to give up the sense of it as a once-nearly-possessed language, therefore still a foreign language, teasing him to utter it. Jonson had a great deal more of Latin, and—perhaps this was a consequence—got used to it; he never cared to import it consciously into his verse. I am talking speculatively and like an impressionable layman. The vocabulary of Shakespeare has been analyzed for its Latin and other constituents by careful scholars; for instance by the late Oxford Professor of Poetry, George Gordon. But in general it is my understanding that the Shakespearean scholars have not speculated upon an issue that would seem very engaging: whether there are not some principles, or habits, which might govern Shakespeare's Latinity as a literary instrument.

It is still a fact, three and a half centuries from Shakespeare, that many words now thoroughly accredited as English are visibly from the Latin; we are conscious of them as of a minority of not quite assimilated words; they bring back our school-sense. And we reflect upon the two large historic accessions of Latin words into English. In the first one, that of the Norman period, the words introduced were French in their immediate identities, but Latin ultimately; the transmission was doubtless as much by oral means as by literature. It is customary to say that this stock of new words had been thoroughly assimilated by the end of the fourteenth century, so that in Chaucer we have a single unified language, with no special consciousness when the words were from the Latin. The foreignness had gone from them. And we think of Chaucer as taking pains if necessary to use them easily, in order to help naturalize them if they were still not quite naturalized. That is the intention we mean sometimes to attribute to him as a patriot.

The other large-scale importation was an incident of the European Renaissance which came by way of the universities in the sixteenth century. In no sense is Renaissance or Rebirth the right name for the general movement more than it is linguistically. The new ideas that filled the undernourished European consciousness were old ideas recovered, classical ideas; but reborn with their original bodies, the classical words. Or they are new ideas developing from the classical ideas and finding classical words to suit. But we recall what had happened to the invading words after the Norman conquest. Were the Renaissance invaders likewise to be assimilated into English and to lose their identity?

In answer I suggest that precisely this event was imminent, that the Latinical words were disappearing as such in the literature that was being written, but that Shakespeare's example more than any other one thing stopped the process. On this supposition, it was Shakespeare who preserved the life of Latin as a foreign language still held tributary to the borrowings of luxurious English writers. Without Shakespeare the Latinical words would probably have been lost. They would have been lost not by being dropped *out of* the language but by being dropped *into* it—as countless other foreign words have been lost within our capacious language and are now used over and over without any sense of their foreignness. Knowing as we do that Shakespeare was of humble birth, did not attend the university, and as an actor was like a man belonging to a trade rather than to a gentle profession, we often wonder where we are to look for the signs of his social inferiority. Perhaps we will imagine that his linguistic strategy was not the aristocratic one. Probably at one time, say just before Shakespeare's birth, it was aristocratic to make a display of one's Latinity; but toward the end of the century it was aristocratic, on the contrary, to make no difference in one's speech between the Latinical and the native elements, and the display of an attainment of so common an order as Latinity rated as vulgar affectation. Was Shakespeare then a generation behind the best usage? But there is no profit for us here. His early plays are of nondescript Latinity, quite *à la mode;* and the special turn his Latinity began to take was a novel and literary move, not a social one.

The dying Hamlet says to Horatio:

> *If thou didst ever hold me in thy heart,*
> *Absent thee from felicity a while,*
> *And in this harsh world draw thy breath in pain*
> *To tell my story.*

It is one of Arnold's "touchstones" of poetry, indisputably a passage of first-rate quality. But its whole distinction is connected with the *absent thee* and the *felicity* of the second line. In Schlegel's first-rate German translation of the plays it comes as a shock to us to discover that both these Latinical items have disappeared, as inadmissible into that language. To an English linguistic sense such a passage does not seem to have been translated when we meet with it in Schlegel. Both the terms are weaker in their Latinical version than they would be in some good native version, but they are strong by their visible opposition to the native context. A German friend tells me that some German professor might conceivably say, *"Absentiren Sie sich"* to a favored pupil, and would be understood, but that the effect would be that of an academic joke. And we may construe Shakespeare's line somewhat in that sense, as the pleasantry of a young Hamlet fresh from the university even though uttered among his last words. But apparently Arnold, who is prepared to take the line quite independent of dramatic setting or linguistic context, did not hold this view of it; it is notorious that he declined any analysis of his touchstones. To him it is one of those locutions resounding incessantly in the memory, and so effective for the feelings that it will serve as a standard of what the noblest poetry must be like.

If Hamlet's speech will not go into German, where there is no Latinity, we can imagine the contrary case when effort is made to bring it into French. This is not a bi-lingual tongue either, but here it is the Latinity which is the staple and the commonplace. We may have had occasion to see what happens, if we consulted Gide's version of the play a few years ago. The Prince of Denmark's French is admirable, and if we say that Hamlet is not himself here, that his mind is suddenly less interesting, that his sea-change is a little ludicrous, it is only after explaining courteously that we happen to have heard his English. Now, we are often told that English is a superior language for poetry, and we must often have felt that this is said too absolutely for politeness, or truth for that matter. Yet it can be said safely that all Shakespeare's effects were possible in English, and that some of the happiest ones are evidently not possible in German or French.

When Lear finds his Fool beside him in the storm, his thought suddenly turns from his own sufferings to the condition of the poor. It is a kingly thought, and leads him to apostrophize privilege everywhere:

> *O, I have ta'en*
> *Too little thought of this. Take physic, pomp;*
> *Expose thyself to feel what wretches feel,*
> *That thou mayst shake the superflux to them*
> *And show the heavens more just.*

There is a slight flurry of Latinity in the *physic, pomp, expose*. But the key to the passage is *superflux,* a word that nobody had used till then, and, to tell the truth, a word that even this usage did not fix securely in the language. It would mean overflow; in Schlegel the German is *das Uberflüssige*. I judge that we all are reminded more or less consciously of Lazarus begging for the crumbs which fall—without being noticed because there is so much food—from the rich man's table. But I believe we should balk at speaking of them as an overflow. We are prepared to accept a bolder metaphor in the Latin than we can take in the English. Especially striking is the collocation of *shake* and *superflux*. The English is a little inhospitable to the stranger, does not make it easy for him. All we can think of really shaking to the poor in this connection would be the tablecloth holding the surplus crumbs; which would not exactly be flowing. The whole image receives more notice and not less from our having these literal questions about it.

Latinical practices as startling as this are unusual in the early plays, and they are also hard to find in the contemporary authors. I suppose nobody would expect to find them in Spenser. In the *Shepheardes Calender* there are passages in straight English talk and rude English meters, and there are other passages in good university language and syllabic meters, both effects quite nicely specialized. In *The Faerie Queene* this beginning has not been followed up. There is no end of innovations in words and the forms of words, but there is no particular consciousness of the Latin as calling for a different response from that of the English and there is a nearly fatal over-all smoothness in the tone; we do not sense any dramatic effect in the shift from one tone to the other. The proportion of Latinical words, if we may indulge in a very simple generalization, is too large for effectiveness.

In Marlowe the Shakespearean practice is sometimes almost hit upon. His

> *See, see where Christ's blood streams in the firmament!*

does not sufficiently develop the opposed contexts. When Faustus exclaims on seeing Helen:

> *Was this the face that launched a thousand ships,*
> *And burnt the topless towers of Ilium?*

we have two bold metaphors about the force of beauty, of which the second somehow does not strike us as quite native English. Then we proceed to note that *topless* is Virgilian, and too far-fetched and "literary" to be a folk-metaphor; *Ilium* is Latinical for Troy, as the place is known to English-speaking folk; and of course syllabic pentameter rates in the sixteenth century as Latinical, or at least Romanic, in comparison with English accentual meters, though it is almost too common to touch us linguistically. And in the scene before the Emperor there is a passage between Faustus and a heckling knight, in which a magical trick is played upon the knight, who expostulates:

> *Thou damned wretch and execrable dog,*
> *Bred in the concave of some monstrous rock,*
> *How darest thou thus abuse a gentleman?*

The gentleman has not only a turn for abuse but a pretty gift for the Latinities. And Faustus explains to the Emperor in prose that he has only "worthily requited this injurious knight." Briefly, we cannot tell what linguistic development might have lain ahead of Marlowe when he died before reaching the age of thirty.

Perhaps I may be credited with looking rather widely though sketchily round to find other evidences of Shakespeare's kind of Latinity. Here I can only say, and provisionally, that so far as I can see we have to give Shakespeare the credit for the strategy in question, and for its persistence in literature. If so, it is a massive disposition within the language that he accomplished, and not a small disposition. Shakespeare, or something else, stopped the reduction of the Latinical words into common words, and held them in a state of perpetual suspension and arrest. They are in the language, but not quite of it. If our language were a political sovereignty, we might say that the native stock had welcomed the immigration of the well-favored foreigners, whose mores, skills, and presences were quite distinct, but had not naturalized them; they became a sort of colony, by no means free of the obligation to work like the regular citizens at practical tasks, and indeed they were specially qualified for expert or precision techniques; but expected also to appear sometimes at the formal occasions of society in costume.

This must be a unique status for so large an element of a language to persist in. One consequence is to give to the dictionary a special importance among English-using peoples. It reinforces, and nowadays it even replaces and shortcuts, the actual study of Latin. For the students of literature, and perhaps even its writers, one of the important services of the dictionary is to show when an English word is of Latin origin, and what the original Latin was and signified. Otherwise I do not know how they would understand Shakespeare, Milton, many writers of the seventeenth century, and occasionally a good modern. Of course the study of Latin independently is better, but it is increasingly a labor that may not be enforced. The best educational argument for it, so far as I know, would be that Latin is still a living language, and lives in Shakespeare and Milton. It is a splendid argument to make to those who already know this by experience, but a difficult one to offer to the uninitiated.

I turn to some other examples from the bi-lingual Shakespeare; there is a wealth of them, and often they are units of considerable length. Here is the Queen telling Laertes about the death of his sister by drowning. Gertrude is a woman perhaps more foolish than vicious, but in the midst of her garrulousness and absurd sequence of pathetic fallacies there are irruptions of Latinity which are regal.

> *Then, on the pendent boughs her coronet weeds*
> *Clambering to hang, an envious sliver broke;*
> *When down her weedy trophies and herself*
> *Fell in the weeping brook. Her clothes spread wide.*
> *And mermaid-like a while they held her up:*
> *Which time she chanted snatches of old tunes,*
> *As one incapable of her own distress,*
> *Or like a creature native and indued*
> *Unto that element: but long it could not be*
> *Till that her garments, heavy with their drink,*
> *Pull'd the poor wretch from her melodious lay*
> *To muddy death.*

We will observe the linguistic ambivalence in *pendent boughs* and *coronet weeds;* the rather sustained though crisp and energetic Latinity of *creature native and indued Unto that element;* and *melodious lay* contending with *muddy death,* a Latinical *-ous* adjective opposed to a folk or *-y* adjective.

We have looked twice at *Hamlet,* which is rich in this kind of Latinity. What will we make of the Sonnets? We can see how much the later ones advance in quality over the early ones, and we have been told that the later ones often closely anticipate the language, in particular, of *Hamlet.* One of the finest is No. 107:

> *Not mine own fears, nor the prophetic soul*
> *Of the wide world dreaming on things to come,*
> *Can yet the lease of my true love control,*
> *Supposed as forfeit to a confined doom.*
>
> *The mortal moon hath her eclipse endured,*
> *And the sad augurs mock their own presage;*
> *Incertainties now crown themselves assured,*
> *And peace proclaims olives of endless age.*
>
> *Now with the drops of this most balmy time*
> *My love looks fresh and Death to me subscribes,*

> *Since, spite of him, I'll live in this poor rime,*
> *While he insults o'er dull and speechless tribes:*
>
> *And thou in this shall find thy monument,*
> *When tyrants' crests and tombs of brass are spent.*

Latinity is frequent in this sonnet, and sometimes sharp. The beginning is vernacular. *Prophetic* (which is Greek if not Latin) is necessary to the sense, but its clang is nearly canceled by *soul* and by the fullness of the pretty image in the next line; this soul of the world is not Spiritus Mundi at all, only the hatefulness of all the gossips who see no future for this affair; but in the third line we have another technical word in *lease,* and, to conclude the quatrain, a shower of Latinity in *control, supposed, forfeit, confined.* The last of these words requires a knowledge of Latin if we are to understand that the doom is appointed to occupy a tract adjoining that of the love affair, so that at a certain point in the lover's course he is bound to step over. In the second quatrain *endured* is pure Latin likewise, meaning lasted out, or lived through; and each line has a Latinical qualification in *presage, assured,* or *proclaims,* though it would be commonplace except by virtue of its context. The third quatrain is the best from our present point of view. The vernacular at the beginning is brought up short in *subscribes;* and it makes a fresh start only to run into *insults.* Indeed, *subscribes* and *insults o'er* give the chief interest to this passage if we know our Latin. *Subscribes to me* is "writes himself under me" or leaves me on top; *insults* is "jumps up on," and puts Death back into his usual relation to his victims (the tribes who do not make poems); and to make the reversal explicit Shakespeare adds a redundant *o'er* to match the earlier *sub-.* The couplets of Shakespeare's sonnets are not usually exciting, though they are necessary to the logic as generalized conclusions. This one is distinguished a little by the crisp work of *tyrants' crests and tombs.* People would know each of these words, but at having the three of them together would feel that there was a certain preoccupation with their Latinity.

Here is a brilliant passage from *Antony and Cleopatra,* which is full of them. Talking with his man Eros, Antony plays with the whimsy that Cleopatra has so robbed him of his substance that he has lost visibility.

> ANT.    *Eros, thou yet behold'st me?*
> EROS.                    *Ay, noble lord.*
> ANT.    *Sometime we see a cloud that's dragonish,*
>             *A vapor sometime like a bear or lion,*
>             *A tower'd citadel, a pendent rock,*
>             *A forked mountain, or blue promontory*
>             *With trees upon 't, that nod unto the world*
>             *And mock our eyes with air. Thou has seen these*
>                         *signs;*
>             *They are black vesper's pageants.*
> EROS.                    *Ay, my lord.*
> ANT.    *That which is now a horse, even with a thought*
>             *The rack dislimns and makes it indistinct*
>             *As water is in water.*

The Latinical effects here are subtle, but still entirely distinct. The context consists of many primitive folk-items: dragon, tower, rock, forked, mountain, blue, trees, eyes, air, black, horse, rack (the scudding cloud-masses in the foreground that blot out the distant effects), and water. The first Latinical item is *vapor,* and not too decisive; but *citadel* accompanies *tower'd,* and *pendent* accompanies *rock; forked mountain* is not necessarily conscious of the Latinity of its second member, but presently there is *blue promontory,* clearly bi-lingual, and *promontory* (a fore-mountain) echoes *mountain,* and gives back to it its own Latinity: *black vesper's pageants* is a climactic compound ending Antony's first period. His second speech is a bi-lingual three-liner. Our interest is in *dislimns* followed by *indistinct* in the same line and even, though this looks unlikely, in the same sense. *Limn* is Latin-via-French, and *tinct* is Latin, both meaning draw or paint. The *dis-* of *dislimns* is privative; so is the *in-* of *indistinct* but not its *dis-*. (If it were, we should have in the word a double negative.) Here that prefix means "apart"; and the two words are fairly synonymous. Our attention focuses principally and longest on these two words in their curious and dangerous relation; and *indistinct* goes back and echoes *dislimns* just as *promontory* echoed *mountain.* The easy tone of the passage masks the achievement, the mastery, which is something of great intricacy.

Now a look at a very late passage of Shakespeare. It is from Prospero's speech when he is explaining to Miranda and Ferdinand the disappearance of the spirits in the midst of the masque which he has commanded; then moralizing the event for their instruction. If Prospero with his enchanter's wand in some sense represents Shakespeare with his dramatic imagination, the passage is Shakespeare's final utterance of his conviction of the general mortality, and his rueful sense that, though life is handsome enough while we live it, yet as its end draws near one sees that it never had a solid substance.

> *Our revels now are ended. These our actors,*
> *As I foretold you, were all spirits, and*
> *Are melted into air, into thin air;*
> *And, like the baseless fabric of this vision,*
> *The cloud-capp'd towers, the gorgeous palaces,*
> *The solemn temples, the great globe itself,*
> *Yea, all which it inherit, shall dissolve,*
> *And, like this insubstantial pageant faded,*
> *Leave not a rack behind. We are such stuff*
> *As dreams are made on; and our little life*
> *Is rounded with a sleep.*

The vision disappeared, and so it will be with the world itself, and ourselves. This is said with some pretty doubling between the vernacular and the Latinity; as if one had better deal with it now one way and again the other way, that is, playfully, gracefully, not too grimly and willfully. The two versions thoroughly interpenetrate each other, though the vernacular is the main one. The actors of the masque *are melted into air,* which is a folkish disposition, and there is a folkish addition in *into thin air.* Yet this same masque is described below as a *vision* made of a *baseless fabric.* The world with its objects and people will *dissolve* (a variation on *melt*) like the *vision,* which becomes an *insubstantial pageant* (whose *melted* appears now as *faded*). The contents of the world are identified by four objects, of which the middle two are *gorgeous palaces* and *solemn temples,* with *cloud-capp'd towers* and *the great globe itself* on the two sides; and the people are *all which it inherit.* The last three lines, after the high-toned *insubstantial pageant,* are in solid vernacular. Our substance is a *stuff* (the equivalent of *fabric*), but the stuff of dreams; that is to say, our life is a dream, and the dream is set in the midst of the long sleep out of which it rises and into which it goes. Would we have this peculiar "view of life" elaborated? It is put better in the vernacular (for the most part) than it could have been put Latinically, or technically, because then the staple would be the philosophical language, and it might be expected to account for itself better. The dream-business uses two common poetic figures; thus, life is but a dream; and not only that, death is but a sleep; so that the dream-idea has a sleep-idea to depend on.

Since these words of Prospero are almost Shakespeare's last words to us, I will not stop without one more remark. Prospero has addressed them to Ferdinand and Miranda, who do not seem particularly appalled; their own dream is just coming to its head. When next we shall discover them, they will be playing at chess and love, and presently, when all the characters come in, Miranda will say:

> *O wonder!*
> *How many goodly creatures are there here!*
> *How beauteous mankind is! O brave new world,*
> *That has such people in it!*

To which Prospero will reply drily:

> *'Tis new to thee.*

Prospero will make his plans to go back with the company to Naples for the wedding, and then to retire to his Milan, where

> *Every third thought shall be my grave.*

His dream has at least had a good ending, and it is time for another dream. Would it not be gross of us to wish different theological views upon Prospero? Since these are in character, and dramatically adequate, we should do well to cultivate Keats's "negative capability," and let well enough alone.

One of the forms that negative capability might take with a poet would be this: to pass slyly back and forth between his two languages, if he is an English poet; as if he could not be expected to arrive at systematic theology with such a variable instrument.

Kenneth Burke

# SYMBOLIC ACTION IN A POEM BY KEATS

We are here set to analyze the "Ode on a Grecian Urn" as a viaticum that leads, by a series of transformations, into the oracle, "Beauty is truth, truth beauty." We shall analyze the Ode "dramatistically," in terms of symbolic action.

To consider language as a means of *information* or *knowledge* is to consider it epistemologically, semantically, in terms of "science." To consider it as a mode of *action* is to consider it in terms of "poetry." For a poem is an act, the symbolic act of the poet who made it—an act of such a nature that, in surviving as a structure or object, it enables us as readers to re-enact it.

"Truth" being the essential word of knowledge (science) and "beauty" being the essential word of art or poetry, we might substitute accordingly. The oracle would then assert, "Poetry is science, science poetry." It would be particularly exhilarating to proclaim them one if there were a strong suspicion that they were at odds (as the assertion that "God's in his heaven, all's right with the world" is really a *counter*-assertion to doubts about God's existence and suspicions that much is wrong). It was the dialectical opposition between the "aesthetic" and the "practical," with "poetry" on one side and utility (business and applied science) on the other that was being ecstatically denied. The *relief* in this denial was grounded in the romantic philosophy itself, a philosophy which gave strong recognition to precisely the *contrast* between "beauty" and "truth."

Perhaps we might put it this way: If the oracle were to have been uttered in the first stanza of the poem rather than the last, its phrasing proper to that place would have been: "Beauty is *not* truth, truth *not* beauty." The five stanzas of successive transformation were necessary for the romantic philosophy of a romantic poet to transcend itself (raising its romanticism to a new order, or new dimension). An abolishing of romanticism through romanticism! (To transcend romanticism through romanticism is, when all is over, to restore in one way what is removed in another.)

But to the poem, step by step through the five stanzas.

As a "way in," we begin with the sweeping periodic sentence that, before the stanza is over, has swiftly but imperceptibly been transmuted in quality from the periodic to the breathless, a cross between interrogation and exclamation:

> Thou still unravish'd bride of quietness,
>     Thou foster-child of silence and slow time,
> Sylvan historian, who canst thus express
>     A flowery tale more sweetly than our rhyme:

What leaf-fring'd legend haunts about thy shape
  Of deities or mortals, or of both,
    In Tempe or the dales of Arcady?
What men or gods are these? What maidens loth?
  What mad pursuit? What struggle to escape?
    What pipes and timbrels? What wild ecstasy?

Even the last quick outcries retain somewhat the quality of the periodic structure with which the stanza began. The final line introduces the subject of "pipes and timbrels," which is developed and then surpassed in Stanza II:

Heard melodies are sweet, but those unheard
  Are sweeter; therefore, ye soft pipes, play on;
Not to the sensual ear, but, more endear'd,
  Pipe to the spirit ditties of no tone:
Fair youth, beneath the trees, thou canst not leave
  Thy song, nor ever can those trees be bare;
    Bold Lover, never, never canst thou kiss,
Though winning near the goal—yet, do not grieve;
  She cannot fade, though thou hast not thy bliss,
    Forever wilt thou love, and she be fair!

If we had only the first stanza of this Ode, and were speculating upon it from the standpoint of motivation, we could detect there tentative indications of two motivational levels. For the lines express a doubt whether the figures on the urn are "deities or mortals"—and the motives of gods are of a different order from the motives of men. This bare hint of such a possibility emerges with something of certainty in the second stanza's development of the "pipes and timbrels" theme. For we explicitly consider a contrast between body and mind (in the contrast between "heard melodies," addressed "to the sensual ear," and "ditties of no tone," addressed "to the spirit").

Also, of course, the notion of inaudible sound brings us into the region of the mystic oxymoron (the term in rhetoric for "the figure in which an epithet of a contrary significance is added to a word: e.g., *cruel kindness; laborious idleness*"). And it clearly suggests a concern with the level of motives-behind-motives, as with the paradox of the prime mover that is itself at rest, being the unmoved ground of all motion and action. Here the poet whose sounds are the richest in our language is meditating upon *absolute* sound, the *essence* of sound, which would be soundless as the prime mover is motionless, or as the "principle" of sweetness would not be sweet, having transcended sweetness, or as the sub-atomic particles of the sun are each, in their isolate purity, said to be devoid of temperature.

Contrast Keats's unheard melodies with those of Shelley:

Music, when soft voices die,
Vibrates in the memory—
Odours, when sweet violets sicken,
Live within the sense they quicken.

Rose leaves, when the rose is dead,
Are heaped for the beloved's bed;
And so thy thoughts, when thou art gone,
Love itself shall slumber on.

Here the futuristic Shelley is anticipating retrospection; he is looking forward to looking back. The form of thought is naturalistic and temporalistic in terms of *past* and *future*. But the form of thought in Keats is mystical, in terms of an *eternal present*. The Ode is striving to move beyond the region of becoming into the realm of *being*. (This is another way of saying that we are here concerned with two levels of motivation.)

In the last four lines of the second stanza, the state of immediacy is conveyed by a development peculiarly Keatsian. I refer not simply to translation into terms of the erotic, but rather to a quality of *suspension* in the erotic imagery, defining an eternal prolongation of the state just prior to fulfilment—not exactly arrested ecstasy, but rather an arrested pre-ecstasy.[1]

Suppose that we had but this one poem by Keats, and knew nothing of its author or its period, so that we could treat it only in itself, as a series of internal transformations to be studied in their development from a certain point, and without reference to any motives outside the Ode. Under such conditions, I think, we should require no further observations to characterize (from the standpoint of symbolic action) the main argument in the second stanza. We might go on to make an infinity of observations about the details of the stanza; but as regards major deployments we should deem it enough to note that the theme of "pipes and timbrels" is developed by the use of mystic oxymoron, and then surpassed (or given a development-atop-the-development) by the stressing of erotic imagery (that had been ambiguously adumbrated in the references to "maidens loth" and "mad pursuit" of Stanza I). And we could note the quality of *incipience* in this imagery, its state of arrest not at fulfilment, but at the point just prior to fulfilment.

Add, now, our knowledge of the poem's place as an enactment in a particular cultural scene, and we likewise note in this second stanza a variant of the identification between death and sexual love that was so typical of 19th-century romanticism and was to attain its musical monument in the Wagnerian *Liebestod*. On a purely dialectical basis, to die in love would be to be born to love (the lovers dying as individual identities that they might be transformed into a common identity). Adding historical factors, one can note the part that capitalist individualism plays in sharpening this consummation (since a property structure that heightens the sense of individual identity would thus make it more imperiously a "death" for the individual to take on the new identity made by a union of two). We can thus see why the love-death equation would be particularly representative of a romanticism that was the reflex of business.

Fortunately, the relation between private property and the love-death equation is attested on unimpeachable authority, concerning the effect of consumption and consummation in a "mutual flame":

> So between them love did shine,
> That the turtle saw his right
> Flaming in the phoenix' sight;
> Either was the other's mine.

---

[1] Mr. G. Wilson Knight, in *The Starlit Dome*, refers to "that recurring tendency in Keats to image a poised form, a stillness suggesting motion, what might be called a 'tiptoe' effect."

> Property was thus appall'd,
> That the self was not the same;
> Single nature's double name
> Neither two nor one was called.

The addition of fire to the equation, with its pun on sexual burning, moves us from purely dialectical considerations into psychological ones. In the lines of Shakespeare, fire is the third term, the ground term for the other two (the synthesis that ends the lovers' roles as thesis and antithesis). Less obviously, the same movement from the purely dialectical to the psychological is implicit in any imagery of a *dying* or a *falling* in common, which when woven with sexual imagery signalizes a "transcendent" sexual consummation. The figure appears in a lover's compliment when Keats writes to Fanny Brawne, thus:

I never knew before, what such a love as you have made me feel, was; I did not believe in it; my Fancy was afraid of it lest it should burn me up. But if you will fully love me, though there may be some fire, 'twill not be more than we can bear when moistened and bedewed with pleasures.

Our primary concern is to follow the transformations of the poem itself. But to understand its full nature as a symbolic act, we should use whatever knowledge is available. In the case of Keats, not only do we know the place of this poem in his work and its time, but also we have material to guide our speculations as regards correlations between poem and poet. I grant that such speculations interfere with the symmetry of criticism as a game. (Criticism as a game is best to watch, I guess, when one confines himself to the single unit, and reports on its movements like a radio commentator broadcasting the blow-by-blow description of a prizefight.) But linguistic analysis has opened up new possibilities in the correlating of producer and product —and these concerns have such important bearing upon matters of culture and conduct in general that no sheer conventions or ideals of criticism should be allowed to interfere with their development.

From what we know of Keats's illness, with the peculiar inclination to erotic imaginings that accompany its fever (as with the writings of D. H. Lawrence) we can glimpse a particular bodily motive expanding and intensifying the lyric state in Keats's case. Whatever the intense *activity* of his thoughts, there was the material *pathos* of his physical condition. Whatever transformations of mind or body he experienced, his illness was there as a kind of constitutional substrate, whereby all aspects of the illness would be imbued with their derivation from a common ground (the phthisic fever thus being at one with the phthisic chill, for whatever the clear contrast between fever and chill, they are but modes of the same illness, the common underlying substance).

The correlation between the state of agitation in the poems and the physical condition of the poet is made quite clear in the poignant letters Keats wrote during his last illness. In 1819 he complains that he is "scarcely content to write the best verses for the fever they leave behind." And he continues: "I want to compose without this fever." But a few months later he confesses, "I am recommended not even to read poetry, much less write it." Or: "I must say that for 6 Months before I was taken ill I had not passed a tranquil day. Either that gloom overspre[a]d me or I was suffering under some passionate feeling, or if I turn'd to versify that exacerbated the poison of either sensation." Keats was "like a sick eagle looking at the sky," as he wrote of his mortality in a kindred poem, "On Seeing the Elgin Marbles."

But though the poet's body was a *patient,* the poet's mind was an *agent.* Thus, as a practitioner of poetry, he could *use* his fever, even perhaps encouraging, though not deliberately, esthetic habits that, in making for the perfection of his lines, would exact payment in the ravages of his body (somewhat as Hart Crane could write poetry only by modes of living that made for the cessation of his poetry and so led to his dissolution).

Speaking of agents, patients, and action here, we might pause to glance back over the centuries thus: in the Aristotelian grammar of motives, action has its reciprocal in passion, hence *passion* is the property of a *patient.* But by the Christian paradox (which made the martyr's action identical with his passion, as the accounts of the martyrs were called both Acts and Passionals), *patience* is the property of a moral *agent.* And this Christian view, as secularized in the philosophy of romanticism, with its stress upon creativeness, leads us to the possibility of a bodily suffering redeemed by a poetic act.

In the third stanza, the central stanza of the Ode (hence properly the fulcrum of its swing) we see the two motives, the action and the passion, in the process of being separated. The possibility raised in the first stanza (which was dubious whether the level of motives was to be human or divine), and developed in the second stanza (which contrasts the "sensual" and the "spirit"), becomes definitive in Stanza III:

> Ah, happy, happy boughs! that cannot shed
> Your leaves, nor ever bid the Spring adieu;
> And, happy melodist, unwearied,
> For ever piping songs for ever new;
> More happy love! more happy, happy love!
> For ever warm and still to be enjoy'd,
> For ever panting, and for ever young;
> All breathing human passion far above,
> That leaves a heart a high-sorrowful and cloy'd,
> A burning forehead, and a parching tongue.

The poem as a whole makes permanent, or fixes in a state of arrest, a peculiar agitation. But within this fixity, by the nature of poetry as a progressive medium, there must be development. Hence, the agitation that is maintained throughout (as a mood absolutized so that it fills the entire universe of discourse) will at the same time undergo internal transformations. In the third stanza, these are manifested as a clear division into two distinct and contrasted realms. There is a transcendental fever, which is felicitous, divinely above "all breathing human passion." And this "leaves" the other level, the level of earthly fever, "a burning forehead and a parching tongue." From the bodily fever, which is a passion, and malign, there has split off a spiritual activity, a wholly benign aspect of the total agitation.

Clearly, a movement has been finished. The poem must, if it is well-formed, take a new direction, growing out of and surpassing the curve that has by now been clearly established by the successive stages from "Is there the possibility of two motivational levels?" through "there are two motivational levels" to "the 'active' motivational level 'leaves' the 'passive' level."

Prophesying, with the inestimable advantage that goes with having looked ahead, what should we expect the new direction to be? First, let us survey the situation. Originally, before the two strands of the fever had been definitely drawn apart, the bodily passion could serve as the scene or ground of the spiritual action. But at the end of the third stanza, we abandon the level of bodily passion. The action is "far above" the passion, it "leaves" the fever. What then would this transcendent act require, to complete it?

It would require a scene of the same quality as itself. An act and a scene belong together. The nature of the one must be a fit with the nature of the other. (I like to call this the "scene-act ratio," or "dramatic ratio.") Hence, the act having now transcended its bodily setting, it will require, as its new setting, a transcendent scene. Hence, prophesying *post eventum,* we should ask that, in Stanza IV, the poem *embody* the transcendental act by endowing it with an appropriate scene.

The scene-act ratio involves a law of dramatic consistency whereby the quality of the act shares the quality of the scene in which it is enacted (the synecdochic relation of container and thing contained). Its grandest variant was in supernatural cosmogonies wherein mankind took on the attributes of gods by acting in cosmic scenes that were themselves imbued with the presence of godhead.[2]

Or we may discern the logic of the scene-act ratio behind the old controversy as to whether "God willed the good because it is good," or "the good is good because God willed it." This strictly theological controversy had political implications. But our primary concern here is with the *dramatistic* aspects of this controversy. For you will note that the whole issue centers in the problem of the *grounds* of God's creative act.

Since, from the purely dramatic point of view, every act requires a scene in which it takes place, we may note that one of the doctrines (that "God willed the good because it is good") is more symmetrical than the other. For by it, God's initial act of creation is itself given a ground, or scene (the objective existence of goodness, which was so real that God himself did not simply make it up, but acted in conformity with its nature when willing it to be the law of his creation). In the scholastic formulas taken over from Aristotle, God was defined as "pure act" (though this pure act was in turn the ultimate ground or *scene* of human acting and willing). And from the standpoint of purely dramatic symmetry, it would be desirable to have some kind of "scene" even for God. This requirement is met, we are suggesting, in the doctrine that "God willed the good *because* it is good." For this word, "because," in assigning a reason for God's willing, gives us in principle

---

2 In an article by Leo Spitzer, "*Milieu* and *Ambiance:* An Essay in Historical Semantics" (September and December 1942 numbers of *Philosophy and Phenomenological Research*), one will find a wealth of material that can be read as illustrative of "dramatic ratio."

a kind of scene, as we may discern in the pun of our word, "ground," itself, which indeterminately applies to either "place" or "cause."

If even theology thus responded to the pressure for dramatic symmetry by endowing God, as the transcendent act, with a transcendent scene of like quality, we should certainly expect to find analogous tactics in this Ode. For as we have noted that the romantic passion is the secular equivalent of the Christian passion, so we may recall Coleridge's notion that poetic action itself is a "dim analogue of Creation." Keats in his way confronting the same dramatistic requirement that the theologians confronted in theirs, when he has arrived at his transcendent act at the end of Stanza III (that is, when the benign fever has split away from the malign bodily counterpart, as a divorcing of spiritual action from sensual passion), he is ready in the next stanza for the imagining of a scene that would correspond in quality to the quality of the action as so transformed. His fourth stanza will concretize, or "materialize," the act, by dwelling upon its appropriate ground.

> Who are these coming to the sacrifice?
>    To what green altar, O mysterious priest,
> Lead'st thou that heifer lowing at the skies,
>    And all her silken flanks with garlands drest?
> What little town, by river or sea shore,
>    Or mountain built with peaceful citadel,
> Is emptied of this folk, this pious morn?
> And, little town, thy streets for evermore
>    Will silent be; and not a soul to tell
>    Why thou art desolate, can e'er return.

It is a vision, as you prefer, of "death" or of "immortality." "Immortality," we might say, is the "good" word for "death," and must necessarily be conceived in terms of death (the necessity that Donne touches upon when he writes, ". . . but thinke that I/Am, by being dead, immortall"). This is why, when discussing the second stanza, I felt justified in speaking of the variations of the love-death equation, though the poem spoke not of love and *death*, but of love *for ever*. We have a deathy-deathless scene as the corresponding ground of our transcendent act. The Urn itself, as with the scene upon it, is not merely an immortal act in our present mortal scene; it was originally an immortal act in a mortal scene quite different. The imagery, of sacrifice, piety, silence, desolation, is that of communication with the immortal or the dead.[3]

---

[3] In imagery there is no negation, or disjunction. Logically, we can say, "this *or* that," "this, *not* that." In imagery we can but say, "this *and* that," "this *with* that," "this-that," etc. Thus, imagistically considered, a commandment cannot be simply a proscription, but is also latently a provocation (a state of affairs that figures in the kind of stylistic scrupulosity and/or curiosity to which Gide's heroes have been particularly sensitive, as "thou shalt not . . ." becomes imaginatively transformed into "what would happen if . . ."). In the light of what we have said about the deathiness of immortality, and the relation between the erotic and the thought of a "dying," perhaps we might be justified in reading the last line of the great "Bright Star!" sonnet as naming states not simply alternative but also synonymous:

And so live ever—or else swoon to death.

Incidentally, we might note that the return to the use of rhetorical questions in the fourth stanza serves well, on a purely technical level, to keep our contact with the mood of the opening stanza, a music that now but vibrates in the memory. Indeed, one even gets the impression that the form of the rhetorical question had never been abandoned; that the poet's questings had been couched as questions throughout. This is tonal felicity at its best, and something much like unheard tonal felicity. For the actual persistence of the rhetorical questions through these stanzas would have been wearisome, whereas their return now gives us an inaudible variation, by making us feel that the exclamations in the second and third stanzas had been questions, as the questions in the first stanza had been exclamations.

But though a lyric greatly profits by so strong a sense of continuousness, or perpetuity, I am trying to stress the fact that in the fourth stanza we *come upon* something. Indeed, this fourth stanza is related to the three foregoing stanzas quite as the sestet is related to the octave in Keats's sonnet, "On First Looking Into Chapman's Homer":

> Much have I travell'd in the realms of gold,
>     And many goodly states and kingdoms seen;
>     Round many western islands have I been
> Which bards in fealty to Apollo hold.
> Oft of one wide expanse had I been told
>     That deep-brow'd Homer ruled as his demesne;
>     Yet did I never breathe its pure serene
> Till I heard Chapman speak out loud and bold;
>
> Then felt I like some watcher of the skies
>     When a new planet swims into his ken;
> Or like stout Cortez when with eagle eyes
>     He stared at the Pacific—and all his men
> Look'd at each other with a wild surmise—
>     Silent, upon a peak in Darien.

I am suggesting that, just as the sestet in this sonnet, *comes upon a scene,* so it is with the fourth stanza of the Ode. In both likewise we end on the theme of silence; and is not the Ode's reference to the thing that "not a soul can tell" quite the same in quality as the sonnet's reference to a "wild surmise"?

Thus, with the Urn as viaticum (or rather, with the *poem* as viaticum, and *in the name* of the Urn), having symbolically enacted a kind of act that transcends our mortality, we round out the process by coming to dwell upon the transcendental ground of this act. The dead world of ancient Greece, as immortalized on an Urn surviving from that period, is the vessel of this deathy-deathless ambiguity. And we have gone dialectically from the "human" to the "divine" and thence to the "ground of the divine" (here tracing in poetic imagery the kind of "dramatistic" course we have considered, on the purely conceptual plane, in the theological speculations about the

---

This use of the love-death equation is as startlingly paralleled in a letter to Fanny Brawne:
    I have two luxuries to brood over in my walks, your loveliness and the hour of my death. O that I could take possession of them both in the same moment.

"grounds" for God's creative act). Necessarily, there must be certain in-adequacies in the conception of this ground, precisely because of the fact that immortality can only be conceived in terms of death. Hence the refer-ence to the "desolate" in a scene otherwise possessing the benignity of the eternal.

The imagery of pious sacrifice, besides its fitness for such thoughts of departure as when the spiritual act splits from the sensual pathos, suggests also a bond of communication between the levels (because of its immortal character in a mortal scene). And finally, the poem, in the name of the Urn, or under the aegis of the Urn, is such a bond. For we readers, by re-enacting it in the reading, use it as a viaticum to transport us into the quality of the scene which it depicts on its face (the scene containing as a fixity what the poem as act extends into a process). The scene *on* the Urn is really the scene *behind* the Urn; the Urn is literally the ground of this scene, but transcen-dentally the scene is the ground of the Urn. The Urn contains the scene out of which it arose.

We turn now to the closing stanza:

> O Attic shape! Fair attitude! with brede
>   Of marble men and maidens overwrought,
> With forest branches and the trodden weed
>   Thou, silent form, dost tease us out of thought
> As doth eternity: Cold Pastoral!
>   When old age shall this generation waste,
>     Thou shalt remain, in midst of other woe
> Than ours, a friend to man, to whom thou say'st,
>   "Beauty is truth, truth beauty,"—that is all
>     Ye know on earth, and all ye need to know.

In the third stanza we were at a moment of heat, emphatically sharing an imagery of loves "panting" and "for ever warm" that was, in the transcen-dental order, companionate to "a burning forehead, and a parching tongue" in the order of the passions. But in the last stanza, as signalized in the marmorean utterance, "Cold Pastoral!" we have gone from transcendental fever to transcendental chill. Perhaps, were we to complete our exegesis, we should need reference to some physical step from phthisic fever to phthisic chill, that we might detect here a final correlation between bodily passion and mental action. In any event we may note that, the mental action having departed from the bodily passion, the change from fever to chill is not a sufferance. For, as only the *benign* aspects of the fever had been left after the split, so it is a wholly benign chill on which the poem ends.[4]

I wonder whether anyone can read the reference to "brede of marble men and maidens overwrought" without thinking of "breed" for "brede" and "excited" for "overwrought." (Both expressions would thus merge notions of sexuality and craftsmanship, the erotic and the poetic.) As for the designat-

[4] In a letter to Fanny Brawne, Keats touches upon the fever-chill contrast in a passage that also touches upon the love-death equation, though here the chill figures in an untrans-figured state:
I fear that I am too prudent for a dying kind of Lover. Yet, there is a great difference between going off in warm blood like Romeo; and making one's exit like a frog in a frost.

ing of the Urn as an "Attitude," it fits in admirably with our stress upon symbolic action. For an attitude is an arrested, or incipient *act*—not just an *object,* or *thing.*

Yeats, in *A Vision,* speaks of "the diagrams in Law's *Boehme,* where one lifts a paper to discover both the human entrails and the starry heavens." This equating of the deeply without and the deeply within (as also with Kant's famous remark) might well be remembered when we think of the sky that the "watcher" saw in Keats's sonnet. It is an internal sky, attained through meditations induced by the reading of a book. And so the oracle, whereby truth and beauty are proclaimed as one, would seem to derive from a profound inwardness.

Otherwise, without these introductory mysteries, "truth" and "beauty" were at odds. For whereas "beauty" had its fulfilment in romantic poetry, "truth" was coming to have its fulfilment in science, technological accuracy, accountancy, statistics, actuarial tables, and the like. Hence, without benefit of the rites which one enacts in a sympathetic reading of the Ode (rites that remove the discussion to a different level), the enjoyment of "beauty" would involve an esthetic kind of awareness radically in conflict with the kind of awareness deriving from the practical "truth." And as regards the tactics of the poem, this conflict would seem to be solved by "estheticizing" the true rather than by "verifying" the beautiful.

Earlier in our essay, we suggested reading "poetry" for "beauty" and "science" for "truth," with the oracle deriving its *liberating* quality from the fact that it is uttered at a time when the poem has taken us to a level where earthly contradictions do not operate. But we might also, in purely conceptual terms, attain a level where "poetry" and "science" cease to be at odds; namely: by translating the two terms into the "grammar" that lies behind them. That is: we could generalize the term "poetry" by widening it to the point where we could substitute for it the term "act." And we could widen "science" to the point where we could substitute "scene." Thus we have:

| "beauty" | equals | "poetry" | equals | "act" |
| "truth" | equals | "science" | equals | "scene" |

We would equate "beauty" with "act," because it is not merely a decorative thing, but an assertion, an affirmative, a creation, hence in the fullest sense an act. And we would equate "truth" or "science" with the "scenic" because science is a knowledge of *what is*—and *all that is* comprises the over-all universal *scene.* Our corresponding transcendence, then, got by "translation" into purely grammatical terms, would be: "Act is scene, scene act." We have got to this point by a kind of purely conceptual transformation that would correspond, I think, to the transformations of imagery leading to the oracle in the Ode.

"Act is scene, scene act." Unfortunately, I must break the symmetry a little. For poetry, as conceived in idealism (romanticism) could not quite be equated with *act,* but rather with *attitude.* For idealistic philosophies, with their stress upon the subjective, place primary stress upon the *agent* (the individual, the ego, the will, etc.). It was medieval scholasticism that placed primary stress upon the *act.* And in the Ode the Urn (which is the vessel or representative of poetry) is called an "attitude," which is not outright an act, but an incipient or arrested act, a *state of mind,* the property of an *agent.* Keats, in calling the Urn an attitude, is *personifying* it. Or we might use the italicizing resources of dialectic by saying that for Keats, beauty (poetry) was not so much "the *act* of an agent" as it was "the act of an *agent.*"

Perhaps we can re-enforce this interpretation by examining kindred strategies in Yeats, whose poetry similarly derives from idealistic, romantic sources. Indeed, as we have noted elsewhere,[5] Yeats's vision of immortality in his Byzantium poems but carries one step further the Keatsian identification with the Grecian Urn:

> Once out of nature I shall never take
> My bodily form from any natural thing,
> But such a form as Grecian goldsmiths make
> Of hammered gold and gold enamelling . . .

Here certainly the poet envisions immortality as "esthetically" as Keats. For he will have immortality as a golden bird, a fabricated thing, a work of Grecian goldsmiths. Here we go in the same direction as the "overwrought" Urn, but farther along in that direction.

The ending of Yeats's poem, "Among School Children," helps us to make still clearer the idealistic stress upon agent:

> Labour is blossoming or dancing where
> The body is not bruised to pleasure soul,
> Nor beauty torn out of its own despair,
> Nor blear-eyed wisdom out of midnight oil.
> O chestnut tree, great rooted blossomer,
> Are you the leaf, the blossom or the bole?
> O body swayed to music, O brightening glance,
> How can we know the dancer from the dance?

Here the chestnut tree (as personified agent) is the ground of unity or continuity for all its scenic manifestations; and with the agent (dancer) is merged the act (dance). True, we seem to have here a commingling of act, scene, and agent, all three. Yet it is the *agent* that is "foremost among the equals." Both Yeats and Keats, of course, were much more "dramatistic" in their thinking than romantic poets generally, who usually center their efforts upon the translation of *scene* into terms of *agent* (as the materialistic science that was the dialectical counterpart of romantic idealism preferred conversely to translate *agent* into terms of *scene,* or in other words, to treat "consciousness" in terms of "matter," the "mental" in terms of the "physical," "people" in terms of "environment").

To review briefly: The poem begins with an ambiguous fever which in the course of the further development is "separated out," splitting into a bodily fever and a spiritual counterpart. The bodily passion is the malign aspect of the fever, the mental action its benign aspect. In the course of the development, the malign passion is transcended and the benign active partner, the intellectual exhilaration, takes over. At the beginning, where

[5] "On Motivation in Yeats" (*The Southern Review,* Winter 1942).

the two aspects were ambiguously one, the bodily passion would be the "scene" of the mental action (the "objective symptoms" of the body would be paralleled by the "subjective symptoms" of the mind, the bodily state thus being the other or ground of the mental state). But as the two become separated out, the mental action transcends the bodily passion. It becomes an act in its own right, making discoveries and assertions not grounded in the bodily passion. And this quality of action, in transcending the merely physical symptoms of the fever, would thus require a different ground or scene, one more suited in quality to the quality of the transcendent act.

The transcendent act is concretized, or "materialized," in the vision of the "immortal" scene, the reference in Stanza IV to the original scene of the Urn, the "heavenly" scene of a dead, or immortal, Greece (the scene in which the Urn was originally enacted and which is also fixed on its face). To indicate the internality of this vision, we referred to a passage in Yeats relating the "depths" of the sky without to the depths of the mind within; and we showed a similar pattern in Keats's account of the vision that followed his reading of Chapman's Homer. We suggested that the poet is here coming upon a new internal sky, through identification with the Urn as act, the same sky that he came upon through identification with the enactments of Chapman's translation.

This transcendent scene is the level at which the earthly laws of contradiction no longer prevail. Hence, in the terms of this scene, he can proclaim the unity of truth and beauty (of science and art), a proclamation which he needs to make precisely because here was the basic split responsible for the romantic agitation (in both poetic and philosophic idealism). That is, it was gratifying to have the oracle proclaim the unity of poetry and science because the values of technology and business were causing them to be at odds. And from the perspective of a "higher level" (the perspective of a dead or immortal scene transcending the world of temporal contradictions) the split could be proclaimed once more a unity.

At this point, at this stage of exaltation, the fever has been replaced by chill. But the bodily passion has completely dropped out of account. All is now mental action. Hence, the chill (as in the ecstatic exclamation, "Cold Pastoral!") is proclaimed only in its benign aspect.

We may contrast this discussion with explanations such as a materialist of the Kretschmer school might offer. I refer to accounts of motivation that might treat disease as cause and poem as effect. In such accounts, the disease would not be "passive," but wholly active; and what we have called the mental action would be wholly passive, hardly more than an epiphenomenon, a mere symptom of the disease quite as are the fever and the chill themselves. Such accounts would give us no conception of the essential matter here, the intense linguistic activity.

*Mark Schorer*                                I
## TECHNIQUE AS DISCOVERY

Modern criticism, through its exacting scrutiny of literary texts, has demonstrated with finality that in art beauty and truth are indivisible and one. The Keatsian overtones of these terms are mitigated and an old dilemma solved if for beauty we substitute form, and for truth, content. We may, without risk of loss, narrow them even more, and speak of technique and subject matter. Modern criticism has shown us that to speak of content as such is not to speak of art at all, but of experience; and that it is only when we speak of the *achieved* content, the form, the work of art as a work of art, that we speak as critics. The difference between content, or experience, and achieved content, or art, is technique.

When we speak of technique, then, we speak of nearly everything. For technique is the means by which the writer's experience, which is his subject matter, compels him to attend to it; technique is the only means he has of discovering, exploring, developing his subject, of conveying its meaning, and, finally, of evaluating it. And surely it follows that certain techniques are sharper tools than others, and will discover more; that the writer capable of the most exacting technical scrutiny of his subject matter will produce works with the most satisfying content, works with thickness and resonance, works which reverberate, works with maximum meaning.

We are no longer able to regard as seriously intended criticism of poetry which does not assume these generalizations; but the case for fiction has not yet been established. The novel is still read as though its content has some value in itself, as though the subject matter of fiction has greater or lesser value in itself, and as though technique were not a primary but a supplementary element, capable perhaps of not unattractive embellishments upon the surface of the subject, but hardly of its essence. Or technique is thought of in blunter terms than those which one associates with poetry, as such relatively obvious matters as the arrangement of events to create plot; or, within plot, of suspense and climax; or as the means of revealing character motivation, relationship, and development; or as the use of point of view, but point of view as some nearly arbitrary device for the heightening of dramatic interest through the narrowing or broadening of perspective upon the material, rather than as a means toward the positive definition of theme. As for the resources of language, these, somehow, we almost never think of as a part of the technique of fiction—language as used to create a certain texture and tone which in themselves state and define themes and meanings; or language, the counters of our ordinary speech, as forced, through conscious manipulation, into all those larger meanings which our ordinary

Reprinted from *The Hudson Review*, 1948, by permission of the editors and the author. Copyright 1948 by *The Hudson Review*, Inc.

speech almost never intends. Technique in fiction, all this is a way of saying, we somehow continue to regard as merely a means to organizing material which is "given" rather than as the means of exploring and defining the values in an area of experience which, for the first time *then,* are being given.

Is fiction still regarded in this odd, divided way because it is really less tractable before the critical suppositions which now seem inevitable to poetry? Let us look at some examples: two well-known novels of the past, both by writers who may be described as "primitive," although their relative innocence of technique is of a different sort—Defoe's *Moll Flanders* and Emily Brontë's *Wuthering Heights;* and three well-known novels of this century—*Tono-Bungay,* by a writer who claimed to eschew technique; *Sons and Lovers,* by a novelist who, because his ideal of subject matter ("the poetry of the immediate present") led him at last into the fallacy of spontaneous and unchangeable composition, in effect eschewed technique; and *A Portrait of the Artist as a Young Man,* by a novelist whose practice made claims for the supremacy of technique beyond those made by anyone in the past or by anyone else in this century.

Technique in fiction is, of course, all those obvious forms of it which are usually taken to be the whole of it, and many others; but for the present purposes, let it be thought of in two respects particularly: the uses to which language, as language, is put to express the quality of the experience in question; and the uses of point of view not only as a mode of dramatic delimitation, but more particularly, of thematic definition. Technique is really what T. S. Eliot means by "convention"—any selection, structure, or distortion, any form or rhythm imposed upon the world of action; by means of which—it should be added—our apprehension of the world of action is enriched or renewed. In this sense, everything is technique which is not the lump of experience itself, and one cannot properly say that a writer has no technique or that he eschews technique, for, being a writer, he cannot do so. We can speak of good and bad technique, of adequate and inadequate, of technique which serves the novel's purpose, or disserves.

## II

In the prefatory remarks to *Moll Flanders,* Defoe tells us that he is not writing fiction at all, but editing the journals of a woman of notorious character, and rather to instruct us in the necessities and the joys of virtue than to please us. We do not, of course, take these professions seriously, since nothing in the conduct of the narrative indicates that virtue is either more necessary or more enjoyable than vice. On the contrary, we discover that Moll turns virtuous only after a life of vice has enabled her to do so with security; yet it is precisely for this reason that Defoe's profession of didactic purpose has interest. For the actual morality which the novel enforces is the morality of any commercial culture, the belief that virtue pays —in worldly goods. It is a morality somewhat less than skin deep, having no relation to motives arising from a sense of good and evil, least of all, of evil-*in*-good, but exclusively from the presence or absence of food, drink, linen, damask, silver, and timepieces. It is the morality of measurement, and without in the least intending it, *Moll Flanders* is our classic revelation of the mercantile mind: the morality of measurement, which Defoe has completely neglected to measure. He fails not only to evaluate this material in his announced way, but to evaluate it at all. His announced purpose is, we admit, a pious humbug, and he meant us to read the book as a series of scandalous events; and thanks to his inexhaustible pleasure in excess and exaggeration, this element in the book continues to amuse us. Long before the book has been finished, however, this element has also become an absurdity; but not half the absurdity as that which Defoe did not intend at all—the notion that Moll could live a rich and full life of crime, and yet, repenting, emerge spotless in the end. The point is, of course, that she has no moral being, nor has the book any moral life. Everything is external. Everything can be weighed, measured, handled, paid for in gold, or expiated by a prison term. To this, the whole texture of the novel testifies: the bolts of goods, the inventories, the itemized accounts, the landlady's bills, the lists, the ledgers: all this, which taken together comprises what we call Defoe's method of circumstantial realism.

He did not come upon that method by any deliberation; it represents precisely his own world of value, the importance of external circumstance to Defoe. The point of view of Moll is indistinguishable from the point of view of her creator. We discover the meaning of the novel (at unnecessary length, without economy, without emphasis, with almost none of the distortions or the advantages of art) in spite of Defoe, not because of him. Thus the book is not the true chronicle of a disreputable female, but the true allegory of an impoverished soul—the author's; not an anatomy of the criminal class, but of the middle class. And we read it as an unintended comic revelation of self and of a social mode. Because he had no adequate resources of technique to separate himself from his material, thereby to discover and to define the meanings of his material, his contribution is not to fiction but to the history of fiction, and to social history.

The situation in *Wuthering Heights* is at once somewhat the same and yet very different. Here, too, the whole novel turns upon itself, but this time to its estimable advantage; here, too, is a revelation of what is perhaps the author's secret world of value, but this time, through what may be an accident of technique, the revelation is meaningfully accomplished. Emily Brontë may merely have stumbled upon the perspectives which define the form and the theme of her book. Whether she knew from the outset, or even at the end, what she was doing, we may doubt; but what she did and did superbly we can see.

We can assume, without at all becoming involved in the author's life but merely from the tone of somnambulistic excess which is generated by the writing itself, that this world of monstrous passion, of dark and gigantic emotional and nervous energy, is for the author, or was in the first place, a world of ideal value; and that the book sets out to persuade us of the moral magnificence of such unmoral passion. We are, I think, expected, in the first place, to take at their own valuation these demonic beings, Heathcliff and Cathy: as special creatures, set apart from the cloddish world about them by their heightened capacity for feeling, set apart, even, from the ordinary objects of human passion as, in their transcendent, sexless relationship, they identify themselves with an uncompromising landscape and cosmic force. Yet this is absurd, as much of the detail that surrounds it ("Other dogs lurked in other recesses") is absurd. The novelist Emily Brontë had to discover these absurdities to the girl Emily; her technique had to evaluate them for what they were, so that we are persuaded that it is not Emily who is mistaken in her estimate of her characters, but they who are mistaken in their estimate of themselves. The theme of the moral magnificence of unmoral passion is an impossible theme to sustain, and what interests us is that it was device—and this time, mere, mechanical device—which taught Emily Brontë that, the needs of her temperament to the contrary, all personal longing and reverie to the contrary, perhaps—that this was indeed not at all what her material must mean as art. Technique objectifies.

To lay before us the full character of this passion, to show us how it first comes into being and then comes to dominate the world about it and the life that follows upon it, Emily Brontë gives her material a broad scope in time, lets it, in fact, cut across three generations. And to manage material which is so extensive, she must find a means of narration, points of view, which can encompass that material, and, in her somewhat crude concept of motive, justify its telling. So she chooses a foppish traveller who stumbles into this world of passionate violence, a traveller representing the thin and conventional emotional life of the far world of fashion, who wishes to hear the tale; and for her teller she chooses, almost inevitably, the old family retainer who knows everything, a character as conventional as the other, but this one representing not the conventions of fashion, but the conventions of the humblest moralism. What has happened is, first, that she has chosen as her narrative perspective those very elements, conventional emotion and conventional morality, which her hero and heroine are meant to transcend with such spectacular magnificence; and second, that she has permitted this perspective to operate throughout a long period of time. And these two elements compel the novelist to see what her unmoral passions come to. Moral magnificence? Not at all; rather, a devastating spectacle of human waste; ashes. For the time of the novel is carried on long enough to show Heathcliff at last an emptied man, burned out by his fever ragings, exhausted and will-less, his passion meaningless at last. And it goes even a little further, to Lockwood, the fop, in the graveyard, sententiously contemplating headstones. Thus in the end the triumph is all on the side of the cloddish world, which survives.

Perhaps not all on that side. For, like Densher at the end of *The Wings of the Dove,* we say, and surely Hareton and the second Cathy say, "We shall never be again as we were!" But there is more point in observing that a certain body of materials, a girl's romantic daydreams, have, through the most conventional devices of fiction, been pushed beyond their inception in fancy to their meanings, their conception as a written book—that they, that is, are not at all as they were.

### III

Technique alone objectifies the materials of art; hence technique alone evaluates those materials. This is the axiom which demonstrates itself so devastatingly whenever a writer declares, under the urgent sense of the importance of his materials (whether these are autobiography, or social ideas, or personal passions)—whenever such a writer declares that he cannot linger with technical refinements. That art will not tolerate such a writer H. G. Wells handsomely proves. His enormous literary energy included no respect for the techniques of his medium, and his medium takes its revenge upon his bumptiousness. "I have never taken any very great pains about writing. I am outside the hierarchy of conscious and deliberate writers altogether. I am the absolute antithesis of Mr. James Joyce. . . . Long ago, living in close conversational proximity to Henry James, Joseph Conrad, and Mr. Ford Madox Hueffer, I escaped from under their immense artistic preoccupations by calling myself a journalist." Precisely. And he escaped—he disappeared—from literature into the annals of an era.

Yet what confidence! "Literature," Wells said, "is not jewelry, it has quite other aims than perfection, and the more one thinks of 'how it is done' the less one gets it done. These critical indulgences lead along a fatal path, away from every natural interest towards a preposterous emptiness of technical effort, a monstrous egotism of artistry, of which the later work of Henry James is the monumental warning. 'It,' the subject, the thing or the thought, has long since disappeared in these amazing works; nothing remains but the way it has been 'manipulated.' " Seldom has a literary theorist been so totally wrong; for what we learn as James grows for us and Wells disappears is that without what he calls "manipulation," there *is* no "it," no "subject" in art. There is again only social history.

The virtue of the modern novelist—from James and Conrad down—is not only that he pays so much attention to his medium, but that, when he pays most, he discovers through it a new subject matter, and a greater one. Under the "immense artistic preoccupations" of James and Conrad and Joyce, the form of the novel changed, and with the technical change, analogous changes took place in substance, in point of view, in the whole conception of fiction. And the final lesson of the modern novel is that technique is not the secondary thing that it seemed to Wells, some external machination, a mechanical affair, but a deep and primary operation; not only that technique *contains* intellectual and moral implications, but that it *discovers* them. For a writer like Wells, who wished to give us the intellectual and the moral history of our times, the lesson is a hard one: it tells us that the order of intellect and the order of morality do not exist at all, in art, except as they are organized in the order of art.

Wells's ambitions were very large. "Before we have done, we will have all life within the scope of the novel." But that is where life already is, within the scope of the novel; where it needs to be brought is into novels. In Wells we have all the important topics in life, but no good novels. He was not asking too much of art, or asking that it include more than it happily can; he was not asking anything of it—as art, which is all that it can give, and that is everything.

A novel like *Tono-Bungay,* generally thought to be Wells's best, is therefore instructive. "I want to tell—*myself,*" says George, the hero, "and my impressions of the thing as a whole"—the thing as a whole being the collapse of traditional British institutions in the twentieth century. George "tells himself" in terms of three stages in his life which have rough equivalents in modern British social history, and this is, to be sure, a plan, a framework; but it is the framework of Wells's abstract thinking, not of his craftsmanship, and the primary demand which one makes of such a book as this, that means be discovered whereby the dimensions of the hero contain the experiences he recounts, is never met. The novelist flounders through a series of literary imitations—from an early Dickensian episode, through a kind of Shavian interlude, through a Conradian episode, to a Jules Verne vision at the end. The significant failure is in that end, and in the way that it defeats not only the entire social analysis of the bulk of the novel, but Wells's own ends as a thinker. For at last George finds a purpose in science. "I decided that in power and knowledge lay the salvation of my life, the secret that would fill my need; that to these things I would give myself."

But science, power, and knowledge are summed up at last in a destroyer. As far as one can tell Wells intends no irony, although he may here have come upon the essence of the major irony in modern history. The novel ends in a kind of meditative rhapsody which denies every value that the book had been aiming toward. For of all the kinds of social waste which Wells has been describing, this is the most inclusive, the final waste. Thus he gives us in the end not a novel, but a hypothesis; not an individual destiny, but a theory of the future; and not his theory of the future, but a nihilistic vision quite opposite from everything that he meant to represent. With a minimum of attention to the virtues of technique, Wells might still not have written a good novel; but he would at any rate have established a point of view and a tone which would have told us what he meant.

To say what one means in art is never easy, and the more intimately one is implicated in one's material, the more difficult it is. If, besides, one commits fiction to a therapeutic function which is to be operative not on the audience but on the author, declaring, as D. H. Lawrence did, that "One sheds one's sicknesses in books, repeats and presents again one's emotions to be master of them," the difficulty is vast. It is an acceptable theory only with the qualification that technique, which objectifies, is under no other circumstances so imperative. For merely to repeat one's emotions, merely to look into one's heart and write, is also merely to repeat the round of emotional bondage. If our books are to be exercises in self-analysis, then technique must—and alone can—take the place of the absent analyst.

Lawrence, in the relatively late Introduction to his *Collected Poems*, made that distinction of the amateur between his "real" poems and his "composed" poems, between the poems which expressed his demon directly and created their own form "willy-nilly," and the poems which, through the hocus-pocus of technique, he spuriously put together and could, if necessary, revise. His belief in a "poetry of the immediate present," poetry in which nothing is fixed, static, or final, where all is shimmeriness and impermanence and vitalistic essence, arose from this mistaken notion of technique. And from this notion, an unsympathetic critic like D. S. Savage can construct a case which shows Lawrence driven "concurrently to the dissolution of personality and the dissolution of art." The argument suggests that Lawrence's early, crucial novel, *Sons and Lovers,* is another example of meanings confused by an impatience with technical resources.

The novel has two themes: the crippling effects of a mother's love on the emotional development of her son; and the "split" between kinds of love, physical and spiritual, which the son develops, the kinds represented by two young women, Clara and Miriam. The two themes should, of course, work together, the second being, actually, the result of the first: this "split" is the "crippling." So one would expect to see the novel developed, and so Lawrence, in his famous letter to Edward Garnett, where he says that Paul is left at the end with the "drift towards death," apparently thought he had developed it. Yet in the last few sentences of the novel, Paul rejects his desire for extinction and turns towards "the faintly humming, glowing town," to life—as nothing in his previous history persuades us that he could unfalteringly do.

The discrepancy suggests that the book may reveal certain confusions between intention and performance.

The first of these is the contradiction between Lawrence's explicit characterizations of the mother and father and his tonal evaluations of them. It is a problem not only of style (of the contradiction between expressed moral epithets and the more general texture of the prose which applies to them) but of point of view. Morel and Lawrence are never separated, which is a way of saying that Lawrence maintains for himself in this book the confused attitude of his character. The mother is a "proud, *honorable* soul," but the father has a "small, *mean* head." This is the sustained contrast; the epithets are characteristic of the whole, and they represent half of Lawrence's feelings. But what is the other half? Which of these characters is given his real sympathy—the hard, self-righteous, aggressive, demanding mother who comes through to us, or the simple, direct, gentle, downright, fumbling, ruined father? There are two attitudes here. Lawrence (and Morel) loves his mother, but he also hates her for compelling his love; and he hates his father with the true Freudian jealousy, but he also loves him for what he is in himself, and he sympathizes more deeply with him because his wholeness has been destroyed by the mother's domination, just as his, Lawrence-Morel's, has been.

This is a psychological tension which disrupts the form of the novel and obscures its meaning, because neither the contradiction in style nor the confusion in point of view is made to right itself. Lawrence is merely repeating his emotions, and he avoids an austerer technical scrutiny of his material because it would compel him to master them. He would not let the artist be stronger than the man.

The result is that, at the same time that the book condemns the mother, it justifies her; at the same time that it shows Paul's failure, it offers rationalizations which place the failure elsewhere. The handling of the girl, Miriam, if viewed closely, is pathetic in what it signifies for Lawrence, both as man and artist. For Miriam is made the mother's scapegoat, and in a different way from the way that she was in life. The central section of the novel is shot through with alternate statements as to the source of the difficulty: Paul is unable to love Miriam wholly, and Miriam can love only his spirit. The contradictions appear sometimes within single paragraphs, and the point of view is never adequately objectified and sustained to tell us which is true. The material is never seen as material; the writer is caught in it exactly as firmly as he was caught in his experience of it. "That's how women are with me," said Paul. "They want me like mad, but they don't want to belong to me." So he might have said, and believed it; but at the end of the novel, Lawrence is still saying that, and himself believing it.

For the full history of this technical failure, one must read *Sons and Lovers* carefully and then learn the history of the manuscript from the book called *D. H. Lawrence: A Personal Record,* by one E. T., who was Miriam in life. The basic situation is clear enough. The first theme—the crippling effects of the mother's love—is developed right through to the end; and then suddenly, in the last few sentences, turns on itself, and Paul gives himself to life, not death. But all the way through, the insidious rationalizations of the second theme have crept in to destroy the artistic coherence of the work. A "split" would occur in Paul; but as the split is treated, it is superimposed upon rather than developed in support of the first theme. It is a rationalization made from it. If Miriam is made to insist on spiritual love, the meaning and the power of theme one are reduced; yet Paul's weakness is disguised. Lawrence could not separate the investigating analyst, who must be objective, from Lawrence, the subject of the book; and the sickness was not healed, the emotion not mastered, the novel not perfected. All this, and the character of a whole career, would have been altered if Lawrence had allowed his technique to discover the fullest meaning of his subject.

*A Portrait of the Artist as a Young Man,* like *Tono-Bungay* and *Sons and Lovers,* is autobiographical, but unlike these it analyzes its material rigorously, and it defines the value and the quality of its experience not by appended comment or moral epithet, but by the texture of the style. The theme of *A Portrait,* a young artist's alienation from his environment, is explored and evaluated through three different styles and methods as Stephen Dedalus moves from childhood through boyhood into maturity. The opening pages are written in something like the stream of consciousness of *Ulysses,* as the environment impinges directly on the consciousness of the infant and the child, a strange, opening world which the mind does not yet subject to questioning, selection, or judgment. But this style changes very soon, as the boy begins to explore his surroundings; and as his sensuous experience of the world is enlarged, it takes on heavier and heavier rhythms and a fuller and fuller body of sensuous detail, until it reaches a crescendo of romantic opulence in the emotional climaxes which mark Stephen's rejection of domestic and religious values. Then gradually the style subsides into the austere intellectuality of the final sections, as he defines to himself the outlines of the artistic task which is to usurp his maturity.

A highly self-conscious use of style and method defines the quality of experience in each of these sections, and, it is worth pointing out in connection with the third and concluding section, the style and method evaluate the experience. What has happened to Stephen is, of course, a progressive alienation from the life around him as he progressed in his initiation into it, and by the end of the novel, the alienation is complete. The final portion of the novel, fascinating as it may be for the developing aesthetic creed of Stephen-Joyce, is peculiarly bare. The life experience was not bare, as we know from *Stephen Hero;* but Joyce is forcing technique to comment. In essence, Stephen's alienation is a denial of the human environment; it is a loss; and the austere discourse of the final section, abstract and almost wholly without sensuous detail or strong rhythm, tells us of that loss. It is a loss so great that the texture of the notation-like prose here suggests that the end is really all an illusion, that when Stephen tells us and himself that he is going forth to forge in the smithy of his soul the uncreated conscience of his race, we are to infer from the very quality of the icy, abstract void he now inhabits, the implausibility of his aim. For *Ulysses* does not create the conscience of the race; it creates our consciousness.

In the very last two or three paragraphs of the novel, the style changes once more, reverts from the bare, notative kind to the romantic prose of Stephen's adolescence. "Away! Away! The spell of arms and voices: the white arms of roads, their promise of close embraces and the black arms of tall ships that stand against the moon, their tale of distant nations. They are held out to say: We are alone—come." Might one not say that the austere ambition is founded on adolescent longing? That the excessive intellectual severity of one style is the counterpart of the excessive lyric relaxation of the other? And that the final passage of *A Portrait* punctuates the illusory nature of the whole ambition?

For *Ulysses* does not create a conscience. Stephen, in *Ulysses,* is a little older, and gripped now by guilt, but he is still the cold young man divorced from the human no less than the institutional environment. The environment of urban life finds a separate embodiment in the character of Bloom, and Bloom is as lost as Stephen, though touchingly groping for moorings. Each of the two is weakened by his inability to reach out, or to do more than reach out to the other. Here, then, is the theme again, more fully stated, as it were in counterpoint.

But if Stephen is not much older, Joyce is. He is older as an artist not only because he can create and lavish his godlike pity on a Leopold Bloom, but also because he knows now what both Stephen and Bloom mean, and *how much,* through the most brilliant technical operation ever made in fiction, they can be made to mean. Thus *Ulysses,* through the imaginative force which its techniques direct, is like a pattern of concentric circles, with the immediate human situation at its center, this passing on and out to the whole dilemma of modern life, this passing on and out beyond that to a vision of the cosmos, and this to the mythical limits of our experience. If we read *Ulysses* with more satisfaction than any other novel of this century, it is because its author held an attitude toward technique and the technical scrutiny of subject matter which enabled him to order, within a single work and with superb coherence, the greatest amount of our experience.

## IV

In the United States during the last twenty-five years, we have had many big novels but few good ones. A writer like James T. Farrell apparently assumes that by endless redundancy in the description of the surface of American life, he will somehow write a book with the scope of *Ulysses*. Thomas Wolfe apparently assumed that by the mere disgorging of the raw material of his experience he would give us at last our epic. But except in a physical sense, these men have hardly written novels at all.

The books of Thomas Wolfe were, of course, journals, and the primary role of his publisher in transforming these journals into the semblance of novels is notorious. For the crucial act of the artist, the unique act which is composition, a sympathetic editorial blue pencil and scissors were substituted. The result has excited many people, especially the young, and the ostensibly critical have observed the prodigal talent with the wish that it might have been controlled. Talent there was, if one means by talent inexhaustible verbal energy, excessive response to personal experience, and a great capacity for auditory imitativeness, yet all of this has nothing to do with the novelistic quality of the written result; until the talent is controlled, the material organized, the content achieved, there is simply the man and his life. It remains to be demonstrated that Wolfe's conversations were any less interesting as novels than his books, which is to say that his books are without interest as novels. As with Lawrence, our response to the books is determined, not by their qualities as novels, but by our response to him and his qualities as a temperament.

This is another way of saying that Thomas Wolfe never really knew what he was writing *about*. *Of Time and the River* is merely a euphemism for "Of a Man and his Ego." It is possible that had his conception of himself and of art included an adequate respect for technique and the capacity to pursue it, Wolfe would have written a great novel on his true subject— the dilemma of romantic genius; it was his true subject, but it remains his undiscovered subject, it is the subject which *we* must dig out for him, because he himself had neither the lamp nor the pick to find it in and mine it out of the labyrinths of his experience. Like Emily Brontë, Wolfe needed a point of view beyond his own which would separate his material and its effect.

With Farrell, the situation is opposite. He knows quite well what his subject is and what he wishes to tell us about it, but he hardly needs the novel to do so. It is significant that in sheer clumsiness of style no living writer exceeds him, for his prose is asked to perform no service beyond communication of the most rudimentary kind of fact. For his ambitions, the style of the newspaper and the lens of the documentary camera would be quite adequate, yet consider the diminution which Leopold Bloom, for example, would suffer, if he were to be viewed from these, the technical perspectives of James Farrell. Under the eye of this technique, the material does not yield up enough; indeed, it shrinks.

More and more writers in this century have felt that naturalism as a method imposes on them strictures which prevent them from exploring through all the resources of technique the full amplifications of their subjects, and that thus it seriously limits the possible breadth of aesthetic meaning and response. James Farrell is almost unique in the complacency with which he submits to the blunt techniques of naturalism; and his fiction is correspondingly repetitive and flat.

That naturalism had a sociological and disciplinary value in the nineteenth century is obvious; it enabled the novel to grasp materials and make analyses which had eluded it in the past, and to grasp them boldly; but even then it did not tell us enough of what, in Virginia Woolf's phrase, is "really real," nor did it provide the means to the maximum of reality coherently contained. Even the Flaubertian ideal of objectivity seems, today, an unnecessarily limited view of objectivity, for as almost every good writer of this century shows us, it is quite as possible to be objective about subjective states as it is to be objective about the circumstantial surfaces of life. Dublin, in *Ulysses,* is a moral setting: not only a city portrayed in the naturalistic fashion of Dickens' London, but also a map of the modern psyche with its oblique and baffled purposes. The second level of reality in no way invalidates the first, and a writer like Joyce shows us that, if the artist truly respects his medium, he can be objective about both at once. What we need in fiction is a devoted fidelity to every technique which will help us to discover and to evaluate our subject matter, and more than that, to discover the amplifications of meaning of which our subject matter is capable.

Most modern novelists have felt this demand upon them. André Gide allowed one of his artist-heroes to make an observation which considerably resembles an observation we have quoted from Wells. "My novel hasn't got a subject. . . . Let's say, if you prefer it, it hasn't got *one* subject. . . . 'A slice of life,' the naturalist school said. The great defect of that school is that it always cuts its slice in the same direction; in time, lengthwise. Why not in breadth? Or in depth? As for me I should like not to cut at all. Please understand; I should like to put everything into my novel." Wells, with his equally large blob of potential material, did not know how to cut it to the novel's taste; Gide cut, of course—in every possible direction. Gide and others. And those "cuts" are all the new techniques which modern fiction has given us. None, perhaps, is more important than that inheritance from French symbolism which Huxley, in the glittering wake of Gide, called "the musicalization of fiction." Conrad anticipated both when he wrote that the novel "must strenuously aspire to the plasticity of sculpture, to the colour of painting, and to the magic suggestiveness of music—which is the art of arts," and when he said of that early but wonderful piece of symbolist fiction, *Heart of Darkness,* "It was like another art altogether. That sombre theme had to be given a sinister resonance, a tonality of its own, a continued vibration that, I hoped, would hang in the air and dwell on the ear after the last note had been struck." The analogy with music, except as a metaphor, is inexact, and except as it points to techniques which fiction can employ as fiction, not very useful to our sense of craftsmanship. It has had an approximate exactness in only one work, Joyce's final effort, an effort unique in literary history, *Finnegans Wake,* and here, of course, those readers willing to approach the "ideal" effort Joyce demands, discovering an inexhaustible wealth and scope, are most forcibly reminded of the primary importance of technique to subject, and of their indivisibility.

The techniques of naturalism inevitably curtail subject and often leave it in its original area, that of undefined social experience. Those of our writers who, stemming from this tradition, yet, at their best, achieve a novelistic definition of social experience—writers like the occasional Sherwood Anderson, William Carlos Williams, the occasional Erskine Caldwell, Nathanael West, and Ira Wolfert in *Tucker's People*—have done so by pressing naturalism far beyond itself, into positively Gothic distortions. The structural machinations of Dos Passos and the lyrical interruptions of Steinbeck are the desperate maneuvers of men committed to a method of whose limitations they despair. They are our symbolists *manqué*, who end as allegorists.

Our most accomplished novels leave no such impressions of desperate and intentional struggle, yet their precise technique and their determination to make their prose work in the service of their subjects have been the measure of their accomplishment. Hemingway's *The Sun Also Rises* and Wescott's *The Pilgrim Hawk* are works of art not because they may be measured by some external, neoclassic notion of form, but because their forms are so exactly equivalent with their subjects, and because the evaluation of their subjects exists in their styles.

Hemingway has recently said that his contribution to younger writers lay in a certain necessary purification of the language; but the claim has doubtful value. The contribution of his prose was to his subject, and the terseness of style for which his early work is justly celebrated is no more valuable, as an end in itself, than the baroque involutedness of Faulkner's prose, or the cold elegance of Wescott's. Hemingway's early subject, the exhaustion of value, was perfectly investigated and invested by his bare style, and in story after story, no meaning at all is to be inferred from the fiction except as the style itself suggests that there is no meaning in life. This style, more than that, was the perfect technical substitute for the conventional commentator; it expresses and it measures that peculiar morality of the stiff lip which Hemingway borrowed from athletes. It is an instructive lesson, furthermore, to observe how the style breaks down when Hemingway moves into the less congenial subject matter of social affirmation: how the style breaks down, the effect of verbal economy as mute suffering is lost, the personality of the writer, no longer protected by the objectification of an adequate technique, begins its offensive intrusion, and the entire structural integrity slackens. Inversely, in the stories and the early novels, the technique was the perfect embodiment of the subject and it gave that subject its astonishing largeness of effect and of meaning.

One should correct Buffon and say that style is the subject. In Wescott's *Pilgrim Hawk,* a novel which bewildered its many friendly critics by the apparent absence of subject, the subject, the story, is again in the style itself. This novel, which is a triumph of the sustained point of view, is only bewildering if we try to make a story out of the narrator's observations upon others; but if we read his observations as oblique and unrecognized observations upon himself the story emerges with perfect coherence, and it reverberates with meaning, is as suited to continuing reflection as the greatest lyrics.

The rewards of such respect for the medium as the early Hemingway and the occasional Wescott have shown may be observed in every good writer we have. The involutions of Faulkner's style are the perfect equivalent of his involved structures, and the two together are the perfect representation of the moral labyrinths he explores, and of the ruined world which his novels repeatedly invoke and in which these labyrinths exist. The cultivated sensuosity of Katherine Anne Porter's style has charm in itself, of course, but no more than with these others does it have aesthetic value in itself; its values lie in the subtle means by which sensuous details become symbols, and in the way that the symbols provide a network which is the story, and which at the same time provides the writer and us with a refined moral insight by means of which to test it. When we put such writers against a writer like William Saroyan, whose respect is reserved for his own temperament, we are appalled by the stylistic irresponsibility we find in him, and by the almost total absence of theme, or defined subject matter, and the abundance of unwarranted feeling. Such a writer inevitably becomes a sentimentalist because he has no means by which to measure his emotion. Technique, at last, is measure.

These writers, from Defoe to Porter, are of unequal and very different talent, and technique and talent are, of course, after a point, two different things. What Joyce gives us in one direction, Lawrence, for all his imperfections as a technician, gives us in another, even though it is not usually the direction of art. Only in some of his stories and in a few of his poems, where the demands of technique are less sustained and the subject matter is not autobiographical, Lawrence, in a different way from Joyce, comes to the same aesthetic fulfilment. Emily Brontë, with what was perhaps her intuitive grasp of the need to establish a tension between her subject matter and her perspective upon it, achieves a similar fulfilment; and, curiously, in the same way and certainly by intuition alone, Hemingway's early work makes a moving splendor from nothingness.

And yet, whatever one must allow to talent and forgive in technique, one risks no generalization in saying that modern fiction at its best has been peculiarly conscious of itself and of its tools. The technique of modern fiction, at once greedy and fastidious, achieves as its subject matter not some singleness, some topic or thesis, but the whole of the modern consciousness. It discovers the complexity of the modern spirit, the difficulty of personal morality, and the fact of evil—all the untractable elements under the surface which a technique of the surface alone can not approach. It shows us—in Conrad's words, from *Victory*—that we all live in an "age in which we are camped like bewildered travellers in a garish, unrestful hotel," and while it puts its hard light on our environment, it penetrates, with its sharp weapons, the depths of our bewilderment. These are not two things, but only an adequate technique can show them as one. In a realist like Farrell, we have the environment only, which we know from the newspapers; in a subjectivist like Wolfe, we have the bewilderment only, which we record in our own diaries and letters. But the true novelist gives them to us together, and thereby increases the effect of each, and reveals each in its full significance.

Elizabeth Bowen, writing of Lawrence, said of modern fiction, "We want the naturalistic surface, but with a kind of internal burning. In Lawrence every bush burns." But the bush burns brighter in some places than in others, and it burns brightest when a passionate private vision finds its objectification in exacting technical search. If the vision finds no such objectification, as in Wolfe and Saroyan, there is a burning without a bush. In our committed realists, who deny the resources of art for the sake of life, whose technique forgives both innocence and slovenliness—in Defoe and Wells and Farrell—there is a bush but it does not burn. There, at first glance, the bush is only a bush; and then, when we look again, we see that, really, the thing is dead.

*Allen Tate*

# TENSION IN POETRY

I

Many poems that we ordinarily think of as good poetry—and some, besides, that we neglect—have certain common features that will allow us to invent, for their sharper apprehension, the name of a single quality. I shall call that quality tension. In abstract language, a poetic work has distinct quality as the ultimate effect of the whole, and that whole is the "result" of a configuration of meaning which it is the duty of the critic to examine and evaluate. In setting forth this duty as my present procedure I am trying to amplify a critical approach that I have used on other occasions, without wholly giving up the earlier method, which I should describe as the isolation of the general ideas implicit in the poetic work.

Towards the end of this essay I shall cite examples of "tension," but I shall not say that they exemplify tension only, or that other qualities must be ignored. There are all kinds of poetry, as many as there are good poets, as many even as there are good poems, for poets may be expected to write more than one kind of poetry; and no single critical insight may impute an exclusive validity to any one kind. In all ages there are schools demanding that one sort only be written—their sort: political poetry for the sake of the cause; picturesque poetry for the sake of the home town; didactic poetry for the sake of the parish; even a generalized personal poetry for the sake of the reassurance and safety of numbers. This last I suppose is the most common variety, the anonymous lyricism in which the common personality exhibits its commonness, its obscure yet standard eccentricity, in a language that seems always to be deteriorating; so that today many poets are driven to inventing private languages, or very narrow ones, because public speech has become heavily tainted with mass feeling.

Mass language is the medium of "communication," and its users are less interested in bringing to formal order what is sometimes called the "affective state" than in arousing that state.

Once you have said that everything is One it is obvious that literature is the same as propaganda; once you have said that no truth can be known apart from the immediate dialectical process of history it is obvious that all contemporary artists must prepare the same fashionplate. It is clear too that the One is limited in space as well as time, and the no less Hegelian Fascists are right in saying that all art is patriotic.

What Mr. William Empson calls patriotic poetry sings not merely in behalf of the State; you will find it equally in a ladylike lyric and in much of the political poetry of our time. It is the poetry of the mass language, very different from the "language of the people" which interested the late W. B. Yeats. For example:

> What from the splendid dead
> We have inherited—
> Furrows sweet to the grain, and the weed subdued—
> See now the slug and the mildew plunder.
> Evil does overwhelm
> The larkspur and the corn;
> We have seen them go under.

From this stanza by Miss Millay we infer that her splendid ancestors made the earth a good place that has somehow gone bad—and you get the reason from the title: "Justice Denied in Massachusetts." How Massachusetts could cause a general desiccation, why (as we are told in a footnote to the poem) the execution of Sacco and Vanzetti should have anything to do with the rotting of the crops, it is never made clear. These lines are mass language: they arouse an affective state in one set of terms, and suddenly an object quite unrelated to those terms gets the benefit of it; and this effect, which is usually achieved, as I think it is here, without conscious effort, is sentimentality. Miss Millay's poem was admired when it first appeared about ten years ago, and is no doubt still admired, by persons to whom it communicates certain feelings about social justice, by persons for whom the lines are the occasion of feelings shared by them and the poet. But if you do not share those feelings, as I happen not to share them in the images of desiccated nature, the lines and even the entire poem are impenetrably obscure.

I am attacking here the fallacy of communication in poetry. (I am not attacking social justice.) It is no less a fallacy in the writing of poetry than of critical theory. The critical doctrine fares ill the further back you apply it; I suppose one may say—if one wants a landmark—that it began to prosper after 1798; for, on the whole, nineteenth-century English verse is a poetry of communication. The poets were trying to use verse to convey ideas and feelings that they secretly thought could be better conveyed by science (consult Shelley's *Defense*), or by what today we call, in a significantly bad poetic phrase, the Social Sciences. Yet possibly because the poets believed the scientists to be tough, and the poets joined the scientists in thinking the poets tender, the poets stuck to verse. It may scarcely be said that we change this tradition of poetic futility by giving it a new name, Social Poetry. May a poet hope to deal more adequately with sociology than with physics? If he seizes upon either at the level of scientific procedure, has he not abdicated his position as poet?

At a level of lower historical awareness than that exhibited by Mr. Edmund Wilson's later heroes of the Symbolist school, we find the kind of verse that I have been quoting, verse long ago intimidated by the pseudo-rationalism of the Social Sciences. This sentimental intimidation has been so complete that, however easy the verse looked on the page, it gave up all claim to sense. (I assume here what I cannot now demonstrate, that Miss Millay's poem is obscure but that Donne's "Second Anniversarie" is not.) As another example of this brand of obscurity I have selected at random a nineteenth-century lyric, "The Vine," by James Thomson:

> The wine of love is music,
>   And the feast of love is song:
> When love sits down to banquet,
>   Love sits long:
>
> Sits long and rises drunken,
>   But not with the feast and the wine;
> He reeleth with his own heart,
>   That great rich Vine.

The language here appeals to an existing affective state; it has no coherent meaning either literally or in terms of ambiguity or implication; it may be wholly replaced by any of its several paraphrases, which are already latent in our minds. One of these is the confused image of a self-intoxicating man-about-town. Now good poetry can bear the closest literal examination of every phrase, and is its own safeguard against our irony. But the more closely we examine this lyric, the more obscure it becomes; the more we trace the implications of the imagery, the denser the confusion. The imagery adds nothing to the general idea that it tries to sustain; it even deprives that idea of the dignity it has won at the hands of a long succession of better poets going back, I suppose, to Guinizelli:

> *Al cor gentil ripara sempre Amore*
> *Come alla selva augello in la verdura . . .*

What I want to make clear is the particular kind of failure, not the degree, in a certain kind of poetry. Were we interested in degrees we might give comfort to the nineteenth century by citing lines from John Cleveland or Abraham Cowley, bad lyric verse no better than "The Vine," written in an age that produced some of the greatest English poetry. Here are some lines from Cowley's "Hymn: to light," a hundred-line inventory of some of the offices performed by the subject in a universe that still seems to be on the whole Ptolemaic; I should not care to guess the length the poem might have reached under the Copernican system. Here is one of the interesting duties of light:

> Nor amidst all these Triumphs dost thou scorn
>   The humble glow-worm to adorn,
>   And with those living spangles gild,
> (O Greatness without Pride!) the Bushes of the Field.

Again:

> The Violet, springs little Infant, stands,
>   Girt in thy purple Swadling-bands:
>   On the fair Tulip thou dost dote;
> Thou cloath'st it in a gay and party-colour'd Coat.

This, doubtless, is metaphysical poetry; however bad the lines may be—they are pretty bad—they have no qualities, bad or good, in common with "The Vine." Mr. Ransom has given us, in a remarkable essay, "Shakespeare at Sonnets" [1] (*The World's Body,* 1938), an excellent description of this kind of poetry: "The impulse to metaphysical poetry . . . consists in committing the feelings in the case . . . to their determination within the elected figure." That is to say, in metaphysical poetry the logical order is explicit; it must be coherent; the imagery by which it is sensuously embodied must have at least the appearance of logical determinism: perhaps the appearance only, because the varieties of ambiguity and contradiction possible beneath the logical surface are endless, as Mr. Empson has demonstrated in his elucidation of Marvell's "The Garden." Here it is enough to say that the development of imagery by extension, its logical determinants being an Ariadne's thread that the poet will not permit us to lose, is the leading feature of the poetry called metaphysical.

But to recognize it is not to evaluate it; and I take it that Mr. Ransom was giving us a true Aristotelian definition of a *genus,* in which the identification of a type does not compel us to discern the implied values. Logical extension of imagery is no doubt the key to the meaning of Donne's "Valediction: forbidding mourning"; it may equally initiate inquiry into the ludicrous failure of "Hymn: to light," to which I now return.

Although "The Vine" and "Hymn: to light" seem to me equally bad poetry, Cowley's failure is somewhat to be preferred; its negative superiority lies in a firmer use of the language. There is no appeal to an affective state; the leading statement can be made perfectly explicit: God is light, and light is life. The poem is an analytical proposition exhibiting the properties inherent in the major term; that is, exhibiting as much of the universe as Cowley could get around to before he wearied of logical extension. But I think it is possible to infer that good poetry could have been written in Cowley's language; and we know that it was. Every term, even the verbs converted into nouns, denotes an object, and, in the hands of a good poet, would be amenable to controlled distortions of literal representation. But here the distortions are uncontrolled. Everything is in this language that a poet needs except the poetry, or the imagination, or what I shall presently illustrate under the idea of tension.

I have called "Hymn: to light" an analytical proposition. That is the form in which the theme must have appeared to Cowley's mind; that is to say, simple analysis of the term *God* gave him, as it gave everybody else in Christendom, the proposition: God is light. (Perhaps, under neo-Platonic influence, the prime Christian symbol, as Professor Fletcher and others have shown in reducing to their sources the powers of the Three Blessed Ladies of *The Divine Comedy.*) But in order to write his poem Cowley had to develop the symbol by synthetic accretion, by adding to light properties not inherent in its simple analysis:

> The Violet, springs little Infant, stands,
> Girt in thy purple Swadling-bands . . .

[1] His rejection of Shakespeare's sonnets seems to be a result of deductive necessity in his premises, or of the courage of mere logic; but the essay contains valuable insights into the operation of the metaphysical "conceit."

The image, such as it is, is an addition to the central figure of light, an assertion of a hitherto undetected relation among the objects, light, diapers, and violets—a miscellany that I recommend to the consideration of Mr. E. E. Cummings, who could get something out of it that Cowley did not intend us to get. If you will think again of "The Vine," you will observe that Thomson permits, in the opposite direction, an equal license with the objects *de*noted by his imagery, with the unhappy results that we have already seen.

"The Vine" is a failure in denotation. "Hymn: to light" is a failure in connotation. The language of "The Vine" lacks objective content. Take "music" and "song" in the first two lines; the context does not allow us to apprehend the terms in extension; that is, there is no reference to objects that we may distinguish as "music" and "song"; the wine of love could have as well been song, its feast music. In "Hymn: to light," a reduction to their connotations of the terms *violet, swadling-bands,* and *light* (the last being represented by the pronoun *thou*) yields a clutter of images that may be unified only if we forget the firm denotations of the terms. If we are going to receive as valid the infancy of the violet, we must ignore the metaphor that conveys it, for the metaphor renders the violet absurd; by ignoring the diaper, and the two terms associated with it, we cease to read the passage, and begin for ourselves the building up of acceptable denotations for the terms of the metaphor.

Absurd: but on what final ground I call these poems absurd I cannot state as a principle. I appeal to the reader's experience, and invite him to form a judgment of his own. It is easy enough to say, as I shall say in detail in a moment, that good poetry is a unity of all the meanings from the furthest extremes of intension and extension. Yet our recognition of the action of this unified meaning is the gift of experience, of culture, of, if you will, our humanism. Our powers of discrimination are not deductive powers, though they may be aided by them; they wait rather upon the cultivation of our total human powers, and they represent a special application of those powers to a single medium of experience—poetry.

I have referred to a certain kind of poetry as the embodiment of the fallacy of communication: it is a poetry that communicates the affective state, which (in terms of language) results from the irresponsible denotations of words. There is a vague grasp of the "real" world. The history of this fallacy, which is as old as poetry but which towards the end of the eighteenth century began to dominate not only poetry, but other arts as well—its history would probably show that the poets gave up the language of denotation to the scientists, and kept for themselves a continually thinning flux of peripheral connotations. The companion fallacy, to which I can give only the literal name, the fallacy of mere denotation, I have also illustrated from Cowley: this is the poetry which contradicts our most developed human insights in so far as it fails to use and direct the rich connotation with which language has been informed by experience.

## II

We return to the inquiry set for this discussion: to find out whether there is not a more central achievement in poetry than that represented by either of the extreme examples that we have been considering. I proposed as descriptive of that achievement, the term *tension*. I am using the term not as a general metaphor, but as a special one, derived from lopping the prefixes off the logical terms *ex*tension and *in*tension. What I am saying, of course, is that the meaning of poetry is its "tension," the full organized body of all the extension and intension that we can find in it. The remotest figurative significance that we can derive does not invalidate the extensions of the literal statement. Or we may begin with the literal statement and by stages develop the complications of metaphor: at every stage we may pause to state the meaning so far apprehended, and at every stage the meaning will be coherent.

The meanings that we select at different points along the infinite line between extreme intension and extreme extension will vary with our personal "drive," or "interest," or "approach": the Platonist will tend to stay pretty close to the end of the line where extension, and simple abstraction of the object into a universal, is easiest, for he will be a fanatic in morals or some kind of works, and will insist upon the shortest way with what will ever appear to him the dissenting ambiguities at the intensive end of the scale. The Platonist (I do not say that his opponent is the Aristotelian) might decide that Marvell's "To His Coy Mistress" recommends immoral behavior to the young men, in whose behalf he would try to suppress the poem. That, of course, would be one "true" meaning of "To His Coy Mistress," but it is a meaning that the full tension of the poem will not allow us to entertain exclusively. For we are compelled, since it is there, to give equal weight to an intensive meaning so rich that, without contradicting the literal statement of the lover-mistress convention, it lifts that convention into an insight into one phase of the human predicament—the conflict of sensuality and asceticism.

I should like to quote now, not from Marvell, but a stanza from Donne that I hope will reinforce a little what I have just said and connect it with some earlier remarks.

> Our two soules therefore, which are one,
>   Though I must goe, endure not yet
> A breach, but an expansion,
>   Like gold to aiery thinnesse beate.

Here Donne brings together the developing imagery of twenty lines under the implicit proposition: the unity of two lovers' souls is a non-spatial entity, and is therefore indivisible. That, I believe, is what Mr. John Crowe Ransom would call the logic of the passage; it is the abstract form of its extensive meaning. Now the interesting feature here is the logical contradiction of embodying the unitary, non-spatial soul in a spatial image: the malleable gold is a plane whose surface can always be extended mathematically by one-half towards infinity; the souls are this infinity. The finite image of the gold, in extension, logically contradicts the intensive meaning (infinity) which it conveys; but it does not invalidate that meaning. We have seen that Cowley compelled us to ignore the denoted diaper in order that we might take seriously the violet which it pretended to swathe. But in

Donne's "Valediction: forbidding mourning" the clear denotation of the gold contains, by intension, the full meaning of the passage. If we reject the gold, we reject the meaning, for the meaning is wholly absorbed into the image of the gold. Intension and extension are here one, and they enrich each other.

Before I leave this beautiful object, I should like to notice two incidental features in further proof of Donne's mastery. "Expansion"—a term denoting an abstract property common to many objects, perhaps here one property of a gas: it expands visibly the quality of the beaten gold.

> . . . endure not yet
> a breach . . .

But if the lovers' souls are the formidable, inhuman entity that we have seen, are they not superior to the contingency of a breach? Yes and no: both answers are true answers; for by means of the sly "yet" Donne subtly guards himself against our irony, which would otherwise be quick to scrutinize the extreme metaphor. The lovers have not endured a breach, but they are simple, miserable human beings, and they may quarrel tomorrow.[2]

Now all this meaning and more, and it is all one meaning, is embedded in that stanza: I say more because I have not exhausted the small fraction of significance that my limited powers have permitted me to see. For example, I have not discussed the rhythm, which is of the essential meaning; I have violently isolated four lines from the meaning of the whole poem. Yet, fine as it is, I do not think the poem the greatest poetry; perhaps only very little of Donne makes that grade, or of anybody else. Donne offers many examples of tension in imagery, easier for the expositor than greater passages in Shakespeare.

But convenience of elucidation is not a canon of criticism. I wish now to introduce other kinds of instance, and to let them stand for us as sort of Arnoldish touchstones to the perfection that poetic statement has occasionally reached. I do not know what bearing my comment has had, or my touchstones may have, upon the larger effects of poetry or upon long poems. The long poem is partly a different problem. I have of necessity confined both commentary and illustration to the slighter effects that seemed to me commensurate with certain immediate qualities of language. For, in the long run, whatever the poet's "philosophy," however wide may be the extension of his meaning—like Milton's Ptolemaic universe in which he didn't believe—by his language shall you know him; the quality of his language is the valid limit of what he has to say.

I have not searched out the quotations that follow: they at once form the documentation and imply the personal bias from which this inquiry has grown. Only a few of the lines will be identified with the metaphysical technique, or, in Mr. Ransom's fine phrase, the metaphysical strategy. Strategy would here indicate the point on the intensive-extensive scale at

---

2 Mr. F. O. Matthiessen informs me that my interpretation here, which detaches the "yet" from the developing figure, is not the usual one. Mr. Matthiessen refers the phrase to the gold, for which in his view it prepares the way.

which the poet deploys his resources of meaning. The metaphysical poet as a rationalist begins at or near the extensive or denoting end of the line; the romantic or Symbolist poet at the other, intensive end; and each by a straining feat of the imagination tries to push his meanings as far as he can towards the opposite end, so as to occupy the entire scale. I have offered one good and one bad example of the metaphysical strategy, but only defective examples of the Symbolist, which I cited as fallacies of mass language: Thomson was using language at its mass level, unhappily ignorant of the need to embody his connotations in a rational order of thought. (I allude here also, and in a quite literal sense, to Thomson's personal unhappiness, as well as to the excessive pessimism and excessive optimism of other poets of his time.) The great Symbolist poets, from Rimbaud to Yeats, have heeded this necessity of reason. It would be a hard task to choose between the two strategies, the Symbolist and the metaphysical; both at their best are great, and both are incomplete.

These touchstones, I believe, are not poetry of the extremes, but poetry of the center: poetry of tension, in which the "strategy" is diffused into the unitary effect.

> Ask me no more whither doth hast
> The Nightingale when *May* is past:
> For in your sweet dividing throat
> She winters, and keeps warm her note.

.    .    .

> O thou Steeled Cognizance whose leap commits
> The agile precincts of the lark's return . . .

.    .    .

> That time of year thou mayst in me behold
> When yellow leaves, or none, or few do hang
> Upon those boughs which shake against the cold,
> Bare ruined choirs where late the sweet birds sang.

.    .    .

> Beauty is but a flower
> Which wrinkles will devour;
> Brightness falls from the air,
> Queens have died young and fair,
> Dust hath closed Helen's eye.
> I am sick, I must die.
>     Lord, have mercy upon us!

.    .    .

> And then may chance thee to repent
> The time that thou hast lost and spent
>     To cause thy lovers sigh and swoon;
> Then shalt thou know beauty but lent,
>     And wish and want as I have done.

.    .    .

> We have lingered in the chambers of the sea
> By seagirls wreathed with seaweed red and brown
> Till human voices wake us and we drown.

.    .    .

I am of Ireland
And the Holy Land of Ireland
And time runs on, cried she.
Come out of charity
And dance with me in Ireland.

.            .            .

And my poor fool is hanged! No, no, no life!
Why should a dog, a horse, a rat, have life
And thou no breath at all? Thou'lt come no more,
Never, never, never, never, never!—
Pray you undo this button; thank you, sir.—
Do you see this? Look on her, —look, —her lips, —
Look there, look there!

.            .            .

'Tis madness to resist or blame
The force of angry heavens flame:
   And, if we would speak true,
   Much to the Man is due,
Who, from his private Gardens, where
He liv'd reserved and austere,
   As if his highest plot
   To plant the Bergamot,
Could by industrious Valour climbe
To ruin the great Work of Time,
   And cast the Kingdome old
   Into another Mold.

.            .            .

Cover her face; mine eyes dazzle; she died young.


### III

There are three more lines that I wish to look at: a tercet from *The Divine Comedy*. I know little of either Dante or his language; yet I have chosen as my final instance of tension—the instance itself will relieve me of the responsibility of the term—not a great and difficult passage, but only a slight and perfect one. It is from a scene that has always been the delight of the amateur reader of Dante; we can know more about it with less knowledge than about any other, perhaps, in the poem. The damned of the Second Circle are equivocally damned: Paolo and Francesca were illicit lovers but their crime was incontinence, neither adultery nor pandering, the two crimes of sex for which Dante seems to find any real theological reprobation, for they are committed with the intent of injury.

You will remember that when Dante first sees the lovers they are whirling in a high wind, the symbol here of lust. When Francesca's conversation with the poet begins, the wind dies down, and she tells him where she was born, in these lines:

> *Siede la terra dove nata fui*
> *Sulla marina dove il Po discende*
> *Per aver pace co' seguaci sui.*

Courtney Landon renders the tercet:

> The town where I was born sits on the shore,
> Whither the Po descends to be at peace
> Together with the streams that follow him.

But it misses a good deal; it misses the force of *seguaci* by rendering it as a verb. Professor Grandgent translates the third line: "To have peace with its pursuers," and comments: "The tributaries are conceived as chasing the Po down to the sea." Precisely; for if the *seguaci* are merely followers, and not pursuers also, the wonderfully ordered density of this simple passage is sacrificed. For although Francesca has told Dante where she lives, in the most directly descriptive language possible, she has told him more than that. Without the least imposition of strain upon the firmly denoted natural setting, she fuses herself with the river Po near which she was born. By a subtle shift of focus we see the pursued river as Francesca in Hell: the pursuing tributaries are a new visual image for the pursuing winds of lust. A further glance yields even more: as the winds, so the tributaries at once pursue and become one with the pursued; that is to say, Francesca has completely absorbed the substance of her sin—she is the sin; as, I believe it is said, the damned of the *Inferno* are plenary incarnations of the sin that has put them there. The tributaries of the Po are not only the winds of lust by analogy of visual images; they become identified by means of sound:

> . . . *discende*
> *Per aver pace co' seguaci sui.*

The sibilants dominate the line; they are the hissing of the wind. But in the last line of the preceding tercet Francesca has been grateful that the wind has subsided so that she can be heard—

> *Mentre che il vento, come fa, si tace.*

After the wind has abated, then, we hear in the silence, for the first time, its hiss, in the susurration to the descending Po. The river is thus both a visual and an auditory image, and since Francesca is her sin and her sin is embodied in this image, we are entitled to say that it is a sin that we can both hear and see.

*William Empson*

# AMBIGUITY OF THE FOURTH TYPE

An ambiguity of the fourth type occurs when two or more meanings of a statement do not agree among themselves, but combine to make clear a more complicated state of mind in the author. Evidently this is a vague enough definition which would cover much of the third type, and almost everything in the types which follow; I shall only consider here its difference from the third type.

Reprinted from *Seven Types of Ambiguity* by William Empson, by permission of New Directions, Publishers. All rights reserved.

One is conscious of the most important aspect of a thing, not the most complicated; the subsidiary complexities, once they have been understood, merely leave an impression in the mind that they were to such-and-such an effect and they are within reach if you wish to examine them. I put into the third type cases where one was intended to be mainly conscious of a verbal subtlety; in the fourth type the subtlety may be as great, the pun as distinct, the mixture of modes of judgment as puzzling, but they are not in the main focus of consciousness because the stress of the situation absorbs them, and they are felt to be natural under the circumstances. Of course, different readers apply their consciousness in different ways, and a line which taken alone would be of the third type may become of the fourth type in its setting; but the distinction, I think, is usually clear.

> *I never saw that you did painting need,*
> *And therefore to your fair no painting set,*
> *I found (or thought I found) you did exceed,*
> *The barren tender of a Poet's debt:*
> *And therefore have I slept in your report,*
> *That you yourself being extant well might show,*
> *How far a modern quill doth come too short,*
> *Speaking of worth, what worth in you doth grow,*
> *This silence for my sin you did impute,*
> *Which shall be most my glory being dumb,*
> *For I impair not beauty being mute,*
> *When others would give life, and bring a tomb.*
> > *There lives more life in one of your fair eyes,*
> > *Than both your Poets can in praise devise.*
> > > Sonnets, lxxxiii.

Shakespeare is the writer upon whom ingenuity has most often been misapplied; and if his syntax appears ambiguous, it may be because the Elizabethan rules of punctuation trusted to the reader's intelligence and were more interested in rhetoric than in grammar. One must pause before shadowing with irony this noble compound of eulogy and apology. But one may notice its position in the sequence (Shakespeare seems to have been taunted for his inferiority, and is being abandoned for the rival poet); the mixture of extraordinary claims and bitter humility with which it is surrounded; and that the two adjacent Sonnets say: "Thou truly fair wert truly sympathised In true plain words by thy truth-telling friend," and "You to your beauteous blessings add a curse, Being fond on praise, which makes your praises worse." It is not true that the feeling must be simple because it is deep; irony is similar to this kind of lyrical self-abandonment, or they relieve similar situations; by the energy with which such an adoration springs forward one can measure the objections which it is overriding, by the sharpness of what is treated as an ecstasy one may guess that it would otherwise have been pain.

Line 2, then, goes both with line 1 and line 3. Taking it with line 1, Shakespeare was only concerned for the young man's best interests: "I did not praise you in verse because I could not see that your reputation could be set any higher by my praise." Even for this, the primary, meaning there are two implications; either *never* "until you told me to praise you," an order accepted humbly but with some echo of *being fond on praise,* or *never* "until I found you out"; "At one time I had not yet discovered that your cheeks needed rouge, and your character whitewash"; "When I first loved you I did not realise that you had this simple and touching desire for flattery."

The first line may also stand alone, as an introduction, with these meanings, so that line 2 goes with line 3; for this version one would put a comma after *therefore;* "And so, when no painting had been set to your fairness" (paint to your cheeks or to a portrait, praise to your beauty or to your virtue, apology to your vices), "I found that you exceeded" (in beauty, in virtue, or in wildness of life); "And so, judging you simply, not foreseeing the defences I should have to build up against feeling harshly of you, it came to me as a shock to know you as you are." The first version is much the stronger, both because *I found* is parallel to *I never saw* and because *exceed* wants to pass over the comma and take the fourth line as its object; indeed, I put the second version down less from conviction than because I cannot now read the line without thinking of it.[1]

For the various senses of line 4 we must first consider the meaning of *tender,* which is almost wholly limited into its legal sense by *debt;* "offered payment of what is due." This is coloured, however, by "tender regard" (I *Henry IV,* V. iv. 49); also the meaning "person who looks after" may be fancied in the background. Taking the word as object of *exceed,* we have: "I found you were worth more than the normal compliments due from a poet hired to write eulogies of you," "I found that you exceeded what I could express of beauty in verse," "I found your tenderness towards me exceeded the barren tenderness I owed you as your tame poet," "I found that you were more to me than the person who would see to it that the hired poet wrote adequate praises." These assume the *poet's debt* is a debt owed *by* a poet. Taking it as owed *to* a poet, we have: "I have found that you gave me more than you need have done," "I found that you treated me more as a friend than as a hired poet," and "I found you felt for me more generously than I felt for you, when I merely looked after my job and wrote eulogies of you." I am being verbose here to show the complexity of the material; the resultant ideas from all these permutations are only two: "You were treating me as a friend, not as a poet," and "You were more than I could describe." Here *tender* is the object of *exceed,* but, stressing the comma after *exceed,* *tender* may be either, as a mere echo, a second object of *found,* "I found only the barren tender," "You did *not* treat me more as a friend than as a poet, so I stopped writing" (*or thought I found* is now a more generous doubt), or may be a comment in apposition to the whole first three lines: "This was merely my business; I thought your beauty and virtue so excessive because that was the proper thing; to be expected from a poet in love; to be expected from a professional poet trying to win favour at Court." Most people in reading the line only recognise the meaning, "You were more than I could describe," but they are made to feel also in the word *barren* a more dreary and more petty way of feeling about the matter, they know there is some bitterness which this wave of generosity has submerged.

[1] One must, I think, either say that the comma after *exceed* is a misprint or that it is intended to attract attention to the word and suggest that W. H. exceeded in more ways than one. But the complexity of feeling is still there if it is a misprint.

*Therefore* in line 5 seems parallel to *therefore* in line 2, so that it could refer to *found* or *saw*. Or with a larger rhythm, the fifth line refers to the whole first quatrain and starts a new one. Alternatively, *therefore* may refer forward to line 6: "for this reason . . . in order that." *Report* is either what people in general say or what Shakespeare says, or what Shakespeare writes, about him; thus *I have slept in your report* means either "I have stopped writing about you," or "I have stopped contradicting rumours about you," or "I have bolstered up my faith in you by accepting the public's good opinion of you." *That* means "in order that" (you might show well), "the fact that" (I have slept, which your being extant well shows), or "for fear that" (your being extant might show how far a modern quill comes too short). *Extant* means visible, or successful and respected, or the subject of scandal. *How* and *what* follow *show* and *speaking* respectively, but for variations of grammar which leave them detached they may be regarded as introducing an exclamation and a question. The last line of the quatrain evidently refers backwards as its main meaning: "A modern quill comes too short when attempting to write of as much worth as is in you"; it can also refer forwards, but in trying to regard it in this way one is bothered by a modern usage which could take it alone; "and, talking of worth, *are* you worth anything, now, frankly?" This is not an Elizabethan idiom and was certainly not intended, but its coarseness is hard to keep out of one's mind, because the version which takes line 8 with line 9 is very similar to it: "I was describing all the worth I could find in you without the effort of flattery, and this amounted to the silences of which you, being fond on praise, have been complaining." If you like you may call this version ridiculous, and hurriedly place a colon at the end of the second quatrain; but please notice that the line may still be read as: "I was afraid that a modern quill might come short of a high standard of worth in describing all the worth that it can find in you."

This seems to me a good illustration of the difference between the third type of ambiguity and the fourth. Shakespeare was exquisitely conscious of such subsidiary uses of grammar and the jokes that could be made out of bad stops (if example is needed, consider Quince in Act V, scene i, of the *Dream*); but I do not think he was conscious of these alternatives (certainly I do not think that the reader who is apprehending the result as poetry should be conscious of these alternatives) in a clear-cut way as if they were jokes. They do not need to be separated out to give their curious and harrowing overtone to the quatrain; and once they have been separated out, they can only be connected with the mood of the poem if you hold clearly in mind the third quatrain which is their reconciliation. I might first paraphrase the second. "I have not written or talked about you fully, as the absence, or the particular kind, or the excess of scandal about you shows; *either* because your reality was already a sufficient expression of your beauty and virtue, *or* in order that you might still make a good show in the eyes of the world, as you might not if I were to describe you as I now know you, *or* for fear that the contrast between you and your description might be bad for the literary reputation of the Elizabethans, *or* for fear that the contrast between what this time and previous times could produce in the way of beauty and virtue might be bad for the Elizabethan reputation as a whole."

It would be possible to regard line 12, which clinches the third quatrain, as an antithesis: "When others would bring life, I in fact bring a tomb." This might be Shakespeare's *tomb;* "I do not flatter you but I bring you the devotion of a lifetime." More probably it is W. H.'s; "I do not attempt to flatter you at the moment; I bring you the sad and reserved gift of an eternal praise." We may extract from this some such meaning as: "I do not describe your beauty or your faithlessness, but my love for you." However, there are two other ways of taking the syntax which destroy this antithesis: "When others would bring life, I, if I wrote about you, would bring a tomb," and "When others would try to write about you, would try to give you life, and thereby bring you a tomb"; for both these the *tomb* must imply some action which would *impair beauty*. The normal meaning is given by Sonnet xvii:

> *Who will beleeve my verse in time to come*
> *If it were fild with your most high deserts?*
> *Though yet Heaven knowes it is but as a tombe*
> *Which hides your life, and shows not halfe your parts.*

This first use of the word has no doubt that it is eulogy; the Sonnet is glowing and dancing with his certitude. But when the metaphor is repeated, this time without being explained, it has grown dark with an incipient double meaning; "I should fail you, now that you have behaved so badly to me, if I tried to express you in poetry; I should give you myself, and draw from my readers, a cold and limited judgment, praise you without sincerity, or blame you without thinking of the living man." ("Simply the thing I am Shall make me live"; Shakespeare continually draws on a generosity of this kind. It is not "tout comprendre," in his view, it is merely to feel how a man comes to be a working system, which necessarily excites a degree of sympathy.)[2]

A literary conundrum is tedious, and these meanings are only worth detaching in so far as they are dissolved into the single mood of the poem. Many people would say that they cannot all be dissolved, that an evidently delicate and slender Sonnet ought not to take so much explaining, whatever its wealth of reference and feeling, that Shakespeare, if all this is true, wrote without properly clarifying his mind. One might protest *via* the epithet "natural," which has stuck to Shakespeare through so many literary fashions; that he had a wide rather than a sharp focus to his mind; that he snatched ideas almost at random from its balanced but multitudinous activity; that this is likely to be more so rather than less in his personal poetry; and that in short (as Macaulay said in a very different connection) the reader must take such grammar as he can get and be thankful. One might apologise by saying that people have always read obscure meanings into Shakespeare, secure in the feeling, "If it means less, why is it so beautiful?" and that this

---

[2] The *tomb* is formal praise such as would be written on a tombstone, whereas the real merits of the man are closely connected with his faults, which can't be mentioned in a formal style of praise. I am not now sure that the ambiguities of word and syntax add a great deal to what is clear enough as the theme. That the feeling behind the poem is ambivalent would not, I suppose, be denied.

Maybe I should explain that I put another complete analysis of a Shakespeare Sonnet (xvi) in the second chapter on the ground that it has much less background of rudeness to W. H. than this later one.

analysis can only be offered as another mode of approaching so mysterious a totality, another glance at the effects of language. Or it may boldly be said that the composition of feeling, which never falls apart among these ambiguities (it is, on any interpretation, pained, bitter, tender and admiring; Shakespeare is being abandoned by W. H., and stiffly apologising for not having been servile to him), rises and is clinched plainly in the final couplet; we are reminded of the references to the roving eye glancing round for new conquests; Shakespeare includes the whole ambiguity in his enthusiasm; the worth and sin, the beauty and painting, are all delightful to him, and too subtle to be grasped.

*A Valediction: of weeping* weeps for two reasons, which may not at first sight seem very different; because their love when they are together, which they must lose, is so valuable, and because they are "nothing" when they are apart. There is none of the Platonic pretence Donne keeps up elsewhere, that their love is independent of being together; he can find no satisfaction in his hopelessness but to make as much of the actual situation of parting as possible; and the language of the poem is shot through with a suspicion which for once he is too delicate or too preoccupied to state unambiguously, that when he is gone she will be unfaithful to him. Those critics who say the poem is sincere, by the way, and therefore must have been written to poor Anne, know not what they do.

> *Let me powre forth*
> *My teares before thy face, whil'st I stay here,*
> *For thy face coins them, and thy stampe they beare,*
> *And by this Mintage they are something worth,*
>   *For thus they be*
>   *Pregnant of thee,*
> *Fruits of much grief they are, emblemes of more,*
> *When a teare falls, that thou falst which it bore,*
> *So thou and I are nothing then, when on a divers shore.*[3]

"Allow me this foolishness; let me cry thoroughly while I can yet see your face, because my tears will be worth nothing, may, in fact, not flow at all, when once I have lost sight of you." "Let me plunge, at this dramatic moment, into my despair, so that by its completeness I may be freed from it, and my tears may be coined into something more valuable."

The metaphor of coining is suitable at first sight only "because your worth and your beauty are both royal," but other deductions from it can be made. In that his *teares* will not reflect her *face* unless he *stays here*, it may imply "because it is only when I am seeing your beauty that it matters so much to me; I only shed valuable tears about you when I am at your side." There is a shift of the metaphor in this, brought out by line 3, from the *teares* as molten metal which must be *stamped* with her value to the *teares* themselves as the completed *coin;* "because," then, "you are so fruitful of unhappiness"; and in either case, far in the background, in so far as she is not really such a queenly figure, "because you are public, mercenary, and illegal." [4]

[3] The three verses of the poem are quoted and examined separately.
[4] I doubt now whether Donne would have minded leaving these conceivable implications lying about, even if the poem were in fact written for his wife. He might well have feared that she would throw up her reckless marriage.

In each of the three verses of the poem the two short middle lines are
separated only by commas from the lines before and after them; Professor
Grierson on the two occasions that he has corrected this has accurately
chosen the more important meaning, and unnecessarily cut off the less. In
this verse, *for thus they be* may be a note to give the reasons why the tears
are *something worth,* or may be parallel to *for thy face coins them,* so that
it leads on to the rest of the stanza. Going backwards, "Let me pour out
at once the tears I shall have to shed sooner or later, because if I do it now
they will reflect your face and become valuable because they contain you";
going forwards, "Let me pour forth my tears before your face, because they
are epitomes of you in this way, that they are born in sorrow, and are signs
that there is more sorrow to come after." *Pregnant* because they are like her,
in that they *fall* and are *emblems of grief,* and give true information about
her (as in "a pregnant sentence"), because they are round and large like a
pregnancy, because they hold a reflection of her inside them, and because,
if they are wept in her presence, they will carry her more completely with
them, and so do him more good. It is this last obscure sense, that he is
getting rid of her, or satisfying her, or getting his feeling for her into a
more manageable form, by a storm of emotion in her presence, that gives
energy to the metaphor of *pregnancy,* and logic to the second alternative—
the idea that she normally causes sorrow.

Corresponding to these alternative meanings of *for thus, that thou* means
"the fact that you" and "that particular case of you." "The tears are emblems of more grief by foreshadowing, when they fall, that you will fall who
were the cause of them" (if *which* refers to a person it should be the subject
of *bore*), or, beginning a new sentence at *when,* "when a tear falls, that
reflection of you which it carries in it falls too" (*which* now refers to a thing
and so can be the object).

And corresponding to these again, there is a slight variation in the meaning of *so,* according as the last line stands alone or follows on from the one
before. "These tears by falling show that you will fall who were the cause
of them. And therefore, because you will fall when we are separated, when
we are separated we shall both become nothing," or "When the reflection of
you is detached from my eye and put on a separate tear it falls; in the same
way we shall ourselves fall and be nothing when we are separated by water."

All these versions imply that their love was bound to lead to unhappiness;
the word *fall* expects unfaithfulness, as well as negation, from her absence;
*then* means both "when you fall" and "when we are separated," as if they
were much the same thing; and *nothing* (never name her, child, if she be
nought, advised Mrs. Quickly) says the same of himself also, when a channel
divides them deeper, but no less salt, than their pool of tears.

> *On a round ball,*
> *A workeman that hath copies by, can lay*
> *An Europe, Afrique, and an Asia,*
> *And quickly make that, which was nothing,* **All,**
>   *So doth each teare*
>   *Which thee doth weare,*
> *A globe, yea world by that impression grow*
> *Till my teares mixed with thine do overflow*
> *This world, by waters sent from thee, my heaven dissolved so,*

The first four lines are defining the new theme, and their grammar is straightforward. Then the *teare* may be active or passive, like the *workeman* or like the *ball;* on the face of it, it is like the *ball,* but *so doth* may treat it as like the *workeman.* For *doth* may be a separate verb as well as an auxiliary of *grow;* while, in any case, *grow* may either mean "turn into" or "grow larger." The *globe* and the *world* may be either the *teare* or *thee.* The other meanings of *impression* [Chapter V] would be possible here. Either, then, "In the same way each tear that wears you, who are a whole world yourself or at least the copy of one, grows into a world," or "And so does every tear that wears you; each tear, that is, grows, so as to include everything, or to produce a great deal more water"; it is only this second, vaguer meaning which gives a precise meaning to *till,* and suggests, instead of a mere heap of world-tears, such a flood as descended upon the wickedness of the antediluvians.

*Which thee doth weare* suggests by the order of the words a more normal meaning, that her *teares* are jewels and she is *wearing* them; this is inverted by the grammar, so as to leave an impression that she is uniquely and unnaturally under the control of her tears, or even has no existence independent of them.

The last line but one may stand alone, with *overflow* meaning simply "flow excessively," or "flow into each other," so as to spoil each other's shape, and then the last line, by itself, means, "In the same way, the necessities of this, the real, world have dissolved my precarious heaven by means of, or into, tears." Or making *world* the object of *overflow,* it may mean, according as *this world* is the real world or the *teares,* either "we produce more and more tears till we drown the world altogether, and can no longer see things like ordinary people," or "my tear reflects you and so is a world till one of your tears falls on it, spoils its shape and leaves only a splash"; it is she who has made the *world* which is his *heaven,* and she who destroys it. The rest of the line then says, "in the same way my happiness in our love has been dissolved, by this meeting with your tears," making *heaven* the subject of the intransitive verb *dissolved.* But *my heaven* may be in apposition to *thee; dissolved* may be a participle; and *so* may be not "in the same way" but "so completely, so terribly"; it is not merely his memory and idea and understanding of her, it is the actual woman herself, as she was when they were happy together, who is *dissolving* under his eyes into the *tears* of this separation; *dissolved,* it has already happened. The waters are falling that were above the firmament; the heaven and crystalline spheres, which were she, are broken; she is no longer the person he made her, and will soon be made into a different person by another lover. These broken pieces of grammar which may be fitted together in so many ways are lost phrases jerked out whilst sobbing, and in the reading, "so my heaven dissolved this world," which though far in the background is developed in the following stanza, there is a final echo of unexplained reproach.

> *O more than Moone,*
> *Draw not up seas to drowne me in thy spheare,*
> *Weep me not dead, in thine armes, but forbeare*
> *To teach the sea, what it may doe too soone,*
> *    Let not the winde*
> *    Example finde,*

> *To do me more harm, then it purposeth,*
> *Since thou and I sigh one another's breath,*
> *Whoe'er sighs most, is cruellest, and hasts the other's death.*

She is *Moone,* with a unifying reference to the first line of the poem, because she draws up the tides of weeping both from him and from herself, a power not necessarily to her credit, but at any rate deserving adoration; the moon, too, is female, inconstant, chaste because though bright cold, and has *armes* in which the new moon holds the old one. Some of the lyrical release in the line may be explained as because it is deifying her, and remembering the Sidney tradition, even now after so many faults in her have been implied, and are still being implied. She is *more than Moone* because she is more valuable to him than anything in the real world to which he is being recalled; because she has just been called either the earth or the heavens and they are larger than the moon; as controlling tides more important or more dangerous than those of the sea; as making the world more hushed and glamourous than does moonlight; as being more inconstant, or as being more constant, than the moon; as being able to draw tides right up to her own sphere; as shining by her own light; and as being more powerful because closer.

*In thy spheare* may be taken with *me,* "don't drown me, whether with my tears or your own, now that I am still fairly happy and up in your sphere beside you; don't trouble to draw up the seas so high, or be so cruel as to draw up the seas so high, that they drown me now, since to-morrow they will drown me easily, when I am thrown down into the world"; may be taken alone, as "your sphere of influence," your sort of drowning, "don't *you* go drowning me; I have the whole sea to drown me when I take ship to-morrow"; or may be taken with *Moone,* "you, far in your sphere, high and safe from sorrow in your permanence and your power to change, do not drown a poor mortal who is not in your sphere, to whom these things matter more deeply."

The machinery of interpretation is becoming too cumbrous here, in that I cannot see how these meanings come to convey tenderness rather than the passion of grief which has preceded them, how they come to mark a particular change of tone, a return towards control over the situation, which makes them seem more vividly words actually spoken. It is a question of the proportions in which these meanings are accepted, and their interactions; it is not surprising that the effect should be what it is, but I do not know that it could have been foreseen. Perhaps it is enough to say that the request, in its fantastic way, is more practical, and draws its point from the immediate situation.

*Weep me not dead* means: "do not make me cry myself to death; do not kill me with the sight of your tears; do not cry for me as for a man already dead, when, in fact, I am in your arms," and, with a different sort of feeling, "do not exert your power over the sea so as to make it drown me by sympathetic magic"; there is a conscious neatness in the ingenuity of the phrasing, perhaps because the same idea is being repeated, which brings out the change of tone in this verse. *What it may doe too soone,* since the middle lines may as usual go forwards or backwards, may be said of the *sea* or of the *winde;* if of the *winde* the earlier syntax may be "forbeare in order to teach the sea to be calm"; this gives point to the crude logic, which has in any case a sort of lyrical ease, of "do not weep, but forbeare to weep." The *sea* is going to separate them; it *may* be going to drown him; and so it *may* drown him, for all he cares, when he has lost her. The *winde purposeth* to blow him from her, and if she doesn't stop sighing she will *teach* it to do *more harm,* and upset the boat. One may notice the contrast between the danger and discomfort of this prospect, also the playfulness or brutality of the request, and the cooing assured seductive murmur of the sound *doe too soone;* by this time he is trying to soothe her.

I always think of this poem as written before Donne's first voyage with Essex, which he said he undertook to escape from "the queasy pain of loving and being loved"; the fancy is trivial but brings out the change of tone in the last two lines. In itself the notion is a beautiful one, "our sympathy is so perfect that any expression of sorrow will give more pain to the other party than relief to its owner, so we ought to be trying to cheer each other up," but to say this is to abandon the honest luxuriance of sorrow with which they have been enlivening their parting, to try to forget feeling in a bright, argumentative, hearty quaintness (the good characters in Dickens make the orphan girl smile through her tears in this way); the language itself has become flattened and explanatory: so that he almost seems to be feeling for his hat. But perhaps I am libelling this masterpiece; all one can say is that its passion exhausts itself; it achieves at the end the sense of reality he was looking for, and some calm of mind.[5]

This poem is ambiguous because his feelings were painfully mixed, and because he felt that at such a time it would be ungenerous to spread them out clearly in his mind; to express sorrow at the obvious fact of parting gave an adequate relief to his disturbance, and the variety of irrelevant, incompatible ways of feeling about the affair that were lying about in his mind were able so to modify, enrich, leave their mark upon this plain lyrical relief as to make it something more memorable.

I hope I have now made clear what the fourth type is like when it really gets under way; I shall add some much slighter cases which seemed illuminating.

> *What if this present were the world's last night?*
> *Mark in my heart, O Soule, where thou dost dwell,*
> *The picture of Christ crucified, and tell*
> *Whether that countenance can thee affright,*
> *Teares in his eyes quench the amasing light,*
> *Blood fills his frownes, which from his pierc'd head fell.*
> *And can that tongue adjudge thee unto hell,*
> *Which prayed forgivenesse for his foes fierce spight?*
> *No, no; but as in my idolatrie*
> *I said to all my profane mistresses,*
> *Beauty, of pitty, foulness onely is*
> *A sign of rigour; so I say to thee,*

5 It seems at least possible that they may choose to do each other less harm than they could; he seems therefore to have cured himself of some of the earlier suspicions. I still think that all this analysis is correct.

> *To wicked spirits are horrid shapes assign'd,*
> *This beauteous form assures a piteous mind.*
> > DONNE, Holy Sonnets, xiii.

In one's first reading of the first line, the dramatic idea is of Donne pausing in the very act of sin, stricken and swaddled by a black unexpected terror: suppose the end of the world came *now*? The preacher proceeds to comfort us after this shock has secured our attention. But looking back, and taking for granted the end's general impression of security, the first line no longer conflicts with it. "Why, this *may* be the last night, but God is loving. What if it were?" In the first notion one must collect one's mind to answer the Lord suddenly, and Donne, in fact, shuffles up an old sophistry from Plato, belonging to the lyrical tradition he rather despised, and here even more absurdly flattering to the person addressed and doubtful as to its general truth than on the previous occasions he has found it handy. Is a man in the last stages of torture so beautiful, even if blood hides his frowns? Never mind about that, he is pleased, we have carried it off all right; the great thing on these occasions is to have a ready tongue.[6]

A similar doubt as to emphasis runs through the *Apparition*, and almost leaves one in doubt between two moods; an amused pert and fanciful contempt, written up with more elaboration than it deserves, so as to give him an air of being detached from her and interested in literature; and the scream of agony and hatred by which this is blown aside.

> Then *thy* sicke taper *will begin to* winke

is a bumping line full of guttering and oddity, but brisk with a sense of power over her. This has reached a certain intensity by the time we get to

> *thinke*
> *Thou call'st for more,*
> *And* in false sleepe *will from thee* shrinke.

with the stresses in the line almost equal; Crashaw uses a similar rhythm to convey a chanting and mystical certainty,

> *And in her* first ranks *make thee* room.

Donne's version conveys: "I am speaking quite seriously, with conviction, but with personal indifference, to this toad."

> *And* then *poore* Aspen wretch, neglected *thou*
> *All in a cold quicksilver sweat wilt lye*
> *A veryer ghost than I.*

The stress is on *neglected;* "you would be glad to get me back now if you could." But

> *since my love is spent*
> *I had* rather *thou shouldst* painfully *repent*
> *Than by my threatenings rest still innocent.*

---

[6] I leave in my expression of distaste for the poem, but it has little to do with the ambiguity in question.

What a placid epigrammatical way of stopping, we are to think, and how trivial the affair is made by this final admission that she is innocent! He would not say that if he cared for her any more.

But, after all, the first line calls her a *murderess,* and the way most people read the poem makes the poet more seriously involved;

> *Then* thy *sicke taper will begin to winke*

("As does mine now; you have left me ill and exhausted," and the last part of the line gabbles with fury.)

> *And in false sleepe will from* thee *shrinke*

("as you, if I can credit it, as you have shrunk from *me;* with a disgust which I shall yet turn to terror.")

> *And* then *poore Aspen wretch, neglected* thou

(It is almost a childish cry; "I find it *intolerable* to be so neglected.")

> *A veryer ghost than* I

("Than I am now," not "than I shall be then"); that his *love* is *spent* has become pathetically unbelievable;

> *I had rather* thou *shouldst painfully repent*

("As I am repenting, in agony"); and *innocent* has become a scream of jealous hatred at her hypocrisy, of an impotent desire to give any pain he can find.

The meaning of an English sentence is largely decided by the accent, and yet one learns in conversation to put the accent in several places at once; it may be possible to read the poem so as to combine these two ways of underlining it. But these last two cases are curious in that the alternative versions seem particularly hard to unite into a single vocal effect. You may be intended, while reading a line one way, to be conscious that it could be read in another; so that if it is to be read aloud it must be read twice; or you may be intended to read it in some way different from the colloquial speech-movement so as to imply both ways at once. Different styles of reading poetry aloud use these methods in different proportions, but perhaps these two last examples from Donne respectively demand the two methods in isolation. The following example from Hopkins shows the first case being forcibly included in the second.

> *Margaret, are you grieving*
> *Over Goldengrove unleafing?*
> *Leaves, like the things of man, you*
> *With your fresh thoughts care for, can you?*
> *Ah, as the heart grows older*
> *It will come to such sights colder*
> *By and by, nor spare a sigh*
> *Though world of wanwood leafmeal lie;*
> *And yet you will weep and know why.*

> *Now no matter, child, the name.*
> *Sorrow's springs àre the same.*
> *Nor mouth had, no, nor mind express'd,*
> *What heart heard of, ghost guess'd:*
> *It is the blight man was born for,*
> *It is Margaret you mourn for.*

*Will weep* may mean: "insist upon weeping, now or later," or "shall weep in the future." *Know* in either case may follow *will*, like *weep*, "you insist upon knowing, or you shall know," or may mean: "you already know why you weep, why you shall weep, or why you insist upon weeping," or thirdly, may be imperative, "listen and I shall tell you why you weep, or shall weep, or shall insist upon weeping, or insist upon weeping already." Mr. Richards, from whom I copy this (*Practical Criticism,* p. 83), considers that the ambiguity of *will* is removed by the accent which Hopkins placed upon it; it seems to me rather that it is intensified. Certainly, with the accent on *weep* and *and, will* can only be the auxiliary verb, and with the accent on *will* its main meaning is "insist upon." But the future meaning also can be imposed upon this latter way of reading the line if it is the tense which is being stressed, if it insists on the contrast between the two sorts of weeping, or, including *know* with *weep,* between the two sorts of knowledge. Now it is useful that the tense should be stressed at this crucial point, because it is these two contrasts and their unity which make the point of the poem.

It seems difficult to enjoy the accent on *are,* which the poet has inserted; I take it to mean: "Sorrow's springs, always the same, independent of our attitude to them and of our degree of consciousness of them, exist," permanently and as it were absolutely.

The two sorts of knowledge, intuitive and intellectual, form ambiguities again in the next couplet; this may help to show they are really there in the line about *will. Mouth* and *mind* may belong to *Margaret* or somebody else; *what heart heard of* goes both forwards and backwards; and *ghost,* which in its grammatical position means both the profundities of the unconsciousness and the essentially conscious spirit, brings to mind both immortality and a dolorous haunting of the grave. "Nobody else's mouth had told her, nobody else's mind had hinted to her, about the fact of mortality, which yet her own imagination had already invented, which her own spirit could foresee." "Her mouth had never mentioned death; she had never stated the idea to herself so as to be conscious of it; but death, since it was a part of her body, since it was natural to her organs, was known at sight as a portent by the obscure depths of her mind." My point is not so much that these two are mixed up as that the poet has shown precisely by insisting that they were *the same,* that he knew they were distinguishable.

A much fainter example of the sort of ambiguity in question is supplied by one of Pope's great passages about dowagers, which possesses in a high degree the sensuous beauty that is supposed to have been beyond his powers:

> *As hags hold sabbats, not for joy but spite,*
> *So these their merry miserable night;*
> *So round and round the ghosts of beauty glide,*
> *And haunt the places where their honour died.*

*See how the world its veterans rewards.*
*A youth of frolics, an old age of cards.*
*Fair to no purpose, artful to no end,*
*Young without lovers, old without a friend;*
*A fop her passion, and her prize a sot;*
*Alive ridiculous, and dead forgot.*

Essay on Women, Ep. II. 245.

An impression of febrile and uncontrollable hatred is given to the terrible climax of this passage by the flat, indifferent little words, *fop, sot,* which, if they are to fill out the line, to give it weight, as its meaning and position demand, cannot be dropped with the analytical contempt with which they appear on the printed page; must be hurled at a person conceived as in front of you, to whom you know they are intolerable. Never was the couplet more of a rocking-horse if each line is considered separately; but all the inertia of this flatness is needed to give him strength; never was the couplet given more delicacy of modulation than is here imposed by the mere weight and passion of the sense conveyed. What is so compelling about the passage is the combination within it of two sharply distinguished states of mind; the finicking precision with which the subject-matter is handled; the pity, bitterness, and terror with which the subject-matter must be conceived.

In the third type, two such different moods would both be included, laid side by side, made relevant as if by a generalisation; in the fourth type they react with one another to produce something different from either, and here the reaction is an explosion.

I spoke of "sensuous beauty," thinking of the second couplet quoted, to which a more verbal analysis can be applied. The dowagers may *glide round and round* because they are still dancing, or merely, since they are fixed to the card-table in the next couplet, because they go on and on, in rotation, to the same drawing-rooms. In this way they may at once be conceived as still dancing and yet as at an age when, in those days, they would have had to stop. They are first spoken of as *ghosts* of their dead *beauty,* and will then be thought of as still dancing, since such *ghosts* would still be echoing what they had done in life; but in the next line they are *ghosts* of their dead *honour, haunting* a *place* only, and that not so much the ballroom as the card-table. (These *places,* however, are practically the same, so there is an independent ambiguity as to whether they lost their *honour* by cheating at the card-table or making assignations in the ballroom.) The result of this is that the two lines cannot run as simply as they claim to do; *ghosts* means something different for each line, and you must in each case translate the line back into something said about old ladies, or the transitions will not work. But one is accustomed to this process of immediate translation only in verses of flowery and graceful ornament, so that it is a parody of the manner in which a gallant compliment would have been paid to the ladies, and has a ghastly air of being romantic and charming.

I must not deny that the *ghost* of a dead *beauty* might haunt the place where her *honour* had died, as she might haunt the place where anything that interested her had happened. If you read it like this, there is a touch of that form of wit which caps a sentence with the unexpected word; "you might think she was most distressed at losing her beauty; but no, it's her conscience that troubles the old woman, and well it may." However, I find it very difficult to read the lines like this; they stand too completely parallel and apart, and read like one blow after another.

Or you may say from this parallelism that *beauty* and *honour* are treated as necessary corollaries of one another, the two names being used in the two lines only for variety (as if from the old dictionary interest in synonyms); so that *ghosts of beauty* are the same as *ghosts of honour*, and had necessarily to lose their properties in the same place. Beauty and honour, then, are identical, so that we find ourselves, to our justifiable surprise, in Spenser's fairy-story world of sensuous idealism. There is a sort of subterranean resonance in the verses from the clash of this association; with a feverish anger, like the screws of a liner racing above water, Pope finds himself indeed hag-ridden by these poor creatures; they excite in him feelings irrelevantly powerful, of waste, of unavoidable futility, which no bullying of its object can satisfy.

Wordsworth was not an ambiguous poet; the cult of simplicity moved its complexity back into the subconscious, poisoned only the sources of thought, in the high bogs of the mountains, and stated as simply as possible the fundamental disorders of the mind. But he sometimes uses what may be called philosophical ambiguities when he is not sure how far this process can tolerably be pushed. In the third type we found minor uses of ambiguity for jokes; the fourth type includes its electoral applications. Thus the degree of pantheism implied by some of Wordsworth's most famous passages depends very much on the taste of the reader, who can impose grammar without difficulty to uphold his own views.

> *For I have learnt*
> *To look on nature, not as in the hour*
> *Of thoughtless youth; but hearing oftentimes*
> *The still, sad music of humanity,*
> *Nor harsh nor grating, though of ample power*
> *To chasten and subdue. And I have felt*
> *A presence that disturbs me with the joy*
> *Of elevated thoughts; a sense sublime*
> *Of something far more deeply interfused,*
> *Whose dwelling is the light of setting suns,*
> *And the round ocean and the living air,*
> *And the blue sky, and in the mind of man:*
> *A motion and a spirit, that impels*
> *All thinking things, all objects of all thought,*
> *And rolls through all things.*
>
> Tintern Abbey.

It is not sufficient to say that these lines convey with great beauty the mood intended; Wordsworth seems to have believed in his own doctrines and wanted his readers to know what they were. It is reasonable, then, to try to extract from this passage definite opinions on the relations of God, man, and nature, and on the means by which such relations can be known.

There are several points of difficulty in the grammar when one tries to do this. It is not certain what is *more deeply interfused* than what. It is not certain whether the *music of humanity* is the same as the *presence;* they are separated by the word *and* and a full stop. We may notice, too, that the word *in* seems to distinguish, though but faintly, the *mind of man* from the *light,* the *ocean,* the *air* and the *sky;* this tends to separate the *motion* and the *spirit* form from the *presence* and the *something;* but they may, again, all be identical with the *music.* Wordsworth may then have *felt* a *something far more deeply interfused* than the *presence* that *disturbed* him; we seem here to have God revealing himself in particular to the mystic, but being in a more fundamental sense immanent in his whole creation.[7] Or the *something* may be in apposition to the *presence* (the *sense* equal to the *joy);* so that both are "more" *deeply interfused* than the *music of humanity,* but apparently in the same way. This version only conceives God as immanent in his creation, and as affecting the poet in the same way as he affects everything else; or as only imagined by the poet as immanent in creation, in the same way as the *music of humanity* is imagined as immanent. Thus, the first version is Christian, the second in part pantheistic, in part agnostic. Again, the *something* may possibly dwell only in the natural objects mentioned, ending at *sky;* the *motion* and the *spirit* are then not thought of at all as *interfused* into nature, like the *something;* they are things active *in the mind of man.* At the same time they are similar to the *something;* thus Wordsworth either *feels* them or *feels a sense* of them. With this reading the voice would rise in some triumph at the words *mind of man;* man has a spirit immanent in nature in the same way as is the spirit of God, and is decently independent from him. Or the *something* may also *dwell in the mind of man,* and have the *motion* and the *spirit* in apposition to it; under this less fortunate arrangement a God who is himself nature subjects us at once to determinism and predestination.

So far I have been examining grammatical ambiguities, but the last three lines also admit of doubt, as to the purpose of what seems an irrelevant distinction. Whether man or some form of God is subject here, he distinguishes between *things* which are objects or subjects of *thought,* these he *impels;* and *things* which are neither objects nor subjects of *thought,* through these he merely *rolls.* (I am not sure what is the logical status of the *things* not the objects of *thought* about which Wordsworth is *thinking* here; after all, he is not thinking very hard, so it may be all right.) The only advantage I can see in this distinction is that it makes the *spirit* at once intelligent and without intelligence; at once God and nature; allows us to think of him as the second, without compromising his position as the first.[8]

---

7 Or one may stand for paganism (the local deity of a bit of lake scenery, say) and the other for the more puzzling doctrine (far more deeply interfused) on which Wordsworth would support it.

8 Critics have disliked the meanness and fussiness of this passage, and I wish that I had something wise and reconciling to say after all these years. Miss M. C. Bradbrook wrote that the nouns after the full stop are all obviously in apposition, because the theme is the transcendence of the subject-object relationship. It is, I suppose, almost certain that Wordsworth meant the grammar to run on like this. But surely, even if clauses are in apposition, they must be supposed to be somehow distinguishable, or why do they have to be said one after another? One could give a much more sympathetic account of the philosophical background of Wordsworth, and no doubt if I. A. Richards' *Coleridge on Imagination* had been already published I would have written differently. But the more seriously one takes the doctrine, it seems to me, the more this expression of it seems loose rhetoric.

And, indeed, whether or not a great deal of wisdom is enshrined in these lines, lines just as muddled, superficially speaking, may convey a mode of using their antinomies, and so act as creeds. The reason why one grudges Wordsworth this source of strength is that he talks as if he owned a creed by which his half-statements might be reconciled, whereas, in so far as his creed was definite, he found these half-statements necessary to keep it at bay. There is something rather shuffling about this attempt to be uplifting yet non-denominational, to put across as much pantheism as would not shock his readers. I must protest again that I enjoy the lines very much, and find, like everybody else, that I remember them; probably it was necessary for Wordsworth to shuffle, if he was to maintain his peculiar poetical attitude. And, of course, by considering the example in this chapter, I have shown that I regard the shuffling as a deeply-rooted necessity, not conscious at the time when it was achieved. But, perhaps, this last example may show how these methods can be used to convict a poet of holding muddled opinions rather than to praise the complexity of the order of his mind. To the more fruitful sorts of muddle I must proceed in my next chapter.

# 2. THE USES OF THE SOCIO-CULTURAL MILIEU

## The Theory

*David Daiches*

## FICTION AND CIVILIZATION

There are many approaches to the criticism of fiction, from the purely formal to the purely historical. And no approach which brings out some truth about the novels under consideration can be entirely unprofitable. But with facts about fiction, as with historical facts, there are degrees of usefulness; and the fundamental critical question is concerned with gauging these degrees, or at least with relating them to each other. One might say generally that those facts are likely to be most important which have most relevance to the question of value, but it is difficult to assess this relevance objectively, for it varies so in the hands of different critics. If, therefore, we affirm dogmatically that that critical approach is most useful which involves relating the art of fiction at any given time to the civilization of which it is a part, and endeavoring to see all other questions of form, technique, style, and subject matter against the background of this relationship, we are aware that this may not appear a self-evident truth to all and that to those to whom it does not so appear it would be impossible to prove. For such a belief implies not only the view that relations are as much facts as what are more usually denoted by that term, but also that to see the results of different human activities as separate phenomena rather than as part of a process is an unsatisfactory, if not a perverse, occupation. In other words, in the definition of an event the context is part of the definition. This is either an axiom or nothing. You cannot prove causality and you cannot disprove an atomic view of history; you can only feel the one to be obvious, the other to be absurd. No one has ever disproved Bishop Berkeley with complete philosophical adequacy—but nobody believes him.

So much controversy about critical methods has resulted from the critics' failure to make clear their axioms that this point seems worth stressing. If you are a literary atomist and believe that all critical statements about a work that have any value are concerned simply with the relations between the parts and the whole within that particular work, that the frame of reference for the critic is rigorously bound by the terms presented by or implied in the work, then you will do well to make this view clear at the outset so that those who disagree will know with what they are disagreeing. And, similarly, if you hold the view that the wider the context with reference to which a truth is stated the more significant that truth is, you ought to be explicit about it. For we are here dealing with a fundamental divergence about axioms, and one school of critics can only be intelligible to the other if this divergence is wholly understood. Though the two critical processes are so different, the history of criticism has shown that one man need not confine himself throughout his career as a critic to one method. Many have written histories of literature within a fairly wide context and produced in addition formal studies of individual works which ignore that wider context completely; but the relation between the two has always been obscure.

There are advantages and disadvantages on both sides. For those who hold the maximum-context view there is always the consideration that the maximum context can never be attained; that all relevant material (which would be the sum of human activity and its causes) can never be confined within the scope of any one discussion, and therefore one can only approximate, in varying degree, to the ideal without any prospect of ever attaining it. On the other hand, those who endeavor to limit the context to the given work have to realize that every term they use or their author uses, every reaction counted on by the author and undergone by the critic, depends on the civilization that lies behind both author and critic to give it meaning, so that the "work in itself" becomes an abstraction—a convenient formula with no real correspondence to anything in the world of experience. Thus the first type of critic can only approximate to a goal which, though real, is yet unattainable, while the second can achieve an end which, though attainable, is yet unreal. (This, however, is no necessary disproof of the second critic's possible contention that it is profitable to proceed as though his end were real.) The holder of the maximum-context view can also urge that his critical method includes, or ought to include, the other, so that he is doing what the other critic is doing and more. You can, for example, make a formal analysis of a work while recognizing the importance of the wider context in determining the actual meaning of the text and also its meaning in terms of anticipated reaction on the part of the reader—emotional patterns, etc.; while the other critic can never claim that his method may include the former—indeed, it is often his boast that it does not. This, perhaps, is as near as we can come to a logical proof of the superior usefulness of the former method, though it may be replied that inclusiveness is no necessary proof of such superiority.

The critic who endeavors to see literature as a process rather than as a series of phenomena, and as a process which is bound up with an infinite series of ever wider processes, ought to realize that however wide his context, it is but a fraction of what it might be. This will save him from the fallacy of believing that it is possible in the criticism of literature to employ either a purely deductive or a purely inductive method. He has neither fixed premises nor all the relevant data. He can neither start with a complete view of civilization and work down to the individual work of art nor can he start with the particular work of art and work up to civilization as a whole; he must try both methods and give neither his complete trust. This, perhaps, may be given as an excuse for the lack of system in the present work; for the alternation between generalizations and particular investigations. The main object is to indicate relevance and to show how understanding depends on awareness of relevance. That appreciation depends on understanding and that a theory of value can come only after appreciation, hardly need stating.

It is perhaps easier to adopt this approach in the criticism of fiction than in the discussion of any of the other arts, for the storyteller creates an imaginary world which can easily be set side by side with the real world. Such a juxtaposition can serve a variety of purposes, from the crude comparison of true with false through such terms as "realism," "naturalism," and "romanticism," and from comparisons of the same kind made through the use of the same terms with an infinite number of degrees of sophistication, to considerations of the nature of the relation between the two which have little or nothing to do with the true-false distinction. But so long as this comparison concerns only the events of the story, it can yield comparatively little. The patterning of those events, their relation to each other within the story, the attitude to them which emerges, the mood which surrounds them, the tone in which they are related, and the style of the writing are all equally relevant. This becomes clearest in the criticism of a work like *Ulysses,* where to discuss the events narrated without reference to style and tone as equally if not more relevant would be patently absurd. The separation of the story from the way in which it is told, of plot from style, is an artificial procedure which may be useful at times but which can never yield the most important truths about a work. What *Ulysses* really is, as a piece of fiction and as an illuminating product of a certain stage of civilization, could never be learned by discussing these aspects of the story separately; and this is equally true, though perhaps less easy to see, of all fiction. Indeed, if we look back on the major critical blunders of great critics of the past we can see most of them— Dr. Johnson on *Lycidas* for example—as primarily due to this separation of different aspects of the work and the treating of them as each capable of independent appraisement.

The universality of great works of fiction does not imply their ability to be isolated from all contexts but rather their ability to retain their value in many different contexts. Indeed, there are here two different tasks for the maximum-context critic; one is to investigate the relation between the work and the world of which the author was a part and the other to inquire into the circumstances of appreciation by investigating the relation between the work and the worlds of which readers have been a part. We must always remember that an explanation of origins does not explain present value. Psychologists may tell us that a certain author wrote a certain novel in order to escape the implications of his own way of life; sociologists may tell us that another author wrote as he did as a result of certain social attitudes which belonged to his class. These are interesting and important facts, but they imply no necessary judgments about the value of the works at the present time. Confusion between origin and value is perhaps the commonest critical error of the present day.

Explanation of origin, however, can serve some very fundamental purposes. If we know just what it is in the civilization of his time that led the author to adopt the attitude he did, to shape the work the way he did, to tell this story in this way and no other, then we understand what we may call the logic of the work; we can see what its real principle of unity is; we can see the work as a whole and be sure of seeing the right whole. And only then are we qualified to talk about appreciation and value. Thus there is a connection between origin and value, though not the direct one that some critics seem to postulate. Of course, some may maintain that it is not necessary or desirable to see the right whole in the sense just indicated, but that every man ought to get what he can out of the work, which is, and ought to be, different for each reader. Here again is a view that one can reject only by choice, not on proof. Those who wish to regard literature as simply a series of exercising-grounds for their own personalities, incapable of objective definition or evaluation, may of course do so: you cannot prove to those who wish to equate criticism with autobiography that such an equation is unhealthy. But we know what we would say in any other branch of inquiry where the inquirers handed out autobiography for results.

Those who regard literary criticism as possessing at least some objectivity will see the importance of finding out what the right whole really is. Is *Hamlet* a propaganda tract against believing in ghosts or a serious psychological study of a certain type of mind in a certain situation patterned in a definite way? Is *Alice in Wonderland* a child's adventure story or a Freudian joke? Of course, a work may be very many different things at the same time, but it is important to know which is the essential thing, what it is that determines the pattern and the scale of emphases, what is the real work, and what are the by-products of it. The purely formal critic always tends to think that he knows what the work in question is simply because it is in print before him. But he is much mistaken. The printed text may stand for any number of different works, as the history of criticism abundantly shows. What the real work is and what gives the principle of organization to the whole can be certainly determined only by investigating the relation of the printed words to the civilization that produced them.

What is a great work of fiction? One might answer this question in purely formal terms by talking about plot, style, characterization, unity, etc. But these aspects of a novel are not wholly objective. You can always find them if you know that they are there; and you can nearly always find them if you think you know that they are there. Give a critic an unpublished manuscript and tell him it is a youthful piece of Flaubert's, and he will find qualities in it that he would never find if told that it was by some wholly obscure writer. There is a story told of an American student who sent some of Shakespeare's sonnets to a publisher, which were returned with a letter informing the sender that these poems of his were crude and immature and he had little if any real poetical gift. This is by no means to say that there are no permanent and objective qualities in literature; but it does imply that there can be, and often is, great confusion as to what the work in question really is. What is this artistic whole about which we are asking questions? The work itself will never be able to answer that question unless we place it in the context of the civilization that produced it.

Our question, then—what is a great work of fiction?—cannot be answered simply by the usual kind of critical analysis. A wider investigation must precede this, directed toward finding out what particular works of fiction actually are. Only then can a formal analysis be applied—after the object of the analysis has been determined. But the situation is not simply that the maximum-context critic tells us what the work is and then the formal critic sits down to analyze it and to tell us whether it is good or bad. The two activities are not separate: they neither operate independently nor follow chronologically. The true critic tries to work toward the middle from both ends at once, as scientific investigation proceeds by a combination of hypothesis and experiment.

What, then, is a great work of fiction? After we have worked from the wider context inward and from the work outward, we shall probably find that the greatest works are those which, while fulfilling all the formal requirements, most adequately reflect the civilization of which they are a product. This does not conflict with the traditional view that great art presents the universal through the particular. Civilizations are macrocosms of human nature, and what illustrates the former will best illustrate aspects of the latter. The psychological terms we apply to individual types of character have their perfect counterpart in the terms (which may or may not be psychological) which we apply to states of civilization. There will always be aspects of human character and emotion as an illumination of which the decadent bourgeoisie, the struggling proletariat, the atrophied landed gentry, and similar phenomena of civilization will always be adequate myths long after these phenomena have passed away. If ever they cease to be so, a great deal of past literature will have ceased to possess literary value—an eventuality which is of course possible but remote.

*Ulysses* is not shown to be a bad work of art because we have demonstrated that it took its origin from a defeatist desire to retreat from the contemporary situation; on the contrary, such retreat was one of the most important features of intellectual bourgeois life at the time, and Joyce illustrates it with such brilliance and subtlety and with such formal perfection that *Ulysses* is one of the great novels of civilization. The state of civilization can, of course, have a wholly evil effect on a writer's art; it might lead to deliberate falsification or distortion which spoils the work as art. *The Little Minister* or *Sentimental Tommy* represent certain features of a state of civilization, but they are not on that account great works of fiction. The distortion is obvious and deliberate and leads to formal defects, such as tragic premises being followed by a comic solution. It is, in part at least, a question of degree. If the work reflects something basic and fundamental in the contemporary state of civilization, it is not only a more impressive work, a truer work, and, by some interesting natural law of genius, a more adequate work formally than one which reflects some surface attitude or minor subsidiary development, but it also has more permanent contacts with the experience of later generations, however much civilization may have changed. One can, of course, impose a moral judgment in order to discriminate further and say that the attitude underlying *Ulysses* is bad or unhealthy, even if it does get to the basis of a state of civilization. We all make such judgments in evaluating literature, consciously or not, and it would be wise to realize at what stage they come in. They are not, however, judgments to be ashamed of or to try to suppress: to discriminate between valuable and less valuable attitudes is a necessary and praiseworthy activity in any context. But we should know these judgments for what they are and realize that they will differ in different times and places.

If civilizations are macrocosms of human nature, individual characters are microcosms of civilizations; and if this were not so, the creation and criticism of art would have had very different histories. This twofold fact is the most substantial of the many bridges which link art as a personal activity and a personal enjoyment with art as the typical product of a civilization. We are likely to be led astray by the abstractness of the term "civilization"—a term which, of course, really refers to attitudes and actions of people. And this brings us back to a main point concerning the relation between fiction and civilization. Civilization is the attitudes and actions of people, and fiction uses the attitudes and actions of people as the raw material out of which to construct the kind of pattern we call a novel. No other art does this quite so directly; not even other forms of literature. Thus the critic of fiction is in a peculiarly advantageous position for discussing the relation of his art to things in general, because there is one concrete aspect of that relation ready to begin with.

The whole question is much more than the academic one of trying to find out what is the right way of criticizing literature. In the academic sense there is perhaps no right way. To each individual the right way will be the one which gives him most satisfaction—the greatest sense of intellectual adventure; the historically minded will always prefer facts and dates; the geometrically minded will talk of premises and probability and plot; and the philosopher and the aesthete will have their own interests and their own terminology. But while critical fashions change, intellectual curiosity remains: we all should like to know the most we can about the objects of our inquiry. And this, in brief, is the object of the maximum-context critic—to learn the most he can about the work he is investigating and to find a way of integrating his diverse knowledge. If knowledge is useless abstracted from all context, it is equally useless, however manifold, without adequate integration. Critical impressionism, like critical atomism, develops as a reaction against prematurely closed systems; but, after all, the search for a system is the search for the integration of knowledge, which is the endeavor to make knowledge useful. Such an endeavor surely needs no defense.

And so when we talk of fiction and civilization we are not only indicating a context wide enough to supply us with the maximum amount of knowledge but we are also indicating a way of capitalizing on that knowledge. We want to know why and how men do what they do and what the relations between their different activities are. We want to see things as a whole, yet as a real whole—the whole that they are, not the whole that they might be. We also want to know (though so few nowadays admit it) what to seek and what to avoid; and as the normative emerges naturally from the descriptive, if only the latter is true and adequate and well organized, this also is an aim of the maximum-context critic's activity.

Unfortunate as we are in many respects in living in the present world rather than at some time in the past, we are at least fortunate in this: that we are living at a time when the state of civilization is patent to all. No intelligent observer who has not allowed wishful thinking to master altogether his intellectual processes can deny that we are living in the midst of the disintegration of a civilization, or, to put it in a less terrifying manner (though it is terrifying), in a transitional stage between two civilizations. Rarely if ever has the nature of the contemporary situation been so clear to observers. We are thus in a position to discuss recent and contemporary activity of all kinds with full awareness of the nature of the context. This is an opportunity that the literary critic must find too tempting to miss, no matter how much temerity he may display in attempting to take advantage of it. We can look back on the recent past, knowing what it has been leading to, and analyze it with the familiarity of a contemporary, yet with the knowledge which hitherto has been reserved for the future historian. While as a rule the contemporary cannot see the wood for the trees and the historian cannot see the trees for the wood, here is a situation which seems to offer a chance of seeing clearly both the individual trees and the wood as a whole. It is a consciousness of this that has tempted the present study, however inadequately it may have achieved this double vision.

'For to study fiction in a transitional civilization is as fascinating a task as any critic can set himself. How have the major fiction writers of the time reflected this transitional quality, how have they reacted to it, and what is the nature of their work as a result? These are the questions which the preceding pages endeavor, in some slight degree, to answer. And this is the link that binds the several chapters together. An attempt has been made to show that even purely technical innovations in the modern novel are related to this major question and that no aspect of the novelist's art is free from the implications of the civilization of which, whatever the writer's purpose, it is a part. Indeed, one of the most interesting things to observe in recent fiction—especially in the fiction of the 1920's—is the way in which the novelist unconsciously rationalizes an impulse which comes, not from some personal discovery in style or technique, but from the state of civilization, or, more directly, from the state of culture, which is one aspect of civilization. If the artist were aware of the true origin and nature of his impulse he would probably be a much less effective artist, for self-consciousness of that kind has never been very good for art. That is one reason why the contemporary proletarian novel is not particularly good literature, though it serves many valuable purposes. It will have most chance of becoming good literature only when it is the natural reflex of the existing state of culture, not a deliberate attempt to point forward to a new one. Which is another way of saying that no real literary revival can come until after the transition is over.

# The Uses

*Christopher Caudwell*

## GEORGE BERNARD SHAW:

A STUDY OF THE

BOURGEOIS SUPERMAN

*A good man fallen among Fabians.* Lenin

Shaw in his life acquired general recognition among the ordinary members of the "middle class" both here and in America, as representative of Socialist thought. The case of Shaw is in many ways interesting and significant; it is a proof of how stubborn is the bourgeois illusion. The bourgeois may be familiar with Marxism and keenly critical of the social system, and anxious to change it, and yet all this leads only to an ineffectual beating of the air because he believes that man is in himself free.

Shaw is an ex-anarchist, a vegetarian, a Fabian, and, of late years, a Social Fascist: he is inevitably an *Utopian* socialist. His idea of Utopia was expounded in *Back to Methuselah,* a paradise of Ancients who spend their days in *thought* and despise the butterfly young who engage in the *active* work of artistic creation and science.

Shaw then exposed the weakness as well as the essence of his characteristically bourgeois brand of socialism. It represents the primacy of pure contemplation. In pure contemplation man is alone, is apparently exempt from co-operation, is wrapped in a private world; and he is then believed, by bourgeois thought, to be wholly free. Is not this the illusion of the scientist? No, for science is not *pure* thought, it is thought allied to action, testing all its cogitations at the bar of reality. It is thought as thought ought to be, passing always in dialectic movement between knowing and being, between dream and outer reality. Shaw abhors this kind of thought. He abhors modern science not as he might do for its human weaknesses, but hating it for its essence, for its social qualities, for all that is good in its active creative rôle.

This is a familiar spectacle: the intellectual attempting to dominate hostile reality by "pure" thought. It is a human weakness to believe that by retiring into his imagination man can elicit categories or magical spells which will

Reprinted from *Studies in a Dying Culture,* 1938, by Christopher Caudwell, by permission of Dodd, Mead & Company, New York, N.Y. (Christopher Caudwell was the pseudonym of Christopher St. John Sprigg.)

enable him to subjugate reality contemplatively. It is the error of the "theoretical" man, of the prophet, of the mystic, of the metaphysician, in its pathological form the error of the neurotic. It is the trace of the primitive believer in magic that remains in us all. In Shaw it takes a characteristically bourgeois form. He sees that truth brings freedom, but he refuses to see that this understanding is a social product and not a thing that one clever man can find alone. Shaw still believes that out of his Platonic soul man can extract pure wisdom in the form of world-dominating Ideas, and out of debate and ratiocination, without social action, beat out a new and higher consciousness.

It is notable that the real artist, like the real scientist, never makes this mistake. Both find themselves repeatedly pushed into contact with reality; they desire and seek reality outside them.

Reality is a large, tough, and—as man gets to know it—increasingly complex substance. To know it requires the socially pooled labours of generations of men. So complex has science already grown that a man can only hope to grasp completely a small corner of it. The old dream of all-knowledge for one mind has vanished. Men must be content to co-operate by giving a few stitches in the vast tapestry, and even these few stitches may be as complex as the earlier large design of a Newton or a Darwin.

Now Shaw with his bourgeois individualism is impatient at the restriction science sets on the domination of reality by one acute intellect. Shaw cannot hope to master the apparatus of science, therefore he sweeps it all away as mumbo-jumbo. It is nonsense, Shaw says,. that the sun is ninety million miles away from the earth. Natural Selection is preposterous. And so instead of these concepts reached with so much labour, Shaw puts forward ideas drawn purely from his desires like those of any Hindoo mystic theorising about the world. Sweeping aside all science as nonsense, he rewrites the history of reality in terms of a witch-doctor's "life-force" and a jam-to-morrow God. Shavian cosmology is barbarous; it is idealistic. Shaw dominates this tough, distressing, gritty environment by the familiar neurotic method, by imposing on it a series of fictional delusions of a wish-fulfilment type. This is not because Shaw is foolish but precisely because he is possessed of a naturally acute intellect. Its very acuteness has given him a pride which makes him feel he ought to be able to dominate all knowledge without social aid, by pure cerebration. He will not recognise, except cursorily, the social nature of knowledge. So we get in his cosmology an effect like that of an exceptionally brilliant medicine man theorising about life. Since the average intellectual is still infected with similarly barbaric theorising, it is not surprising that he does not detect the essential crudity of all Shaw's philosophy. Bourgeois speaks to bourgeois.

It is barbarous to believe in action without thought, that is the Fascist heresy. But it is equally barbarous to believe in thought without action, the bourgeois intellectual heresy. Thought is immobilised—or rather races like a machine with nothing to bite on—once it is declutched from action, for thought is an aid to action. Thought guides action, but it learns *how* to guide *from* action. Being must historically and always precede knowing, for knowing evolves as an extension of being.

Shaw's instinctive bourgeois belief in the primacy of lonely thought is of course evidenced not only in his ludicrous cosmology and repulsive Utopia, but also in his Butlerian biology, in which the various animals decide whether they want long necks and so forth, and by concentrating their minds on this aim, succeed in growing them. Ludicrous as this Butlerian neo-Lamarckianism is, it has enormous emotional influence on the bourgeois mind. It appeals to it so powerfully that sober scientists, even while admitting that no atom of evidence can be found for this hypothesis and all kinds of evidence for the opposite standpoint, yet insist on giving it a provisional approval, because it seems so "nice" to them. To a mind obsessed with bourgeois concepts of liberty and the autonomy of the individual mind, such a conception seems to promise a kind of substitute for the paradise which determinism denies him.

This would be unimportant if Shaw's Fabianism did not pervade all his work, robbing it of artistic as well as of political value. Believing in the solitary primacy of thought, all his plays are devoid of humanity, because they represent human beings as walking intellects. Fortunately they are not, or the human race would long ago have perished in some dream-fantasy of logic and metaphysics. Human beings are mountains of unconscious being, walking the old grooves of instinct and simple life, with a kind of occasional phosphorescence of consciousness at the summit. And this conscious phosphorescence derives its value and its power from the emotions, from the instincts; only its form is derived from the intellectual shapes of thought. Age by age man strives to make this consciousness more intense, the artist by subtilising and intensifying the emotions, the scientist by making fuller and more real the thought form, and in both cases this is done by burning more being in the thin flame. Shaw, however, is obsessed with the "pure" flame, phosphorescence separate from being. The ideas thus abstracted become empty and petty and strike with a remote tinkling sound in the ears. Shaw's plays become an "unearthly ballet of bloodless categories."

This mixed thought and feeling of consciousness is not the source of social power, only a component of it. Society with its workshops, its buildings, its material solidity, is always present below real being and is a kind of vast reservoir of the unknown, unconscious and irrational in every man, so that of everyone we can say his conscious life is only a fitful gleam on the mass of his whole existence. Moreover, there is a kind of carapacious toughness about the conscious part of society which resists change, even while, below these generalisations, changes in material and technique and real detailed being are going on. This gives rise in every man to a tension which is a real dynamic force in society, producing artists, poets, prophets, madmen, neurotics and all the little uncertainties, irrationalities, impulses, sudden unreasoning emotions, all the delights and horrors, everything that makes life the thing it is, enrapturing the artist and terrifying the neurotic. It is the sum of the uneasy, the anti-conservative, the revolutionary. It is everything which cannot be content with the present but causes lovers to tire of love, children to flee their happy parental circle, men to waste themselves in apparently useless effort.

This source of all happiness and woe is the disparity between man's being and man's consciousness, which drives on society and makes life vital. Now all this tension, everything below the dead intellectual sphere, is blotted out in Shaw. The Life Love, which is his crude theological substitute for this real active being, is itself intellectually conceived. Thus his characters are inhuman; all their conflicts occur on the rational plane, and none of their conflicts are ever resolved—for how can logic ever resolve its eternal antimonies, which can only be synthesised in action? This tension creates "heroes" like Caesar and Joan of Arc, who, in response to the unformulated guidance of experience, call into existence tremendous talent forces of whose nature they can know nothing, yet history itself seems to obey them. Such heroes are inconceivable to Shaw. He is bound to suppose that all they brought about they consciously willed. Hence these heroes appear to him as the neat little figures of a bourgeois history book, quite inhuman, and regarding their lives as calmly as if they were examination papers on the "currents of social change." These plays are not dramas. This is not art, it is mere debate and just as unresolved, just as lacking in tragic finality, temporal progress or artistic unity as is all debate.

For this reason, too, Shaw is a kind of intellectual aristocrat, and no one who is not capable of declaring his motives rationally and with the utmost acuity on instant demand appears in his plays, except as a ludicrous or second-rate figure. The actors are nothing; the thinkers are everything. Even a man who in real life would be powerful, formidable and quite brainless —the "armourer" of *Major Barbara*—has to be transformed into a brilliant theoretician before (as Shaw thinks) he can be made impressive on the stage. But we all know and admire characters devoid of the ability for intellectual formulation who yet seem in their influence upon reality nobler, grander, more powerful and effective than any of our intellectual friends. We know well enough in life at all events, that thought alone does not suffice to drive on the world, and recognise this in our homage to "illusory" "irrational" art, art that speaks to the mere experience of us, stirring it into a fleeting and purely emotional consciousness. None of these characters, who in war, art, statesmanship and ethics, have been of significance in the world's history, appears in Shaw's plays. He is incapable of drawing a character who is impressive without being a good arguer in bourgeois dialectic. This weakness naturally shows itself in his proletarians. Like the proletarians in the Army hostel of Major Barbara, they are simply caricatures. Only by being "educated," like the chauffeur in *Man and Superman,* can they become respectable.

It therefore follows that Shaw's ideal world is a world not of communism, but like Wells's is a world ruled by intellectual Samurai guiding the poor muddled workers; a world of Fascism. For bourgeois intellectuals obsessed with a false notion of the nature of liberty are by the inherent contradictions of their notion at length driven to liberty's opposite, Fascism. Shaw's Utopia is a planned world imposed from above in which the organisation is in the hands of a bureaucracy of intellectuals. Such a world is negated by the world of communism, in which all participate in ruling, and active intellectuals, no longer divorced from being, learn from the conscious worker just as much as the workers demand guidance from thought. The fatal class gap between thought and action is bridged. This world, with its replaceable officials not specially trained for the task, is the opposite of the old Fabian dream or nightmare, the class Utopia in which the ruling class now takes the form of a permanent, intellectual, trained bureaucracy, wielding the powers of State for the "good" of the proletariat. This world was a pleasant dream of the middle class, which neither owned the world, like the capitalist, nor had the certainty of one day owning it like the proletariat. It is an unrealisable dream which yet holds the intellectual away from the proletariat and makes him a bulwark of reaction and Fascism. Shaw is still obsessed with the idea of liberty as a kind of medicine which a man of goodwill can impose on the "ignorant" worker from without. That liberty would be medicine for the bourgeois, not the worker. He does not see that neither intellectual nor worker possesses as yet this priceless freedom to give, both are confined within the categories of their time, and communism is the active creation of true liberty which cannot yet be given by anybody to anybody. It is a voyage of discovery, but we are certain of one thing. The liberty which the Roman, the feudal lord and the bourgeois achieved, proved illusory, simply because they believed that a ruling class could find it, and impose it on society. But we can see that they failed and man is still everywhere in chains, because they did not share the pursuit of liberty with their slaves, their serfs, or the exploited proletariat; and they did not do so because to have done so would have been to cease to be a ruling class, a thing impossible until productive forces had developed to a stage where ruling classes were no longer necessary. Therefore, before the well-meaning intellectual, such as Shaw, seeks this difficult liberty, he must first help to change the system of social relations to one in which all men and not a class have the reins of society in their hands. To achieve liberty a man must govern himself; but since he lives in society, and society lives by and in its productive relations, this means that for men to achieve liberty society must govern its productive relations. For a man to rule himself presupposes that society is not ruled by a class from which he himself is excluded. The search for liberty only begins in the classless state, when society, being completely self-governing, can learn the difficult ways of freedom. But how can this be achieved when its destiny is planned by a class, or controlled by the higgling of a market, or even arranged by a company of elegant Samurai? How can the intellectual Samurai ever agree, since no two philosophers have ever agreed about absolute truth and justice? Only one referee has ever been found for the interminable *sic et mon* of thought—action. But in a world where thought rules and action must hold its tongue, how can the issue ever be resolved? Action permeates every pore of society: its life is the action of every man. Society is torn apart as soon as its form is determined by the thought of a few which is privileged and separate from the action of the many.

Since Shaw implicitly denies the elementary truth that thought flows from being, and that man changes his consciousness by changing his social relations, which change is the result of the pressure of real being below those relations, Shaw must necessarily deny the efficacy of revolutionary action as compared with the activities of propaganda. Like Wells he believes that preaching alone will move the world. But the world moves, and though it moves through and with preaching, it does not follow that all preaching moves it, but only that that preaching moves it which moves with the law of motion of the world, which marches along the line of action, and cuts down the grain of events. Yet a bourgeois intellectual always believes that whatever he conceives as absolute truth and justice—vegetarianism or equal incomes or anti-vaccination—can be imposed on the world by successful argument. Hence Shaw's plays.

But here Shaw is faced with a dilemma. He is to impose his absolute truths on the world by the process of logical debate. But the world of non-thinkers or half-thinkers on which he imposes it are necessarily an inferior race of creatures—the mere labourers, the nit-wit aggregation of the non-intellectuals, the plastic amorphous mass whom the intellectual lords of creation save from disaster by their godlike commands. How can one drill sense into these creatures? What will appeal to their infantile frivolous minds? One must of course treat them as one treats children, one must sugar the pill of reason with paradox, humour, with lively and preposterous incident.

Thus Shaw, whom a belief in the primacy of intellectual consciousness prevented from becoming an artist, was by this same belief prevented from becoming a serious thinker or a real force in contemporary consciousness. He became the world's buffoon; because his messages were always wrapped in the sugar of humour, they were taken as always laughable. The British bourgeois, who ignored Marx, vilified Lenin and threw its Tom Manns into prison, regarded Shaw with a tolerant good-humour as a kind of court jester. The people he had depreciated depreciated him. The sugar he put on his pill prevented the pill from acting.

Marx by contrast did not attempt to make *Das Kapital* appealing to the tired brains of the British bourgeoisie. He did not attempt to become a best-seller, or veil his views in West End successes. He did not give humorous interviews to the contemporary press. His name was known only to a few Englishmen of his time, while that of Shaw is known to millions. But because he gave his message seriously, treating the race of men as his equals, his message was received seriously and well. Because he did not believe that thought rules the world, but that thought must follow the grain of action, his thought has been more world-creating than that of any single man. Not only has it called into existence a new civilisation over a sixth of the world's surface, but in all other countries all revolutionary elements are oriented round Marx's thought; all contemporary politics are of significance only in so far as they are with Marx or against him.

It is no answer to say that Marx's is a greater intellect than Shaw's. Doubtless if Shaw had been Marx he would have been Marx. No one has devised a standard for measuring intellects in themselves, since intellects do not exist in themselves, but only in their overt mentation. Shaw and Marx were both men of keen intellect, as evidenced in their writings, and both were aware, from experience, of the breakdown of greedy bourgeois social relations; but the mind of one was able to leap forward to the future, the other is prisoned always in the categories of the bourgeoisdom it despises. Because Shaw gave his message condescendingly and flippantly, treating the race of men as his inferiors, his message has been much read and little noted, and the message itself betrays all the falsehood and unreality of the attitude which settled its delivery.

Shaw read Marx early in life, and he was given therefore the alternative of being a dangerous revolutionary instead of a popular reformist who would dream of a world saved by a converted middle class. He decided that although

Marx had shown him the shame and falsities of bourgeois life, he would refuse to recognise the necessity for the overthrow of this decaying class by the class of the future. From that moment Shaw was divided against himself.

This decision is explained by his personal history. Born into a middle-class family that had fallen from affluence and social position to embarrass-ment, the ambitious young Shaw, impressed from childhood with the necessity for retrieving the former Shavian status, came to London to gain suc-cess. Here he existed for a time by writing, as poor as any worker. But thanks to the possession of a dress-suit and a gift for playing on the piano, he was still able to mix in refined Kensington circles. Faced with proletarianisation, he clung to the bourgeois class. In the same way, faced with the problem of ideological proletarianisation in his reading of Marx, he resisted it, and adhered to Fabianism, with its bourgeois traditions and its social respecta-bility.

This problem and his answer to it, decided his ideology and also his art. His knowledge of Marx enabled him to attack destructively all bourgeois institutions. But he was never able to give any answer to the question: *What shall we do here and now to improve them besides talking?* This prob-lem, in the veiled form of "tainted money," comes up in his work repeatedly —in *Widowers' Houses, Major Barbara, Mrs. Warren's Profession*—and always it is *patched up.* We must accept things as they are until the system is changed. But no immediate steps besides talking are ever to be taken to change the system. Major Barbara, horrified at first by finding the Christ she believes in has sold out to capital, ends all the same by marrying the manager of the armament factory whose proprietor has bought Him. Shaw himself, who discovered the ruling class was rotten to the core, and built on the exploitation of the workers, yet ends by marrying ideologically money, respectability, fame, peaceful reformism and ultimately even Mussolini. He who takes no active steps to change the system, helps to maintain the system.

Yet just because Shaw has read Marx, he understands the essential con-tradictions of this solution. For this reason his plays are full of deliberately forced conversions, unconvincing *dénouements,* and a general escape from reality through the medium of fantasy and humour. Shaw dealt quite simply in his life with the problem of tainted goods that arose from the sufferings of animals. Meat and sera, one resulting from the slaughter and the other from the vivisection of animals, must not be used, even though in spite of one's abstention the wicked business goes merrily on. But he cannot make that renouncement in the case of money and of all the intangibles of bourgeois respectability—fame as a Fabian intellectual instead of suppres-sion as a dangerous revolutionary. Meat and sera are not essential to the life of society, and therefore it is possible to abstain from them. In bourgeois society money is what holds society together: no one can ever eat without it; therefore it is impossible to "abstain" from it. But this in itself exposes the futility of Shaw's bourgeois abstaining approach to the problem, like that of the pacifist who will not fight but continues to be fed at the expense of the community. Shaw's ambivalent attitude to social evils reveals his cowardice before the prime evil, the very hinge of society, which he will accept, while he abstains from the lesser evils. Thus his vegetarianism acts as a kind of compensation for his betrayal on the larger issue, and a symbol of his whole reformist approach. He will abstain; he will criticise; but he will not act. This last refusal infects his criticism and makes his abstention an active weapon of reaction. And so, all through his plays and prefaces, money is the god, without which we are nothing, are powerless and helpless. "Get money, and you can be virtuous; without it you cannot even start to be good." Shaw repeats this so often and so loudly that he seems anxious to convince himself as well as others. "Renounce it," he asks, "and what help is your altruism? Even if you throw it in the gutter, some scoundrel will pick it up. Wait till the system is changed."

But how is it to be changed? Shaw has no convincing answer. There is no need to accuse Shaw of conscious dishonesty. Shaw is helplessly imprisoned in the categories of bourgeois thought. He could not see, that because being conditions knowing, the bourgeois class for all their "cleverness" are doomed to collapse and the workers for all their "stupidity" are able to play an active creative rôle in building a new civilisation on the wreckage of the old. Faced with this choice—*worker or bourgeois*—the bourgeois—with all the brilliance of bourgeois culture behind him—seemed to Shaw preferable to the other, ignorant, "irrational" and "brutalised" by poverty. Hence arose his life problem, how to persuade this bourgeois class to renounce its sins. He had to convert them, or fold his hands in despair; and yet in his heart he did not believe in their future, for he had read Marx.

This decision, conditioned by his class and his experience, led to all his difficulties. He could never really bring himself to believe in a bourgeois class regenerated by Fabianism, and events made still clearer its hopelessness and its decay. Hence, more and more, his plays become futile and unresolved. Civilisation is driven "On the Rocks" or is in the "Apple Cart." Relief is found in the faith of a Life Force making inevitably for a Utopia (*Back to Methuselah*). Or as in *St. Joan* he tries to comfort himself by turning to a period when this class he has committed himself to, this bourgeois class, played an active creative part: he draws St. Joan as the heroine and prophet of bourgeois individuality, amid a dying medievalism. In *Heartbreak House* he records simply a Tchekovian detachment and disillusion. Evidently all Shaw's failings, all the things that prevented him from fulfilling the artistic and intellectual promise of his native gifts, arise in a most direct fashion from his fatal choice of the bourgeois class at a period of history when the choice was wrong. From this choice springs the unreality of his plays, their lack of dramatic resolutions, the substitution of debate for dialectic, the belief in life forces and thought Utopias, the bungling treatment of human beings in love, the lack of scientific knowledge, and the queer strain of mountebank in all Shaw says, as of a man who in mocking others is also mocking himself because he despises himself but despises others more.

Shaw performed a useful function in exposing the weakness of the bourgeois class. He exposes the rottenness of its culture and at the same time commits the future to its hands, but neither he nor his readers can believe in the success of that; and so he represents symbolically bourgeois intelligence as it is to-day, shamefaced and losing confidence in itself. He plays this active part, that he is one of the forces of defeatism and despair which help the decay of a world that has had its day. This disintegration is no more than pathological without the active forces of revolution which can shatter the rotten structure and build it anew. This confidence Shaw has never achieved, nor the insight that is needed for it. He stands by the side of Wells, Lawrence, Proust, Huxley, Russell, Forster, Wassermann, Hemingway, and Galsworthy as typical of their age, men who proclaim the disillusionment of bourgeois culture with itself, men themselves disillusioned and yet not able to wish for anything better or gain any closer grasp of this bourgeois culture whose pursuit of liberty and individualism led men into the mire. Always it is their freedom they are defending. This makes them pathetic rather than tragic figures, for they are helpless, not because of overwhelming circumstances but because of their own illusion.

*Edmund Wilson*
## FLAUBERT'S POLITICS

Gustave Flaubert has figured for decades as the great glorifier and practitioner of literary art at the expense of human affairs both public and personal. We have heard about his asceticism, his nihilism, his consecration to the search for *le mot juste*. His admirers have tended to praise him on the same assumption on which his critics have found him empty and sterile: the assumption that he had no moral or social interests. At most, *Madame Bovary* has been taken as a parable of the romantic temperament.

Really Flaubert owed his superiority to those of his contemporaries—Gautier, for example, who professed the same literary creed—to the seriousness of his concern with the large questions of human destiny. It was a period when the interest in history was intense; and Flaubert, in his intellectual tastes as well as in his personal relations, was almost as close to the historians Michelet, Renan and Taine, and to the historical critic Sainte-Beuve, as to Gautier and Baudelaire. In the case of Taine and Sainte-Beuve, he came to deplore their preoccupation in their criticism with the social aspects of literature at the expense of all its other values; but he himself seems always to see humanity in social terms and historical perspective. His point of view may be gauged pretty accurately from his comments in one of his letters on Taine's *History of English Literature:* "There is something else in art beside the milieu in which it is practiced and the physiological antecedents of the worker. On this system you can explain the series, the group, but never the individuality, the special fact which makes him this person and not another. This method results inevitably in leaving *talent* out of consideration. The masterpiece has no longer any significance except as an historical document. It is the old critical method of La Harpe exactly turned around. People used to believe that literature was an altogether

Reprinted from *The Triple Thinkers* by Edmund Wilson, by permission of Oxford University Press, New York, N. Y., and the author.

personal thing and that books fell out of the sky like meteors. Today they deny that the will and the absolute have any reality at all. The truth, I believe, lies between the two extremes."

But it was also a period in France—Flaubert's lifetime, 1820–81—of alternating republics and monarchies, of bogus emperors and defeated revolutions, when political ideas were in confusion. The French historians of the Enlightenment tradition, which was the tradition of the Revolution, were steadily becoming less hopeful; and a considerable group of the novelists and poets held political and social issues in contempt and staked their careers on art as an end in itself: their conception of their relation to society was expressed in their damnation of the bourgeois, who gave his tone to all the world, and their art was a defiance of him. The Goncourts in their journal have put the attitude on record: "Lying phrases, resounding words, hot air—that's just about all we get from the political men of our time. Revolutions are a simple *déménagement* followed by the moving back of the same ambitions, corruptions and villainies into the apartment which they have just been moved out of—and all involving great breakage and expense. No political morals whatever. When I look about me for a disinterested opinion, I can't find a single one. People take risks and compromise themselves on the chance of getting future jobs. . . . You are reduced, in the long run, to disillusion, to a disgust with all beliefs, a tolerance of any power at all, an indifference to political passion, which I find in all my literary friends, and in Flaubert as in myself. You come to see that you must not die for any cause, that you must live with any government that exists, no matter how antipathetic it may be to you—you must believe in nothing but art and profess only literature. All the rest is a lie and a booby-trap." In the field of art, at least, it was possible, by heroic effort, to prevent the depreciation of values.

This attitude, as the Goncourts say, Flaubert fully shared. "Today," he wrote Louise Colet in 1853, "I even believe that a thinker (and what is an artist if he is not a triple thinker?) should have neither religion nor fatherland nor even any social conviction. It seems to me that absolute doubt is now indicated so clearly that it would be almost an absurdity to want to formulate it." And—"the citizens who work themselves up for or against the Empire or the Republic," he wrote George Sand in 1869, "seem to be just about as useful as the ones who used to argue about efficacious grace and efficient grace." Nothing exasperated him more—and we may sympathize with him today—than the idea that the soul is to be saved by the profession of correct political opinions.

Yet Flaubert is a thundering idealist. "The idea" which turns up in his letters of the fifties—"genius like a powerful horse drags humanity at her tail along the roads of the idea," in spite of all that human stupidity can do to rein her in—is evidently, under its guise of art, none other than the Hegelian "Idea," which served Marx and so many others under a variety of different guises. There are great forces in humanity, Flaubert feels, which the present is somehow suppressing but which may some day be gloriously set free. "The soul is asleep today, drunk with the words she has listened to, but she will experience a wild awakening, in which she will give herself up to the ecstasies of liberation, for there will be nothing more to constrain her, neither government nor religion, not a formula; the republicans of all shades of opinion seem to me the most ferocious pedagogues, with their dreams of organizations, of legislations, of a society constructed like a convent."

When he reasons about society—which he never does except in his letters —his conceptions seem incoherent. But Flaubert, who believed that the artist should be a triple thinker and who was certainly one of the great minds of his time, was the kind of imaginative writer who works dramatically in images and does not deal at all in ideas. His informal expressions of his general opinions are as unsystematized and impromptu as his books are well-built and precise. But it is worth while to quote a few from his letters, because, though they are so very far from formulating a social philosophy— when George Sand accused him of not having one, he admitted it—they do indicate the instincts and emotions which are the prime movers in the world of his art.

Flaubert is opposed to the socialists because he regards them as materialistic and because he dislikes their authoritarianism, which he says derives straight from the tradition of the Church. Yet they have "denied *pain,* have blasphemed three-quarters of modern poetry, the blood of Christ, which quickens in us." And: "O socialists, there is your ulcer: the ideal is lacking to you; and that very matter which you pursue slips through your fingers like a wave; the adoration of humanity for itself and by itself (which brings us to the doctrine of the useful in Art, to the theories of public safety and reason of state, to all the injustices and all the intolerances, to the immolation of the right, to the leveling of the Beautiful), that cult of the belly, I say, breeds wind (pardon the pun)." One thing he makes clear by reiteration through the various periods of his life: his disapproval of the ideal of equality. What is wanted, he keeps insisting, is "justice"; and behind this demand for justice is evidently Flaubert's resentment, arising from his own experience, against the false reputations, the undeserved rewards and the stupid repressions of the Second Empire. And he was skeptical of popular education and opposed to universal suffrage.

Yet among the contemporaries whom he admired most were democrats, humanitarians, and reformers. "You are certainly the French author," he wrote Michelet, "whom I have read and reread most"; and he said of Victor Hugo that Hugo was the living man "in whose skin" he would be happiest to be. George Sand was one of his closest friends: "Un Coeur Simple" was written for her—apparently to answer her reproach that art was "not merely criticism and satire" and to show her that, he, too, had a heart.

When we come to Flaubert's books themselves, we find a much plainer picture of things.

It is not true, as is sometimes supposed, that he disclaimed any moral intention. He deliberately refrained in his novels from commenting on the action in his own character: "the artist ought not to appear in his work any more than God in nature." But, like God, he rules his universe through law; and the reader, from what he hears and sees, must infer the moral system.

What *are* we supposed to infer from Flaubert's work? His general historical point of view is, I believe, pretty well known. He held that "the three great evolutions of humanity" had been *"paganisme, christianisme, muflisme* (muckerism)," and that Europe was in the third of these phases. Paganism he depicted in *Salammbô* and in the short story "Hérodias." The Carthaginians of *Salammbô* had been savage barbarians: they had worshiped serpents, crucified lions, sacrificed their children to Moloch and trampled armies down with herds of elephants; but they had slaughtered, lusted and agonized superbly. Christianity is exemplified in the two saints' legends, *La Tentation de Saint Antoine* and "La Légende de Saint Julien l'Hospitalier." The Christian combats his lusts, he expiates human cruelty; but this attitude, too, is heroic: Saint Anthony, who inhabits the desert, Saint Julien, who lies down with the leper, have pushed to their furthest limits the virtues of abnegation and humility. But when we come to the *muflisme* of the nineteenth century—in *Madame Bovary* and *L'Education Sentimentale*—all is meanness, mediocrity and timidity.

The villain here is, of course, the bourgeois; and it is true that these two novels of Flaubert damn the contemporary world as flatly as the worlds of Salammbô and Saint Anthony have been roundly and dogmatically exalted. But in these pictures of modern life there is a greater complexity of human values and an analysis of social processes which does not appear in the books about the past.

This social analysis of Flaubert's has, it seems to me, been too much disregarded, and this has resulted in the underestimation of one of his greatest books, *L'Education Sentimentale*.

In *Madame Bovary,* Flaubert criticizes the nostalgia for the exotic which played such a large part in his own life and which led him to write *Salammbô* and *Saint Antoine.* What cuts Flaubert off from the other romantics and makes him primarily a social critic is his grim realization of the futility of dreaming about the splendors of the Orient and the brave old days of the past as an antidote to bourgeois society. Emma Bovary, the wife of a small country doctor, is always seeing herself in some other setting, imagining herself someone else. She will never face her situation as it is, with the result that she is eventually undone by the realities she has been trying to ignore. The upshot of all Emma's yearnings for a larger and more glamorous life is that her poor little daughter, left an orphan by Emma's suicide and the death of her father, is sent to work in a cotton mill.

The socialist of Flaubert's time might perfectly have approved of this: while the romantic individualist deludes himself with dreams in the attempt to evade bourgeois society and only succeeds in destroying himself, he lets humanity fall a victim to the industrial-commercial processes, which, unimpeded by his dreaming, go on.

Flaubert had more in common and had perhaps been influenced more by the socialist thought of his day than he would ever have allowed himself to confess. In his novels, it is never the nobility, who are indistinguishable for mediocrity from the bourgeoisie, but the peasants and working people whom he habitually uses as touchstones to bring out the meanness and speciousness of the bourgeois. One of the most memorable scenes in *Madame Bovary* is the agricultural exhibition at which the pompous local dignitaries award a medal to an old farm servant for forty-five years of service on the same farm. Flaubert has told us about the bourgeois at length, made us listen to a long speech by a town councilor on the flourishing state of France; and now he describes the peasant—scared by the flags and the drums and by the gentlemen in black coats and not understanding what is wanted of her. Her long and bony hands, with which she has worked all her life in greasy wool, stable dust and lye, still seem dirty, although she has just washed them, and they hang half open, as if to present the testimony of her toil. There is no tenderness or sadness in her face: it has a rigidity almost monastic. And her long association with animals has given her something of their placidity and dumbness. "So she stood before those florid bourgeois, that half-century of servitude." And the heroine of "Un Coeur Simple," a domestic servant who devotes her whole life to the service of a provincial family and gets not one ray of love in return, has a similar dignity and pathos.

But it is in *L'Education Sentimentale* that Flaubert's account of society comes closest to socialist theory. Indeed, his presentation here of the Revolution of 1848 parallels in so striking a manner Marx's analysis of the same events in *The Eighteenth Brumaire of Louis Napoleon* that it is worth while to bring together into the same focus the diverse figures of Flaubert and Marx in order to see how two great minds of the last century, pursuing courses so apparently divergent, arrived at identical interpretations of the happenings of their own time.

When we do this, we become aware that Marx and Flaubert started from very similar assumptions and that they were actuated by moral aims almost equally uncompromising. Both implacably hated the bourgeois, and both were resolved at any cost of worldly success to keep outside the bourgeois system. And Marx, like Flaubert, shared to some degree the romantic bias in favor of the past. Karl Marx can, of course, hardly be said to have had a very high opinion of any period of human history; but in comparison with the capitalist nineteenth century, he betrayed a certain tenderness for Greece and Rome and the Middle Ages. He pointed out that the slavery of the ancient world had at least purchased the "full development" of the masters and that a certain Antipater of Thessalonica had joyfully acclaimed the invention of the water wheel for grinding corn because it would set free the female slaves who had formerly had to do this work, whereas the bourgeois economists had seen in machinery only a means for making the workers work faster and longer in order "to transform a few vulgar and half-educated upstarts into 'eminent cotton spinners,' 'extensive sausage makers' and 'influential blacking dealers.'" And he had also a soft spot for the feudal system before the nobility had revolted against the Crown and while the rights of all classes, high and low, were still guaranteed by the king. Furthermore, the feudal lords, he insisted, had spent their money lavishly when they had it, whereas it was of the essence of capitalism that the capitalist saved his money and invested it, only to save and reinvest the profits.

Karl Marx's comment on his time was the Communist Manifesto. What is the burden of the great social novel of Flaubert? Frédéric Moreau, the hero of *L'Education Sentimentale,* is a sensitive and intelligent young man with an income; but he has no stability of purpose and is capable of no emotional integrity. He becomes so aimlessly, so will-lessly, involved in love affairs with different types of women that he is unable to make anything real out of any of them: they trip each other up until in the end he is left with nothing. He is most in love from the very beginning with the virtuous wife of a sort of glorified drummer, who is engaged in more or less shady business enterprises; but, what with his timidity and her virtue, he never gets anywhere with her—and even though she loves him in return—and leaves her in the hands of the drummer. Flaubert makes it plain to us, however, that Frédéric and the vulgar husband at bottom represent the same thing: Frédéric is only the more refined as well as the more incompetent side of the middle-class mediocrity of which the promoter is the more flashy and active.

And so in the case of the other characters, the representatives of journalism, art and drama and of the various political factions of the time, and the remnants of the old nobility, Frédéric finds the same shoddiness and lack of principle which are gradually revealed in himself—the same qualities which render so odious to him the banker, M. Dambreuse, the type of the rich and powerful class. M. Dambreuse is always ready to trim his sails to any political party, monarchist or republican, which seems to have a chance of success. "Most of the men who were there," Flaubert writes of the guests at M. Dambreuse's house, "had served at least four governments; and they would have sold France or the human race in order to guarantee their fortune, to spare themselves a difficulty or anxiety, or even from simple baseness, instinctive adoration of force." *"Je me moque des affaires!"* cries Frédéric when the guests at M. Dambreuse's are complaining that criticism of the government hurts business; but he always comes back to hoping to profit by M. Dambreuse's investments and position.

The only really sympathetic characters in *L'Education Sentimentale* are, again, the representatives of the people. Rosanette, Frédéric's mistress, is the daughter of poor workers in the silk mills, who sold her at fifteen to an old bourgeois. Her liaison with Frédéric is a symbol of the disastrously unenduring union between the proletariat and the bourgeoisie, of which Marx, in *The Eighteenth Brumaire,* had written. After the suppression of the workers' insurrection duing the June days of '48, Rosanette gives birth to a weakly child, which dies while Frédéric is already arranging a love affair with the dull wife of the banker. Frédéric believes that Mme. Dambreuse will be able to advance his interests. And bourgeois socialism gets a very Marxist treatment—save in one respect, which we shall note in a moment—in the character of Sénécal, who is eternally making himself unpleasant about communism and the welfare of the masses, for which he is ready to fight to the last barricade. When Sénécal, however, gets a job as foreman in a pottery factory, he turns out to be an inexorable little tyrant; and when it begins to appear, after the putting down of the June riots, that the reaction is sure to triumph, he begins to decide, like our fascists today, that the strong centralization of the government is already itself a kind of communism and that authority is in itself a great thing.

On the other hand, there is the clerk Dussardier, a strapping and stupid fellow and one of the few honest characters in the book. When we first see him, he has just knocked down a policeman in a political brawl on the street. Later, when the National Guard, of which Dussardier is a member, turns against the proletariat in the interests of law and order, Dussardier fells one of the insurgents from the top of a barricade and gets at the same time a bullet in the leg, thereby becoming a great hero of the bourgeois. But Dussardier himself is unhappy. The boy he had knocked down had wrapped the tricolor around him and shouted to the National Guard: "Are you going to fire on your brothers?" Dussardier isn't at all sure that he oughtn't to have been on the other side. His last appearance is at the climax of the story, constitutes, indeed, the climax: he turns up in a proletarian street riot, which the cavalry and police are putting down. Dussardier refuses to move on, crying *"Vive la République!";* and Frédéric comes along just in time to see one of the policemen kill him. Then he recognizes the policeman: it is the socialist, Sénécal.

*L'Education Sentimentale,* unpopular when it first appeared, is likely, if we read it in our youth, to prove baffling and even repellent. It sounds as if it were going to be a love story, but the love affairs turn out so consistently to be either unfulfilled or lukewarm that we find ourselves irritated or depressed. Is it a satire? It is too real for a satire. Yet it does not seem to have the kind of vitality which we are accustomed to look for in a novel.

Yet, although we may rebel, as we first read it, against *L'Education Sentimentale,* we find afterwards that it has stuck in our crop. If it is true, as Bernard Shaw has said, that *Das Kapital* makes us see the nineteenth century "as if it were a cloud passing down the wind, changing its shape and fading as it goes," so that we are never afterward able to forget that "capitalism, with its wage slavery, is only a passing phase of social development, following primitive communism, chattel slavery and feudal serfdom into the past"—so Flaubert's novel plants deep in our mind an idea which we never quite get rid of—the suspicion that our middle-class society of businessmen, bankers and manufacturers, and people who live on or deal in investments, so far from being redeemed by its culture, has ended by cheapening and invalidating culture: politics, science and art—and not only these but the ordinary human relations: love, friendship and loyalty to cause—till the whole civilization has seemed to dwindle.

√ But fully to appreciate the book, one must have had time to see something of life and to have acquired a certain interest in social as distinct from personal questions. Then, if we read it again, we are amazed to find that the tone no longer seems really satiric and that we are listening to a sort of muted symphony of which the timbres had been inaudible before. There are no hero, no villain, to arouse us, no clowns to amuse us, no scenes to wring our hearts. Yet the effect is deeply moving. It is the tragedy of nobody in particular, but of the poor human race itself reduced to such ineptitude, such cowardice, such commonness, such weak irresolution—arriving, with so many fine notions in its head, so many noble words on its lips, at a failure which is all the more miserable because those who have failed are hardly conscious of having done so.

Going back to *L'Education Sentimentale,* we come to understand Mr. F. M. Ford's statement that you must read it fourteen times. Though it is less attractive on the surface than *Madame Bovary* and perhaps others of Flaubert's books, it is certainly the one which he put the most into. And once we have got the clue to all the immense and complex drama which unrolls itself behind the detachment and the monotony of the tone, we find it as absorbing and satisfying as a great play or a great piece of music.

The one conspicuous respect in which Flaubert's criticism of the events of 1848 *diverges* from that of Marx has been thrown into special relief by the recent events of our own time. For Marx, the evolution of the socialist into a policeman would have been due to the bourgeois in Sénécal; for Flaubert, it is a natural development of socialism. Flaubert distrusted, as I have mentioned in quoting from his letters, the authoritarian aims of the socialists. For him, Sénécal, given his bourgeois hypocrisy, was still carrying out a socialist principle—or rather, his behavior as a policeman and his yearnings toward socialist control were both derived from his impulse toward tyranny.

Today we must recognize that Flaubert had observed something of which Marx was not aware. We have had the opportunity to see how even a socialism which has come to power as the result of a proletarian revolution has bred a political police of almost unprecedented ruthlessness and all-pervasiveness—how the socialism of Marx himself, with its emphasis on dictatorship rather than on democratic processes, has contributed to produce this disaster. Here Flaubert, who believed that the artist should aim to be without social convictions, has been able to judge the tendencies of political doctrines as the greatest of doctrinaires could not; and here the role of Flaubert is justified.

The war of 1870 was a terrible shock to Flaubert: the nervous disorders of his later years have been attributed to it. He had the Prussians in his house at Croisset and had to bury his manuscripts. When he made a trip to Paris after the Commune, he came back to the country deeply shaken. "This would never have happened," he said when he saw the wreck of the Tuileries, "if they had only understood *L'Education Sentimentale*." What he meant, one supposes, was that, if they had understood the falsity of their politics, they would never have wreaked so much havoc for their sake. "Oh, how tired I am," he writes George Sand, "of the ignoble worker, the inept bourgeois, the stupid peasant and the odious ecclesiastic."

But in his letters of this period, which are more violent than ever, we see him taking a new direction. The effect of the Commune on Flaubert, as on so many of the other French intellectuals, was to bring out the class-conscious bourgeois in him. Basically bourgeois his life had always been, with his mother and his little income. He had, like Frédéric Moreau himself, been "cowardly in his youth," he wrote George Sand. "I was *afraid* of life." And even moving amongst what he regarded as the grandeurs of the ancient world, he remains a moderate modern Frenchman who seems to be indulging in immoderation self-consciously and in the hope of horrifying other Frenchmen. Marcel Proust has pointed out that Flaubert's imagery, even when he is not dealing with the world of the bourgeois, tends itself to be rather banal. It was the enduring tradition of French classicism which had saved him from the prevailing cheapness: by discipline and objectivity, by heroic application to the mastery of form, he had kept his world at a distance. But now when a working-class government had held Paris for two months and a half and had wrecked monuments and shot bourgeois hostages, Flaubert found himself as fierce against the Communards as any respectable "grocer." "My opinion is," he wrote George Sand, "that the whole Commune ought to have been sent to the galleys, that those sanguinary idiots ought to have been made to clean up the ruins of Paris, with chains around their necks like convicts. That would have wounded *humanity,* though. They treat the mad dogs with tenderness, but not the people who have gotten bitten." He raises his old cry for "justice." Universal suffrage, that "disgrace to the human spirit," must first of all be done away with; but among the elements which must be given their due importance he now includes "race and even money" along with "intelligence" and "education."

For the rest, certain political ideas emerge—though, as usual, in a state of confusion. "The mass, the majority, are always idiotic. I haven't got many convictions, but that one I hold very strongly. Yet the mass must be respected, no matter how inept it is, because it contains the germs of an incalculable fecundity. Give it liberty, but not power. I don't believe in class distinctions any more than you do. The castes belong to the domain of archaeology. But I do believe that the poor hate the rich and that the rich are afraid of the poor. That will go on forever. It is quite useless to preach the gospel of love to either. The most urgent need is to educate the rich, who are, after all, the strongest." "The only reasonable thing to do—I always come back to that—is a government of mandarins, provided that the mandarins know something and even that they know a great deal. The people is an eternal minor, and it will always (in the hierarchy of social elements) occupy the bottom place, because it is unlimited number, mass. It gets us nowhere to have large numbers of peasants learn to read and no longer listen to their priest; but it is infinitely important that there should be a great many men like Renan and Littré who can live and be listened to. Our salvation now is in a *legitimate aristocracy,* by which I mean a majority which will be made up of something other than numerals." Renan himself and Taine were having recourse to similar ideas of the salvation of society through an "élite." In Flaubert's case, it never seems to have occurred to him that the hierarchy of mandarins he is proposing and his project for educating the rich are identical with the ideas of Saint-Simon, which he had rejected years before with such scorn on the ground that they were too authoritarian. The Commune has stimulated in Flaubert a demand for his own kind of despotism.

He had already written in 1869: "It's no longer a question of imagining the best form of government possible, because they are all alike, but to make sure that science prevails. That is the most urgent problem. Everything else will inevitably follow. The purely intellectual type of man has done more for the human race than all the Saint Vincent de Pauls in the world! And politics will remain idiotic forever as long as it does not derive from science. The government of a country ought to be a department of the Institute, and the least important of all." "Politics," he reiterated in 1871, "must become a positive science, as war has already become"; and, "The French Revolution must cease to be a dogma and become part of the domain of science, like all the rest of human affairs." Marx and Engels were not reasoning otherwise; but they believed, as Flaubert could not do, in a coming of age of the proletariat which would make possible the application of social science. For Flaubert, the proletariat had been pathetic and too stupid to do anything effective; the Commune threw him into such a panic that he reviled them as criminals and brutes. At one moment he writes to George Sand, "The International may end by winning out, but not in the way that it hopes, not in the way that people are afraid of"; and then, two days later, "the International will collapse, because it is on the wrong path. No ideas, nothing but envy!"

Finally, he wrote her in 1875: "The words 'religion' or 'Catholicism,' on the one hand, 'progress,' 'fraternity,' 'democracy,' on the other, no longer answer the spiritual needs of the day. The dogma of equality—a new thing —which the radicals have been crying up, has been proved false by the experiments of physiology and by history. I do not at the present time see any way of setting up a new principle, any more than of still respecting the old ones. So I search, without finding it, for the central idea from which all the rest ought to depend."

In the meantime, his work becomes more misanthropic. "Never, my dear old chap," he had written Ernest Feydeau, "have I felt so colossal a disgust for mankind. I'd like to drown the human race under my vomit." He writes a political comedy, *Le Candidat*, the only piece that he has yet composed which has not a single even faintly sympathetic character. The rich parvenu who is running for deputy sacrifices his daughter's happiness and allows himself to be cuckolded by his wife as well as humiliates himself by every form of truckling and trimming, in order to win the election. The audiences would not have it; and the leading actor, as the atrocious central character, came off the stage in tears. One cannot blame them: reading the play today, in spite of some amusing and mordant scenes, it proves too horrid to take even from Flaubert.

Then he embarked on *Bouvard et Pécuchet*, which occupied him—with only one period of relief, when he indulged his suppressed kindliness and idealism in the relatively human *Trois Contes*—for most of the rest of his life. Here two copyists retire from their profession and set out to cultivate the arts and sciences. They make a mess of them all. The book contains an even more withering version of the events of 1848, in which the actors and their political attitudes are reduced to the scale of performing fleas. When Bouvard and Pécuchet find that everything has "cracked in their hands," they go back to copying again. Flaubert did not live to finish the book; but the reader was to have been supplied in a second part with a sort of encyclopaedia made up entirely of absurd statements and foolish sentiments extracted from the productions they were to copy.

*Bouvard et Pécuchet* has somewhat mystified Flaubert's critics, who have usually taken it as a caricature of the bourgeois like *L'Education Sentimentale*—in which case what would have been the point of doing the same thing over again and simply making everything smaller and drier? M. René Dumesnil, the Flaubert expert, believes that *Bouvard et Pécuchet* was to have had a larger application. The encyclopaedia of silly ideas was to have been not merely a credo of the bourgeois: it was to have contained also the ineptitudes of great men, of writers whom Flaubert admired, and, also, selections from Flaubert himself—certainly, in the first part of the book, Flaubert caricatures his own notions about politics and society along with those of everybody else. Bouvard and Pécuchet were to realize the stupidity of their neighbors and to learn their own limitations and to be left with a profound impression of general human imbecility and ignorance. They were themselves to compile the monument to human inanity.

If this theory is true—and Flaubert's manuscripts bear it out—Flaubert had lifted the onus of blame from the bourgeois and for the first time written a satire on humanity itself of the type of *Gulliver's Travels*. The bourgeois has ceased to preach to the bourgeois: as the first big cracks begin to show in the structure of the nineteenth century, he shifts his complaint to the incompetence of humanity, for he is unable to believe in, or even to conceive, any non-bourgeois way out.

*Lionel Trilling*

## THE PRINCESS CASAMASSIMA I

In 1888, on the second of January, which in any year is likely to be a sad day, Henry James wrote to his friend William Dean Howells that his reputation had been dreadfully injured by his last two novels. The desire for his productions, he said, had been reduced to zero, editors no longer asked for his work, they even seemed ashamed to publish the stories they had already bought. But James was never without courage. "However, I don't despair," he wrote, "for I think I am now really in better form than I ever have been in my life and I propose yet to do many things." And then, no doubt with the irony all writers use when they dare to speak of future recognition, but also, surely, with the necessary faith, he concludes the matter: "Very likely too, some day, all my buried prose will kick off its various tombstones at once."

And so it happened. The "some day" has arrived and we have been hearing the clatter of marble as James's buried prose kicks off its monuments in a general resurrection. On all sides James is being given the serious and joyous interest he longed for in his lifetime.

One element of our interest must be the question of how some of James's prose ever came to be buried at all. It is not hard to understand why certain of James's books did not catch the contemporary fancy. But the two books on which James placed the blame for his diminishing popularity were *The Bostonians* and *The Princess Casamassima*, and of all James's novels these are the two which are most likely to make an immediate appeal to the reader of today. That they should not have delighted their contemporary public, but on the contrary should have turned it against James, makes a lively problem in the history of taste.[1]

Reprinted from the "Introduction" to *The Princess Casamassima*, by Henry James, by permission of The Macmillan Company and the author. Copyright 1948 by The Macmillan Company, New York, N. Y.

[1] Whoever wishes to know what the courage of the artist must sometimes be could do no better than to read the British reviews of *The Bostonians* and *The Princess Casamassima*.

In the masterpieces of his late years James became a difficult writer. This is the fact and nothing is gained for James by denying it. He himself knew that these late works were difficult; he wished them to be dealt with as if they were difficult. When a young man from Texas—it was Mr. Stark Young—inquired indirectly of James how he should go about reading his novels, James did not feel that this diffidence was provincial but happily drew up lists which would lead the admirable young man from the easy to the hard. But the hostility with which *The Bostonians* and *The Princess Casamassima* were received cannot be explained by any difficulty either of manner or intention, for in these books there is none. The prose, although personally characteristic, is perfectly in the tradition of the nineteenth-century novel. It is warm, fluent, and on the whole rather less elaborate and virtuose than Dickens' prose. The motives of the characters are clear and direct—certainly they are far from the elaborate punctilio of the late masterpieces. And the charge that is sometimes made against the later work, that it exists in a social vacuum, clearly does not pertain here. In these novels James is at the point in his career at which society, in the largest and even the grossest sense, is offering itself to his mind with great force. He understands society as crowds and police, as a field of justice and injustice, reform and revolution. The social texture of his work is grainy and knotted with practicality and detail. And more: his social observation is of a kind that we must find startlingly prescient when we consider that it was made some sixty years ago.

It is just this prescience, of course, that explains the resistance of James's contemporaries. What James saw he saw truly, but it was not what the readers of his time were themselves equipped to see. That we now are able to share his vision required the passage of six decades and the events which brought them to climax. Henry James in the eighties understood what we have painfully learned from our grim glossary of wars and concentration camps, after having seen the state and human nature laid open to our horrified inspection. "But I have the imagination of disaster—and see life as ferocious and sinister": James wrote this to A. C. Benson in 1896, and what so bland a young man as Benson made of the statement, what anyone then was likely to make of it, is hard to guess. But nowadays we know that such an imagination is one of the keys to truth.

It was, then, "the imagination of disaster" that cut James off from his contemporaries and it is what recommends him to us now. We know something about the profound disturbance of the sexual life which seems to go along with hypertrophy of the will and how this excess of will seems to be a response to certain maladjustments in society and to direct itself back upon them; D. H. Lawrence taught us much about this, but Lawrence himself never attempted a more daring conjunction of the sexual and the political life than Henry James succeeds with in *The Bostonians*. We know much about misery and downtroddenness and of what happens when strong

---

In a single year James brought out two major works; he thought they were his best to date and expected great things of them; he was told by the reviewers that they were not really novels at all; he was scorned and sneered at and condescended to and dismissed. In adjacent columns the ephemeral novels of the day were treated with gentle respect. The American press rivaled the British in the vehemence with which it condemned *The Bostonians,* but it was more tolerant of *The Princess Casamassima.*

and gifted personalities are put at a hopeless disadvantage, and about the possibilities of extreme violence, and about the sense of guilt and unreality which may come to members of the upper classes and the strange complex efforts they make to find innocence and reality, and about the conflict between the claims of art and of social duty—these are among the themes which make the pattern of *The Princess Casamassima*. It is a novel which has at its very center the assumption that Europe has reached the full of its ripeness and is passing over into rottenness, that the peculiarly beautiful light it gives forth is in part the reflection of a glorious past and in part the phosphorescence of a present decay, that it may meet its end by violence and that this is not wholly unjust, although never before has the old sinful continent made so proud and pathetic an assault upon our affections.

## II

*The Princess Casamassima* belongs to a great line of novels which runs through the nineteenth century as, one might say, the very backbone of its fiction. These novels, which are defined as a group by the character and circumstance of their heroes, include Stendhal's *The Red and the Black*, Balzac's *Père Goriot* and *Lost Illusions*, Dickens' *Great Expectations*, Flaubert's *Sentimental Education;* only a very slight extension of the definition is needed to allow the inclusion of Tolstoi's *War and Peace* and Dostoevski's *The Idiot*.

The defining hero may be known as the Young Man from the Provinces. He need not come from the provinces in literal fact, his social class may constitute his province. But a provincial birth and rearing suggest the simplicity and the high hopes he begins with—he starts with a great demand upon life and a great wonder about its complexity and promise. He may be of good family but he must be poor. He is intelligent, or at least aware, but not at all shrewd in worldly matters. He must have acquired a certain amount of education, should have learned something about life from books, although not the truth.

The hero of *The Princess Casamassima* conforms very exactly to type. The province from which Hyacinth Robinson comes is a city slum. "He sprang up at me out of the London pavement," says James in the preface to the novel in the New York Edition. In 1883, the first year of his long residence in England, James was in the habit of prowling the streets, and they yielded him the image "of some individual sensitive nature or fine mind, some small obscure creature whose education should have been almost wholly derived from them, capable of profiting by all the civilization, all the accumulation to which they testify, yet condemned to see things only from outside—in mere quickened consideration, mere wistfulness and envy and despair."

Thus equipped with poverty, pride, and intelligence, the Young Man from the Provinces stands outside life and seeks to enter. This modern hero is connected with the tales of the folk. Usually his motive is the legendary one of setting out to seek his fortune, which is what the folk tale says when it means that the hero is seeking himself. He is really the third and youngest son of the woodcutter, the one to whom all our sympathies go, the gentle and misunderstood one, the bravest of all. He is likely to be in some doubt about his parentage; his father the woodcutter is not really his father. Our hero has, whether he says so or not, the common belief of children that there is some mystery about his birth; his real parents, if the truth were known, are of great and even royal estate. Julien Sorel of *The Red and the Black* is the third and youngest son of an actual woodcutter, but he is the spiritual son of Napoleon. In our day the hero of *The Great Gatsby* is not really the son of Mr. Gatz; he is said to have sprung "from his Platonic conception of himself," to be, indeed, "the son of God." And James's Hyacinth Robinson, although fostered by a poor dressmaker and a shabby fiddler, has an English lord for his real father.

It is the fate of the Young Man to move from an obscure position into one of considerable eminence in Paris or London or St. Petersburg, to touch the life of the rulers of the earth. His situation is as chancy as that of any questing knight of medieval romance. He is confronted by situations whose meanings are dark to him, in which his choice seems always decisive. He understands everything to be a "test." Parsifal at the castle of the Fisher King is not more uncertain about the right thing to do than the Young Man from the Provinces picking his perilous way through the irrationalities of the society into which he has been transported. That the Young Man be introduced into great houses and involved with large affairs is essential to his story, which must not be confused with the cognate story of the Sensitive Young Man. The provincial hero must indeed be sensitive, and in proportion to the brassiness of the world; he may even be an artist; but it is not his part merely to be puzzled and hurt; he is not the hero of *The Way of All Flesh* or *Of Human Bondage* or *Mooncalf.* Unlike the merely sensitive hero, he is concerned to know how the political and social world are run and enjoyed; he wants a share of power and pleasure and in consequence he takes real risks, often of his life. The "swarming facts" that James tells us Hyacinth is to confront are "freedom and ease, knowledge and power, money, opportunity, and satiety."

The story of the Young Man from the Provinces is thus a strange one, for it has its roots both in legend and in the very heart of the modern actuality. From it we have learned most of what we know about modern society, about class and its strange rituals, about power and influence and about money, the hard fluent fact in which modern society has its being. Yet through the massed social fact there runs the thread of legendary romance, even of downright magic. We note, for example, that it seems necessary for the novelist to deal in transformation. Some great and powerful hand must reach down into the world of seemingly chanceless routine and pick up the hero and set him down in his complex and dangerous fate. Pip meets Magwitch on the marsh, a felon-godfather; Pierre Bezuhov unexpectedly inherits the fortune that permits this uncouth young man to make his tour of Russian society; powerful unseen forces play around the proud head of Julien Sorel to make possible his astonishing upward career; Rastignac, simply by being one of the boarders at the Maison Vauquer which also shelters the great Vautrin, moves to the very center of Parisian intrigue; James Gatz rows out to a millionaire's yacht, a boy in dungarees, and becomes Jay Gatsby, an Oxford man, a military hero.

Such transformations represent, with only slight exaggeration, the literal fact that was to be observed every day. From the late years of the eighteenth century through the early years of the twentieth, the social structure of the West was peculiarly fitted—one might say designed—for changes in fortune that were magical and romantic. The upper-class ethos was strong enough to make it remarkable that a young man should cross the borders, yet weak enough to permit the crossing in exceptional cases. A shiftless boy from Geneva, a starveling and a lackey, becomes the admiration of the French aristocracy and is permitted by Europe to manipulate its assumptions in every department of life: Jean Jacques Rousseau is the father of all the Young Men from the Provinces, including the one from Corsica.

The Young Man's story represents an actuality, yet we may be sure that James took special delight in its ineluctable legendary element. James was certainly the least primitive of artists, yet he was always aware of his connection with the primitive. He set great store by the illusion of probability and verisimilitude, but he knew that he dealt always with illusion; he was proud of the devices of his magic. Like any primitive storyteller, he wished to hold the reader against his will, to *enchant,* as we say. He loved what he called "the story as story"; he delighted to work, by means of the unusual, the extravagant, the melodramatic, and the supernatural, upon what he called "the blessed faculty of wonder"; and he understood primitive story to be the root of the modern novelist's art. F. O. Matthiessen speaks of the fairy tale quality of *The Wings of the Dove;* so sophisticated a work as *The Ambassadors* can be read as one of those tales in which the hero finds that nothing is what it seems and that the only guide through the world must be the goodness of his heart.

Like any great artist of story, like Shakespeare or Balzac or Dickens or Dostoevski, James crowds probability rather closer than we nowadays like. It is not that he gives us unlikely events but that he sometimes thickens the number of interesting events beyond our ordinary expectation. If this, in James or in any storyteller, leads to a straining of our sense of verisimilitude, there is always the defense to be made that the special job of literature is, as Marianne Moore puts it, the creation of "imaginary gardens with real toads in them." The reader who detects that the garden is imaginary should not be led by his discovery to a wrong view of the reality of the toads. In settling questions of reality and truth in fiction, it must be remembered that, although the novel in certain of its forms resembles the accumulative and classificatory sciences, which are the sciences most people are most at home with, in certain other of its forms the novel approximates the sciences of experiment. And an experiment is very like an imaginary garden which is laid out for the express purpose of supporting a real toad of fact. The apparatus of the researcher's bench is not nature itself but an artificial and extravagant contrivance, much like a novelist's plot, which is devised to force or foster a fact into being. This seems to have been James's own view of the part that is played in his novels by what he calls "romance." He seems to have had an analogy with experiment very clearly in mind when he tells us that romance is "experience liberated, so to speak; experience disengaged, disembroiled, disencumbered, exempt from the conditions that usually attach to it." Again and again he speaks of the contrivance of a novel in ways which will make it seem like illegitimate flummery to the reader who is committed only to the premises of the naturalistic novel, but which the intelligent scientist will understand perfectly.

Certainly *The Princess Casamassima* would seem to need some such defense as this, for it takes us, we are likely to feel, very far along the road to romance, some will think to the very point of impossibility. It asks us to accept a poor young man whose birth is darkly secret, his father being a dissipated but authentic English lord, his mother a French courtesan-seamstress who murders the father; a beautiful American-Italian princess who descends in the social scale to help "the people"; a general mingling of the very poor with persons of exalted birth; and then a dim mysterious leader of revolution, never seen by the reader, the machinations of an underground group of conspirators, an oath taken to carry out an assassination at some unspecified future day, the day arriving, the hour of the killing set, the instructions and the pistol given.

Confronted by paraphernalia like this, even those who admire the book are likely to agree with Rebecca West when, in her exuberant little study of James, she tells us that it is "able" and " meticulous" but at the same time "distraught" and "wild," that the "loveliness" in it comes from a transmutation of its "perversities"; she speaks of it as a "mad dream" and teases its vast unlikelihood, finding it one of the big jokes in literature that it was James, who so prided himself on his lack of naïveté, who should have brought back to fiction the high implausibility of the old novels which relied for their effects on dark and stormy nights, Hindu servants, mysterious strangers, and bloody swords wiped on richly embroidered handkerchiefs.

Miss West was writing in 1916, when the English naturalistic novel, with its low view of possibility, was in full pride. Our notion of political possibility was still to be changed by a small group of quarrelsome conspiratorial intellectuals taking over the control of Russia. Even a loyal Fabian at that time could consider it one of the perversities of *The Princess Casamassima* that two of its lower-class characters should say of a third that he had the potentiality of becoming Prime Minister of England; today Paul Muniment sits in the Cabinet and is on the way to Downing Street. In the thirties the book was much admired by those who read it in the light of knowledge of our own radical movements; it then used to be said that although James had dreamed up an impossible revolutionary group he had nonetheless managed to derive from it some notable insights into the temper of radicalism; these admirers grasped the toad of fact and felt that it was all the more remarkably there because the garden is so patently imaginary.

Yet an understanding of James's use of "romance"—and there is "romance" in Hyacinth's story—must not preclude our understanding of the striking literal accuracy of *The Princess Casamassima*. James himself helped to throw us off the scent when in his preface to the novel he told us that he made no research into Hyacinth's subterranean politics. He justified this by saying that "the value I wished most to render and the effect I wished most to produce were precisely those of our not knowing, of society's not knowing, but only guessing and suspecting and trying to ignore, what 'goes on' irreconcilably, subversively, beneath the vast smug surface." And he concludes the preface with the most beautifully arrogant and truest thing a novelist ever said about his craft: "What it all came back to was, no doubt, something like *this* wisdom—that if you haven't, for fiction, the root of the matter in you, haven't the sense of life and the penetrating imagination, you are a fool in the very presence of the revealed and assured; but that if you *are* so armed, you are not really helpless, not without your resource, even before mysteries abysmal." If, to learn about the radical movement of his time, James really did no more than consult his penetrating imagination—which no doubt was nourished like any other on conversation and the daily newspaper—then we must say that in no other novelist did the root of the matter go so deep and so wide. For the truth is that there is not a political event of *The Princess Casamassima*, not a detail of oath or mystery or danger, which is not confirmed by multitudinous records.

### III

We are inclined to flatter our own troubles with the belief that the late nineteenth century was a peaceful time. But James knew its actual violence. England was, to be sure, rather less violent than the Continent, but the history of England in the eighties was one of profound social unrest often intensified to disorder. In March of 1886, the year in which *The Princess Casamassima* appeared in book form, James wrote to his brother William of a riot in his street, of ladies' carriages being stopped and the "occupants hustled, rifled, slapped, and kissed." He does not think that the rioters were unemployed workingmen, more likely that they were "the great army of roughs and thieves." But he says that there is "immense destitution" and that "everyone is getting poorer—from causes which, I fear, will continue." In the same year he wrote to Charles Eliot Norton that the state of the British upper class seems to be "in many ways very much the same rotten and *collapsible* one of the French aristocracy before the revolution."

James envisaged revolution, and not merely as a convenience for his fiction. But he imagined a kind of revolution with which we are no longer familiar. It was not a Marxian revolution. There is no upsurge of an angry proletariat led by a disciplined party which plans to head a new strong state. Such a revolution has its conservative aspect—it seeks to save certain elements of bourgeois culture for its own use, for example, science and the means of production and even some social agencies. The revolutionary theory of *The Princess Casamassima* has little in common with this. There is no organized mass movement; there is no disciplined party but only a strong conspiratorial center. There are no plans for taking over the state and almost no ideas about the society of the future. The conspiratorial center plans only for destruction, chiefly personal terrorism. But James is not naïvely representing a radical Graustark; he is giving a very accurate account of anarchism.

In 1872, at its meeting in The Hague, the First International voted the expulsion of the anarchists. Karl Marx had at last won his long battle with Bakunin. From that point on, "scientific socialism" was to dominate revolutionary thought. Anarchism ceased to be a main current of political theory. But anarchism continued as a force to be reckoned with, especially in the Latin countries, and it produced a revolutionary type of great courage and sometimes of appealing interest. Even in decline the theory and action of anarchism dominated the imagination of Europe.

It is not possible here to give a discriminating account of anarchism in all its aspects; to distinguish between the mutation which verges on nihilism and that which is called communist-anarchism, or between its representatives, Sergei Nechayev, who had the character of a police spy, and Kropotkin or the late Carlo Tresca, who were known for their personal sweetness; or to resolve the contradiction between the violence of its theory and action and the gentle world toward which these are directed. It will have to be enough to say that anarchism holds that the natural goodness of man is absolute and that society corrupts it, and that the guide to anarchist action is the desire to destroy society in general and not merely a particular social form.

When, therefore, Hyacinth Robinson is torn between his desire for social justice and his fear lest the civilization of Europe be destroyed, he is dealing reasonably with anarchist belief. "The unchaining of what is today called the evil passions and the destruction of what is called public order" was the consummation of Bakunin's aim which he defended by saying that "the desire for destruction is at the same time a creative desire." It was not only the state but all social forms that were to be demolished according to the doctrine of *amorphism;* any social form held the seeds of the state's rebirth and must therefore be extirpated. Intellectual disciplines were social forms like any other. At least in its early days anarchism expressed hostility toward science. Toward the arts the hostility was less, for the early leaders were often trained in the humanities and their inspiration was largely literary; in the nineties there was a strong alliance between the French artists and the anarchist groups. But in the logic of the situation art was bound to come under the anarchist fire. Art is inevitably associated with civil peace and social order and indeed with the ruling classes. Then too any large intense movement of moral-political action is likely to be jealous of art and to feel that it is in competition with the full awareness of human suffering. Bakunin on several occasions spoke of it as of no account when the cause of human happiness was considered. Lenin expressed something of the same sort when, after having listened with delight to a sonata by Beethoven, he said that he could not listen to music too often. "It affects your nerves, makes you want to say stupid, nice things, and stroke the heads of people who could create such beauty while living in this vile hell. And you mustn't stroke anyone's head—you might get your hand bitten off." And similarly the Princess of James's novel feels that her taste is but the evidence of her immoral aristocratic existence and that art is a frivolous distraction from revolution.

The nature of the radicals in *The Princess Casamassima* may, to the modern reader, seem a distortion of fact. The people who meet at the Sun and Moon to mutter their wrongs over their beer are not revolutionists and scarcely radicals; most of them are nothing more than dull malcontents. Yet they represent with complete accuracy the political development of a large part of the working class of England at the beginning of the eighties. The first great movement of English trade unionism had created an aristocracy of labor largely cut off from the mass of the workers, and the next great movement had not yet begun; the political expression of men such as met at the Sun and Moon was likely to be as fumbling as James represents it.

James has chosen the occupations of these men with great discrimination. There are no factory workers among them; at that time anarchism did not attract factory workers so much as the members of the skilled and relatively sedentary trades: tailors, shoemakers, weavers, cabinetmakers, and ornamental-metal workers. Hyacinth's craft of bookbinding was no doubt chosen because James knew something about it and because, being at once a fine and a mechanic art, it perfectly suited Hyacinth's fate, but it is to the point that bookbinders were largely drawn to anarchism.

When Paul Muniment tells Hyacinth that the club of the Sun and Moon is a "place you have always overestimated," he speaks with the authority of one who has connections more momentous. The anarchists, although of course they wished to influence the masses and could on occasion move them to concerted action, did not greatly value democratic or quasi-democratic mass organizations. Bakunin believed that "for the international organization of all Europe one hundred revolutionists, strongly and seriously bound together, are sufficient." The typical anarchist organization was hierarchical and secret. When in 1867 Bakunin drew up plans of organization, he instituted three "orders": a public group to be known as the International Alliance of Social Democracy; then above this and not known to it the Order of National Brothers; above this and not known to it the Order of International Brothers, very few in number. James's Muniment, we may suppose, is a National Brother.

For the indoctrination of his compact body of revolutionists, Bakunin, in collaboration with the amazing Sergei Nechayev, compiled *The Revolutionary Catechism*. This vade mecum might be taken as a guidebook to *The Princess Casamassima*. It instructs the revolutionist that he may be called to live in the great world and to penetrate into any class of society: the aristocracy, the church, the army, the diplomatic corps. It tells how one goes about compromising the wealthy in order to command their wealth, just as the Princess is compromised. There are instructions on how to deal with people who, like James's Captain Sholto, are drawn to the movement by questionable motives; on how little one is to trust the women of the upper classes who may be seeking sensation or salvation—the Princess calls it reality—through revolutionary action. It is a ruthless little book: eventually Bakunin himself complains that nothing—no private letter, no wife, no daughter—is safe from the conspiratorial zeal of his co-author Nechayev.

The situation in which Hyacinth involves himself, his pledge to commit an assassination upon demand of the secret leadership, is not the extreme fancy of a cloistered novelist, but a classic anarchist situation. Anarchism could arouse mass action, as in the riots at Lyon in 1882, but typically it showed its power by acts of terror committed by courageous individuals glad to make personal war against society. Bakunin canonized for anarchism the Russian bandit Stenka Razin; Balzac's Vautrin and Stendhal's Valbayre (of *Lamiel*) are prototypes of anarchist heroes. Always ethical as well as instrumental in its theory, anarchism conceived assassination not only as a way of advertising its doctrine and weakening the enemy's morale, but also as punishment or revenge or warning. Of the many assassinations or attempts at assassination that fill the annals of the late years of the century, not all were anarchist, but those that were not were influenced by anarchist example. In 1878 there were two attempts on the life of the Kaiser, one on the King of Spain, one on the King of Italy; in 1880 another attempt on the King of Spain; in 1881 Alexander II of Russia was killed after many attempts; in 1882 the Phoenix Park murders were committed, Lord Frederick Cavendish, Secretary for Ireland, and Undersecretary Thomas Burke being killed by extreme Irish nationalists; in 1883 there were several dynamite conspiracies in Great Britain and in 1885 there was an explosion in the House of Commons; in 1883 there was an anarchist plot to blow up, all at once, the Emperor Wilhelm, the Crown Prince, Bismarck and Moltke. These are but a few of the terroristic events of which James would have been aware in the years just before he began *The Princess Casamassima,* and later years brought many more.

Anarchism never established itself very firmly in England as it did in Russia, France, and Italy. In these countries it penetrated to the upper classes. The actions of the Princess are not unique for an aristocrat of her time, nor is she fabricating when she speaks of her acquaintance with revolutionists of a kind more advanced than Hyacinth is likely to know. In Italy she would have met on terms of social equality such notable anarchists as Count Carlo Cafiero and the physician Enrico Malatesta, who was the son of a wealthy family. Kropotkin was a descendant of the Ruriks and, as the novels of James's friend Turgenev testify, extreme radicalism was not uncommon among the Russian aristocracy. In France in the eighties and still more markedly in the nineties there were artistic, intellectual, and even aristocratic groups which were closely involved with the anarchists.

The great revolutionary of *The Princess Casamassima* is Hoffendahl, whom we never see although we feel his real existence. Hoffendahl is, in the effect he has upon others, not unlike what is told of Bakunin himself in his greatest days, when he could enthrall with his passion even those who could not understand the language he spoke in. But it is possible that James also had the famous Johann Most in mind. Most figured in the London press in 1881 when he was tried because his newspaper, *Freiheit,* exulted in the assassination of the Czar. He was found guilty of libel and inciting to murder and sentenced to sixteen months at hard labor. The jury that convicted him recommended mercy on the ground that he was a foreigner and "might be suffering violent wrong." The jury was right— Most had suffered in the prisons of Germany after a bitter youth. It is not clear whether he, like James's Hoffendahl, had had occasion to stand firm under police torture, but there can be no doubt of his capacity to do so. After having served his jail sentence, he emigrated to America, and it has been said of him that terrorist activities in this country centered about him. He was implicated in the Haymarket Affair and imprisoned for having incited the assassin of President McKinley; Emma Goldman and Alexander Berkman were his disciples, and they speak of him in language such as Hyacinth uses of Hoffendahl. It is worth noting that Most was a bookbinder by trade.

In short, when we consider the solid accuracy of James's political detail at every point, we find that we must give up the notion that James could move only in the thin air of moral abstraction. A writer has said of *The Princess Casamassima* that it is "a capital example of James's impotence in matters sociological." The very opposite is so. Quite apart from its moral and aesthetic authority, *The Princess Casamassima* is a brilliantly precise representation of social actuality.

IV

In his preface to *The Princess* in the New York Edition, James tells us of a certain autobiographical element that went into the creation of Hyacinth Robinson. "To find his possible adventures interesting," James says, "I had only to conceive his watching the same public show, the same innumerable appearances I had myself watched and of watching very much as I had watched."

This, at first glance, does not suggest a very intense connection between author and hero. But at least it assures us that at some point the novel is touched by the author's fantasy about himself. It is one of the necessities of the successful modern story that the author shall have somewhere entrusted his personal fantasy to the tale; but it may be taken as very nearly a rule that the more the author disguises the personal nature of his fantasy, the greater its force will be. Perhaps he is best off if he is not wholly aware that he is writing about himself at all: his fantasy, like an actual dream, is powerful in the degree that its "meaning" is hidden.

If Hyacinth does indeed express James's personal fantasy, we are led to believe that the fantasy has reference to a familial situation. James puts an insistent emphasis upon his hero's small stature. Hyacinth's mere size is decisive in the story. It exempts him from certain adult situations; for example, where Paul Muniment overcomes the class barrier to treat the Princess as a woman, taking so full an account of her sexual existence and his own that we expect him to make a demand upon her, Hyacinth is detached from the sexual possibility and disclaims it. The intention is not to show him as unmanly but as too young to make the claims of maturity; he is the child of the book, always the very youngest person. And this child-man lives in a novel full of parental figures. Hyacinth has no less than three sets of parents: Lord Frederick and Florentine, Miss Pynsent and Mr. Vetch, Eustache Poupin and Madame Poupin, and this is not to mention the French-revolutionary grandfather and the arch-conspirator Hoffendahl; and even Millicent Henning appears, for one memorable Sunday, in a maternal role. The decisive parental pair are, of course, the actual parents, Lord Frederick and Florentine, who represent—some will feel too schematically—the forces which are in conflict in Hyacinth. Undertaking to kill the Duke as a step in the destruction of the ruling class, Hyacinth is in effect plotting the murder of his own father; and one reason that he comes to loathe the pledged deed is his belief that, by repeating poor Florentine's action, he will be bringing his mother to life in all her pitiful shame.

It is as a child that Hyacinth dies; that is, he dies of the withdrawal of love. James contrives with consummate skill the lonely circumstance of

Hyacinth's death. Nothing can equal for delicacy of ironic pathos the incidents of the last part of the book, in which Hyacinth, who has his own death warrant in his pocket, the letter ordering the assassination, looks to his adult friends for a reason of love which will explain why he does not have to serve it on himself, or how, if he must serve it, he can believe in the value of his deed. But the grown-up people have occupations from which he is excluded and they cannot believe in his seriousness. Paul Muniment and the Princess push him aside, not unkindly, only condescendingly, only as one tells a nice boy that there are certain things he cannot understand, such things as power and love and justification.

The adult world last represents itself to Hyacinth in the great scene of lust in the department store. To make its point the crueler, James has previously contrived for Hyacinth a wonderful Sunday of church and park with Millicent Henning;[2] Millicent enfolds Hyacinth in an undemanding, protective love that is not fine or delicate but for that reason so much the more useful; but when in his last hunt for connection Hyacinth seeks out Millicent in her shop, he sees her standing "still as a lay-figure" under Captain Sholto's gaze, exhibiting "the long grand lines" of her body under pretense of "modeling" a dress. And as Hyacinth sees the Captain's eyes "travel up and down the front of Millicent's person," he knows that he has been betrayed.

So much manipulation of the theme of parent and child, so much interest in lost protective love, suggests that the connection of Hyacinth and his author may be more intense than at first appears. And there is one consideration that reinforces the guess that this fantasy of a child and his family has a particular and very personal relation to James in his own family situation. The matter which is at issue in *The Princess Casamassima,* the dispute between art and moral action, the controversy between the glorious unregenerate past and the regenerate future, was not of merely general interest to Henry James, nor, indeed, to any of the notable members of the James family. Ralph Barton Perry in his *Thought and Character of William James* finds the question so real and troubling in William's life that he devotes a chapter to it. William, to whom the antithesis often represented itself as between Europe-art and America-action, settled in favor of America and action. Henry settled, it would seem, the other way—certainly in favor of art. But whether Henry's option necessarily involved, as William believed, a decision in favor of the past, a love of the past for, as people like to say, the past's sake, may be thought of as the essential matter of dispute between William and Henry.

The dispute was at the very heart of their relationship. They had the

2 The reviewer for *The Athenaeum* remarked it as "an odd feature of the book that nearly all the action, or nearly all of which the date is indicated, takes place on Sundays." The observation was worth making, for it suggests how certain elements of the book's atmosphere are achieved: what better setting for loneliness and doubt than Sunday in a great city? And since the action of the book must depend on the working schedule of the working-class characters, who, moreover, live at considerable distance from one another, what more natural than that they should meet on Sundays? But the reviewer thinks that "possibly a London week-day suggests a life too strenuous to be lived by the aimless beings whom Mr. James depicts." The "aimless beings" note was one that was struck by most of the more-or-less liberal reviewers.

matter out over the years. But in the having-out William was the aggressor, and it is impossible to suppose that his statement of the case did not cause Henry pain. William came to suspect that the preoccupation with art was very close to immorality. He was perhaps not so wrong as the clichés in defense of art would make him out to be; his real error lay in his not knowing what art, as a thing to contemplate or as a thing to make, implied for his brother. His suspicion extended to Henry's work. He was by no means without sympathy for it, but he thought that Henry's great gifts were being put at the service of the finicking and refined; he was impatient of what was not robust in the same way he was. Henry, we may be sure, would never have wanted a diminution of the brotherly frankness that could tell him that *The Bostonians* might have been very fine if it had been only a hundred pages long; but the remark and others of similar sort could only have left his heart a little sore.

When, then, we find Henry James creating for his Hyacinth a situation in which he must choose between political action and the fruits of the creative spirit of Europe, we cannot but see that he has placed at the center of his novel a matter whose interest is of the most personal kind. Its personal, its familial, nature is emphasized by Alice James's share in the dispute, for she and William were at one against their brother in aggressively holding a low view of England, and William's activism finds a loud and even shrill echo in Alice, whose passionate radicalism was, as Henry said of her, "her most distinguishing feature." But far more important is the father's relation to the family difference. The authority of the elder Henry James could be fairly claimed by both his sons, for he was brilliantly contradictory on the moral status of art. If William could come to think of art as constituting a principle which was antagonistic to the principle of life, his father had said so before him. And Henry could find abundant support for his own position in his father's frequent use of the artist as one who, because he seeks to create and not to possess, most closely approximates in mankind the attributes of divinity.

*The Princess Casamassima* may, then, be thought of as an intensely autobiographical book, not in the sense of being the author's personal record but in the sense of being his personal act. For we may imagine that James, beautifully in control of his novel, dominant in it as almost no decent person can be in a family situation, is continuing the old dispute on his own terms and even taking a revenge. Our imagination of the "revenge" does not require that we attribute a debasing malice to James—quite to the contrary, indeed, for the revenge is gentle and innocent and noble. It consists, this revenge, only in arranging things in such a way that Paul Muniment and the Princess shall stand for James's brother and sister and then so to contrive events as to show that, at the very moment when this brilliant pair think they are closest to the conspiratorial arcanum, the real thing, the true center, they are in actual fact furthest from it.[3] Paul and

---

3 When I say that Paul and the Princess "stand for" William and Alice, I do not mean that they are portraits of William and Alice. It is true that, in the conditioning context of the novel, Paul suggests certain equivalences with William James: in his brisk masculinity, his intelligence, his downright common sense and practicality, most of all in his relation to Hyacinth. What we may most legitimately guess to be a representation is the

the Princess believe themselves to be in the confidence of *Them,* the People Higher Up, the International Brothers, or whatever, when really they are held in suspicion in these very quarters. They condescend to Hyacinth for his frivolous concern with art, but Hyacinth, unknown to them, has received his letter of fatal commission; he has the death warrant in his pocket, another's and his own; despite his having given clear signs of lukewarmness to the cause, he is trusted by the secret powers where his friends are not. In his last days Hyacinth has become aware of his desire no longer to bind books but to write them: the novel can be thought of as Henry James's demonstrative message, to the world in general, to his brother and sister in particular, that the artist quite as much as any man of action carries his ultimate commitment and his death warrant in his pocket. "Life's nothing," Henry James wrote to a young friend, "—unless heroic and sacrificial."

James even goes so far as to imply that the man of art may be close to the secret center of things when the man of action is quite apart from it. Yet Hyacinth cannot carry out the orders of the people who trust him. Nor of course can he betray them—the pistol which, in the book's last dry words, "would certainly have served much better for the Duke," Hyacinth turns upon himself. A vulgar and facile progressivism can find this to be a proof of James's "impotence in matters sociological"—"the problem remains unsolved." Yet it would seem that a true knowledge of society comprehends the reality of the social forces it presumes to study and is aware of contradictions and consequences; it knows that sometimes society offers an opposition of motives in which the antagonists are in such a balance of authority and appeal that a man who so wholly perceives them as to embody them in his very being cannot choose between them and is therefore destroyed. This is known as tragedy.

## V

We must not misunderstand the nature of Hyacinth's tragic fate. Hyacinth dies sacrificially, but not as a sacrificial lamb, wholly innocent; he dies as a human hero who has incurred a certain amount of guilt.

The possibility of misunderstanding Hyacinth's situation arises from our

---

*ratio* of the characters—Paul:Hyacinth : : William:Henry. The Princess has Alice's radical ideas; she is called "the most remarkable woman in Europe," which in effect is what Henry James said Alice would have been if the full exercise of her will and intellect had not been checked by her illness. But such equivalence is not portraiture and the novel is not a family *roman à clef.* And yet the matter of portraiture cannot be so easily settled, for it has been noticed by those who are acquainted with the life and character of Alice James that there are many points of similarity between her and Rosy Muniment. Their opinions are, to be sure, at opposite poles, for Rosy is a staunch Tory and a dreadful snob, but the very patness of the opposition may reasonably be thought significant. In mind and pride of mind, in outspokenness, in will and the license given to will by illness, there is similarity between the sister of Paul and the sister of William and Henry. There is no reason why anyone interested in Henry James should not be aware of this, provided that it not be taken as the negation of Henry's expressed love for Alice and William—provided, too, that it be taken as an aspect of his particular moral imagination, a matter which is discussed later.

modern belief that the artist is one of the types of social innocence. Our competitive, acquisitive society ritualistically condemns what it practices— with us money gives status, yet we consider a high regard for money a debasing thing and we set a large value on disinterested activity. Hence our cult of the scientist and the physician, who are presumed to be free of the acquisitive impulses. The middle class, so far as it is liberal, admires from varying distances the motives and even the aims of revolutionists: it cannot imagine that revolutionists have anything to "gain" as the middle class itself understands gain. And although sometimes our culture says that the artist is a subversive idler, it is nowadays just as likely to say that he is to be admired for his innocence, for his activity is conceived as having no end beyond itself except possibly some benign social purpose, such as "teaching people to understand each other."

But James did not see art as, in this sense, innocent. We touch again on autobiography, for on this point there is a significant connection between James's own life and Hyacinth's.

In Chapter XXV of *A Small Boy and Others,* his first autobiographic volume, James tells how he was initiated into a knowledge of style in the Galerie d'Apollon of the Louvre. As James represents the event, the varieties of style in that gallery assailed him so intensely that their impact quite transcended aesthetic experience. For they seemed to speak to him not visually at all but in some "complicated sound" and as a "deafening chorus"; they gave him what he calls "a general sense of glory." About this sense of glory he is quite explicit. "The glory meant ever so many things at once, not only beauty and art and supreme design, but history and fame and power, the world in fine raised to the richest and noblest expression."

Hazlitt said that "the language of poetry naturally falls in with the language of power," and goes on to develop an elaborate comparison between the processes of the imagination and the processes of autocratic rule. He is not merely indulging in a flight of fancy or a fashion of speaking; no stancher radical democrat ever lived than Hazlitt and no greater lover of imaginative literature, yet he believed that poetry has an affinity with political power in its autocratic and aristocratic form and that it is not a friend of the democratic virtues. We are likely not to want to agree with Hazlitt; we prefer to speak of art as if it lived in a white bungalow with a garden, had a wife and two children, and were harmless and quiet and cooperative. But James is of Hazlitt's opinion; his first great revelation of art came as an analogy with the triumphs of the world; art spoke to him of the imperious will, with the music of an army with banners. Perhaps it is to the point that James's final act of imagination, as he lay dying, was to call his secretary and give her as his last dictation what purported to be an autobiographical memoir by Napoleon Bonaparte.

But so great an aggression must carry some retribution with it, and as James goes on with the episode of the Galerie d'Apollon, he speaks of the experience as having the effect not only of a "love-philtre" but also of a "fear-philtre." Aggression brings guilt and then fear. And James concludes the episode with the account of a nightmare in which the Galerie figures; he calls it "the most appalling and yet most admirable" nightmare of his life. He dreamed that he was defending himself from an intruder, trying to keep the door shut against a terrible invading form; then suddenly there came "the great thought that I, in my appalled state, was more appalling than the awful agent, creature or presence"; whereupon he opened the door and, surpassing the invader for "straight aggression and dire intention," pursued him down a long corridor in a great storm of lightning and thunder; the corridor was seen to be the Galerie d'Apollon. We do not have to presume very far to find the meaning in the dream, for James gives us all that we might want; he tells us that the dream was important to him, that, having experienced art as "history and fame and power," his arrogation seemed a guilty one and represented itself as great fear which he overcame by an inspiration of straight aggression and dire intention and triumphed in the very place where he had had his imperious fantasy. An admirable nightmare indeed. One needs to be a genius to counterattack nightmare; perhaps this is the definition of genius.

When James came to compose Hyacinth's momentous letter from Venice, the implications of the analogue of art with power had developed and become clearer and more objective. Hyacinth has had his experience of the glories of Europe, and when he writes to the Princess his view of human misery is matched by a view of the world "raised to the richest and noblest expression." He understands no less clearly than before "the despotisms, the cruelties, the exclusions, the monopolies and the rapacities of the past." But now he recognizes that "the fabric of civilization as we know it" is inextricably bound up with this injustice; the monuments of art and learning and taste have been reared upon coercive power. Yet never before has he had the full vision of what the human spirit can accomplish to make the world "less impracticable and life more tolerable." He finds that he is ready to fight for art—and what art suggests of glorious life—against the low and even hostile estimate which his revolutionary friends have made of it, and this involves of course some reconciliation with established coercive power.

It is easy enough, by certain assumptions, to condemn Hyacinth and even to call him names. But first we must see what his position really means and what heroism there is in it. Hyacinth recognizes what very few people wish to admit, that civilization has a price, and a high one. Civilizations differ from one another as much in what they give up as in what they acquire; but all civilizations are alike in that they renounce something for something else. We do right to protest this in any given case that comes under our notice and we do right to get as much as possible for as little as possible; but we can never get everything for nothing. Nor, indeed, do we really imagine that we can. Thus, to stay within the present context, every known theory of popular revolution gives up the vision of the world "raised to the richest and noblest expression." To achieve the ideal of widespread security, popular revolutionary theory condemns the ideal of adventurous experience. It tries to avoid doing this explicitly and it even, although seldom convincingly, denies that it does it at all. But all the instincts or necessities of radical democracy are against the superbness and arbitrariness which often mark great spirits. It is sometimes said in the interests of an ideal or abstract completeness that the choice need not be made, that security can be imagined to go with richness and nobility of expression. But we have not seen it in the past and nobody really strives to imagine it in the future. Hyacinth's choice is made under the pressure of the counterchoice made by Paul and the Princess; their "general rectification" implies a civilization from which the idea of life raised to the richest and noblest expression will quite vanish.

There have been critics who said that Hyacinth is a snob and the surrogate of James's snobbery. But if Hyacinth is a snob, he is of the company of Rabelais, Shakespeare, Scott, Dickens, Balzac, and Lawrence, men who saw the lordliness and establishment of the aristocrat and the gentleman as the proper condition for the spirit of man, and who, most of them, demanded it for themselves, as poor Hyacinth never does, for "it was not so much that he wished to enjoy as that he wished to know; his desire was not to be pampered but to be initiated." His snobbery is no other than that of John Stuart Mill when he discovered that a grand and spacious room could have so enlarging an effect upon his mind; when Hyacinth at Medley had his first experience of a great old house, he admired nothing so much as the ability of a thing to grow old without loss but rather with gain of dignity and interest; "the spectacle of long duration unassociated with some sordid infirmity or poverty was new to him; for he had lived with people among whom old age meant, for the most part, a grudged and degraded survival." Hyacinth has Yeats's awareness of the dream that a great house embodies, that here the fountain of life "overflows without ambitious pains,"

> And mounts more dizzy high the more it rains
> As though to choose whatever shape it wills
> And never stoop to a mechanical
> Or servile shape, at others' beck and call.

But no less than Yeats he has the knowledge that the rich man who builds the house and the architect and artists who plan and decorate it are "bitter and violent men" and that the great houses "but take our greatness with our violence" and our "greatness with our bitterness." [4]

By the time Hyacinth's story draws to its end, his mind is in a perfect equilibrium, not of irresolution but of awareness. His sense of the social horror of the world is not diminished by his newer sense of the glory of the world. On the contrary, just as his pledge of his life to the revolutionary cause had in effect freed him to understand human glory, so the sense of the glory quickens his response to human misery—never, indeed, is he so sensitive to the sordid life of the mass of mankind as after he has had the revelation of art. And just as he is in an equilibrium of awareness, he is also in an equilibrium of guilt. He has learned something of what may lie behind abstract ideals, the envy, the impulse to revenge and to dominance. He is the less inclined to forgive what he sees because, as we must remember, the triumph of the revolution presents itself to him as a certainty and the act of revolution as an ecstasy. There is for him as little doubt of the revolution's success as there is of the fact that his mother had murdered his father. And when he thinks of revolution, it is as a tremendous tide, a

---

[4] "Ancestral Houses" in *Collected Poems*. The whole poem may be read as a most illuminating companion-piece to *The Princess Casamassima*.

colossal force; he is tempted to surrender to it as an escape from his isolation—one would be lifted by it "higher on the sun-touched billows than one could ever be by a lonely effort of one's own." But if the revolutionary passion thus has its guilt, Hyacinth's passion for life at its richest and noblest is no less guilty. It leads him to consent to the established coercive power of the world, and this can never be innocent. One cannot "accept" the suffering of others, no matter for what ideal, no matter if one's own suffering be also accepted, without incurring guilt. It is the guilt in which every civilization is implicated.

Hyacinth's death, then, is not his way of escaping from irresolution. It is truly a sacrifice, an act of heroism. He is a hero of civilization because he dares do more than civilization does: embodying two ideals at once, he takes upon himself, in full consciousness, the guilt of each. He acknowledges both his parents. By his death he instructs us in the nature of civilized life and by his consciousness he transcends it.

## VI

Suppose that truth be the expression, not of intellect, nor even, as we sometimes now think, of will, but of love. It is an outmoded idea, and yet if it has still any force at all it will carry us toward an understanding of the truth of *The Princess Casamassima*. To be sure, the legend of James does not associate him with love; indeed, it is a fact symptomatic of the condition of American letters that Sherwood Anderson, a writer who himself spoke much of love, was able to say of James that he was the novelist of "those who hate." Yet as we read *The Princess Casamassima* it is possible to ask whether any novel was ever written which, dealing with decisive moral action and ultimate issues, makes its perceptions and its judgments with so much loving-kindness.

Since James wrote, we have had an increasing number of novels which ask us to take cognizance of those whom we call the underprivileged. These novels are of course addressed to those of us who have the money and the leisure to buy books and read them and the security to assail our minds with accounts of the miseries of our fellow men; on the whole, the poor do not read about the poor. And in so far as the middle class has been satisfied and gratified by the moral implications of most of these books, it is not likely to admire Henry James's treatment of the poor. For James represents the poor as if they had dignity and intelligence in the same degree as people of the reading class. More, he assumes this and feels no need to insist that it is so. This is a grace of spirit that we are so little likely to understand that we may resent it. Few of our novelists are able to write about the poor so as to make them something more than the pitied objects of our facile sociological minds. The literature of our liberal democracy pets and dandles its underprivileged characters, and, quite as if it had the right to do so, forgives them what faults they may have. But James is sure that in such people, who are numerous, there are the usual human gradations of understanding, interest, and goodness. Even if my conjecture about the family connection of the novel be wholly mistaken, it will at least suggest what is unmistakably true, that James could write about a workingman quite as if he were as large, willful, and complex as the author of *The Principles of Psychology*. At the same time that everything in the story of *The Princess Casamassima* is based on social difference, everything is also based on the equality of the members of the human family. People at the furthest extremes of class are easily brought into relation because they are all contained in the novelist's affection. In that context it is natural for the Princess and Lady Aurora Langrish to make each other's acquaintance by the side of Rosy Muniment's bed and to contend for the notice of Paul. That James should create poor people so proud and intelligent as to make it impossible for anyone, even the reader who has paid for the privilege, to condescend to them, so proud and intelligent indeed that it is not wholly easy for them to be "good," is, one ventures to guess, an unexpressed, a never-to-be-expressed reason for finding him "impotent in matters socio-logical." We who are liberal and progressive know that the poor are our equals in every sense except that of being equal to us.

But James's special moral quality, his power of love, is not wholly comprised by his impulse to make an equal distribution of dignity among his characters. It goes beyond this to create his unique moral realism, his particular gift of human understanding. If in his later novels James, as many say he did, carried awareness of human complication to the point of virtuosity, he surely does not do so here, and yet his knowledge of complication is here very considerable. But this knowledge is not an analytical one, or not in the usual sense in which that word is taken, which implies a cool dissection. If we imagine a father of many children who truly loves them all, we may suppose that he will see very vividly their differences from one another, for he has no wish to impose upon them a similarity which would be himself; and he will be quite willing to see their faults, for his affection leaves him free to love them, not because they are faultless but because they are they; yet while he sees their faults he will be able, from long connection and because there is no reason to avoid the truth, to perceive the many reasons for their actions. The discriminations and modifications of such a man would be enormous, yet the moral realism they would constitute would not arise from an analytical intelligence as we usually conceive it but from love.

The nature of James's moral realism may most easily be exemplified by his dealings with the character of Rosy Muniment. Rosy is in many ways similar to Jennie Wren, the dolls' dressmaker of *Our Mutual Friend;* both are crippled, courageous, quaint, sharp-tongued, and dominating, and both are admired by the characters among whom they have their existence. Dickens unconsciously recognizes the cruelty that lies hidden in Jennie, but consciously he makes nothing more than a brusque joke of her habit of threatening people's eyes with her needle. He allows himself to be deceived and is willing to deceive us. But James manipulates our feelings about Rosy into a perfect ambivalence. He forces us to admire her courage, pride, and intellect and seems to forbid us to take account of her cruelty because she directs it against able-bodied or aristocratic people. Only at the end does he permit us the release of our ambivalence—the revelation that Hyacinth doesn't like Rosy and that we don't have to is an emotional relief and a moral enlightenment. But although we by the author's express permission are free to dislike Rosy, the author does not avail himself of the same privilege. In the family of the novel Rosy's status has not changed.

Moral realism is the informing spirit of *The Princess Casamassima* and it yields a kind of social and political knowledge which is hard to come by. It is at work in the creation of the character of Millicent Henning, whose strength, affectionateness, and warm sensuality move James to the series of remarkable prose arias in her praise which punctuate the book; yet while he admires her, he knows the particular corruptions which our civilization is working upon her, for he is aware not only of her desire to pull down what is above her but also of her desire to imitate and conform to it and to despise what she herself is. Millicent is proud of doing nothing with her hands, she despises Hyacinth because he is so poor in spirit as to consent to *make* things and get dirty in the process, and she values herself because she does nothing less genteel than exhibit what others have made; and in one of the most pregnant scenes of the book James involves her in the peculiarly corrupt and feeble sexuality which is associated in our culture with exhibiting and looking at luxurious objects.

But it is in the creation of Paul Muniment and the Princess that James's moral realism shows itself in fullest power. If we seek an explanation of why *The Princess Casamassima* was not understood in its own day, we find it in the fact that the significance of this remarkable pair could scarcely have emerged for the reader of 1886. But we of today can say that they and their relationship constitute one of the most masterly comments on modern life that has ever been made.

In Paul Muniment a genuine idealism coexists with a secret desire for personal power. It is one of the brilliances of the novel that his ambition is never made explicit. Rosy's remark about her brother, "What my brother really cares for—well, one of these days, when you know you'll tell me," is perhaps as close as his secret ever comes to statement. It is conveyed to us by his tone, as a decisive element of his charm, for Paul radiates what the sociologists, borrowing the name from theology, call *charisma,* the charm of power, the gift of leadership. His natural passion for power must never become explicit, for it is one of the beliefs of our culture that power invalidates moral purpose. The ambiguity of Paul Muniment has been called into being by the nature of modern politics in so far as they are moral and idealistic. For idealism has not changed the nature of leadership, but it has forced the leader to change his nature, requiring him to present himself as a harmless and self-abnegating man. It is easy enough to speak of this ambiguity as a form of hypocrisy, yet the opposition between morality and power from which it springs is perfectly well conceived. But even if well conceived, it is endlessly difficult to execute and it produces its own particular confusions, falsifications, and even lies. The moral realist sees it as the source of characteristically modern ironies, such as the liberal exhausting the scrupulosity which made him deprecate all power and becoming extravagantly tolerant of what he had once denounced, or the idealist who takes license from his ideals for the unrestrained exercise of power.

The Princess, as some will remember, is the Christina Light of James's earlier novel, *Roderick Hudson,* and she considers, as Madame Grandoni says of her, "that in the darkest hour of her life, she sold herself for a title and a fortune. She regards her doing so as such a terrible piece of frivolity that she can never for the rest of her days be serious enough to make up for it." Seriousness has become her ruling passion, and in the great sad comedy of the story it is her fatal sin, for seriousness is not exempt from the tendency of ruling passions to lead to error. And yet it has an aspect of heroism, this hunt of hers for reality, for a strong and final basis of life. "Then it's real, it's solid!" she exclaims when Hyacinth tells her that he has seen Hoffendahl and has penetrated to the revolutionary holy of holies. It is her quest for reality that leads her to the poor, to the very poorest poor she can find, and that brings a light of joy to her eye at any news of suffering or deprivation, which must surely be, if anything is, an irrefrangible reality. As death and danger are—her interest in Hyacinth is made the more intense by his pledged death, and she herself eventually wants to undertake the mortal mission. A perfect drunkard of reality, she is ever drawn to look for stronger and stronger drams.

Inevitably, of course, the great irony of her fate is that the more passionately she seeks reality and the happier she becomes in her belief that she is close to it, the further removed she is. Inevitably she must turn away from Hyacinth because she reads his moral seriousness as frivolousness; and inevitably she is led to Paul who, as she thinks, affirms her in a morality which is as real and serious as anything can be, an absolute morality which gives her permission to devaluate and even destroy all that she has known of human good because it has been connected with her own frivolous, self-betraying past. She cannot but mistake the nature of reality, for she believes it is a thing, a position, a finality, a bedrock. She is, in short, the very embodiment of the modern will which masks itself in virtue, making itself appear harmless, the will that hates itself and finds its manifestations guilty and is able to exist only if it operates in the name of virtue, that despises the variety and modulations of the human story and longs for an absolute humanity, which is but another way of saying a nothingness. In her alliance with Paul she constitutes a striking symbol of that powerful part of modern culture that exists by means of its claim to political innocence and by its false seriousness—the political awareness that is not aware, the social consciousness which hates full consciousness, the moral earnestness which is moral luxury.

The fatal ambiguity of the Princess and Paul is a prime condition of Hyacinth Robinson's tragedy. If we comprehend the complex totality that James has thus conceived, we understand that the novel is an incomparable representation of the spiritual circumstances of our civilization. I venture to call it incomparable because, although other writers have provided abundant substantiation of James's insight, no one has, like him, told us the truth in a single luminous act of creation. If we ask by what magic James was able to do what he did, the answer is to be found in what I have identified as the source of James's moral realism. For the novelist can tell the truth about Paul and the Princess only if, while he represents them in their ambiguity and error, he also allows them to exist in their pride and beauty: the moral realism that shows the ambiguity and error cannot refrain from showing the pride and beauty. Its power to tell the truth arises from its power of love. James had the imagination of disaster and that is why he is immediately relevant to us; but together with the imagination of disaster he had what the imagination of disaster often destroys and in our time is daily destroying, the imagination of love.

*Leslie A. Fiedler*
# SAUL BELLOW

With the publication of *Seize the Day*, Saul Bellow has become not merely a writer with whom it is possible to come to terms, but one with whom it is *necessary* to come to terms—perhaps of all our novelists the one we need most to understand, if we are to understand what the novel is doing at the present moment. Bellow has endured the almost ritual indignities of the beginning fictionist: his first novel a little over-admired and read by scarcely anyone; his second novel once more critically acclaimed, though without quite the thrill of discovery, and still almost ignored by the larger public; his third novel, thick, popular, reprinted in the paper-backs and somewhat resented by the first discoverers, who hate seeing what was exclusively theirs pass into the public domain; and now a fourth book: a collection of stories, most of which have appeared earlier, a play, and a new novella.

Suddenly, the novelist whom we have not ceased calling a "young writer" (it is a habit hard to break and the final indignity) is established and forty, a part of our lives and something for the really young to define themselves against. But it has become clear that he will continue to write, that he is not merely the author of a novel or two, but a *novelist;* and this in itself is a triumph, a rarity in recent American literary history and especially among the writers with whom we associate Bellow. We think of the whole line of Jewish-American novelists, so like him in origin and aspiration, of Daniel Fuchs and Henry Roth and Nathanael West, those poets and annalists of the thirties who did not survive their age, succumbing to death or Hollywood or a sheer exhaustion of spirit and subject. Or we think of Bellow's own contemporaries, the *Partisan Review* group, urban Jews growing up under the threat of failure and terror, the depression and Spain and the hopelessly foreseen coming of war. We remember, perhaps, Isaac Rosenfeld or H. J. Kaplan or Oscar Tarcov or Delmore Schwartz or even Lionel Trilling, who had also to be twice-born, committed first to Stalinism and then to disenchantment, but who were capable of using imaginatively only the disenchantment. And remembering these, we recall beginnings not quite fulfilled, achievements which somehow betrayed initial promises. Certain short stories remain in our minds (flanked by all those essays, those explanations and rejoinders and demonstrations of wit): Kaplan's "The Mohammedans," Rosenfeld's "The Pyramids," Schwartz's "In Dreams Begin Re-

Reprinted from *Prairie Schooner*, Summer, 1957, by permission of The University of Nebraska Press and the author. Copyright 1957 by The University of Nebraska Press, Lincoln, Nebraska.

sponsibilities," Trilling's "The Other Margaret"; but where except in *The Dangling Man* and *The Victim* and *Augie March* do the themes and motifs of the group find full novelistic expression?

We must begin to see Bellow, then, as the inheritor of a long tradition of false starts and abject retreats and grey inconclusions. There is a sense in which he fulfills the often frustrated attempt to possess the American imagination and to enter the American cultural scene of a line of Jewish fictionists which goes back beyond the post-war generation through Ben Hecht and Ludwig Lewisohn to Abe Cahan. A hundred, a thousand one-shot novelists, ephemeral successes and baffled eccentrics stand behind him, defining a subject: the need of the Jew in America to make clear his relationship to that country in terms of belonging or protest—and a language: a speech enriched by the dialectic and joyful intellectual play of Jewish conversation.

Bellow's own story is, then, like the archetypal Jewish dream a success story; since, like the standard characters in the tales of my grandfather (socialist though he was!), the novelist, too, has "worked himself up in America." Bellow's success must not be understood, however, as exclusively his own; for he emerges at the moment when the Jews for the first time move into the center of American culture, and he must be seen in the larger context. The background is familiar enough: the gradual breaking up of the Anglo-Saxon domination of our imagination: the relentless urbanization which makes rural myths and images no longer central to our experience; the exhaustion as vital themes of the Midwest and of the movement from the provinces to New York or Chicago or Paris; the turning again from West to East, from our own heartland back to Europe; and the discovery in the Jews of a people essentially urban, essentially Europe-oriented, a ready-made image for what the American longs to or fears he is being forced to become.

On all levels in the years since World War II, the Jewish-American writer feels imposed on him the role of being The American, of registering his experience for his compatriots and for the world as The American Experience. Not only his flirtation with Communism and his disengagement, but his very sense of exclusion, his most intimate awareness of loneliness and flight are demanded of him as public symbols. The Southerner and the Jew, the homosexual out of the miasma of Mississippi and the ex-radical out of the iron landscape of Chicago and New York—these seem the exclusive alternatives, contrasting yet somehow twinned symbols of America at mid-century. *Partisan Review* becomes for Europe and *Life* magazine the mouthpiece of intellectual America, not despite but because of its tiny readership and its specially determined contributors; and in Saul Bellow a writer emerges capable of transforming its obsessions into myths.

He must not, however, be seen only in this context. His appearance as the first Jewish-American novelist to stand at the center of American literature is flanked by a host of matching successes on other levels of culture and sub-culture. What Saul Bellow is for highbrow literature, Salinger is for upper middlebrow, Irwin Shaw for middle middlebrow and Herman Wouk for lower middlebrow. Even on the lowbrow levels, where there has been no such truce with anti-Semitism as prosperity has brought to the middle classes, two young Jews in contriving Superman have invented for the comic books a new version of the Hero, the first purely urban incarnation of the most ancient of mythic figures. The acceptance of Bellow as the leading novelist of his generation must be paired off with the appearance of Marjorie Morningstar on the front cover of *Time.* On all levels, the Jew is in the process of being mythicized into the representative American.

There is a temptation in all this to a kind of assimilation with the most insipid values of bourgeois life in the United States. It is to Bellow's credit that he has at once accepted the full challenge implicit in the identification of Jew with American, and yet has not succumbed to the temptation; that he has been willing to accept the burden of success without which he might have been cut off from the central subject of his time; and that he has accomplished this without essential compromise. In *Augie March,* which is the heart of his work (though technically not as successful as *The Victim* or *Seize the Day*), he has risked the final absurdity: the foot-loose Jewish boy, harried by urban machiavellians, the picaresque *schlimazl* out of Fuchs or Nathanael West, becomes Huck Finn; or, if you will, Huck is transformed into the foot-loose Jewish boy. It is hard to know which way of saying it gives a fuller sense of the absurdity and importance of the transaction. The point is, I think, that the identification saves both halves of the combination from sentimental falsification: Huck Finn, who has threatened for a long time to dissolve into the snub-nosed little rascal, bare-foot and overalled; and the Jewish *schlimazl,* who becomes only too easily the liberals' insufferable victim, say, Noah Ackerman in Irwin Shaw's *The Young Lions.*

The themes of Saul Bellow are not, after all, very different from those of the middlebrow Jewish novelists in step with whom he has "worked himself up"; but in treatment they become transformed. Like Wouk or Shaw, he, too, has written a War Novel: a book about the uncertainty of intellectual and Jew face to face with a commitment to regimentation and violence. But unlike Wouk and Shaw, Bellow has not merely taken the World War I novel of protest and adulterated it with popular front pieties. His intellectual is not shown up like Wouk's Keefer; his Jew does not prove himself as brave and brutal as his anti-Semitic buddies like Shaw's Ackerman or Wouk's Greenspan, whose presumable triumphs are in fact abject surrenders. The longing to relinquish the stereotyped protest of the twenties, no longer quite believed in, is present in Bellow's *Dangling Man,* but present as a *subject:* a temptation to be confronted, not a value to be celebrated.

*Dangling Man* is not an entirely successful book; it is a little mannered, a little incoherent, obviously a first novel. But it is fresh beyond all expecta-tion, unlike any American war book before or since; for Bellow has realized that for his generation the war itself is an anticlimax (too foreknown from a score of older novels to be really lived), that their real experience is the waiting, the dangling, the indecision before the draft. His book therefore ends, as it should, with its protagonist about to leave for camp and writing in his journal: "Hurray for regular hours! And for the supervision of the spirit! Long live regimentation!" In the purest of ironies, the slogans of accommodation are neither accepted nor rejected, but suspended.

Similarly, in *The Victim* Bellow takes up what is, perhaps, the theme *par excellence* of the liberaloid novel of the forties: anti-Semitism. In proletarian novels, though many were written by Jews, this was a subject only peripherally treated; for the Jew in the Communist movement, Judaism was the enemy, Zionism and the Jewish religion the proper butt of satire and dissent. But Hitler had made a difference, releasing a flood of pious protests against discrimination; from Arthur Miller's *Focus* to John Hersey's *The Wall,* via *Gentlemen's Agreement, The Professor's Umbrella,* etc., Jew and Gentile alike took up the subject over and over. In a time when the Worker had been replaced by the Little Man as a focus for undiscriminating sympathy, the Little Jew took his place beside the Little Negro, the Little Chinese, the Little Paraplegic as a favorite victim. Even what passed for War Novels were often merely anti-Semitic fictions in disguise, the war itself being treated only as an occasion for testing a Noble Young Jew under the pressure of ignorant hostility.

In the typical middlebrow novel, it was seldom a real Jew who was exposed to persecution; rather some innocent gentile who by putting on glasses mysteriously came to look Jewish or some high-minded reporter only pretending to be a Jew. In part what is involved is the commercial necessity for finding a gimmick to redeem an otherwise overworked subject; but in part what is at stake is surely a confusion in the liberal, middlebrow mind about what a Jew is anyhow: a sneaking suspicion that Jew-baiting is real but Jews are imaginary, just as, to the same mind, witch-hunting is real but witches only fictions.

In Bellow's book about anti-Semitism, *The Victim,* once more the confusion becomes the subject. It is Asa Leventhal, not the author, who is uncertain of what it means to be a Jew, because he does not know yet what it is to be a man; and neither he nor his author will be content with the simple equation: the victim equals the Jew, the Jew the victim. In *The Victim,* Jew and anti-Semite are each other's prey as they are each other's beloved. At the moment when the Jew in general, when the author himself as well as his protagonist, have moved into situations of security, however tenuous, inflicting injury in their scramble to win that security, Bellow alone among our novelists has had the imagination and the sheer nerve to portray the Jew, the Little Jew, as victimizer as well as victim. Allbee may be mad, a pathological anti-Semite and a bum, but his charge that Leventhal's success was achieved somehow at his expense is not utter nonsense. It is the necessary antidote to the self-pity of the Jew, one part of a total ambiguous picture. In the slow, grey, low-keyed exposition of *The Victim,* Leventhal's violence and his patience, his desire to exculpate himself and his sense of guilt, his haunting by the anti-Semite he haunts, become for us truths, part of our awareness of our place as Jews in the American scene.

As *The Victim* is Bellow's most specifically Jewish book, *Augie March* (in this, as in all other respects, a reaction from the former) is his most generally American. Its milieu is Jewish American, its speech patterns somehow moulded by Yiddish, but its theme is the native theme of *Huckle-*

*berry Finn:* the rejection of power and commitment and success, the pursuit of a primal innocence.[1] It is a strangely non-Jewish book in being concerned not with a man's rise but with his evasion of rising; and yet even in that respect it reminds us of *David Levinsky,* of the criticism of David implicit in the text and entrusted to the Socialist characters. It is as if David had been granted a son, a grandson, to try again—to seek a more genuine Americanism of noncommital. Certainly, Bellow's character is granted a symbolic series of sexual successes to balance off the sexual failures of Cahan's protagonist. But the socialism of Cahan does not move his descendant; it has become in the meanwhile Soviet Communism, an alternative image of material success, and has failed; so that there is left to Augie only the denial of the values of capitalism without a corresponding allegiance, a desire to flee success from scene to scene, from girl to girl, from father to father—in favor of what? The most bitter of Happy Endings as well as the most negative, the truly American Happy Ending: no reunion with the family, no ultimately happy marriage, no return to the native place—only a limitless disponibility guarded like a treasure. It is, of course, the ending of *Huckleberry Finn,* an ending which must be played out as comedy to be tolerable at all; but unlike Twain, Bellow, though he has found the proper tone for his episodes, cannot recapture it for his close. *Augie,* which begins with such rightness, such conviction, does not know how to end; shriller and shriller, wilder and wilder, it finally whirls apart in a frenzy of fake euphoria and exclamatory prose.

*Seize the Day* is a pendant and resolution to *Augie March.* Also a study of success and failure, this time it treats them in contemporary terms rather than classic ones, reworking directly a standard middlebrow theme. Call it "The Death of a Salesman" and think of Arthur Miller. It is the price of failure in a world dedicated to success that Bellow is dealing with now; or more precisely, the self-consciousness of failure in a world where it is not only shameful but rare; or most exactly of all, the bitterness of success and failure become pawns in the deadly game between father and son. Bellow is not very successful when he attempts to deal with the sentimental and erotic relations that are the staples of the great European novels; his women tend to be nympholeptic projections, fantasies based on girls one never had; and his husbands and wives seem convincing only at the moment of parting. But he comes into his own when he turns to the emotional transactions of males inside the family: brother and brother, son and father—or father-hating son and machiavellian surrogate father. It is the muted rage of such relationships that is the emotional stuff of his best work; and in *Seize the Day,* it is the dialogues of Tommy and his old man, Tommy and the sharper Tamkin that move us, prepare us for Tommy's bleakest encounter: with himself and the prescience of his own death.

But how, we are left asking, has Bellow made tragedy of a theme that remains in the hands of Arthur Miller sentimentality and "good theatre"? It is just this magical transformation of the most travestied of middlebrow themes which is Bellow's greatest triumph. That transformation is in part the work of style, a function of language. Bellow is in no sense an experimental writer; the scraps of avant-garde technique which survive in *The Dangling Man* are purged away in *The Victim;* yet he has managed to resist the impulse to lifeless lucidity which elsewhere has taken over in a literature reacting to the linguistic experiments of the twenties. There is always the sense of a living voice in his prose, for his books are all dramatic; and though this sometimes means a deliberate muting of rhetoric for the sake of characterization, it just as often provides occasions for a release of full virtuosity. Muted or released, his language is never dull or merely expedient, but always moves under tension, toward or away from a kind of rich, crazy poetry, a juxtaposition of high and low style, elegance and slang, unlike anything else in English except *Moby-Dick,* though at the same time not unrelated in range and variety to spoken Yiddish.

Since Bellow's style is based on a certain conversational ideal at once intellectual and informal, dialogue is for him necessarily a distillation of his strongest effects. Sometimes one feels his characters' speeches as the main events of the books in which they occur; certainly they have the impact of words exchanged among Jews, that is to say, the impact of actions, not merely overheard but *felt,* like kisses or blows. Implicit in the direction of his style is a desire to encompass a world larger, richer, more disorderly and untrammelled than that of any other writer of his generation; it is this which impels him toward the picaresque, the sprawling, episodic manner of *Augie March.* But there is a counter impulse in him toward the tight, rigidly organized, underplayed style of *The Victim:* and at his best, I think, as in *Seize the Day,* an ability to balance the two tendencies against each other: hysteria and catalepsy, the centrifugal and the centripetal in a sort of perilous rest.

But the triumphs of Bellow are not mere triumphs of style; sometimes indeed they must survive the collapse of that style into mannerism, mechanical self-parody. Beyond an ear, Bellow possesses a fortunate negative talent: a constitutional inability to dissolve his characters into their representative types, to compromise their individuality for the sake of a point. It is not merely that his protagonists refuse to blur into the generalized Little People, the Victims of sentimental liberalism; but that they are themselves portrayed as being conscious of their struggle against such debasement. That struggle is, indeed, the essence of their self-consciousness, their self-definition. Their invariable loneliness is felt by them and by us not only as a function of urban life and the atomization of culture, but as something *willed:* the condition and result of their search to know what they are.

More, perhaps, than any other recent novelist, Bellow is aware that the collapse of the proletarian novel, which marks the starting place of his own art, has meant more than the disappearance of a convention in the history of fiction. With the disappearance of the proletarian novel as a form there has taken place the gradual dissolution of the last widely shared definition of man: man as the product of society. If man seems at the moment extraordinarily lonely, it is not only because he finds it hard to communicate with his fellows, but because he has lost touch with any overarching definition of himself.

This Bellow realizes; as he realizes that it is precisely in such loneliness, once man learns not to endure but to *become* that loneliness, that man can rediscover his identity and his fellowship with others. We recognize the Bellow character because he is openly what we are in secret, because he is us without our customary defenses. Such a protagonist lives nowhere except in the City; he camps temporarily in boarding houses or lonely hotels, sits by himself at the corner table of some seedy restaurant or climbs back-breaking stairways in search of another whose existence no one will admit. He is the man whose wife is off visiting her mother or has just left him; the man who returns to find his house in disorder or inhabited by a squalid derelict; the man who flees his room to follow the funeral of someone he never knew.

He is essential man, man stripped of success and belongness, even of failure; he is man disowned by his father, unrecognized by his son, man without woman, man face to face with himself, which means for Bellow face to face not with a fact but a question: "What am I?" To which the only answer is: "He who asks!" But such a man is at once the Jew in perpetual exile and Huck Finn in whom are blended with perfect irony the twin American beliefs that the answer to all questions is always over the next horizon and that there is no answer now or ever.

# 3. THE USES OF TRADITION

## The Theory

*T. S. Eliot*

### TRADITION AND THE INDIVIDUAL TALENT

**I**

In English writing we seldom speak of tradition, though we occasionally apply its name in deploring its absence. We cannot refer to "the tradition" or to "a tradition"; at most, we employ the adjective in saying that the poetry of So-and-so is "traditional" or even "too traditional." Seldom, perhaps, does the word appear except in a phrase of censure. If otherwise, it is vaguely approbative, with the implication, as to the work approved, of some pleasing archaeological reconstruction. You can hardly make the word agreeable to English ears without this comfortable reference to the reassuring science of archaeology.

Certainly the word is not likely to appear in our appreciations of living or dead writers. Every nation, every race, has not only its own creative, but its own critical turn of mind; and is even more oblivious of the shortcomings and limitations of its critical habits than of those of its creative genius. We know, or think we know, from the enormous mass of critical writing that has appeared in the French language the critical method or habit of the French; we only conclude (we are such unconscious people) that the French are "more critical" than we, and sometimes even plume ourselves a little with the fact, as if the French were the less spontaneous. Perhaps they are; but we might remind ourselves that criticism is as inevitable as breathing, and that we should be none the worse for articulating what passes in our minds when we read a book and feel an emotion about

Reprinted from *Selected Essays of T. S. Eliot* by permission of Harcourt, Brace & World, Inc. Copyright 1932, 1936, 1950 by Harcourt, Brace & World, Inc., New York, N. Y. Copyright 1960 by T. S. Eliot.

it, for criticizing our own minds in their work of criticism. One of the facts that might come to light in this process is our tendency to insist, when we praise a poet, upon those aspects of his work in which he least resembles any one else. In these aspects or parts of his work we pretend to find what is individual, what is the peculiar essence of the man. We dwell with satisfaction upon the poet's difference from his predecessors, especially his immediate predecessors; we endeavour to find something that can be isolated in order to be enjoyed. Whereas if we approach a poet without this prejudice we shall often find that not only the best, but the most individual parts of his work may be those in which the dead poets, his ancestors, assert their immortality most vigorously. And I do not mean the impressionable period of adolescence, but the period of full maturity.

Yet if the only form of tradition, of handing down, consisted in following the ways of the immediate generation before us in a blind or timid adherence to its successes, "tradition" should positively be discouraged. We have seen many such simple currents soon lost in the sand; and novelty is better than repetition. Tradition is a matter of much wider significance. It cannot be inherited, and if you want it you must obtain it by great labour. It involves, in the first place, the historical sense, which we may call nearly indispensable to any one who would continue to be a poet beyond his twenty-fifth year; and the historical sense involves a perception, not only of the pastness of the past, but of its presence; the historical sense compels a man to write not merely with his own generation in his bones, but with a feeling that the whole of the literature of Europe from Homer and within it the whole of the literature of his own country has a simultaneous existence and composes a simultaneous order. This historical sense, which is a sense of the timeless as well as of the temporal and of the timeless and of the temporal together, is what makes a writer traditional. And it is at the same time what makes a writer most acutely conscious of his place in time, of his own contemporaneity.

No poet, no artist of any art, has his complete meaning alone. His significance, his appreciation is the appreciation of his relation to the dead poets and artists. You cannot value him alone; you must set him, for contrast and comparison, among the dead. I mean this as a principle of aesthetic, not merely historical, criticism. The necessity that he shall conform, that he shall cohere, is not onesided; what happens when a new work of art is created is something that happens simultaneously to all the works of art which preceded it. The existing monuments form an ideal order among themselves, which is modified by the introduction of the new (the really new) work of art among them. The existing order is complete before the new work arrives; for order to persist after the supervention of novelty, the *whole* existing order must be, if ever so slightly, altered; and so the relations, proportions, values of each work of art toward the whole are readjusted; and this is conformity between the old and the new. Whoever has approved this idea of order, of the form of European, of English literature will not find it preposterous that the past should be altered by the present as much as the present is directed by the past. And the poet who is aware of this will be aware of great difficulties and responsibilities.

In a peculiar sense he will be aware also that he must inevitably be judged by the standards of the past. I say judged, not amputated, by them; not judged to be as good as, or worse or better than, the dead; and certainly not judged by the canons of dead critics. It is a judgment, a comparison, in which two things are measured by each other. To conform merely would be for the new work not really to conform at all; it would not be new, and would therefore not be a work of art. And we do not quite say that the new is more valuable because it fits in; but its fitting in is a test of its value —a test, it is true, which can only be slowly and cautiously applied, for we are none of us infallible judges of conformity. We say: it appears to conform, and is perhaps individual, or it appears individual, and may conform; but we are hardly likely to find that it is one and not the other.

To proceed to a more intelligible exposition of the relation of the poet to the past: he can neither take the past as a lump, an indiscriminate bolus, nor can he form himself wholly on one or two private admirations, nor can he form himself wholly upon one preferred period. The first course is inadmissible, the second is an important experience of youth, and the third is a pleasant and highly desirable supplement. The poet must be very conscious of the main current, which does not at all flow invariably through the most distinguished reputations. He must be quite aware of the obvious fact that art never improves, but that the material of art is never quite the same. He must be aware that the mind of Europe—the mind of his own country—a mind which he learns in time to be much more important than his own private mind—is a mind which changes, and that this change is a development which abandons nothing *en route,* which does not superannuate either Shakespeare, or Homer, or the rock drawing of the Magdalenian draughtsmen. That this development, refinement perhaps, complication certainly, is not, from the point of view of the artist, any improvement. Perhaps not even an improvement from the point of view of the psychologist or not to the extent which we imagine; perhaps only in the end based upon a complication in economics and machinery. But the difference between the present and the past is that the conscious present is an awareness of the past in a way and to an extent which the past's awareness of itself cannot show.

Some one said: "The dead writers are remote from us because we *know* so much more than they did." Precisely, and they are that which we know.

I am alive to a usual objection to what is clearly part of my programme for the *métier* of poetry. The objection is that the doctrine requires a ridiculous amount of erudition (pedantry), a claim which can be rejected by appeal to the lives of poets in any pantheon. It will even be affirmed that much learning deadens or perverts poetic sensibility. While, however, we persist in believing that a poet ought to know as much as will not encroach upon his necessary receptivity and necessary laziness, it is not desirable to confine knowledge to whatever can be put into a useful shape for examinations, drawing-rooms, or the still more pretentious modes of publicity. Some can absorb knowledge, the more tardy must sweat for it. Shakespeare acquired more essential history from Plutarch than most men could from the whole British Museum. What is to be insisted upon is that the poet must develop or procure the consciousness of the past and that he should continue to develop this consciousness throughout his career.

What happens is a continual surrender of himself as he is at the moment to something which is more valuable. The progress of an artist is a continual self-sacrifice, a continual extinction of personality.

There remains to define this process of depersonalization and its relation to the sense of tradition. It is in this depersonalization that art may be said to approach the condition of science. I, therefore, invite you to consider, as a suggestive analogy, the action which takes place when a bit of finely filiated platinum is introduced into a chamber containing oxygen and sulphur dioxide.

## II

Honest criticism and sensitive appreciation are directed not upon the poet but upon the poetry. If we attend to the confused cries of the newspaper critics and the *susurrus* of popular repetition that follows, we shall hear the names of poets in great numbers; if we seek not Blue-book knowledge but the enjoyment of poetry, and ask for a poem, we shall seldom find it. I have tried to point out the importance of the relation of the poem to other poems by other authors, and suggested the conception of poetry as a living whole of all the poetry that has ever been written. The other aspect of this Impersonal theory of poetry is the relation of the poem to its author. And I hinted, by an analogy, that the mind of the mature poet differs from that of the immature one not precisely in any valuation of "personality," not being necessarily more interesting, or having "more to say," but rather by being a more finely perfected medium in which special, or very varied, feelings are at liberty to enter into new combinations.

The analogy was that of the catalyst. When the two gases previously mentioned are mixed in the presence of a filament of platinum, they form sulphurous acid. This combination takes place only if the platinum is present; nevertheless the newly formed acid contains no trace of platinum, and the platinum itself is apparently unaffected; has remained inert, neutral, and unchanged. The mind of the poet is the shred of platinum. It may partly or exclusively operate upon the experience of the man himself; but, the more perfect the artist, the more completely separate in him will be the man who suffers and the mind which creates; the more perfectly will the mind digest and transmute the passions which are its material.

The experience, you will notice, the elements which enter the presence of the transforming catalyst, are of two kinds: emotions and feelings. The effect of a work of art upon the person who enjoys it is an experience different in kind from any experience not of art. It may be formed out of one emotion, or may be a combination of several; and various feelings, inhering for the writer in particular words or phrases or images, may be added to compose the final result. Or great poetry may be made without the direct use of any emotion whatever: composed out of feelings solely. Canto XV of the *Inferno* (Brunetto Latini) is a working up of the emotion evident in the situation; but the effect, though single as that of any work of art, is obtained by considerable complexity of detail. The last quatrain gives an image, a feeling attaching to an image, which "came," which did not develop simply out of what precedes, but which was probably in suspension in the poet's mind until the proper combination arrived for it to add itself to. The poet's mind is in fact a receptacle for seizing and storing up numberless feelings, phrases, images, which remain there until all the particles which can unite to form a new compound are present together.

If you compare several representative passages of the greatest poetry you see how great is the variety of types of combination, and also how completely any semi-ethical criterion of "sublimity" misses the mark. For it is not the "greatness," the intensity, of the emotions, the components, but the intensity of the artistic process, the pressure, so to speak, under which the fusion takes place, that counts. The episode of Paolo and Francesca employs a definite emotion, but the intensity of the poetry is something quite different from whatever intensity in the supposed experience it may give the impression of. It is no more intense, furthermore, than Canto XXVI, the voyage of Ulysses, which has not the direct dependence upon an emotion. Great variety is possible in the process of transmutation of emotion: the murder of Agamemnon, or the agony of Othello, gives an artistic effect apparently closer to a possible original than the scenes from Dante. In the *Agamemnon*, the artistic emotion approximates to the emotion of an actual spectator; in *Othello* to the emotion of the protagonist himself. But the difference between art and the event is always absolute; the combination which is the murder of Agamemnon is probably as complex as that which is the voyage of Ulysses. In either case there has been a fusion of elements. The ode of Keats contains a number of feelings which have nothing particular to do with the nightingale, but which the nightingale, partly, perhaps, because of its attractive name, and partly because of its reputation, served to bring together.

The point of view which I am struggling to attack is perhaps related to the metaphysical theory of the substantial unity of the soul: for my meaning is, that the poet has, not a "personality" to express, but a particular medium, which is only a medium and not a personality, in which impressions and experiences combine in peculiar and unexpected ways. Impressions and experiences which are important for the man may take no place in the poetry, and those which become important in the poetry may play quite a negligible part in the man, the personality.

I will quote a passage which is unfamiliar enough to be regarded with fresh attention in the light—or darkness—of these observations:

> *And now methinks I could e'en chide myself*
> *For doating on her beauty, though her death*
> *Shall be revenged after no common action.*
> *Does the silkworm expend her yellow labours*
> *For thee? For thee does she undo herself?*
> *Are lordships sold to maintain ladyships*
> *For the poor benefit of a bewildering minute?*
> *Why does yon fellow falsify highways,*
> *And put his life between the judge's lips,*
> *To refine such a thing—keeps horse and men*
> *To beat their valours for her? . . .*

In this passage (as is evident if it is taken in its context) there is a combination of positive and negative emotions: an intensely strong attraction toward beauty and an equally intense fascination by the ugliness which is contrasted with it and which destroys it. This balance of contrasted emotion is in the dramatic situation to which the speech is pertinent, but that situation alone is inadequate to it. This is, so to speak, the structural emotion, provided by the drama. But the whole effect, the dominant tone, is due to the fact that a number of floating feelings, having an affinity to this emotion by no means superficially evident, have combined with it to give us a new art emotion.

It is not in his personal emotions, the emotions provoked by particular events in his life, that the poet is in any way remarkable or interesting. His particular emotions may be simple, or crude, or flat. The emotion in his poetry will be a very complex thing, but not with the complexity of the emotions of people who have very complex or unusual emotions in life. One error, in fact, of eccentricity in poetry is to seek for new human emotions to express; and in this search for novelty in the wrong place it discovers the perverse. The business of the poet is not to find new emotions, but to use the ordinary ones and, in working them up into poetry, to express feelings which are not in actual emotions at all. And emotions which he has never experienced will serve his turn as well as those familiar to him. Consequently, we must believe that "emotion recollected in tranquillity" is an inexact formula. For it is neither emotion, nor recollection, nor, without distortion of meaning, tranquillity. It is a concentration, and a new thing resulting from the concentration, of a very great number of experiences which to the practical and active person would not seem to be experiences at all; it is a concentration which does not happen consciously or of deliberation. These experiences are not "recollected," and they finally unite in an atmosphere which is "tranquil" only in that it is a passive attending upon the event. Of course this is not quite the whole story. There is a great deal, in the writing of poetry, which must be conscious and deliberate. In fact, the bad poet is usually unconscious where he ought to be conscious, and conscious where he ought to be unconscious. Both errors tend to make him "personal." Poetry is not a turning loose of emotion, but an escape from emotion; it is not the expression of personality, but an escape from personality. But, of course, only those who have personality and emotions know what it means to want to escape from these things.

### III

ὁ δὲ νοῦς ἴσως Θειότερόν τι χαὶ ἀπαθές ἐστιν.

This essay proposes to halt at the frontier of metaphysics or mysticism, and confine itself to such practical conclusions as can be applied by the responsible person interested in poetry. To divert interest from the poet to the poetry is a laudable aim: for it would conduce to a juster estimation of actual poetry, good and bad. There are many people who appreciate the expression of sincere emotion in verse, and there is a smaller number of people who can appreciate technical excellence. But very few know when there is an expression of *significant* emotion, emotion which has its life in the poem and not in the history of the poet. The emotion of art is impersonal. And the poet cannot reach this impersonality without surrendering himself wholly to the work to be done. And he is not likely to know what is to be done unless he lives in what is not merely the present, but the present moment of the past, unless he is conscious, not of what is dead, but of what is already living.

*T. S. Eliot*

# MILTON (I)

While it must be admitted that Milton is a very great poet indeed, it is something of a puzzle to decide in what his greatness consists. On analysis, the marks against him appear both more numerous and more significant than the marks to his credit. As a man, he is antipathetic. Either from the moralist's point of view, or from the theologian's point of view, or from the psychologist's point of view, or from that of the political philosopher, or judging by the ordinary standards of likeableness in human beings, Milton is unsatisfactory. The doubts which I have to express about him are more serious than these. His greatness as a poet has been sufficiently celebrated, though I think largely for the wrong reasons, and without the proper reservations. His misdeeds as a poet have been called attention to, as by Mr. Ezra Pound, but usually in passing. What seems to me necessary is to assert at the same time his greatness—in that what he could do well he did better than anyone else has ever done—and the serious charges to be made against him, in respect of the deterioration—the peculiar kind of deterioration—to which he subjected the language.

Many people will agree that a man may be a great artist, and yet have a bad influence. There is more of Milton's influence in the badness of the bad verse of the eighteenth century than of anybody's else: he certainly did more harm than Dryden and Pope, and perhaps a good deal of the obloquy which has fallen on these two poets, especially the latter, because of their influence, ought to be transferred to Milton. But to put the matter simply in terms of "bad influence" is not necessarily to bring a serious charge: because a good deal of the responsibility, when we state the problem in these terms, may devolve on the eighteenth-century poets themselves for being such bad poets that they were incapable of being influenced except for ill. There is a good deal more to the charge against Milton than this; and it appears a good deal more serious if we affirm that Milton's poetry could *only* be an influence for the worse, upon any poet whatever. It is more serious,

Contributed to *Essays and Studies* of The English Association, Oxford University Press, 1936. Reprinted from *On Poetry and Poets* by T. S. Eliot, by permission of Farrar, Straus and Cudahy, Inc., New York, N. Y. Copyright 1957 by T. S. Eliot.

also, if we affirm that Milton's bad influence may be traced much farther than the eighteenth century, and much farther than upon bad poets: if we say that it was an influence against which we still have to struggle.

There is a large class of persons, including some who appear in print as critics, who regard any censure upon a "great" poet as a breach of the peace, as an act of wanton iconoclasm, or even hoodlumism. The kind of derogatory criticism that I have to make upon Milton is not intended for such persons, who cannot understand that it is more important, in some vital respects, to be a *good* poet than to be a *great* poet; and of what I have to say I consider that the only jury of judgment is that of the ablest poetical practitioners of my own time.

The most important fact about Milton, for my purpose, is his blindness. I do not mean that to go blind in middle life is itself enough to determine the whole nature of a man's poetry. Blindness must be considered in conjunction with Milton's personality and character, and the peculiar education which he received. It must also be considered in connexion with his devotion to, and expertness in, the art of music. Had Milton been a man of very keen senses—I mean of *all* the five senses—his blindness would not have mattered so much. But for a man whose sensuousness, such as it was, had been withered early by book-learning, and whose gifts were naturally aural, it mattered a great deal. It would seem, indeed, to have helped him to concentrate on what he could do best.

At no period is the visual imagination conspicuous in Milton's poetry. It would be as well to have a few illustrations of what I mean by visual imagination. From *Macbeth:*

> *This guest of summer,*
> *The temple-haunting martlet, does approve*
> *By his loved mansionry that the heaven's breath*
> *Smells wooingly here: no jutty, frieze,*
> *Buttress, nor coign of vantage, but this bird*
> *Hath made his pendent bed and procreant cradle:*
> *Where they most breed and haunt, I have observed*
> *The air is delicate.*

It may be observed that such an image, as well as another familiar quotation from a little later in the same play,

> *Light thickens, and the crow*
> *Makes wing to the rooky wood*

not only offer something to the eye, but, so to speak, to the common sense. I mean that they convey the feeling of being in a particular place at a particular time. The comparison with Shakespeare offers another indication of the peculiarity of Milton. With Shakespeare, far more than with any other poet in English, the combinations of words offer perpetual novelty; they enlarge the meaning of the individual words joined: thus "procreant cradle," "rooky wood." In comparison, Milton's images do not give this sense of particularity, nor are the separate words developed in significance. His language is, if one may use the term without disparagement, *artificial* and *conventional*.

> O'er the smooth enamel'd green . . .
>                    . . . paths of this drear wood
> The nodding horror of whose shady brows
> Threats the forlorn and wandering passenger.

("Shady brow" here is a diminution of the value of the two words from their use in the line from *Dr. Faustus*

> Shadowing more beauty in their airy brows.)

The imagery in *L'Allegro* and *Il Penseroso* is all general:

> While the ploughman near at hand,
> Whistles o'er the furrowed land,
> And the milkmaid singeth blithe,
> And the mower whets his scythe,
> And every shepherd tells his tale,
> Under the hawthorn in the dale.

It is not a particular ploughman, milkmaid, and shepherd that Milton sees (as Wordsworth might see them); the sensuous effect of these verses is entirely on the ear, and is joined to the concepts of ploughman, milkmaid, and shepherd. Even in his most mature work, Milton does not infuse new life into the word, as Shakespeare does.

> The sun to me is dark
> And silent as the moon,
> When she deserts the night
> Hid in her vacant interlunar cave.

Here *interlunar* is certainly a stroke of genius, but is merely combined with "vacant" and "cave," rather than giving and receiving life from them. Thus it is not so unfair, as it might at first appear, to say that Milton writes English like a dead language. The criticism has been made with regard to his involved syntax. But a tortuous style, when its peculiarity is aimed at precision (as with Henry James), is not necessarily a dead one; only when the complication is dictated by a demand of verbal music, instead of by any demand of sense.

> Thrones, dominations, princedoms, virtues, powers,
> If these magnific titles yet remain
> Not merely titular, since by decree
> Another now hath to himself engrossed
> All power, and us eclipsed under the name
> Of King anointed, for whom all this haste
> Of midnight march, and hurried meeting here,
> This only to consult how we may best
> With what may be devised of honours new
> Receive him coming to receive from us
> Knee-tribute yet unpaid, prostration vile,
> Too much to one, but double how endured,
> To one and to his image now proclaimed?

With which compare:

However, he didn't mind thinking that if Cissy should prove all that was likely enough their having a subject in common couldn't but practically conduce; though the moral of it all amounted rather to a portent, the one that Haughty, by the same token, had done least to reassure him against, of the extent to which the native jungle harboured the female specimen and to which its ostensible cover, the vast level of mixed growths stirred wavingly in whatever breeze, was apt to be identifiable but as an agitation of the latest redundant thing in ladies' hats.

This quotation, taken almost at random from *The Ivory Tower,* is not intended to represent Henry James at any hypothetical "best," any more than the noble passage from *Paradise Lost* is meant to be Milton's hypothetical worst. The question is the difference of intention, in the elaboration of styles both of which depart so far from lucid simplicity. The sound, of course, is never irrelevant, and the style of James certainly depends for its effect a good deal on the sound of a voice, James's own, painfully explaining. But the complication, with James, is due to a determination not to simplify, and in that simplification lose any of the real intricacies and by-paths of mental movement; whereas the complication of a Miltonic sentence is an active complication, a complication deliberately introduced into what was a previously simplified and abstract thought. The dark angel here is not *thinking* or conversing, but making a speech carefully prepared for him; and the arrangement is for the sake of musical value, not for significance. A straightforward utterance, as of a Homeric or Dantesque character, would make the speaker very much more real to us; but reality is no part of the intention. We have in fact to read such a passage not analytically, to get the poetic impression. I am not suggesting that Milton has no idea to convey which he regards as important: only that the syntax is determined by the musical significance, by the auditory imagination, rather than by the attempt to follow actual speech or thought. It is at least more nearly possible to distinguish the pleasure which arises from the *noise,* from the pleasure due to other elements, than with the verse of Shakespeare, in which the auditory imagination and the imagination of the other senses are more nearly fused, and fused together with the thought. The result with Milton is, in one sense of the word, *rhetoric.* That term is not intended to be derogatory. This kind of "rhetoric" is not necessarily bad in its influence; but it may be considered bad in relation to the historical life of a language as a whole. I have said elsewhere that the living English which was Shakespeare's became split up into two components one of which was exploited by Milton and the other by Dryden. Of the two, I still think Dryden's development the healthier, because it was Dryden who preserved, so far as it was preserved at all, the tradition of conversational language in poetry: and I might add that it seems to me easier to get back to healthy language from Dryden than it is to get back to it from Milton. For what such a generalization is worth, Milton's influence on the eighteenth century was much more deplorable than Dryden's.

If several very important reservations and exceptions are made, I think that it is not unprofitable to compare Milton's development with that of

*deliberate*

James Joyce. The initial similarities are musical taste and abilities, followed by musical training, wide and curious knowledge, gift for acquiring languages, and remarkable powers of memory perhaps fortified by defective vision. The important difference is that Joyce's imagination is not naturally of so purely auditory a type as Milton's. In his early work, and at least in part of *Ulysses,* there is visual and other imagination of the highest kind; and I may be mistaken in thinking that the later part of *Ulysses* shows a turning from the visible world to draw rather on the resources of phantasmagoria. In any case, one may suppose that the replenishment of visual imagery during later years has been insufficient; so that what I find in *Work in Progress* is an auditory imagination abnormally sharpened at the expense of the visual. There is still a little to be seen, and what there is to see is worth looking at. And I would repeat that with Joyce this development seems to me largely due to circumstances: whereas Milton may be said never to have seen anything. For Milton, therefore, the concentration on sound was wholly a benefit. Indeed, I find, in reading *Paradise Lost,* that I am happiest where there is least to visualize. The eye is not shocked in his twilit Hell as it is in the Garden of Eden, where I for one can get pleasure from the verse only by the deliberate effort not to visualize Adam and Eve and their surroundings.

I am not suggesting any close parallel between the "rhetoric" of Milton and the later style of Joyce. It is a different music; and Joyce always maintains some contact with the conversational tone. But it may prove to be equally a blind alley for the future development of the language.

A disadvantage of the rhetorical style appears to be, that a dislocation takes place, through the hypertrophy of the auditory imagination at the expense of the visual and tactile, so that the inner meaning is separated from the surface, and tends to become something occult, or at least without effect upon the reader until fully understood. To extract everything possible from *Paradise Lost,* it would seem necessary to read it in two different ways, first solely for the sound, and second for the sense. The full beauty of his long periods can hardly be enjoyed while we are wrestling with the meaning as well; and for the pleasure of the ear the meaning is hardly necessary, except in so far as certain key-words indicate the emotional tone of the passage. Now Shakespeare, or Dante, will bear innumerable readings, but at each reading all the elements of appreciation can be present. There is no interruption between the surface that these poets present to you and the core. While therefore, I cannot pretend to have penetrated to any "secret" of these poets, I feel that such appreciation of their work as I am capable of points in the right direction; whereas I cannot feel that my appreciation of Milton leads anywhere outside of the mazes of sound. That, I feel, would be the matter for a separate study, like that of Blake's prophetic books; it might be well worth the trouble, but would have little to do with my interest in the poetry. So far as I perceive anything, it is a glimpse of a theology that I find in large part repellent, expressed through a mythology which would have better been left in the Book of *Genesis,* upon which Milton has not improved. There seems to me to be a division, in Milton, between the philosopher or theologian and the poet; and, for the latter,

I suspect also that this concentration upon the auditory imagination leads to at least an occasional levity. I can enjoy the roll of

> *. . . Cambula, seat of Cathaian Can*
> *And Samarchand by Oxus, Temir's throne,*
> *To Paquin of Sinaean kings, and thence*
> *To Agra and Lahor of great Mogul*
> *Down to the golden Chersonese, or where*
> *The Persian in Ecbatan sate, or since*
> *In Hispahan, or where the Russian Ksar*
> *On Mosco, or the Sultan in Bizance,*
> *Turchestan-born . . . ,*

and the rest of it, but I feel that this is not serious poetry, not poetry fully occupied about its business, but rather a solemn game. More often, admittedly, Milton uses proper names in moderation, to obtain the same effect of magnificence with them as does Marlowe—nowhere perhaps better than in the passage from *Lycidas:*

> *Whether beyond the stormy Hebrides,*
> *Where thou perhaps under the whelming tide*
> *Visit'st the bottom of the monstrous world;*
> *Or whether thou to our moist vows deny'd*
> *Sleep'st by the fable of Bellerus old,*
> *Where the great vision of the guarded Mount*
> *Looks toward Namancos and Bayona's hold . . .*

than which for the single effect of grandeur of sound, there is nothing finer in poetry.

I make no attempt to appraise the "greatness" of Milton in relation to poets who seem to me more comprehensive and better balanced; it has seemed to me more fruitful for the present to press the parallel between *Paradise Lost* and *Work in Progress;* and both Milton and Joyce are so exalted in their own kinds, in the whole of literature, that the only writers with whom to compare them are writers who have attempted something very different. Our views about Joyce, in any case, must remain at the present time tentative. But there are two attitudes both of which are necessary and right to adopt in considering the work of any poet. One is when we isolate him, when we try to understand the rules of his own game, adopt his own point of view: the other, perhaps less usual, is when we measure him by outside standards, most pertinently by the standards of language and of something called Poetry, in our own language and in the whole history of European literature. It is from the second point of view that my objections to Milton are made: it is from this point of view that we can go so far as to say that, although his work realizes superbly one important element in poetry, he may still be considered as having done damage to the English language from which it has not wholly recovered.

*T. S. Eliot*

# MILTON (II)

Samuel Johnson, addressing himself to examine Milton's versification, in the *Rambler* of Saturday, January 12, 1751, thought it necessary to excuse his temerity in writing upon a subject already so fully discussed. In justification of his essay this great critic and poet remarked: "There are, in every age, new errors to be rectified, and new prejudices to be opposed." I am obliged to phrase my own apology rather differently. The errors of our own times have been rectified by vigorous hands, and the prejudices opposed by commanding voices. Some of the errors and prejudices have been associated with my own name, and of these in particular I shall find myself impelled to speak; it will, I hope, be attributed to me for modesty rather than for conceit if I maintain that no one can correct an error with better authority than the person who has been held responsible for it. And there is, I think, another justification for my speaking about Milton, besides the singular one which I have just given. The champions of Milton in our time, with one notable exception, have been scholars and teachers. I have no claim to be either: I am aware that my only claim upon your attention, in speaking of Milton or of any other great poet, is by appeal to your curiosity, in the hope that you may care to know what a contemporary writer of verse thinks of one of his predecessors.

I believe that the scholar and the practitioner in the field of literary criticism should supplement each other's work. The criticism of the practitioner will be all the better, certainly, if he is not wholly destitute of scholarship; and the criticism of the scholar will be all the better if he has some experience of the difficulties of writing verse. But the orientation of the two critics is different. The scholar is more concerned with the understanding of the masterpiece in the environment of its author: with the world in which that author lived, the temper of his age, his intellectual formation, the books which he had read, and the influences which had moulded him. The practitioner is concerned less with the author than with the poem; and with the poem in relation to his own age. He asks: Of what *use* is the poetry of this poet to poets writing to-day? Is it, or can it become, a living force in English poetry still unwritten? So we may say that the scholar's interest is in the permanent, the practitioner's in the immediate. The scholar can teach us where we should bestow our *admiration* and *respect:* the practitioner should be able, when he is the right poet talking about the right poet, to make an old masterpiece actual, give it contemporary importance, and persuade his audience that it is interesting, exciting,

The Henrietta Hertz Lecture, delivered to the British Academy, 1947 and subsequently at the Frick Museum, New York. Reprinted from *On Poetry and Poets* by T. S. Eliot, by permission of Farrar, Straus and Cudahy, Inc., New York, N. Y. Copyright 1957 by T. S. Eliot.

enjoyable, and *active*. I can give only one example of contemporary criticism of Milton, by a critic of the type to which I belong if I have any critical pretensions at all: that is the Introduction to Milton's *English Poems* in the "World Classics" series, by the late Charles Williams. It is not a comprehensive essay; it is notable primarily because it provides the best prolegomenon to *Comus* which any modern reader could have; but what distinguishes it throughout (and the same is true of most of Williams's critical writing) is the author's warmth of feeling and his success in communicating it to the reader. In this, so far as I am aware, the essay of Williams is a solitary example.

I think it is useful, in such an examination as I propose to make, to keep in mind some critic of the past, of one's own type, by whom to measure one's opinions: a critic sufficiently remote in time, for his local errors and prejudices to be not identical with one's own. That is why I began by quoting Samuel Johnson. It will hardly be contested that as a critic of poetry Johnson wrote as a practitioner and not as a scholar. Because he was a poet himself, and a good poet, what he wrote about poetry must be read with respect. And unless we know and appreciate Johnson's poetry we cannot judge either the merits or the limitations of his criticism. It is a pity that what the common reader to-day has read, or has remembered, or has seen quoted, are mostly those few statements of Johnson's from which later critics have vehemently dissented. But when Johnson held an opinion which seems to us wrong, we are never safe in dismissing it without inquiring why he was wrong; he had his own "errors and prejudices," certainly, but for lack of examining them sympathetically we are always in danger of merely countering error with error and prejudice with prejudice. Now Johnson was, in his day, very much a modern: he was concerned with how poetry should be written in his own time. The fact that he came towards the end, rather than the beginning of a style, the fact that his time was rapidly passing away, and that the canons of taste which he observed were about to fall into desuetude, does not diminish the interest of his criticism. Nor does the likelihood that the development of poetry in the next fifty years will take quite different directions from those which to me seem desirable to explore, deter me from asking the questions that Johnson implied: How should poetry be written now? and what place does the answer to this question give to Milton? And I think that the answers to these questions may be different now from the answers that were correct twenty-five years ago.

There is one prejudice against Milton, apparent on almost every page of Johnson's *Life of Milton,* which I imagine is still general: we, however, with a longer historical perspective, are in a better position than was Johnson to recognize it and to make allowance for it. This is a prejudice which I share myself: an antipathy towards Milton the man. Of this in itself I have nothing further to say: all that is necessary is to record one's awareness of it. But this prejudice is often involved with another, more obscure: and I do not think that Johnson had disengaged the two in his own mind. The fact is simply that the Civil War of the seventeenth century, in which Milton is a symbolic figure, has never been concluded. The Civil War is not ended: I question whether any serious civil war ever does end. Throughout that period English society was so convulsed and divided that the effects are still felt. Reading Johnson's essay one is always aware that Johnson was obstinately and passionately of another party. No other English poet, not Wordsworth, or Shelley, lived through or took sides in such momentous events as did Milton; of no other poet is it so difficult to consider the poetry simply as poetry, without our theological and political dispositions, conscious and unconscious, inherited or acquired, making an unlawful entry. And the danger is all the greater because these emotions now take different vestures. It is now considered grotesque, on political grounds, to be of the party of King Charles; it is now, I believe, considered equally grotesque, on moral grounds, to be of the party of the Puritans; and to most persons to-day the religious views of both parties may seem equally remote. Nevertheless, the passions are unquenched, and if we are not very wide awake their smoke will obscure the glass through which we examine Milton's poetry. Something has been done, certainly, to persuade us that Milton was never really of any party, but disagreed with everyone. Mr. Wilson Knight, in *Chariot of Wrath*, has argued that Milton was more a monarchist than a republican, and not in any modern sense a "democrat," and Professor Saurat has produced evidence to show that Milton's theology was highly eccentric, and as scandalous to Protestants as to Catholics—that he was, in fact, a sort of Christadelphian, and perhaps not a very orthodox Christadelphian at that; while on the other hand Mr. C. S. Lewis has opposed Professor Saurat by skilfully arguing that Milton, at least in *Paradise Lost,* can be acquitted of heresy even from a point of view so orthodox as that of Mr. Lewis himself. On these questions I hold no opinion: it is probably beneficial to question the assumption that Milton was a sound Free Churchman and member of the Liberal Party; but I think that we still have to be on guard against an unconscious partisanship if we aim to attend to the poetry for the poetry's sake.

So much for our prejudices. I come next to the positive objection to Milton which has been raised in our own time, that is to say, the charge that he is an unwholesome influence. And from this I shall proceed to the permanent strictures of reproof (to employ a phrase of Johnson's) and, finally, to the grounds on which I consider him a great poet and one whom poets to-day might study with profit.

For a statement of the *generalized* belief in the unwholesomeness of Milton's influence I turn to Mr. Middleton Murry's critique of Milton in his *Heaven and Earth*—a book which contains chapters of profound insight, interrupted by passages which seem to me intemperate. Mr. Murry approaches Milton after his long and patient study of Keats; and it is through the eyes of Keats that he sees Milton.

Keats *(Mr. Murry writes)* as a poetic artist, second to none since Shakespeare, and Blake, as a prophet of spiritual values unique in our history, both passed substantially the same judgement on Milton: "Life to him would be death to me." And whatever may be our verdict on the development of English poetry since Milton, we must admit the justice of Keats's opinion that Milton's magnificence led nowhere. "English must be kept up," said Keats. To be influenced beyond a certain point by Milton's art, he felt, dammed the creative flow of the English genius in and through itself. In saying this, I think, Keats voiced the very inmost of the English genius. To pass under the spell of Milton is to be condemned to imitate him. It is quite different with Shakespeare. Shakespeare baffles and liberates; Milton is perspicuous and constricts.

This is a very confident affirmation, and I criticize it with some diffidence because I cannot pretend to have devoted as much study to Keats, or to have as intimate an understanding of his difficulties, as Mr. Murry. But Mr. Murry seems to me here to be trying to transform the predicament of a particular poet with a particular aim at a particular moment in time into a censure of timeless validity. He appears to assert that the liberative function of Shakespeare and the constrictive menace of Milton are permanent characteristics of these two poets. "To be influenced beyond a certain point" by any one master is bad for any poet; and it does not matter whether that influence is Milton's or another's; and as we cannot anticipate where that point will come, we might be better advised to call it an *un*certain point. If it is not good to remain under the spell of Milton, is it good to remain under the spell of Shakespeare? It depends partly upon what *genre* of poetry you are trying to develop. Keats wanted to write an epic, and he found, as might be expected, that the time had not arrived at which another English epic, comparable in grandeur to *Paradise Lost,* could be written. He also tried his hand at writing plays: and one might argue that *King Stephen* was more blighted by Shakespeare than *Hyperion* by Milton. Certainly, *Hyperion* remains a magnificent fragment which one re-reads; and *King Stephen* is a play which we may have read once, but to which we never return for enjoyment. Milton made a great epic impossible for succeeding generations; Shakespeare made a great poetic drama impossible; such a situation is inevitable, and it persists until the language has so altered that there is no danger, because no possibility, of imitation. Anyone who tries to write poetic drama, even to-day, should know that half of his energy must be exhausted in the effort to escape from the constricting toils of Shakespeare: the moment his attention is relaxed, or his mind fatigued, he will lapse into bad Shakespearian verse. For a long time after an epic poet like Milton, or a dramatic poet like Shakespeare, nothing can be done. Yet the effort must be repeatedly made; for we can never know in advance when the moment is approaching at which a new epic, or a new drama, will be possible; and when the moment does draw near it may be that the genius of an individual poet will perform the last mutation of idiom and versification which will bring that new poetry into being.

I have referred to Mr. Murry's view of the bad influence of Milton as generalized, because it is implicitly the whole personality of Milton that is in question: not specifically his beliefs, or his language or versification, but the beliefs as realized in that particular personality, and his poetry as the expression of it. By the *particular* view of Milton's influence as bad, I mean that view which attends to the language, the syntax, the versification, the imagery. I do not suggest that there is here a complete difference of subject matter: it is the difference of approach, the difference of the focus of interest, between the philosophical critic and the literary critic. An incapacity for the abstruse, and an interest in poetry which is primarily a technical

interest, dispose my mind towards the more limited and perhaps more
superficial task. Let us proceed to look at Milton's influence from this point
of view, that of the writer of poetry in our own time.

The reproach against Milton, that his technical influence has been bad,
appears to have been made by no one more positively than by myself. I find
myself saying, as recently as 1936, that this charge against Milton "appears
a good deal more serious if we affirm that Milton's poetry could *only* be an
influence for the worse, upon any poet whatever. It is more serious, also, if
we affirm that Milton's bad influence may be traced much farther than
the eighteenth century, and much farther than upon bad poets: if we say
that it was an influence against which we still have to struggle."

In writing these sentences I failed to draw a threefold distinction, which
now seems to me of some importance. There are three separate assertions
implied. The first is, that an influence has been bad in the past: this is to
assert that good poets, in the eighteenth or nineteenth century, would have
written better if they had not submitted themselves to the influence of Milton. The second assertion is, that the contemporary situation is such that
Milton is a master whom we should avoid. The third is, that the influence of
Milton, or of any particular poet, can be *always* bad, and that we can predict
that wherever it is found at any time in the future, however remote, it will
be a bad influence. Now, the first and third of these assertions I am no
longer prepared to make, because, detached from the second, they do not
appear to me to have any meaning.

For the first, when we consider one great poet of the past, and one or
more other poets, upon whom we say he has exerted a bad influence, we
must admit that the responsibility, if there be any, is rather with the poets
who were influenced than with the poet whose work exerted the influence.
We can, of course, show that certain tricks or mannerisms which the imi-
tators display are due to conscious or unconscious imitation and emulation,
but that is a reproach against their injudicious choice of a model and not
against their model itself. And we can never prove that any particular poet
would have written better poetry if he had escaped that influence. Even
if we assert, what can only be a matter of faith, that Keats would have
written a very great epic poem if Milton had not preceded him, is it sensible
to pine for an unwritten masterpiece, in exchange for one which we possess
and acknowledge? And as for the remote future, what can we affirm about
the poetry that will be written then, except that we should probably be
unable to understand or to enjoy it, and that therefore we can hold no
opinion as to what "good" and "bad" influences will *mean* in that future?
The only relation in which the question of influence, good and bad, is
significant, is the relation to the immediate future. With that question I
shall engage at the end. I wish first to mention another reproach against
Milton, that represented by the phrase "dissociation of sensibility."

I remarked many years ago, in an essay on Dryden, that:

In the seventeenth century a dissociation of sensibility set in, from which we
have never recovered; and this dissociation, as is natural, was due to the influence
of the two most powerful poets of the century, Milton and Dryden.

The longer passage from which this sentence is taken is quoted by Dr. Tillyard in his *Milton*. Dr. Tillyard makes the following comment:

Speaking only of what in this passage concerns Milton, I would say that there is here a mixture of truth and falsehood. Some sort of dissociation of sensibility in Milton, not necessarily undesirable, has to be admitted; but that he was responsible for any such dissociation in others (at least till this general dissociation had inevitably set in) is untrue.

I believe that the general affirmation represented by the phrase "dissociation of sensibility" (one of the two or three phrases of my coinage—like "objective correlative"—which have had a success in the world astonishing to their author) retains some validity; but I now incline to agree with Dr. Tillyard that to lay the burden on the shoulders of Milton and Dryden was a mistake. If such a dissociation did take place, I suspect that the causes are too complex and too profound to justify our accounting for the change in terms of literary criticism. All we can say is, that something like this did happen; that it had something to do with the Civil War; that it would even be unwise to say it was caused by the Civil War, but that it is a consequence of the same causes which brought about the Civil War; that we must seek the causes in Europe, not in England alone; and for what these causes were, we may dig and dig until we get to a depth at which words and concepts fail us.

Before proceeding to take up the case against Milton, as it stood for poets twenty-five years ago—the second, and only significant meaning of "bad influence"—I think it would be best to consider what permanent strictures of reproof may be drawn: those censures which, when we make them, we must assume to be made by enduring laws of taste. The essence of the permanent censure of Milton is, I believe, to be found in Johnson's essay. This is not the place in which to examine certain particular and erroneous judgments of Johnson; to explain his condemnation of *Comus* and *Samson* as the application of dramatic canons which to us seem inapplicable; or to condone his dismissal of the versification of *Lycidas* by the specialization, rather than the absence, of his sense of rhythm. Johnson's most important censure of Milton is contained in three paragraphs, which I must ask leave to quote in full.

Throughout all his greater works (*says Johnson*) there prevails an uniform peculiarity of *diction,* a mode and cast of expression which bears little resemblance to that of any former writer; and which is so far removed from common use, that an unlearned reader, when he first opens the book, finds himself surprised by a new language.

This novelty has been, by those who can find nothing wrong with Milton, imputed to his laborious endeavours after words suited to the grandeur of his ideas. *Our language,* says Addison, *sunk under him.* But the truth is, that both in prose and in verse, he had formed his style by a perverse and pedantic principle. He was desirous to use English words with a foreign idiom. This in all his prose is discovered and condemned; for there judgment operates freely, neither softened by the beauty, nor awed by the dignity of his thoughts; but such is the power of his poetry, that his call is obeyed without resistance, the reader feels himself in captivity to a higher and nobler mind, and criticism sinks in admiration.

Milton's style was not modified by his subject; what is shown with greater extent in *Paradise Lost* may be found in *Comus*. One source of his peculiarity was his familiarity with the Tuscan poets; the disposition of his words is, I think, frequently Italian; perhaps sometimes combined with other tongues. Of him at last, may be said what Jonson said of Spenser, that he *wrote no language,* but has formed what Butler called a *Babylonish dialect,* in itself harsh and barbarous, but made by exalted genius and extensive learning the vehicle of so much instruction and so much pleasure, that, like other lovers, we find grace in its deformity.

This criticism seems to me substantially true: indeed unless we accept it, I do not think we are in the way to appreciate the peculiar greatness of Milton. His style is not a *classic* style, in that it is not the elevation of a *common* style, by the final touch of genius, to greatness. It is, from the foundation, and in every particular, a personal style, not based upon common speech, or common prose, or direct communication of meaning. Of some great poetry one has difficulty in pronouncing just what it is, what infinitesimal touch, that has made all the difference from a plain statement which anyone could make; the slight transformation which, while it leaves a plain statement a plain statement, has always the maximal, never the minimal, alteration of ordinary language. Every distortion of construction, the foreign idiom, the use of a word in a foreign way or with the meaning of the foreign word from which it is derived rather than the accepted meaning in English, every idiosyncrasy is a particular act of violence which Milton has been the first to commit. There is no cliché, no poetic diction in the derogatory sense, but a perpetual sequence of original acts of lawlessness. Of all modern writers of verse, the nearest analogy seems to me to be Mallarmé, a much smaller poet, though still a great one. The personalities, the poetic theories of the two men could not have been more different; but in respect of the violence which they could do to language, and justify, there is a remote similarity. Milton's poety is poetry as the farthest possible remove from prose; his prose seems to me too near to half-formed poetry to be a good prose.

To say that the work of a poet is at the farthest possible remove from prose would once have struck me as condemnatory: it now seems to me simply, when we have to do with a Milton, the precision of its peculiar greatness. As a poet, Milton seems to me probably the greatest of all eccentrics. His work illustrates no general principles of good writing; the only principles of writing that it illustrates are such as are valid only for Milton himself to observe. There are two kinds of poet who can ordinarily be of use to other poets. There are those who suggest, to one or another of their successors, something which they have not done themselves, or who provoke a different way of doing the same thing: these are likely to be not the greatest, but smaller, imperfect poets with whom later poets discover an affinity. And there are the great poets from whom we can learn negative rules: no poet can teach another to write well, but some great poets can teach others some of the things to avoid. They teach us what to avoid, by showing us what great poetry can do without—how *bare* it can be. Of these are Dante and Racine. But if we are ever to make use of Milton we must do so in quite a different way. Even a small poet can learn something from the study of Dante, or from the study of Chaucer: we must perhaps wait for a great poet before we find one who can profit from the study of Milton.

I repeat that the remoteness of Milton's verse from ordinary speech, his invention of his own poetic language, seems to me one of the marks of his greatness. Other marks are his sense of structure, both in the general design of *Paradise Lost* and *Samson,* and in his syntax; and finally, and not least, his inerrancy, conscious or unconscious, in writing so as to make the best display of his talents, and the best concealment of his weaknesses.

The appropriateness of the subject of *Samson* is too obvious to expatiate upon: it was probably the one dramatic story out of which Milton could have made a masterpiece. But the complete suitability of *Paradise Lost* has not, I think, been so often remarked. It was surely an intuitive perception of what he could not do, that arrested Milton's project of an epic on King Arthur. For one thing, he had little interest in, or understanding of, individual human beings. In *Paradise Lost* he was not called upon for any of that understanding which comes from an affectionate observation of men and women. But such an interest in human beings was not required—indeed its *absence* was a necessary condition—for the creation of his figures of Adam and Eve. These are not a man and woman such as any we know: if they were, they would not be Adam and Eve. They were the original *Man* and *Woman,* not types, but prototypes. They have the general characteristics of men and women, such that we can recognize, in the temptation and the fall, the first motions of the faults and virtues, the abjection and the nobility, of all their descendants. They have ordinary humanity to the right degree, and yet are not, and should not be, ordinary mortals. Were they more particularized they would be false, and if Milton had been more interested in humanity, he could not have created them. Other critics have remarked upon the exactness, without defect or exaggeration, with which Moloch, Belial, and Mammon, in the second book, speak according to the particular sin which each represents. It would not be suitable that the infernal powers should have, in the human sense, characters, for a character is always mixed; but in the hands of an inferior manipulator, they might easily have been reduced to *humours.*

The appropriateness of the material of *Paradise Lost* to the genius and the limitations of Milton is still more evident when we consider the visual imagery. I have already remarked, in a paper written some years ago, on Milton's weakness of visual observation, a weakness which I think was always present—the effect of his blindness may have been rather to strengthen the compensatory qualities than to increase a fault which was already present. Mr. Wilson Knight, who has devoted close study to recurrent imagery in poetry, has called attention to Milton's propensity towards images of engineering and mechanics; to me it seems that Milton is at his best in imagery suggestive of vast size, limitless space, abysmal depth, and light and darkness. No theme and no setting, other than that which he chose in *Paradise Lost,* could have given him such scope for the kind of imagery in which he excelled, or made less demand upon those powers of visual imagination which were in him defective.

Most of the absurdities and inconsistencies to which Johnson calls attention, and which, so far as they can justly be isolated in this way, he

properly condemns, will I think appear in a more correct proportion if
we consider them in relation to this general judgment. I do not think that
we should attempt to *see* very clearly any scene that Milton depicts: it
should be accepted as a shifting phantasmagory. To complain, because we
first find the arch-fiend "chain'd on the burning lake," and in a minute or
two see him making his way to the shore, is to expect a kind of consistency
which the world to which Milton has introduced us does not require.

This limitation of visual power, like Milton's limited interest in human
beings, turns out to be not merely a negligible defect, but a positive virtue,
when we visit Adam and Eve in Eden. Just as a higher degree of characterization of Adam and Eve would have been unsuitable, so a more vivid
picture of the earthly Paradise would have been less paradisiacal. For a
greater definiteness, a more detailed account of flora and fauna, could only
have assimilated Eden to the landscapes of earth with which we are familiar.
As it is, the impression of Eden which we retain, is the most suitable, and
is that which Milton was most qualified to give: the impression of *light*—
a daylight and a starlight, a light of dawn and of dusk, the light which,
remembered by a man in his blindness, has a supernatural glory unexperi-
enced by men of normal vision.

We must, then, in reading *Paradise Lost,* not expect to see clearly; our
sense of sight must be blurred, so that our *hearing* may become more acute.
*Paradise Lost,* like *Finnegans Wake* (for I can think of no work which provides a more interesting parallel: two books by great blind musicians, each
writing a language of his own based upon English) makes this peculiar demand for a readjustment of the reader's mode of apprehension. The emphasis is on the sound, not the vision, upon the word, not the idea; and in
the end it is the unique versification that is the most certain sign of Milton's
intellectual mastership.

On the subject of Milton's versification, so far as I am aware, little enough
has been written. We have Johnson's essay in the *Rambler,* which deserves
more study than it has received, and we have a short treatise by Robert
Bridges on *Milton's Prosody.* I speak of Bridges with respect, for no poet
of our time has given such close attention to prosody as he. Bridges catalogues
the systematic irregularities which give perpetual variety to Milton's verse,
and I can find no fault with his analysis. But however interesting these analyses are, I do not think that it is by such means that we gain an appreciation
of the peculiar rhythm of a poet. It seems to me also that Milton's verse is
especially refractory to yielding up its secrets to examination of the single
line. For his verse is not formed in this way. It is the period, the sentence
and still more the paragraph, that is the unit of Milton's verse; and emphasis on the line structure is the minimum necessary to provide a counter-
pattern to the period structure. It is only in the period that the wave-length
of Milton's verse is to be found: it is his ability to give a perfect and unique
pattern to every paragraph, such that the full beauty of the line is found in
its context, and his ability to work in larger musical units than any other
poet—that is to me the most conclusive evidence of Milton's supreme mastery. The peculiar feeling, almost a physical sensation of a breathless leap,
communicated by Milton's long periods, and by his alone, is impossible to
procure from rhymed verse. Indeed, this mastery is more conclusive evi-

dence of his intellectual power, than is his grasp of any *ideas* that he borrowed or invented. To be able to control so many words at once is the token of a mind of most exceptional energy.

It is interesting at this point to recall the general observations upon blank verse, which a consideration of *Paradise Lost* prompted Johnson to make towards the end of his essay.

The music of the English heroic lines strikes the ear so faintly, that it is easily lost, unless all the syllables of every line co-operate together; this co-operation can only be obtained by the preservation of every verse unmingled with another as a distinct system of sounds; and this distinctness is obtained and preserved by the artifice of rhyme. The variety of pauses, so much boasted by the lovers of blank verse, changes the measures of an English poet to the periods of a declaimer; and there are only a few skilful and happy readers of Milton, who enable their audience to perceive where the lines end or begin. *Blank verse,* said an ingenious critic, *seems to be verse only to the eye.*

Some of my audience may recall that this last remark, in almost the same words, was often made, a literary generation ago, about the "free verse" of the period: and even without this encouragement from Johnson it would have occurred to my mind to declare Milton to be the greatest master of free verse in our language. What is interesting about Johnson's paragraph, however, is that it represents the judgment of a man who had by no means a deaf ear, but simply a *specialized* ear, for verbal music. Within the limits of the poetry of his own period, Johnson is a very good judge of the relative merits of several poets as writers of blank verse. But on the whole, the blank verse of his age might more properly be called unrhymed verse; and nowhere is this difference more evident than in the verse of his own tragedy *Irene:* the phrasing is admirable, the style elevated and correct, but each line cries out for a companion to rhyme with it. Indeed, it is only with labour, or by occasional inspiration, or by submission to the influence of the older dramatists, that the blank verse of the nineteenth century succeeds in making the absence of rhyme inevitable and right, with the rightness of Milton. Even Johnson admitted that he could not wish that Milton had been a rhymer. Nor did the nineteenth century succeed in giving to blank verse the flexibility which it needs if the tone of common speech, talking of the topics of common intercourse, is to be employed; so that when our more modern practitioners of blank verse do not touch the sublime, they frequently sink to the ridiculous. Milton perfected non-dramatic blank verse and at the same time imposed limitations, very hard to break, upon the use to which it may be put if its greatest musical possibilities are to be exploited.

I come at last to compare my own attitude, as that of a poetical practitioner perhaps typical of a generation twenty-five years ago, with my attitude to-day. I have thought it well to take matters in the order in which I have taken them to discuss first the censures and detractions which I believe to have permanent validity, and which were best made by Johnson, in order to make clearer the causes, and the justification, for hostility to Milton on the part of poets at a particular juncture. And I wished to make clear those excellences of Milton which particularly impress me, before explaining why I think that the study of his verse might at last be of benefit to poets.

I have on several occasions suggested, that the important changes in the idiom of English verse which are represented by the names of Dryden and Wordsworth, may be characterized as successful attempts to escape from a poetic idiom which had ceased to have a relation to contemporary speech. This is the sense of Wordsworth's Prefaces. By the beginning of the present century another revolution in idiom—and such revolutions bring with them an alteration of metric, a new appeal to the ear—was due. It inevitably happens that the young poets engaged in such a revolution will exalt the merits of those poets of the past who offer them example and stimulation, and cry down the merits of poets who do not stand for the qualities which they are zealous to realize. This is not only inevitable, it is right. It is even right, and certainly inevitable, that their practice, still more influential than their critical pronouncements, should attract their own readers to the poets by whose work they have been influenced. Such influence has certainly contributed to the taste (if we can distinguish the *taste* from the *fashion*) for Donne. I do not think that any modern poet, unless in a fit of irresponsible peevishness, has ever denied Milton's consummate powers. And it must be said that Milton's diction is not a poetic diction in the sense of being a debased currency: when he violates the English language he is imitating nobody, and he is inimitable. But Milton does, as I have said, represent poetry at the extreme limit from prose; and it was one of our tenets that verse should have the virtues of prose, that diction should become assimilated to cultivated contemporary speech, before aspiring to the elevation of poetry. Another tenet was that the subject-matter and the imagery of poetry should be extended to topics and objects related to the life of a modern man or woman; that we were to seek the non-poetic, to seek even material refractory to transmutation into poetry, and words and phrases which had not been used in poetry before. And the study of Milton could be of no help here: it was only a hindrance.

We cannot, in literature, any more than in the rest of life, live in a perpetual state of revolution. If every generation of poets made it their task to bring poetic diction up to date with the spoken language, poetry would fail in one of its most important obligations. For poetry should help, not only to refine the language of the time, but to prevent it from changing too rapidly: a development of language at too great a speed would be a development in the sense of a progressive deterioration, and that is our danger to-day. If the poetry of the rest of this century takes the line of development which seems to me, reviewing the progress of poetry through the last three centuries, the right course, it will discover new and more elaborate patterns of a diction now established. In this search it might have much to learn from Milton's extended verse structure; it might also avoid the danger of a *servitude* to colloquial speech and to current jargon. It might also learn that the music of verse is strongest in poetry which has a definite meaning expressed in the properest words. Poets might be led to admit that a knowledge of the literature of their own language, with a knowledge of the literature and the grammatical construction of other languages, is a very valuable part of the poet's equipment. And they might, as I have already hinted, devote some study to Milton as, outside the theatre, the greatest master in our language of freedom within form. A study of

*Samson* should sharpen anyone's appreciation of the justified irregularity, and put him on guard against the pointless irregularity. In studying *Paradise Lost* we come to perceive that the verse is continuously animated by the departure from, and return to, the regular measure; and that, in comparison with Milton, hardly any subsequent writer of blank verse appears to exercise any freedom at all. We can also be led to the reflection that a monotony of unscannable verse fatigues the attention even more quickly than a monotony of exact feet. In short, it now seems to me that poets are sufficiently liberated from Milton's reputation, to approach the study of his work without danger, and with profit to their poetry and to the English language.

*F. R. Leavis*

# THE GREAT TRADITION

*". . . not dogmatically but deliberately . . ."*
Johnson, *Preface to Shakespeare*

The great English novelists are Jane Austen, George Eliot, Henry James and Joseph Conrad—to stop for the moment at that comparatively safe point in history. Since Jane Austen, for special reasons, needs to be studied at considerable length, I confine myself in this book to the last three. Critics have found me narrow, and I have no doubt that my opening proposition, whatever I may say to explain and justify it, will be adduced in reinforcement of their strictures. It passes as fact (in spite of the printed evidence) that I pronounce Milton negligible, dismiss "the Romantics," and hold that, since Donne, there is no poet we need bother about except Hopkins and Eliot. The view, I suppose, will be as confidently attributed to me that, except Jane Austen, George Eliot, James and Conrad, there are no novelists in English worth reading.

The only way to escape misrepresentation is never to commit oneself to any critical judgment that makes an impact—that is, never to *say* anything. I still, however, think that the best way to promote profitable discussion is to be as clear as possible with oneself about what one sees and judges, to try and establish the essential discriminations in the given field of interest, and to state them as clearly as one can (for disagreement, if necessary). And it seems to me that in the field of fiction some challenging discriminations are very much called for; the field is so large and offers such insidious temptations to complacent confusions of judgment and to critical indolence. It is of the field of fiction belonging to Literature that I am thinking, and I am thinking in particular of the present vogue of the Victorian age. Trollope, Charlotte Yonge, Mrs. Gaskell, Wilkie Collins, Charles Reade, Charles and Henry Kingsley, Marryat, Shorthouse[1]—one after another the minor novel-

Reprinted from *The Great Tradition* (1948) by F. R. Leavis, by permission of Chatto & Windus, Ltd., London.

ists of that period are being commended to our attention, written up, and publicized by broadcast, and there is a marked tendency to suggest that they not only have various kinds of interest to offer but that they are living classics. (Are not they all in the literary histories?) There are Jane Austen, Mrs. Gaskell, Scott, "the Brontës," [2] Dickens, Thackeray, George Eliot, Trollope and so on, all, one gathers, classical novelists.

It is necessary to insist, then, that there are important distinctions to be made, and that far from all of the names in the literary histories really belong to the realm of significant creative achievement. And as a recall to a due sense of differences it is well to start by distinguishing the few really great—the major novelists who count in the same way as the major poets, in the sense that they not only change the possibilities of the art for practitioners and readers, but that they are significant in terms of the human awareness they promote; awareness of the possibilities of life.[3]

---

[1] The novelist who has not been revived is Disraeli. Yet, though he is not one of the great novelists, he is so alive and intelligent as to deserve permanent currency, at any rate in the trilogy *Coningsby, Sybil* and *Tancred:* his own interests as expressed in these books—the interests of a supremely intelligent politician who has a sociologist's understanding of civilization and its movement in his time—are so mature.

[2] It is tempting to retort that there is only one Brontë. Actually, Charlotte, though claiming no part in the great line of English fiction (it is significant that she couldn't see why any value should be attached to Jane Austen), has a permanent interest of a minor kind. She had a remarkable talent that enabled her to do something firsthand and new in the rendering of personal experience, above all in *Villette.*

The genius, of course, was Emily. I have said nothing about *Wuthering Heights* because that astonishing work seems to me a kind of sport. It may, all the same, very well have had some influence of an essentially undetectable kind: she broke completely, and in the most challenging way, both with the Scott tradition that imposed on the novelist a romantic resolution of his themes, and with the tradition coming down from the eighteenth century that demanded a plane-mirror reflection of the surface of "real" life. Out of her a minor tradition comes, to which belongs, most notably, *The House with the Green Shutters.*

[3] Characteristic of the confusion I am contending against is the fashion (for which the responsibility seems to go back to Virginia Woolf and Mr. E. M. Forster) of talking of *Moll Flanders* as a "great novel." Defoe was a remarkable writer, but all that need be said about him as a novelist was said by Leslie Stephen in *Hours in a Library* (First Series). He made no pretension to practising the novelist's art, and matters little as an influence. In fact, the only influence that need be noted is that represented by the use made of him in the nineteen-twenties by the practitioners of the fantastic *conte* (or pseudo-moral fable) with its empty pretence of significance.

Associated with this use of Defoe is the use that was made in much the same *milieu* of Sterne, in whose irresponsible (and nasty) trifling, regarded as in some way extraordinarily significant and mature, was found a sanction for attributing value to other trifling.

The use of Bunyan by T. F. Powys is quite another matter. It is a mark of the genuine nature of Mr. Powys's creative gift (his work seems to me not to have had due recognition) that he has been able to achieve a kind of traditional relation to Bunyan—especially, of course, in *Mr. Weston's Good Wine.* Otherwise there is little that can be said with confidence about Bunyan as an influence. And yet we know him to have been for two centuries one of the most frequented of all classics, and in such a way that he counts immeasurably in the English-speaking consciousness. It is, perhaps, worth saying that his influence would tend strongly to reinforce the un-Flaubertian quality of the line of English classical fiction (Bunyan, Lord David Cecil might point out—see pp. 191-2 below—was a Puritan), as well as to co-operate with the Jonsonian tradition of morally significant typicality in characters.

To insist on the pre-eminent few in this way is not to be indifferent to tradition; on the contrary, it is the way towards understanding what tradition is. "Tradition," of course, is a term with many forces—and often very little at all. There is a habit nowadays of suggesting that there is a tradition of "the English Novel," and that all that can be said of the tradition (that being its peculiarity) is that "the English Novel" can be anything you like. To distinguish the major novelists in the spirit proposed is to form a more useful idea of tradition (and to recognize that the conventionally established view of the past of English fiction needs to be drastically revised). It is in terms of the major novelists, those significant in the way suggested, that tradition, in any serious sense, has its significance.

To be important historically is not, of course, to be necessarily one of the significant few. Fielding deserves the place of importance given him in the literary histories, but he hasn't the kind of classical distinction we are also invited to credit him with. He is important not because he leads to Mr. J. B. Priestley but because he leads to Jane Austen, to appreciate whose distinction is to feel that life isn't long enough to permit of one's giving much time to Fielding or any to Mr. Priestley.

Fielding made Jane Austen possible by opening the central tradition of English fiction. In fact, to say that the English novel began with him is as reasonable as such propositions ever are. He completed the work begun by *The Tatler* and *The Spectator,* in the pages of which we see the drama turning into the novel—that this development should occur by way of journalism being in the natural course of things. To the art of presenting character and *moeurs* learnt in that school (he himself, before he became a novelist, was both playwright and periodical essayist) he joined a narrative habit the nature of which is sufficiently indicated by his own phrase, "comic epic in prose." That the eighteenth century, which hadn't much lively reading to choose from, but had much leisure, should have found *Tom Jones* exhilarating is not surprising; nor is it that Scott, and Coleridge, should have been able to give that work superlative praise. Standards are formed in comparison, and what opportunities had they for that? But the conventional talk about the "perfect construction" of *Tom Jones* (the late Hugh Walpole brought it out triumphantly and you may hear it in almost any course of lectures on "the English Novel") is absurd. There can't be subtlety of organization without richer matter to organize, and subtler interests, than Fielding has to offer. He is credited with range and variety and it is true that some episodes take place in the country and some in Town, some in the churchyard and some in the inn, some on the high-road and some in the bed-chamber, and so on. But we haven't to read a very large proportion of *Tom Jones* in order to discover the limits of the essential interests it has to offer us. Fielding's attitudes, and his concern with human nature, are simple, and not such as to produce an effect of anything but monotony (on a mind, that is, demanding more than external action) when exhibited at the length of an "epic in prose." What he *can* do appears to best advantage in *Joseph Andrews. Jonathan Wild,* with its famous irony, seems to me mere hobbledehoydom (much as one applauds the determination to explode the gangster-hero), and by *Amelia* Fielding has gone soft.

We all know that if we want a more inward interest it is to Richardson we must go. And there is more to be said for Johnson's preference, and his emphatic way of expressing it at Fielding's expense, than is generally recognized. Richardson's strength in the analysis of emotional and moral states is in any case a matter of common acceptance; and *Clarissa* is a really impressive work. But it's no use pretending that Richardson can ever be made a current classic again. The substance of interest that he too has to offer is in its own way extremely limited in range and variety, and the demand he makes on the reader's time is in proportion—and absolutely—so immense as to be found, in general, prohibitive (though I don't know that I wouldn't sooner read through again *Clarissa* than *A la recherche du temps perdu*). But we can understand well enough why his reputation and influence should have been so great throughout Europe; and his immediately relevant historical importance is plain: he too is a major fact in the background of Jane Austen.

The social gap between them was too wide, however, for his work to be usable by her directly: the more he tries to deal with ladies and gentlemen, the more immitigably vulgar he is. It was Fanny Burney who, by transposing him into educated life, made it possible for Jane Austen to absorb what he had to teach her. Here we have one of the important lines of English literary history—Richardson-FannyBurney-JaneAusten. It is important because Jane Austen is one of the truly great writers, and herself a major fact in the background of other great writers. Not that Fanny Burney is the only other novelist who counts in her formation; she read all there was to read, and took all that was useful to her—which wasn't only lessons.[4] In fact, Jane Austen, in her indebtedness to others, provides an exceptionally illuminating study of the nature of originality, and she exemplifies beautifully the relations of "the individual talent" to tradition. If the influences bearing on her hadn't comprised something fairly to be called tradition she couldn't have found herself and her true direction; but her relation to tradition is a creative one. She not only makes tradition for those coming after, but her achievement has for us a retroactive effect: as we look back beyond her we see in what goes before, and see because of her, potentialities and significances brought out in such a way that, for us, she creates the tradition we see leading down to her. Her work, like the work of all great creative writers, gives a meaning to the past.

Having, in examination-papers and undergraduate essays, come much too often on the proposition that "George Eliot is the first modern novelist," I finally tracked it down to Lord David Cecil's *Early Victorian Novelists*. In so far as it is possible to extract anything clear and coherent from the variety of things that Lord David Cecil says by way of explaining the phrase, it is this: that George Eliot, being concerned, not to offer "primarily an entertainment," but to explore a significant theme—a theme significant in its bearing on the "serious problems and preoccupations of mature life" (p. 291)—breaks with "those fundamental conventions both of form and matter within which the English novel up till then had been constructed" (p. 288). What account, then, are we to assume of Jane Austen? Clearly, one that

---

4 For the relation of Jane Austen to other writers see the essay by Q. D. Leavis, "A Critical Theory of Jane Austen's Writings," in *Scrutiny*, Vol. X, No. 1.

appears to be the most commonly held: she creates delightful characters ("Compare Jane Austen's characterization with Scott's" [5]—a recurrent examination-question) and lets us forget our cares and moral tensions in the comedy of pre-eminently civilized life. The idea of "civilization" invoked appears to be closely related to that expounded by Mr. Clive Bell.[6]

Lord David Cecil actually compares George Eliot with Jane Austen. The passage is worth quoting because the inadequate ideas of form ("composition") and moral interest it implies—ideas of the relation between "art" and "life" as it concerns the novelist—are very representative. (Its consistency with what has been said about George Eliot earlier in the same essay isn't obvious, but that doesn't disturb the reader by the time he has got here.)

It is also easy to see why her form doesn't satisfy us as Jane Austen's does. Life is chaotic, art is orderly. The novelist's problem is to evoke an orderly composition which is also a convincing picture of life. It is Jane Austen's triumph that she solves this problem perfectly, fully satisfies the rival claims of life and art. Now George Eliot does not. She sacrifices life to art. Her plots are too neat and symmetrical to be true. We do not feel them to have grown naturally from their situation like a flower, but to have been put together deliberately and calculatedly like a building. (p. 322)

Jane Austen's plots, and her novels in general, were put together very "deliberately and calculatedly" (if not "like a building").[7] But her interest in "composition" is not something to be put over against her interest in life; nor does she offer an "aesthetic" value that is separable from moral significance. The principle of organization, and the principle of develop-

---

[5] Scott was primarily a kind of inspired folk-lorist, qualified to have done in fiction something analogous to the ballad-opera: the only live part of *Redgauntlet* now is "Wandering Willie's Tale," and "The Two Drovers" remains in esteem while the heroics of the historical novels can no longer command respect. He was a great and very intelligent man; but, not having the creative writer's interest in literature, he made no serious attempt to work out his own form and break away from the bad tradition of the eighteenth-century romance. Of his books, *The Heart of Midlothian* comes the nearest to being a great novel, but hardly *is* that: too many allowances and deductions have to be made. Out of Scott a bad tradition came. It spoiled Fenimore Cooper, who had new and first-hand interests and the makings of a distinguished novelist. And with Stevenson it took on "literary" sophistication and fine writing.

[6] "'As for the revolt against Nature,' he continued, 'that, too, has its uses. If it conduces to the cult of the stylized, the conventionalized, the artificial, just for their own sakes, it also, more broadly, makes for civilization.'

"'Civilization?' I asked. 'At what point between barbarism and decadence does civilization reign? If a civilized community be defined as one where you find aesthetic preoccupations, subtle thought, and polished intercourse, is civilization necessarily desirable? Aesthetic preoccupations are not inconsistent with a wholly inadequate conception of the range and power of art; thought may be subtle and yet trivial; and polished intercourse may be singularly uninteresting.'"—L. H. Myers, *The Root and the Flower*, p. 418.

Myers hasn't the great novelist's technical interest in method and presentment; he slips very easily into using the novel as a *vehicle*. That is, we feel that he is not primarily a novelist. Yet he is sufficiently one to have made of *The Root and the Flower* a very remarkable novel. Anyone seriously interested in literature is likely to have found the first reading a memorable experience and to have found also that repeated re-readings have not exhausted the interest.

[7] See "'Lady Susan' into 'Mansfield Park'" by Q. D. Leavis in *Scrutiny*, Vol. X, No. 2.

ment, in her work is an intense moral interest of her own in life that is in the first place a preoccupation with certain problems that life compels on her as personal ones.[8] She is intelligent and serious enough to be able to impersonalize her moral tensions as she strives, in her art, to become more fully conscious of them, and to learn what, in the interests of life, she ought to do with them. Without her intense moral preoccupation she wouldn't have been a great novelist.

This account of her would, if I had cared to use the formula, have been my case for calling Jane Austen, and not anyone later, "the first modern novelist." In applying it to George Eliot, Lord David Cecil says: "In fact, the laws conditioning the form of George Eliot's novels are the same laws that condition those of Henry James and Wells and Conrad and Arnold Bennett." I don't know what Wells is doing in that sentence; there is an elementary distinction to be made between the *discussion* of problems and ideas, and what we find in the great novelists. And, for all the generous sense of common humanity to be found in his best work, Bennett seems to me never to have been disturbed enough by life to come anywhere near greatness. But it would certainly be reasonable to say that "the laws conditioning the form of Jane Austen's novels are the same laws that condition those of George Eliot and Henry James and Conrad." Jane Austen, in fact, is the inaugurator of the great tradition of the English novel—and by "great tradition" I mean the tradition to which what is great in English fiction belongs.

The great novelists in that tradition are all very much concerned with "form"; they are all very original technically, having turned their genius to the working out of their own appropriate methods and procedures. But the peculiar quality of their preoccupation with "form" may be brought out by a contrasting reference to Flaubert. Reviewing Thomas Mann's *Der Tod in Venedig*, D. H. Lawrence [9] adduces Flaubert as figuring to the world the "will of the writer to be greater than and undisputed lord over the stuff he writes." This attitude in art, as Lawrence points out, is indicative of an attitude in life—or towards life. Flaubert, he comments, "stood away from life as from a leprosy." For the later Aesthetic writers, who, in general, represent in a weak kind of way the attitude that Flaubert maintained with a perverse heroism, "form" and "style" are ends to be sought for themselves, and the chief preoccupation is with elaborating a beautiful style to apply to the chosen subject. There is George Moore, who in the best circles, I gather (from a distance), is still held to be among the very greatest masters of prose, though—I give my own limited experience for what it is worth— it is very hard to find an admirer who, being pressed, will lay his hand on his heart and swear he has read one of the "beautiful" novels through. "The novelist's problem is to evolve an orderly composition which is also a convincing picture of life"—this is the way an admirer of George Moore sees it. Lord David Cecil, attributing this way to Jane Austen, and crediting her with a superiority over George Eliot in "satisfying the rival claims of life and art," explains this superiority, we gather, by a freedom from moral pre-

---

8 D. W. Harding deals illuminatingly with this matter in "Regulated Hatred: An Aspect of the Work of Jane Austen" (see *Scrutiny,* Vol. VIII, No. 4).
9 *Phoenix,* p. 308.

occupations that he supposes her to enjoy. (George Eliot, he tells us, was a Puritan, and earnestly bent on instruction.[10])

As a matter of fact, when we examine the formal perfection of *Emma,* we find that it can be appreciated only in terms of the moral preoccupations that characterize the novelist's peculiar interest in life. Those who suppose it to be an "aesthetic matter," a beauty of "composition" that is combined, miraculously, with "truth to life," can give no adequate reason for the view that *Emma* is a great novel, and no intelligent account of its perfection of form. It is in the same way true of the other great English novelists that their interest in their art gives them the opposite of an affinity with Pater and George Moore; it is, brought to an intense focus, an unusually developed interest in life. For, far from having anything of Flaubert's disgust or disdain or boredom, they are all distinguished by a vital capacity for experience, a kind of reverent openness before life, and a marked moral intensity.

It might be commented that what I have said of Jane Austen and her successors is only what can be said of any novelist of unqualified greatness. That is true. But there *is*—and this is the point—an English tradition, and these great classics of English fiction belong to it; a tradition that, in the talk about "creating characters" and "creating worlds," and the appreciation of Trollope and Mrs. Gaskell and Thackeray and Meredith and Hardy and Virginia Woolf, appears to go unrecognized. It is not merely that we have no Flaubert (and I hope I haven't seemed to suggest that a Flaubert is no more worth having than a George Moore). Positively, there is a continuity from Jane Austen. It is not for nothing that George Eliot admired her work profoundly, and wrote one of the earliest appreciations of it to be published. The writer whose intellectual weight and moral earnestness strike some critics as her handicap certainly saw in Jane Austen something more than an ideal contemporary of Lytton Strachey.[11] What one great original artist learns from another, whose genius and problems are necessarily very different, is the hardest kind of "influence" to define, even when we see it to have been of the profoundest importance. The obvious manifestation of influence is to be seen in this kind of passage:

A little daily embroidery had been a constant element in Mrs. Transome's life; that soothing occupation of taking stitches to produce what neither she nor any one else wanted, was then the resource of many a well-born and unhappy woman.

In short, he felt himself to be in love in the right place, and was ready to endure a great deal of predominance, which, after all, a man could always put down when he liked. Sir James had no idea that he should ever like to put down the predominance of this handsome girl, in whose cleverness he delighted. Why

[10] She is a moralist and a highbrow, the two handicaps going together. "Her humour is less affected by her intellectual approach. Jokes, thank heaven, need not be instructive."— *Early Victorian Novelists,* p. 299.

[11] It is perhaps worth insisting that Peacock is more than that too. He is not at all in the same class as the Norman Douglas of *South Wind* and *They Went.* In his ironical treatment of contemporary society and civilization he is seriously applying serious standards, so that his books, which are obviously not novels in the same sense as Jane Austen's, have a permanent life as light reading—indefinitely re-readable—for minds with mature interests.

not? A man's mind—what there is of it—has always the advantage of being mas-
culine,—as the smallest birch-tree is of a higher kind than the most soaring palm—
and even his ignorance is of a sounder quality. Sir James might not have originated
this estimate; but a kind Providence furnishes the limpest personality with a little
gum or starch in the form of tradition.

The kind of irony here is plainly akin to Jane Austen's—though it is
characteristic enough of George Eliot; what she found was readily assimilated to her own needs. In Jane Austen herself the irony has a serious
background, and is no mere display of "civilization." George Eliot wouldn't
have been interested in it if she hadn't perceived its full significance—its
relation to the essential moral interest offered by Jane Austen's art. And
here we come to the profoundest kind of influence, that which is not manifested in likeness. One of the supreme debts one great writer can owe another
is the realization of unlikeness (there is, of course, no significant unlikeness
without the common concern—and the common seriousness of concern—
with essential human issues). One way of putting the difference between
George Eliot and the Trollopes whom we are invited to consider along with
her is to say that she was capable of understanding Jane Austen's greatness
and capable of learning from her. And except for Jane Austen there was
no novelist to learn from—none whose work had any bearing on her own
essential problems as a novelist.

Henry James also was a great admirer of Jane Austen,[12] and in his case
too there is that obvious aspect of influence which can be brought out by
quotation. And there is for him George Eliot as well, coming between. In
seeing him in an English tradition I am not slighting the fact of his American origin; an origin that doesn't make him less of an English novelist, of
the great tradition, than Conrad later. That he was an American is a fact of
the first importance for the critic, as Mr. Yvor Winters brings out admirably
in his book, *Maule's Curse*.[13] Mr. Winters discusses him as a product of the
New England ethos in its last phase, when a habit of moral strenuousness
remained after dogmatic Puritanism had evaporated and the vestigial moral
code was evaporating too. This throws a good deal of light on the elusive-
ness that attends James's peculiar ethical sensibility. We have, characteristically, in reading him, a sense that important choices are in question
and that our finest discrimination is being challenged, while at the same
time we can't easily produce for discussion any issues that have moral substance to correspond.

It seems relevant also to note that James was actually a New Yorker. In
any case, he belonged by birth and upbringing to that refined civilization of
the old European America which we have learnt from Mrs. Wharton to

12 He can't have failed to note with interest that *Emma* fulfils, by anticipation, a prescrip-
tion of his own: everything is presented through Emma's dramatized consciousness, and
the essential effects depend on that.

13 New Directions, Norfolk, Conn. (1938). To insist that James is in the English tradition
is not to deny that he is in an American tradition too. He is in the tradition that includes
Hawthorne and Melville. He is related to Hawthorne even more closely than Mr. Winters
suggests. A study of the very early work shows Hawthorne as a major influence—as *the*
major influence. The influence is apparent there in James's use of symbolism; and this use
develops into something that characterizes his later work as a whole.

associate with New York. His bent was to find a field for his ethical sensibility in the appreciative study of such a civilization—the "civilization" in question being a matter of personal relations between members of a mature and sophisticated Society. It is doubtful whether at any time in any place he could have found what would have satisfied his implicit demand: the actual fine art of civilized social intercourse that would have justified the flattering intensity of expectation he brought to it in the form of his curiously transposed and subtilized ethical sensibility.

History, it is plain, was already leaving him *déraciné* in his own country, so that it is absurd to censure him, as some American critics have done, for pulling up his roots. He could hardly become deeply rooted elsewhere, but the congenial soil and climate were in Europe rather than in the country of his birth. There is still some idealizing charm about his English country-house [14] in *The Portrait of a Lady,* but that book is one of the classics of the language, and we can't simply regret the conditions that produced something so finely imagined. It is what *The Egoist* is supposed to be. Compare the two books, and the greatness of Henry James as intellectual poet-novelist [15] of "high civilization" comes out in a way that, even for the most innocently deferential reader, should dispose of Meredith's pretensions for ever. James's wit is real and always natural, his poetry intelligent as well as truly rich, and there is nothing bogus, cheap or vulgar about his idealizations: certain human potentialities are nobly celebrated.

That he is a novelist who has closely studied his fellow-craftsmen is plain —and got from them more than lessons in the craft. It is plain, for instance, in *The Portrait of a Lady* that he sees England through literature. We know that he turned an attentive professional eye on the French masters. He has (in his early mature work) an easy and well-bred technical sophistication, a freedom from any marks of provinciality, and a quiet air of knowing his way about the world that distinguish him from among his contemporaries in the language. If from the English point of view he is unmistakably an American, he is also very much a European.

But there could be no question of his becoming a French master in English, and the help he could get from the Continent towards solving his

---

14 Though it has in justice to be remembered that the inhabitants of the house in *The Portrait of a Lady,* the Touchetts, are Americans, and that there is critical significance in the difference between the atmosphere of intellectual aliveness they establish and the quite other English atmosphere of the Warburton home. Moreover Isabel rejects the admirable Lord Warburton for reasons much like those for which the heroine of *An International Episode* rejects the nice English lord, who, by Touchett standards (shall we say?), is not good enough. And in story after story James, with the exasperation of an intellectual writer, expresses his disdainful sense of the utter unintellectuality of the country-house class. He always knew that he hadn't really found the ideal civilization he looked for; so that there is something like a tragic significance in the two juxtaposed notes of this passage from an early letter:

"But don't envy me too much; for the British country-house has at moments, for a cosmopolitanized American, an insuperable flatness. On the other hand, to do it justice, there is no doubt of its being one of the ripest fruits of time . . . of the highest results of civilization."—To Miss Alice James, 15th Dec. 1877: *The Letters of Henry James,* Vol. I, p. 64.

15 See Chapter III.

peculiar problem was obviously limited.[16] It was James who put his finger on the weakness in *Madame Bovary:* the discrepancy between the technical ("aesthetic") intensity, with the implied attribution of interest to the subject, and the actual moral and human paucity of this subject on any mature valuation. His own problem was to justify in terms of an intense interest in sophisticated "civilization" his New England ethical sensibility. The author who offered a congenial study would have to be very different from Flaubert. It was, as a matter of fact, a very English novelist, the living representative of the great tradition—a writer as unlike Flaubert as George Eliot.

George Eliot's reputation being what it is, this suggestion won't recommend itself to everyone immediately. "Like most writers, George Eliot could only create from the world of her personal experience—in her case middle- and lower-class rural England of the nineteenth-century Midlands." [17] Moreover, she was confined by a Puritanism such as James (apart from the fact that he wasn't lower-middle-class) had left a generation or two behind him: "the enlightened person of to-day must forget his dislike of Puritanism when he reads George Eliot." Weighty, provincial, and pledged to the "school-teacher's virtues," she was not qualified by nature or breeding to appreciate high civilization, even if she had been privileged to make its acquaintance. These seem to be accepted commonplaces—which shows how little even those who write about her have read her work.

Actually, though "Puritan" is a word used with many intentions, it is misleading to call her a Puritan at all,[18] and utterly false to say that her

[16] "Your remarks on my French tricks in my letters are doubtless most just, and shall be heeded. But it's an odd thing that such tricks should grow at a time when my last layers of resistance to a long-encroaching weariness and satiety with the French mind and its utterance has fallen from me like a garment. I have done with 'em forever, and am turning English all over. I desire only to feed on English life and the contact of English minds— I wish greatly I knew some. Easy and smooth-flowing as life is in Paris, I would throw it over to-morrow for an even very small chance to plant myself for a while in England. I have got nothing important out of Paris nor am likely to. . . . I know the Théâtre Français by heart!

"Daniel Deronda (Dan'l himself) is indeed a dead, though amiable, failure. But the book is a large affair; I shall write an article of some sort about it. All desire is dead within me to produce something on George Sand."—To William James, 29th July 1876: *The Letters*, Vol. I, p. 51.

[17] All the quotations in this paragraph are from Lord David Cecil.

[18] Unless you specify that, of the definitions Lord David Cecil gives us to choose from, the one you have in mind is that given here: "But the moral code founded on that Puritan theology had soaked itself too deeply into the fibre of her thought and feeling for her to give it up as well. She might not believe in heaven and hell and miracles, but she believed in right and wrong, and man's paramount obligation to follow right, as strictly as if she were Bunyan himself. And her standards of right and wrong were the Puritan standards. She admired truthfulness and chastity and industry and self-restraint, she disapproved of loose living and recklessness and deceit and self-indulgence." I had better confess that I differ (apparently) from Lord David Cecil in sharing these beliefs, admirations and disapprovals, so that the reader knows my bias at once. And they seem to me favourable to the production of great literature. I will add (exposing myself completely) that the enlightenment or aestheticism or sophistication that feels an amused superiority to them leads, in my view, to triviality and boredom, and that out of triviality comes evil (as L. H. Myers notes in the preface to *The Root and the Flower,* and illustrates in the novel itself, especially in the sections dealing with the "Camp").

"imagination had to scrape what nourishment it could from the bare bones of Puritan ethics." There was nothing restrictive or timid about her ethical habit; what she brought from her Evangelical background was a radically reverent attitude towards life, a profound seriousness of the kind that is a first condition of any real intelligence, and an interest in human nature that made her a great psychologist. Such a psychologist, with such a relation to Puritanism, was, of all the novelists open to his study, the one peculiarly relevant to James's interests and problems. That, at any rate, becomes an irresistible proposition when it is added that, in her most mature work, she deals and (in spite of the accepted commonplaces about her) deals consummately, with just that "civilization" which was James's chosen field. To say this is to have the confident wisdom of hindsight, for it can be shown, with a conclusiveness rarely possible in these matters, that James did actually go to school to George Eliot.[19]

That is a fair way of putting the significance of the relation between *The Portrait of a Lady* and *Daniel Deronda* that I discuss in my examination of the latter book. That relation demonstrated, nothing more is needed in order to establish the general relation I posit between the two novelists. James's distinctive bent proclaims itself uncompromisingly in what he does with *Daniel Deronda* (on the good part of which—I call it *Gwendolen Harleth*—*The Portrait of a Lady* is a variation; for the plain fact I point out amounts to that). The moral substance of George Eliot's theme is subtilized into something going with the value James sets on "high civilization"; her study of conscience has disappeared. A charming and intelligent girl, determined to live "finely," confidently exercises her "free ethical sensibility" (Mr. Winters' phrase) and discovers that she is capable of disastrous misvaluation (which is not surprising, seeing not only how inexperienced she is, but how much an affair of inexplicitnesses, overtones and fine shades is the world of discourse she moves in). It is a tragedy in which, for her, neither remorse is involved, nor, in the ordinary sense, the painful growth of conscience, though no doubt her "ethical sensibility" matures.

Along the line revealed by the contrast between the two novels James develops an art so unlike George Eliot's that, but for the fact (which seems to have escaped notice) of the relation of *The Portrait of a Lady* to *Daniel Deronda,* it would, argument being necessary, have been difficult to argue

[19] So footnote 16 above takes on a marked significance—a significance confirmed very strikingly by Percy Lubbock's summary of letters written at about the same time: "In Paris he settled therefore, in the autumn of 1875, taking rooms at 29 Rue du Luxembourg. He began to write *The American,* to contribute Parisian Letters to the *New York Tribune,* and to frequent the society of a few of his compatriots. He made the valued acquaintance of Ivan Turgenev, and through him of the group which surrounded Gustave Flaubert— Edmond de Goncourt, Alphonse Daudet, Guy de Maupassant, Zola and others. But the letters which follow will show the kind of doubts that began to arise after a winter in Paris—doubts of the possibility of Paris as a place where an American imagination could really take root and flourish. He found the circle of literature tightly closed to outside influences; it seemed to exclude all culture but its own after a fashion that aroused his opposition; he speaks sarcastically on one occasion of having watched Turgenev and Flaubert seriously discussing Daudet's *Jack,* while he reflected that none of the three had read, or knew English enough to read, *Daniel Deronda.*"—*The Letters of Henry James,* Vol. I, p. 41.

at all convincingly that there was a significant relation between the novelists. And I had better insist that I am not concerned to establish *indebtedness*. What I have in mind is the fact of the great tradition and the apartness of the two great novelists above the ruck of Gaskells and Trollopes and Merediths. Of the earlier novelists it was George Eliot alone (if we except the minor relevance of Jane Austen) whose work had a direct and significant bearing on his own problem. It had this bearing because she *was* a great novelist, and because in her maturest work she handled with unprecedented subtlety and refinement the personal relations of sophisticated characters exhibiting the "civilization" of the "best society," and used, in so doing, an original psychological notation corresponding to the fineness of her psychological and moral insight. Her moral seriousness was for James very far from a disqualification; it qualified her for a kind of influence that neither Flaubert nor the admired Turgenev could have.

Circumstances discussed above made James peculiarly dependent on literature; the contact with George Eliot's distinctive kind of greatness was correspondingly important for him. It is significant that *Madame de Mauves* (1874), the early story in which he uses something like the theme of *The Portrait of a Lady,* has a wordy quality premonitory (one can't help feeling) of the cobwebbiness that afflicted him in his late phase. We can't doubt that George Eliot counts for something in the incomparably superior concreteness of *The Portrait of a Lady.* In that book, and in its successor, *The Bostonians,* his art is at its most concrete, and least subject to the weakness attendant on his subtlety. It is not derivativeness that is in question, but the relation between two original geniuses. "We cannot attempt to trace," says Mr. Van Wyck Brooks in *The Pilgrimage of Henry James,* "the astonishing development of a creative faculty which, in the course of a dozen years, transcended the simple plot-maker's art of *The American,* the factitious local-colourism of *Roderick Hudson,* and rendered itself capable of the serene beauty of *The Portrait of a Lady,* the masterly assurance of *The Bostonians,* the mature perfection of *Washington Square.*"—It is more than a guess that, in that development, George Eliot had some part.

The reader is likely to comment, I suppose, on the degree in which my treatment of James is taken up with discussing his limitations and the regrettable aspects of his later development. Since it will also be noted that, of my three novelists, he, in terms of space, gets least attention, it might be concluded that a corresponding relative valuation is implied. I had, then, perhaps better say that there is no such relation intended between valuation and length of treatment. I will not, however, deny that, of the three, James seems to me to give decidedly most cause for dissatisfaction and qualification. He is, all the same, one of the great. His registration of sophisticated human consciousness is one of the classical creative achievements: it *added* something as only genius can. And when he is at his best that something is seen to be of great human significance. He creates an ideal civilized sensibility; a humanity capable of communicating by the finest shades of inflection and implication: a nuance may engage a whole complex moral economy and the perceptive response be the index of a major valuation or choice. Even *The Awkward Age,* in which the extremely developed subtlety of treatment is not as remote as one would wish from the hypertrophy that finally overcame him, seems to me a classic; in no other work can we find anything like that astonishing—in so astonishing a measure successful—use of sophisticated "society" dialogue.

In considering James's due status, in fact, it is not easy to say just where the interest of the classical artist turns into the interest of the classical "case." But it seems to me obvious that the "case" becomes in some places boring to the point of unreadableness. Yet there is a tacit conspiracy to admire some of the works that fall, partly, at any rate (wholly, one must conclude, for the admirers who risk explanatory comment on them), under this description. And here is sufficient reason why an attempt to promote a due appreciation of James's genius should give a good deal of discriminatory attention to the tendencies that, as they develop, turn vital subtlety into something else.

When we come to Conrad we can't, by way of insisting that he is indeed significantly "in" the tradition—in and of it, neatly and conclusively relate him to any one English novelist. Rather, we have to stress his foreignness—that he was a Pole, whose first other language was French.[20] I remember remarking to André Chevrillon how surprising a choice it was on Conrad's part to write in English, especially seeing he was so clearly a student of the French masters. And I remember the reply, to the effect that it wasn't at all surprising, since Conrad's work couldn't have been written in French. M. Chevrillon, with the authority of a perfect bilingual, went on to explain in terms of the characteristics of the two languages why it had to be English. Conrad's themes and interests demanded the concreteness and action—the dramatic energy—of English. We might go further and say that Conrad chose to write his novels in English for the reasons that led him to become a British Master Mariner.

I am not, in making this point, concurring in the emphasis generally laid on the Prose Laureate of the Merchant Service. What needs to be stressed is the great novelist. Conrad's great novels, if they deal with the sea at all, deal with it only incidentally. But the Merchant Service is for him both a spiritual fact and a spiritual symbol, and the interests that made it so for him control and animate his art everywhere. Here, then, we have a master of the English language, who chose it for its distinctive qualities and because of the moral tradition associated with it, and whose concern with art—he being like Jane Austen and George Eliot and Henry James an innovator in "form" and method—is the servant of a profoundly serious interest in life. To justify our speaking of such a novelist as in the tradition, that represented by those

---

20 "The politeness of Conrad to James and of James to Conrad was of the most impressive kind. Even if they had been addressing each other from the tribunal of the Académie Française their phrases could not have been more elaborate or delivered more *ore rotundo.* James always addressed Conrad as 'Mon cher confrère,' Conrad almost bleated with the peculiar tone that the Marseillais get into their compliments 'Mon cher maître' . . . Every thirty seconds. When James spoke of me to Conrad he always said: 'Votre ami, le jeune homme modeste.' They always spoke French together, James using an admirably pronounced, correct and rather stilted idiom such as prevailed in Paris in the 'seventies. Conrad spoke with extraordinary speed, fluency and incomprehensibility, a meridional French with as strong a Southern accent as that of garlic in *aioli.* . . . Speaking English he had so strong a French accent that few who did not know him well could understand him at first."— Ford Madox Ford, *Return to Yesterday,* pp. 23–4.

three, we are not called on to establish particular relations with any one of them. Like James, he brought a great deal from outside, but it was of the utmost importance to him that he found a serious art of fiction there in English, and that there *were,* in English, great novelists to study. He drew from English literature what he needed, and learnt in that peculiar way of genius which is so different from imitation. And for us, who have *him* as well as the others, there he is, unquestionably a constitutive part of the tradition, belonging in the full sense.

As being technically sophisticated he may be supposed to have found fortifying stimulus in James, whom he is quite unlike (though James, in his old age, was able to take a connoisseur's interest in *Chance* and appreciate with a professional eye the sophistication of the "doing").[21] But actually, the one influence at all obvious is that of a writer at the other end of the scale from sophistication, Dickens. As I point out in my discussion of him, Conrad is in certain respects so like Dickens that it is difficult to say for just how much influence Dickens counts. He is undoubtedly there in the London of *The Secret Agent,* though—except for the unfortunate *macabre* of the cab-journey, and one or two local mannerisms—he has been transmuted into Conrad. This co-presence of obvious influence with assimilation suggests that Dickens may have counted for more in Conrad's mature art (we don't find much to suggest Dickens in the early adjectival phase) than seems at first probable: it suggests that Dickens may have encouraged the development in Conrad's art of that extraordinary energy of vision and registration in which they are akin. ("When people say that Dickens exaggerates," says Mr. Santayana, "it seems to me that they can have no eyes and no ears. They probably have only *notions* of what things and people are; they accept them conventionally, at their diplomatic value.") We may reasonably, too, in the same way see some Dickensian influence, closely related and of the same order, in Conrad's use of melodrama, or what would have been melodrama in Dickens; for in Conrad the end is a total significance of a profoundly serious kind.

The reason for not including Dickens in the line of great novelists is implicit in this last phrase. The kind of greatness in question has been sufficiently defined. That Dickens was a great genius and is permanently among the classics is certain. But the genius was that of a great entertainer, and he had for the most part no profounder responsibility as a creative artist than this description suggests. Praising him magnificently in a very fine critique,[22] Mr. Santayana, in concluding, says: "In every English-speak-

---

21 Here is the testimony of Conrad's collaborator, Ford Madox Ford: "Conrad had the most unbounded, the most generous and the most understanding admiration for the Master's work but he did not much like James personally. I imagine that was because at bottom James was a New Englander *pur sang,* though he was actually born in New York. James on the other hand liked neither Conrad nor his work very much. . . . James on the other hand never made fun of Conrad in private. Conrad was never for him 'poor dear old' as were Flaubert, Mrs. Humphry Ward, Meredith, Hardy or Sir Edmund Gosse. He once expressed to me as regards Conrad something like an immense respect for his character and achievements. I cannot remember his exact words, but they were something to the effect that Conrad's works impressed him very disagreeably, but he could find no technical fault or awkwardness about them."—*Return to Yesterday,* p. 24.
22 See *Soliloquies in England.*

ing home, in the four quarters of the globe, parents and children would do well to read Dickens aloud of a winter's evening." This note is right and significant. The adult mind doesn't as a rule find in Dickens a challenge to an unusual and sustained seriousness. I can think of only one of his books in which his distinctive creative genius is controlled throughout to a unifying and organizing significance, and that is *Hard Times,* which seems, because of its unusualness and comparatively small scale, to have escaped recognition for the great thing it is. Conrad's views on it, supposing it to have caught his attention, would have been interesting; he was qualified to have written an apt appreciation.

It has a kind of perfection as a work of art that we don't associate with Dickens—a perfection that is one with the sustained and complete serious-ness for which among his productions it is unique. Though in length it makes a good-sized modern novel, it is on a small scale for Dickens: it leaves no room for the usual repetitive overdoing and loose inclusiveness. It is plain that he felt no temptation to these, he was too urgently possessed by his themes; the themes were too rich, too tightly knit in their variety and too commanding. Certain key characteristics of Victorian civilization had clearly come home to him with overwhelming force, embodied in con-crete manifestations that suggested to him connexions and significances he had never realized so fully before. The fable is perfect; the symbolic and representative values are inevitable, and, sufficiently plain at once, yield fresh subtleties as the action develops naturally in its convincing historical way.

In Gradgrind and Bounderby we have, in significant relation, two aspects of Victorian Utilitarianism. In Gradgrind it is a serious creed, devoutly held, and so, if repellent (as the name conveys), not wholly unrespectable; but we are shown Gradgrind as on the most intimate and uncritical terms with Josiah Bounderby, in whom we have the grossest and crassest, the most utterly unspiritual egotism, and the most blatant thrusting and bullying, to which a period of "rugged individualism" gave scope. Gradgrind, in fact, marries his daughter to Bounderby. Yet he is represented as a kind of James Mill; an intellectual who gives his children, on theory, an education that reminds us in a very significant way of the *Autobiography* of the younger Mill. And it is hardly possible to question the justice of this vision of the tendency of James Mill's kind of Utilitarianism, so blind in its onesidedness, so unaware of its bent and its blindness. The generous uncalculating spon-taneity, the warm flow of life, towards which Gradgrindery, practical and intellectual, must be hostile, is symbolized by Sleary's Horse-riding.

The richness in symbolic significance of *Hard Times* is far from ade-quately suggested by this account. The prose is that of one of the greatest masters of English, and the dialogue—very much a test in such an under-taking—is consummate; beautifully natural in its stylization. But there is only one *Hard Times* in the Dickensian *oeuvre.*

Though the greatness of *Hard Times* passed unnoticed, Dickens couldn't fail to have a wide influence. We have remarked his presence in *The Secret Agent.* It is there again, in a minor way, in George Eliot, in some of her less felicitous characterization; and it is there in Henry James, most patently, perhaps, in *The Princess Casamassima,* but most importantly in *Roderick*

*Hudson*.[23] It is there once more, and even more interestingly, in D. H. Lawrence, in *The Lost Girl*. The ironic humour, and the presentation in general, in the first part of that book bear a clear relation to the Dickensian, but are incomparably more mature, and belong to a total serious significance.

I take the opportunity, at this point, to remark parenthetically, that, whereas Dickens's greatness has been confirmed by time, it is quite otherwise with his rival. "It is usual," says Mr. Santayana, "to compare Dickens with Thackeray, which is like comparing the grape with the gooseberry; there are obvious points of resemblance, and the gooseberry has some superior qualities of its own; but you can't make red wine of it." It seems to me that Thackeray's place is fairly enough indicated, even if his peculiar quality isn't precisely defined, by inverting a phrase I found the other day on an examination-paper: "Trollope is a lesser Thackeray." Thackeray is a greater Trollope; that is, he has (apart from some social history) nothing to offer the reader whose demand goes beyond the "creation of characters" and so on. His attitudes, and the essential substance of interest, are so limited that (though, of course, he provides incident and plot) for the reader it is merely a matter of going on and on; nothing has been done by the close to justify the space taken—except, of course, that time has been killed (which seems to be all that even some academic critics demand of a novel). It will be fair enough to Thackeray if *Vanity Fair* is kept current as, in a minor way, a classic: the conventional estimate that puts him among the great won't stand the touch of criticism. The kind of thing that Thackeray is credited with is done at a mature level by James's friend, Howard Sturgis, in *Belchamber*, a novel about Edwardian society (it is, with an appropriateness not always observed in that series, included in *The World's Classics*).

To come back to Conrad and his major quality: he is one of those creative geniuses whose distinction is manifested in their being peculiarly alive in their time—peculiarly alive *to* it; not "in the vanguard" in the manner of Shaw and Wells and Aldous Huxley, but sensitive to the stresses of the changing spiritual climate as they begin to be registered by the most conscious. His interest in the tradition of the Merchant Service as a constructive triumph of the human spirit is correlative with his intense consciousness of the dependence, not only of the distinctive humanities at all levels, but of sanity itself and our sense of a normal outer world, on an analogous creative collaboration. His Robinson Crusoe cannot bear a few days alone on his island, and blows out his brains. We are a long way from Jane Austen, for whom the problem was not to rescue the highly conscious individual from his isolation, but much the contrary. Conrad, of course, was a *déraciné*, which no doubt counts for a good deal in the intensity with which he renders his favourite theme of isolation. But then a state of something like deracination is common to-day among those to whom the question of who the great novelists are is likely to matter. Conrad is representative in the way genius is, which is not the way of those writers in whom journalist-critics acclaim the *Zeitgeist*. (It is relevant to note here that in the early heyday of Wells and Shaw Conrad wrote *Nostromo*—a great creative masterpiece which, among other things, is essentially an implicit comment on

23 See Chapter III.

their preoccupations, made from a very much profounder level of preoccu-pation than theirs. And it is also relevant to venture that in Mr. Arthur Koestler's very distinguished novel, *Darkness at Noon,* we have the work of a writer—also, we note, not born to the language—who knows and admires Conrad, especially the Conrad of *Nostromo* and *Under Western Eyes.*)

Conrad is incomparably closer to us to-day than Hardy and Meredith are. So, for that matter, is George Eliot. I specify Hardy and Meredith because they are both offered to us among the great novelists, and they are both supposed to be philosophically profound about life. It will have been gathered that I think neither can support his reputation. On Hardy (who owes enormously to George Eliot) the appropriately sympathetic note is struck by Henry James: "The good little Thomas Hardy has scored a great success with *Tess of the d'Urbervilles,* which is chock-full of faults and falsity, and yet has a singular charm." This concedes by implication all that properly can be conceded—unless we claim more for *Jude the Obscure,* which, of all Hardy's works of a major philosophic-tragic ambition, comes nearer to sustaining it, and, in its clumsy way—which hasn't the rightness with which the great novelists show their profound sureness of their essential purpose—is impressive.[24] It is all the same a little comic that Hardy should have been taken in the early nineteen-twenties—the Chekhov period—as pre-eminently the representative of the "modern consciousness" or the modern "sense of the human situation." As for Meredith, I needn't add anything to what is said about him by Mr. E. M. Forster,[25] who, having belonged to the original *milieu* in which Meredith was erected into a great master, enjoys peculiar advantages for the necessary demolition-work.

Is there no name later than Conrad's to be included in the great tradi-tion? There is, I am convinced, one: D. H. Lawrence. Lawrence, in the English language, was the great genius of our time (I mean the age, or climatic phase, following Conrad's). It would be difficult to separate the novelist off for consideration, but it was in the novel that he committed himself to the hardest and most sustained creative labour, and he was, as a novelist, the representative of vital and significant development. He might, he has shown conclusively, have gone on writing novels with the kind of

---

[24] Arthur Mizener's essay, *"Jude the Obscure* as a Tragedy," in the Thomas Hardy Cen-tennial Issue of *The Southern Review* (Summer 1940), puts interestingly the case for a serious estimate of the book.

[25] See *Aspects of the Novel.* And here is James on *Lord Ormont and his Aminta:* "More-over, I have vowed not to open *Lourdes* till I shall have closed with a furious final bang the unspeakable Lord Ormont, which I have been reading at the maximum rate of ten pages—ten insufferable and unprofitable pages—a day. It fills me with a critical rage, an artistic fury, utterly blighting in me the indispensable principle of *respect.* I have finished, at this rate, but the first volume—whereof I am moved to declare that I doubt if any equal quantity of extravagant verbiage, of airs and graces, of phrases and attitudes, of obscurities and alembications, ever *started* less their subject, ever contributed less of a statement—told the reader less of what the reader needs to know. All the elaborate predicates of exposition without the ghost of a nominative to hook themselves to; and not a difficulty met, not a figure presented, not a scene constituted—not a dim shadow condensing once either into audible or into visible reality—making you hear for an instant the tap of its feet on the earth. Of course there are pretty things, but for what they are they come so much too dear, and so many of the profundities and tortuosities prove when threshed out to be only pretentious statements of the very simplest propositions."— To Edmund Gosse: *The Letters of Henry James,* Vol. I, p. 224.

"character creation" and psychology that the conventional cultivated reader immediately appreciates—novels that demanded no unfamiliar effort of approach. He might—if his genius had let him. In nothing is the genius more manifest than in the way in which, after the great success—and *succès d'estime*—of *Sons and Lovers* he gives up that mode and devotes himself to the exhausting toil of working out the new things, the developments, that as the highly conscious and intelligent servant of life he saw to be necessary. Writing to Edward Garnett of the work that was to become *Women in Love* he says: "It is *very* different from *Sons and Lovers*: written in another language almost. I shall be sorry if you don't like it, but am prepared. I shan't write in the same manner as *Sons and Lovers* again, I think—in that hard, violent style full of sensation and presentation." [26]

Describing at length what he is trying to do he says:

> You mustn't look in my novel for the old stable *ego* of the character. There is another *ego*, according to whose action the individual is unrecognizable, and passes through, as it were, allotropic states which it needs a deeper sense than any we've been used to exercise, to discover are states of the same single radically unchanged element. (Like as diamond and coal are the same pure simple element of carbon. The ordinary novel would trace the history of the diamond—but I say, 'Diamond, what! This is carbon.' And my diamond might be coal or soot, and my theme is carbon.) You must not say my novel is shaky—it is not perfect, because I am not expert in what I want to do. But it is the real thing, say what you like. And I shall get my reception, if not now, then before long. Again I say, don't look for the development of the novel to follow the lines of certain characters: the characters fall into the form of some other rhythmic form, as when one draws a fiddle-bow across a fine tray delicately sanded, the sand takes lines unknown.[27]

He is a most daring and radical innovator in "form," method, technique. And his innovations and experiments are dictated by the most serious and urgent kind of interest in life. This is the spirit of it:

> Do you know Cassandra in Aeschylus and Homer? She is one of the world's great figures, and what the Greeks and Agamemnon did to her is symbolic of what mankind has done to her since—raped and despoiled her, to their own ruin. It is not your brain that you must trust to, nor your will—but to that fundamental pathetic faculty for receiving the hidden waves that come from the depths of life, and for transferring them to the unreceptive world. It is something which happens below the consciousness, and below the range of the will—it is something which is unrecognizable and frustrated and destroyed.[28]

It is a spirit that, for all the unlikeness, relates Lawrence closely to George Eliot.[29] He writes, again, to Edward Garnett: [30]

> You see—you tell me I am half a Frenchman and one-eighth a Cockney. But that isn't it. I have very often the vulgarity and disagreeableness of the common

26 *The Letters of D. H. Lawrence* (London: William Heinemann Ltd., by permission of Laurence Pollinger Ltd.), p. 172.
27 *Letters*, p. 198.
28 *Letters*, p. 232.
29 Lawrence too has been called a Puritan.
30 *Letters*, p. 190.

people, as you say Cockney, and I may be a Frenchman. But primarily I am a passionately religious man, and my novels must be written from the depth of my religious experience. That I must keep to, because I can only work like that. And my Cockneyism and commonness are only when the deep feeling doesn't find its way out, and a sort of jeer comes instead, and sentimentality and purplism. But you should see the religious, earnest, suffering man in me first, and then the flippant or common things after. Mrs. Garnett says I have no true nobility— with all my cleverness and charm. But that is not true. It is there, in spite of all the littlenesses and commonnesses.

It is this spirit, by virtue of which he can truly say that what he writes must be written from the depth of his religious experience, that makes him, in my opinion, so much more significant in relation to the past and future, so much more truly creative as a technical inventor, an innovator, a master of language, than James Joyce. I know that Mr. T. S. Eliot has found in Joyce's work something that recommends Joyce to him as positively religious in tendency (see *After Strange Gods*). But it seems plain to me that there is no organic principle determining, informing, and controlling into a vital whole, the elaborate analogical structure, the extraordinary variety of technical devices, the attempts at an exhaustive rendering of consciousness, for which *Ulysses* is remarkable, and which got it accepted by a cosmopolitan literary world as a new start. It is rather, I think, a dead end, or at least a pointer to disintegration—a view strengthened by Joyce's own development (for I think it significant and appropriate that *Work in Progress*— *Finnegans Wake,* as it became—should have engaged the interest of the inventor of Basic English).

It is true that we can point to the influence of Joyce in a line of writers to which there is no parallel issuing from Lawrence. But I find here further confirmation of my view. For I think that in these writers, in whom a regrettable (if minor) strain of Mr. Eliot's influence seems to me to join with that of Joyce, we have, in so far as we have anything significant, the wrong kind of reaction against liberal idealism.[31] I have in mind writers in whom Mr. Eliot has expressed an interest in strongly favourable terms: Djuna Barnes of *Nightwood,* Henry Miller, Lawrence Durrell of *The Black Book.* In these writers—at any rate in the last two (and the first seems to me insignificant)—the spirit of what we are offered affects me as being essentially a desire, in Laurentian phrase, to "do dirt" on life. It seems to me important that one should, in all modesty, bear one's witness in these matters. "One must speak for life and growth, amid all this mass of destruction and disintegration." [32] This is Lawrence, and it is the spirit of all his work. It is the spirit of the originality that gives his novels their disconcerting quality, and gives them the significance of works of genius.

I am not contending that he isn't, as a novelist, open to a great deal of criticism, or that his achievement is as a whole satisfactory (the potentiality being what it was). He wrote his later books far too hurriedly. But I know from experience that it is far too easy to conclude that his very aim and intention condemned him to artistic unsatisfactoriness. I am thinking in

31 See D. H. Lawrence's *Fantasia of the Unconscious,* especially Chapter XI.
32 *The Letters of D. H. Lawrence,* p. 256.

particular of two books at which he worked very hard, and in which he developed his disconcertingly original interests and approaches—*The Rainbow* and *Women in Love*. Re-read, they seem to me astonishing works of genius, and very much more largely successful than they did when I read them (say) fifteen years ago. I still think that *The Rainbow* doesn't build up sufficiently into a whole. But I shouldn't be quick to offer my criticism of *Women in Love*, being pretty sure that I should in any case have once more to convict myself of stupidity and habit-blindness on later re-reading. And after these novels there comes, written, perhaps, with an ease earned by this hard work done, a large body of short stories and *nouvelles* that are as indubitably successful works of genius as any the world has to show.

I have, then, given my hostages. What I think and judge I have stated as responsibly and clearly as I can. Jane Austen, George Eliot, Henry James, Conrad, and D. H. Lawrence: the great tradition of the English novel is *there*.

# 4. THE USES OF BIOGRAPHY

## The Theory

*E. M. W. Tillyard*

## THE PERSONAL HERESY (II)

In his brilliant essay on *The Personal Heresy in Criticism* printed in last year's *Essays and Studies of the English Association,* Mr. C. S. Lewis mentioned my *Milton* as a book in which poetry was treated as the expression of personality. And up to a point he may have been right. But as he is hostile to my supposed way of thinking, and as I agree with a good deal of his essay, it seems either that I did not make myself clear or that Mr. Lewis is not entirely right. So I welcome this opportunity of saying what I mean by personality in literature. However, though certain cross-purposes may be straightened by further discussion, I do not say that much of Mr. Lewis's essay is not extremely provocative and controversial. With some of it I disagree; and as the matters of disagreement seem to me well worth dwelling on, I offer the comments that follow. I hope that my being stirred to argue the point with Mr. Lewis may be taken as my warm tribute to his essay's excellence.

As a preliminary, I must express surprise that Mr. Lewis considers the Personal Heresy, as he calls it, a sign of modernity. I should have thought it slightly shop-soiled. Mr. Lewis quotes an ambiguous passage from Mr. T. S. Eliot as supporting it: yet what weight can this passage have in the face of so uncompromising an attack on the Personal Heresy as that author's essay on *Tradition and the Individual Talent*? Here Mr. Eliot says that "the progress of an artist is a continual self-sacrifice, a continual extinction

Reprinted from *The Personal Heresy: A Controversy* (1939) by E. M. W. Tillyard and C. S. Lewis, by permission of the author.

of personality," and that "honest criticism and sensitive appreciation is directed not upon the poet but upon the poetry." And he comes to the conclusion that for the poet the mind of Europe and of his own country is much more important than his own private mind. Now these sentiments are not only close to Mr. Lewis's but they agree with a strong modern tendency, whose limits are not easily drawn, to belittle the individual in comparison with the race, the personal in comparison with the abstract, the Renaissance in comparison with Byzantium. Whatever the fate of this tendency—it may peter out in a few years for all we can tell—at the moment it is modern, and the opposite tendency to cling to the personal, even if fated shortly to prevail, just fails to be modern.

As a second preliminary let me say I entirely accept Mr. Lewis's contention that in the matter of personality you can draw no line between lyric and dramatic poetry. I believe with him that there is a difference between (for example) the poet's feeling towards personal pain and towards pain pictured in his poetry; but within the latter category it makes no difference whether the pain is pictured as happening to the poet speaking for himself in a lyric or to a fictitious personage in a drama.

To turn now to the words "personal" and "personality," it is plain how easy misunderstanding may be if we consider the following sentence of Mr. Lewis's. In commenting on the passage from Keats's *Hyperion* beginning—

> As when, upon a tranced summer-night,
> Those green-rob'd senators of mighty woods,
> Tall oaks . . .

he writes:

It is not relevant that Keats first read about senators (let us say) in a little brown book, in a room smelling of boiled beef, the same day that he pulled out a loose tooth; it is relevant that the senators sat still when the invading Gauls entered the Senate House; it is relevant that Rome really established an empire.

In this passage Mr. Lewis implies that "personal" as a critical term includes every accident however trivial connected with the author. No one can complain that he does so, but I should guess that not a few supporters of the "personal heresy" would simply ignore such trivialities in their conception of personality. They would attach them to the sphere of literary gossip, not to that of criticism. Certainly I should never dream of giving them any critical value in themselves and I should agree that to recall such things when reading poetry would be grossly inappropriate. The most that literary gossip can do in the way of criticism is to keep people off a wrong track. There is a story about Milton that once after his blindness, hearing a lady sing, he said, "Now I swear this lady is handsome." Such an anecdote might have had a critical use at the time when Milton was imagined to be insusceptible to female charm. Now that this error has been generally discarded, the anecdote has no critical value—it is no more than a pleasant piece of literary gossip, and to be conscious of it when we read, for instance, the Chorus's description of Dalila entering like a ship with streamers flying is to abuse both the anecdote and the poetry. If Mr. Lewis in attacking the

personal heresy is wishing to point out that some of the labour spent in
recent years on Johnson and Lamb, for instance, is anecdotal rather than
critical, and that to confound the two spheres is a heresy, then he has my
support.

Of course Mr. Lewis does not confine "personal" to this trivial or acci-
dental sense. He grants that it is possible through poetry to come into
contact with a poet's temperament in the most intimate way. The reader
shares the poet's consciousness. But, according to Mr. Lewis, even so the
personal contact involved is relatively unimportant: first, because the personality with which the reader achieves contact is not the poet's normal
personality but a heightened, temporary, perhaps alien, personality; secondly, because that personality is a means of vision rather than the thing
ultimately seen. The personal heresy consists in the reader's seeing the
poet's *normal* personality in his poetry, and in focusing his eyes on that personality instead of letting them contemplate the universe in a particular way.

Now if it is heretical to hold that part of the value of poetry consists
in gaining contact with the normal personality of the poet, then I am a
heretic. But I shall probably be using the word "normal" in a way Mr.
Lewis would disclaim. When he imagines Keats reading about senators in a
little brown book in a room smelling of boiled beef he attaches these supposed facts to Keats's normal personality. I should do nothing of the sort,
but call them as irrelevant to his normal personality as to the passage of
*Hyperion* under discussion. In other words by "personality" or "normal
personality" I do not mean practical or everyday personality, I mean rather
some mental pattern which makes Keats Keats and not Mr. Smith or Mr.
Jones. (Pattern is of course a bad word because it implies the static, whereas
personality cannot remain fixed: the poet's personality is in the pattern of
the sea rather than in that of a mosaic pavement.) And I believe we read
Keats in some measure because his poetry gives a version of a remarkable
personality of which another version is his life. The two versions are not
the same but they are analogous. Part of our response to poetry is in fact
similar to the stirring we experience when we meet some one whose personality impresses us. Such a person may startle us by the things he does,
but quite outside anything he does there will be a distinction about him
which, though difficult to define, we prize and which has the faculty of
rousing us to some extent from our quotidian selves. This person may be
subject to accidents, such as toothache, irregular habits, or an uncertain
temper, which interfere with our enjoying this distinguished mental pattern
of his; yet we know that the pattern is there. Though subject to change it is
definite enough to be called habitual; it can indeed be looked on as his
normal self underlying the accidents of quotidian existence.

One of the readiest ways of pointing to the function of personality in
poetry is by means of the word style. "Style" readily suggests the mental
pattern of the author, the personality realized in words. Style in poetry is
partly a matter of rhythm; and rhythm, Dr. Richards says very truly in
*Science and Poetry,* "is no matter of tricks with syllables, but directly reflects
personality." Mr. Lewis would probably define style as the poet's credentials
certifying him a person whom you can trust in the quest of bringing back
true reports on the universe; and consider the report far more important

than the credentials. But I should assert myself that experience shows how directly personality revealed through style can constitute the major appeal of poetry. It is pleasant to choose an example from a modern poet who considers poetry an escape from personality rather than an expression of it. In Mr. T. S. Eliot's latest work, *The Rock,* the most successful passages are those where the author's characteristic rhythms and word-arrangements have freest scope, where his style is most obviously recognizable, in other words when he is most himself.

> A Cry from the North, from the West and from the South:
> Whence thousands travel daily to the timekept City;
> Where My Word is unspoken,
> In the land of lobelias and tennis flannels
> The rabbit shall burrow and the thorn revisit,
> The nettle shall flourish on the gravel court,
> And the wind shall say: "Here were decent godless people:
> Their only monument the asphalt road
> And a thousand lost golf balls."

Here the style *is* the poetry. The rhythm has a tense pregnant hush, simple in seeming, however subtle in the attainment, that sets off, that exploits to the utmost, the startling mixture of biblical reference and golf balls. It is entirely individual to the author, it reflects a poetical personality that quickens our pulses, and we value it far more than any heightened apprehension the passage may give us of the things of which it speaks. Mr. Lewis might retort by attaching Mr. Eliot, for all his professions of classicism, to the romantic tradition, and by pointing to his admission that for that tradition the personal theory does not work too badly. So I had better choose a second example not open to this retort; and I cannot do better in illustrating how widely I differ from Mr. Lewis in my conception of the personal sphere in literature than choose the passage from Isaiah to which he refuses all personal quality whatsoever:

And Babylon, the glory of kingdoms, the beauty of the Chaldees' excellency, shall be as when God overthrew Sodom and Gomorrah. It shall never be inhabited, neither shall it be dwelt in from generation to generation: neither shall the Arabian pitch tent there: neither shall the shepherds make their fold there. But wild beasts of the desert shall lie there; and their houses shall be full of doleful creatures; and owls shall dwell there, and satyrs shall dance there. And the wild beasts of the islands shall cry in their desolate houses, and dragons in their pleasant palaces.

First, I am willing to admit with Mr. Lewis that we do not through this passage get in touch with the personality of the original author, or at least, if we see him, it is at best through a mist. But with his remarks on the translator I disagree. Mr. Lewis considers that he was so preoccupied with philological and theological matters that his own personality could find no entrance. This to my mind is to misunderstand not only translation but any art that appears to consist in getting a job of work done. Rule out the possibility of the translator mediating his own self, and you turn much early painting and sculpture, where the artist is fighting to render (as he

thinks) a convincing likeness, into a mere technical exercise. On the contrary, it is precisely when a translator has worked himself up into an excited
desire to do justice to a fine passage or a primitive sculptor is growing
triumphant at surmounting a technical difficulty that his own mental pattern has the chance of manifesting itself. The artist will probably think his
personality is lost in his non-personal activity, but the result may quite
belie his own expectations. The sculptor of the Delphic Charioteer would
have been incredulous if he had been told that his "personality" had in any
way entered into the figure of that impassive, severely draped young man; he
probably thought he had done a good job of work and made a good imitation of the sort of driver who ought to win a chariot race for an illustrious
prince. Yet the statue is like no other statue on earth, and I believe this
unlikeness to be both an important element in the statue's excellence and
to be connected with the sculptor's personality. Similarly the passage from
Isaiah has a quite individual ferocity of rhythm which, if we heed it, will
make the passage far less remote and romantic than Mr. Lewis would have it
be, and incidentally, not too far removed from the immediacy which he
very justly postulates for the original. "For us," says Mr. Lewis, "Babylon is
far away and long ago": possibly, but was it so for a Protestant divine writing not long after the Gunpowder Plot? Not that the translator consciously
or literally thought the passage a prophecy of the fall of the Papacy, and
that he believed dragons would writhe in the ruined halls of the Vatican,
but I suspect that Babylon evoked the Protestant fervour which was a motive
in the translator's mental pattern. Of course a modern reader may let his
mind be guided by the associations that the various evocative words in the
passage have got for him: but this is rather an indulgence of the reader's
own personal proclivities than a proper reading; "personal" in a far less
legitimate sense than in that of trying to establish contact with the mental
pattern of the author.

When I spoke of the sculptor of the Delphic Charioteer having no
notion that his own personality had anything to do with a statue, I was
hinting at a paradox that may go a good way to explaining why people who
may agree at bottom appear to think so differently about personality in
literature. When Mr. Eliot calls poetry "an escape from personality," he
means more than an escape from the accidents that attend a person in
everyday life. He is trying to describe what it feels like when a man succeeds
in writing poetry. The feeling (and other poets confirm Mr. Eliot) brings
with it the impression of a complete abandonment of personality, analogous
to the feeling of "getting out of yourself" that may occur in many non-
literary contexts. Mr. Eliot speaks of the poet "surrendering himself wholly
to the work to be done." The paradox consists in the poet often producing
the most characteristic and personal work through this very process of self-
surrender. The more the poet experiences this abandonment of personality,
the more likely is the reader to hail the poet's characteristic, unmistakable
self. In fact the poet is *ipsissimus cum minime ipse*. Nor will it make the
poet any less personal, if he carefully avoids every vestige of private emotion, if he seeks the utmost objectification. On the contrary, the pattern into
which these apparently alien objects are fitted will express all the more
clearly, with the least risk of encumbrance, the characteristic lines of the

poet's mental pattern. Herein lies the reason why the following passage from Mr. Lewis's essay is no valid argument against the personal theory. In commenting on the lines from *Hyperion* he writes:

It is absolutely essential that each word should suggest not what is private and personal to the poet but what is public, common, impersonal, objective. The common world with its nights, its oaks, and its stars, which we have all seen, and which mean at least *something* the same to all of us, is the bank on which he draws his cheques.

Here Mr. Lewis is assuming that what is true of communication is true of the experience communicated. As far as the former goes, his doctrine is sound, containing the legitimate reproof of the kind of modern verse that draws its cheque on the banks of Albi or Florence or Timbuctoo rather than on the Bank of England. But as regards experience Mr. Lewis is not always right. However public the means of communication, the experience conveyed may (among other things or even chiefly) be a mental pattern peculiar to the poet. Anyhow it is plain enough that those who choose to see only one half of the paradox will never agree with those who choose to see only the other.

However, granted the paradox, there remains another critical sense of the word personal. It is best set forth through Coleridge's comparison of Shakespeare and Milton in the fifteenth chapter of the *Biographia Literaria:*

While the former darts himself forth, and passes into all the forms of human character and passion, the one Proteus of the fire and blood; the other attracts all forms and things to himself, into the unity of his own ideal. All things and modes of action shape themselves anew in the being of Milton; while Shakespeare becomes all things, yet for ever remaining himself.

Now in a sense Shakespeare was just as thorough as Milton in impressing his own personality on the reader. But just because Shakespeare's own mental pattern largely consisted of an almost unexampled power of adapting itself to the shifting experiences of life so as to extract the utmost mental nourishment from them, his personality makes a much less precise effect on us than does the more rigid personality of Milton. When then we talk of the poetry of Milton or of Wordsworth being more personal than that of Shakespeare or of Keats we may be meaning that it expresses a more austerely rigid nature. Now these fluid and rigid natures, although they may both be transmuted into poetry and become thereby accessible, do react differently on the relation between the poet's life and the poet's art. The fluid, adaptable, receptive natures, granted power, are likely to be pure artists and to empty their lives for the sake of their art. Their power, their fierceness go to solving their artistic problems. Flaubert is habitually quoted as an author of this kind. The more rigid natures, who insist, for all their sensibility to impressions, on imposing their own very definite patterns on the world of their vision are likely to be interesting persons in their private lives, apt to do more notable things and to impress themselves on those around them. Thus Wordsworth must needs poke his nose into the French Revolution.

Before drawing some critical deductions from these statements, I wish to say that the above general division of authors into the fluid and empty-lived on the one hand, and the rigid and full-lived on the other, does not invalidate the analogy I postulated above between the mind-pattern as expressed in art and the mind-pattern as expressed in life. True, the analogy between a biography composed of a few dry facts supplemented by a few trivial anecdotes and a beautifully proportioned body of poetry can appear ridiculous. But it may be that the two versions differ less in kind than in completeness. One is a perfect volume; the other consists of a few mutilated pages. The mind-pattern is fully revealed in the poetry; from the biographical material its main lines are indecipherable. And yet the fact that we cannot decipher them does not prove that their trend is not similar to that purged, clarified, and intensified pattern that shows up in the poetry. Even when an author distils almost the whole of himself into his writing (as Flaubert did), what is left of the man, ghost-like and bloodless as it may be, can repeat in some vague sort the mental pattern that has been presented so perfectly in the works. Contact with him might inform us that here is a remarkable personality, but so abstracted from active living as to be unprofitable to pursue. In other words, even the author most depersonalized or sucked dry by his art is potentially a man of note outside the literary sphere.

Still, though the life of the man who has yielded himself to his art should present some analogy with that art, it may, however closely scrutinized, be entirely useless in heightening the appreciation of that art. In fact biographical study will in this case insist on staying on the hither side of criticism in the province of literary anecdotage. It is very likely that Shakespeare's biography, even with the fullest knowledge, would remain as at present in that province. But with the other class, the biography, the *facts* of personality, the data for the mental pattern of the man's life, may substantially help our understanding of the mental pattern as revealed in his art. An extreme example would be William Morris, a much less extreme one, Milton. And if, in writing of Milton, I have forsaken the safe Johnsonian example of not confounding biography and criticism, I would say in defence that I did so because I was writing of Milton, not because I thought they should invariably be so confounded. Yet I grant that the mixture of biography and criticism, even when most justified by the nature of the author, has its besetting danger: it is all too easy for the reader to use biography as an illegitimate short cut into the poet's mental pattern as revealed in his poems. He may arrive thereby at what seems a place higher up on the more difficult road of intensive study of the isolated word, but he will have missed the essential revelation that could only be obtained by the very journey he has shirked. He will, in fact, have been doing something like looking up the answers to a problem when tired of trying to solve it, or using a crib when reading a foreign text. It is when a man believes that the intensive study of the isolated word has gone astray or has been brought to a standstill that he is justified in seeking guidance from biography.

Mr. Lewis's essay raises the whole question of what poetry is about. From the hints he drops I gather that for him poetry is about objects outside the poet's mind, about racial perception, and about God. My business is not with this topic, nor am I clear enough about Mr. Lewis's views to be able to use them as a starting-point. But I wish to make two observations on it before I close. First, I disclaim any intention of limiting the value of poetry to establishing contact with an important personality; and I would refer the reader to an early chapter in my recent book, *Poetry Direct and Oblique,* in which I discuss the things poetry tends to concern. Some of these things, though we accept information about them only because we trust the person who gives it, are different from the personality or mental pattern of the author, described above. They are nearer, at any rate, to the discoveries about the universe that Mr. Lewis expects the poet to make. Secondly, although I have departed from the doctrines of Dr. Richards so far as to admit that the poet tells us things as well as imposes valuable equilibria on our minds, I find Mr. Lewis too rigidly concerned with things and too little heedful of states of mind when he discusses his examples. My disagreement from him can best be illustrated by discussing one of his own instances, Herrick's *Upon Julia's Clothes.* Mr. Lewis discusses half the poem. It may be fairer to take the whole:

> Whenas in silks my Julia goes,
> Then, then, methinks, how sweetly flows
> That liquefaction of her clothes.
> Next, when I cast mine eyes, and see
> That brave vibration each way free;
> Oh, how that glittering taketh me!

Commenting on the first three lines, Mr. Lewis calls them "poetry of an unusually sensuous and simple type," and says that in them "the only experience which has any claim to be poetical experience is an apprehension not of the poet, but of silk." The poet has presented an idea of silk and one of unusual vividness. Now Mr. Lewis expressly excludes from the poetic value of the lines the notion, "With what eyes the poet must have seen silk": that is merly an irrelevant afterthought. I can only conclude that in his opinion the lines concern not a state of mind but a substance called silk, and that they reveal hitherto unapprehended qualities of silk. What are these qualities? Mr. Lewis suggests that the word "liquefaction" is responsible for the vividness with which silk is apprehended. In other words Herrick has made the discovery that compared with certain other textures (felt, for instance) silk resembles in its suppleness a liquid rather than a solid. I cannot believe that Mr. Lewis really holds that the poem's virtue can reside in so elementary an observation, an observation in the power of so many people and not at all requiring the superior penetration of poetic genius. Yet what is the alternative? I can only see (granted silk as the concern of the poem) the vaguely mystical or Platonic notion (common enough in the late nineteenth century) that objects have some essential quality, some true self, which the artist can in some way reveal. Now such interpretations of poetry seem to me justified only if backed by the complete philosophy which they imply. Usually they imply no philosophy; and I doubt, from Mr. Lewis's remarks, whether he really wishes to attach this particular poem to any comprehensive creed. If he does, I have no quarrel with him. If he does not, I think he has failed to attach any value to Herrick's lines.

What I cannot accept in Mr. Lewis's interpretation of the poem is the value he puts on "things." I do not say that the poem does not tell us something, but I do say that what it tells us about silk has a very subordinate share in the poem's total meaning. Silk may have considerable importance as a means, as an end it is negligible. Even the claim of temporal priority made for silk (a claim whose importance I do not admit) is not justified; for before the silk is made vivid to us, we are given through the excited repetition of the words "then, then," the statement of the speaker's excitement at the sight of his Julia in motion. Far from containing the virtue of the poem, the apprehension of silk is but one of a number of factors that go to express a state of mind which readers have somehow shared, and which they have considered in some way valuable. Here are a few of these factors. A fresh and unaffected sensuality pervades the poem. Not only is the speaker's excitement expressed by "then, then," but from the flow of the clothes and their vibration the hint of the body beneath is not absent. The full emphasis and the fall of the third line express how well the spectator's excitement is satisfied by the downward flow of the silk. We may even derive from "liquefaction" a hint of the word "satisfaction." "Liquefaction" is a sophisticated word, and as such is more important than as describing the quality of silk which (incidentally) had been already indicated in the word "flows." More important, probably, than any of the factors noted above is the contrast on which the poem is constructed. The spectator first sees the downward flow of Julia's silks and he experiences satisfaction. He then sees the silks vibrating, perhaps moving in little horizontal eddies, and he is captivated. Even if this contrast means no more than a sense of balance or decorum it is not unimportant in the poem; and anyhow it is something very different from an isolated apprehension of silk.

Now few readers will accept all these observations on Herrick's poem, but I hope most of them will agree that it is complicated and not so very simple and sensuous. And I should be glad to think that they found it initially more reasonable to consider that poem in terms of a state of mind than in terms of a substance called silk. For it is not by any laborious process of induction *after* we have read the poem that we apprehend the qualities of unaffected sensuality, keen observation, sophistication, and sense of decorum. We apprehend them from the rhythm, the vocabulary, the word-arrangement, the pattern of the poem, in fact from the poem's most intimate poetical features. And the fact that such an enumeration is critically only of the most trivial value does not preclude its being on sounder lines than seeing the poem in terms of "things."

To go further, to describe the state of mind these qualities compose is luckily not necessary to my argument, nor need I reopen the question of how far it is the poet's personality we get in touch with through the poem. But I should like to add that seeing a poem in terms of a state of mind need not preclude "Theism or Platonism or Absolute Idealism." If you wish to see God in poetry, you can see Him as readily in the mind of a human being as in a piece of silk.

F. O. *Matthiessen*

## "OUT OF UNHANDSELLED SAVAGE NATURE"

The American with the richest natural gifts as a writer became one largely by accident. In sharpest contrast to Hawthorne's deliberate resolve to be an author of fiction, his embarrassed withdrawal of the still-born *Fanshawe,* and his subsequent long apprenticeship to his craft before collecting his *Tales,* Melville's first book was a record of experience. Undertaken directly upon his return from nearly four years of adventure, it was in print and making his reputation only a little more than a year after he had been discharged from the frigate *United States* as a common seaman. The writing he had done previously amounted to nothing more substantial than two "Fragments from a Writing-Desk," which had been printed in *The Democratic Press* of Lansingburgh, New York, when he was a schoolteacher of nineteen. These are stock dilutions of the *Spectator* tradition, and show no more than that his own formal education, broken off at fifteen by his family's upset finances, had subsequently been extended to include allusions to *Romeo* and *Hamlet,* to Sheridan and Burke and Coleridge, and that his taste was somewhat adulterated by the sentiment of Tom Moore.

If *Typee* had not been an instant success, Melville might well have stopped there, since he had his living to make. But its sequel *Omoo* was clearly called for, and after he became aware of his talents through their exercise, the thought next occurred to him that, having published two narratives of travel that had been regarded with incredulity in many quarters, he might try a romance and see if it could be made to pass for truth. But by the time he had launched on *Mardi* he was married, and his first child was born just before the book appeared. He was compelled, therefore, to undertake a pot-boiler, and turned for his material to another segment of his adventures, his first voyage, the passage to Liverpool he had made at seventeen. That led on naturally to a book about what had happened to him after his life among the cannibals and as a beachcomber in Tahiti; and so he based

Reprinted from *American Renaissance: Art and Expression in the Age of Emerson and Whitman* by **F. O.** Matthiessen, by permission of Oxford University Press, Inc. Copyright 1941 by Oxford University Press, Inc., New York, N.Y.

*White Jacket* on his months in the navy. The one large part of his experience that was still left untapped by all these was the knowledge he had acquired of the whaling industry before he had jumped ship at Typee. *Moby-Dick* ranged farther from his personal history than even *Mardi* had, since the turgid conversations of that romance had often been the debates of his own developing mind, whereas Ahab and his crew were more completely an imaginative projection. When he decided at last to represent life in America, he was no longer writing autobiography even in the loose sense that *Redburn* can be so called; though because of the scantiness of information for Melville's early years, *Pierre* has been unjustifiably so taken by most of his biographers. In the volumes that remained, *Israel Potter*, the bulk of *The Piazza Tales*, *The Confidence Man*, he was not drawing on his own actions at all.

The author of *Typee* was two years older than the author of *Fanshawe*. The author of *Pierre* was thirty-three, the same age as the author of *Twice-Told Tales*, a year older than Thoreau was when he issued the *Week*, three years younger than Whitman when he printed his first *Leaves*, four years younger than the Emerson of the first *Essays*, thirteen years younger than the author of *The Scarlet Letter*. The bursting of Melville's vitality gives the proof of what Emerson had proclaimed in *The American Scholar*: "Not out of those on whom systems of education have exhausted their culture, comes the helpful giant to destroy the old or to build the new, but out of unhandselled savage nature."

In his essay on Hawthorne, Melville exclaimed: "Believe me, my friends, that men not very much inferior to Shakespeare are this day being born on the banks of the Ohio. And the day will come when you shall say, Who reads a book by an Englishman that is a modern?" This was the natural response to Sydney Smith's British arrogance of a generation before: "In the four quarters of the globe, who reads an American book?" [1] Melville's tone is akin here to Whitman's, and may strike us as the extreme of romantic extravagance, as the kind of recklessness that made Carlyle remark that Whitman thought he was a big man because he lived in a big country. Yet without this heady confidence there could hardly have been the renaissance of these years; and Melville and Whitman were right in their intuitions that they were living at the very hour of matured harvest. Emerson was more conscious, in his journal of 1847, of the precarious balance of such periods: "In history, the great moment is when the savage is just ceasing to be a savage . . . that moment of transition,—the foam hangs but a moment on the wave; the sun himself does not pause on the meridian; literature becomes criticism, nervousness, and a gnawing when the first musical triumphant strain has waked the echoes."

In the double excitement of his discovery of both Hawthorne and Shakespeare, Melville felt that other minds might go as far, that there was "hardly a mortal man, who, at some time or other, has not felt as great thoughts

---

[1] In *The Edinburgh Review*, January 1820. Smith was particularly unfortunate in the timing of his question, since Irving had just issued his *Sketch Book;* and with the appearance in the following year of Bryant's first volume of poems and especially of Cooper's *Spy*, the literature of the new nation, as distinct from colonial literature, had begun to find its voice.

in him as any you will find in Hamlet." In the summer that he wrote this, he was responding far more to the abundance of Shakespeare's creative energy than to the corrosion of Hamlet's self-scrutiny. He had not yet lived through the experience of writing the tragedies of Ahab and Pierre. Only through the act of doing what he praised Hawthorne for, through dropping his mind "down into the universe like a plummet," was he to come to something like the fierceness of Hamlet's disillusion. Nervous attritions oppressed him when nearly all that resulted from his two major efforts was violent misunderstanding or neglect. Even during the tension of finishing *Moby-Dick,* he foresaw, in the letter to Hawthorne wherein he dated the beginning of his life from his twenty-fifth year, the year of his return from the sea, that the culmination of powers implied an end. "I feel that I am now come to the inmost leaf of the bulb, and that shortly the flower must fall to the mould."

Among *The Piazza Tales* was "Benito Cereno," one of the most sensitively poised pieces of writing he had ever done. However, by then Melville's more prevailing mood had become that of *The Confidence Man,* where his angrily frustrated satire broke off unfinished with, "Something further may follow of this Masquerade." When he wrote that sentence, he had had a full decade as a professional writer. He seems to have decided that was enough, for though he lived nearly thirty-five years more, he published no more prose.[2] The poems that formed his running commentary on the Civil War were issued in the year after its ending. By that year, too, he had given up any hope of a consular appointment, which, being very little of a party man, he had sought both through Hawthorne and later from the Lincoln administration. He had also had enough of a brief career of lecturing, in the years just prior to the War, on such subjects as "The South Seas," "Travelling," and "Statuary in Rome," as far afield as Chicago and Montreal. Consequently, he accepted the job of outdoor inspector of customs in New York. Unlike Hawthorne, he held his post for twenty years, during which he found time to produce his philosophical poem *Clarel,* finally published in 1876 on money provided by an uncle. Its interminable debates between doubt and faith used for their setting the trip to the Holy Land that he had made in 1856 after writing his last novel. With his retirement from the customhouse in 1885, he had sufficient leisure for issuing two more small volumes of verse, privately printed in only twenty-five copies; and for the final major recrudescence of his prose in *Billy Budd,* which was left in manuscript at his death, and not published until 1924.

In *Moby-Dick* Ishmael meditated, as Melville had in *Typee,* on the fact that "long exile from Christendom and civilization inevitably restores a man to that condition in which God placed him, i.e. what is called savagery," and added, "I myself am a savage." But there were many senses in which

2 In his copy of Arnold's *Essays in Criticism,* which he acquired in 1869, he marked Maurice de Guérin's dictum, "The literary career seems to me unreal, both in its own essence, and in the rewards which one seeks from it, and therefore fatally marred by a secret absurdity." To this Melville added: "This is the first verbal statement of a truth which everyone who thinks in these days must have felt." He also scored a remark on the torture of having to produce: "To a sensitive man like Guérin, to silence his genius is more tolerable than to hackney it."

Melville was not. Of the same racial mixture as Whitman, English on his father's side, Dutch on his mother's, his ancestors had risen far above the Whitmans' plebeian class. There was a weight of wealth and aristocracy behind Melville much greater even than that behind Hawthorne, and he had suffered a much sharper personal experience of family decline. His mother's forebears had been good brewers in Albany from the era of Harmen Van Gansevoort, who had come to this country sometime before 1660, and whose descendants had given the name to Gansevoort Street in New York, at the foot of which, ironically, was the wharf where Melville worked for the government. Melville's grandfather, Peter Gansevoort, had been a distinguished soldier in the Revolution, and his namesake, the uncle who was to provide for *Clarel,* graduated from Princeton, became a banker in Albany, and was an active public figure during the same period when an enterprising Irish Presbyterian immigrant, William James, was founding his family's fortune there in commerce and real estate. Melville's other grandfather, Major Thomas Melville, the subject of Holmes' "The Last Leaf," was, like so many Boston revolutionaries, conservative in everything except his opposition to unjust taxation, and wore his cocked-hat and knee-breeches until his death in 1832.

Melville's father died in that same year, his mind deranged by worry and overwork. He had been an importer of dry-goods, who had established himself first at Albany, and then, prospering, had moved to New York just before his third child, Herman, was born. He believed that "money is the only solid substratum on which man can safely build in this world," and was never deflected towards any other goal. But his business did not recover from a depression in the late twenties; he became deeply involved in debt and was forced to move back to Albany, badly beaten. Within two years after his death, his son Herman had to leave the Albany Academy and become a clerk in the bank. But even less promising prospects lay ahead. In the year of the panic of 1837 the boy shipped for Liverpool, for substantially the same reasons that he attributed to Redburn: "Sad disappointments in several plans which I had sketched for my future life, the necessity of doing something for myself, united to a naturally roving disposition, had now conspired within me, to send me to sea as a sailor."

Redburn's shocked horror at his first glimpse of the suffering and brutality of the world was intensified by the contrast with his family's former well-being. An equally strong contrast was borne in upon the narrator of *Typee,* who, in 1841, was "forced by the united influences of Captain Marryat and hard times" to embark on a whaler. In *Typee* Melville's most serious scrutiny was given to the differences between civilized and savage life, to the frequently contaminating effect of the white man. Even in his relaxed days on the island, when Fayaway slipped off her robe and stood with it in the bow of the canoe as the prettiest mast and sail he had ever seen, another force was working beneath the happy surface of Melville's mind. He could never be a savage; his background of Presbyterian orthodoxy, though in abeyance now, was soon to reassert itself in his meditations on innate depravity.

Melville's early experience had thus compelled his attention to the essential problems of tragedy. The Albany in which he grew up was known as a rich man's town where "the best families live extremely well, enjoying all the conveniences and luxuries of life; but the poor have scarcely the necessaries for subsistence." [3] His rapid initiation into the contrast between aristocratic pretensions and the actual state of masses of people gave him much to ponder concerning the theory and practice of democracy in America. He next made the equally rapid discovery that all the pretensions of civilization might be no better grounded than those on which the French and English missionaries attempted to convert the Polynesians, while actually preparing their ruin at the hands of predatory commerce. This completed his education in skepticism, yet he was a skeptic with a religious and philosophic bias that would not let him rest, but drove him further into speculation on the nature of good and evil than any of his contemporaries had gone. When he demanded, in his essay on Hawthorne, recognition for "those writers who breathe that unshackled, democratic spirit of Christianity in all things," he was just coming to his own full stature. In his examination of both society and religion he became increasingly possessed by Hamlet's problem, by the difference between what seems and what is. What impressed him most in all Shakespeare's tragedies was this same probing "at the very axis of reality." He declared that, "tormented into desperation, Lear, the frantic king, tears off the mask, and speaks the same madness of vital truth." In *Moby-Dick* and *Pierre* he made his great attempt thus to unmask himself and his age.

[3] Quoted from Dr. Morse's standard geography of the time by H. A. Larrabee, "Herman Melville's Early Years in Albany" (*New York History*, April 1934). This is the most substantial study yet to be made of Melville's family background and boyhood environment. Larrabee's conclusion is that Christian Albany furnished a striking example of the typically American contrast between "the *professed* creed, which was largely traditional, theological and imported; and the *practised* one which was native, commercial and opportunist."

# 5. THE USES OF HUMANISM

## *The Theory*

*Douglas Bush*

## THE HUMANIST CRITIC

I have a very simple mind, and my simple creed could be set forth in a paragraph. But it is a matter of strong conviction, and, though a degree of emotional fervor is not an adequate substitute for the intellectual subtlety of modern criticism, I can at least claim to represent the body of common readers in all ages. While my articles of faith are few and elementary, it will take a little space to explain why they are what they are and why I feel strongly about them; and I should like to provide some perspective with a brief sketch of recent developments in scholarship and criticism, however familiar these may be.

Various approaches, old and new, from appreciative impressionism to Marxist dogmatism, have shown both their varying utility and their deficiencies and dangers, but I shall look only at the two chief kinds of criticism, which often lock horns nowadays, the historical and the analytical.

If it is self-evident that works of literature produced in our day are conditioned by the impact of our whole civilization upon the writer, it is no less self-evident that that holds for every writer and work of the past. Logically and ideally, therefore, historical criticism is committed to the knowledge and application of all branches of cultural history. Actually, of course, the historical critic does what he can with those segments of knowledge that he is able to compass. Like the coral animals of bygone theory, he adds his mite to the sum-total of historical learning and criticism and

This paper embodies parts of a discourse on modern critical approaches to literature, the last of a series given by various scholars and critics at the University of Rochester in 1949–50. Reprinted from *The Kenyon Review*, 1951, by permission of the editors and the author. Copyright 1950 by Kenyon College.

expires, having helped, some would say, to build such a coral reef of background and bibliography that no one can get at the work of art itself. Yet the thoroughly justifiable aim is so to re-create all aspects of the past that we can make ourselves virtual contemporaries of an author and understand his intention and achievement in the light of his own age. The method may be most completely successful for those authors who most simply reflect their age, but it is no less essential for those who transcend it. It is only through historical scrutiny that we can distinguish, in both ideas and technique, between the commonplace and the original, between historical and permanent significance. If we see more in a work than its own age saw, or perhaps more than its author saw, historical criticism keeps reinterpretation within bounds; and the historical critic would say that there are such bounds—even if historical interpreters themselves sometimes go off the rails.

Some typical aims and achievements of historical criticism might be illustrated by a couple of examples, and first by a glance at Shakespeare. Whatever the penetrating insights of Lamb, Hazlitt, Keats, and above all Coleridge, romantic criticism was unhistorical and undramatic. Although the final elaboration of the 19th Century attitude, Bradley's *Shakespearean Tragedy,* remains an experience for students, modern criticism has taken a very different line. Historical scholarship re-created the conditions under which Shakespeare worked, and saw him, not as a poet writing dramatic poems to be studied in private, but as a man of the theatre appealing with dramatic immediacy to an Elizabethan audience. This emphasis on the plays as dramas has been developed especially by Professor Stoll, who has combined historical scholarship with wide-ranging aesthetic criticism. It is possible of course to carry the theatrical point of view too far, to slight the total patterns and particular subtleties of image and symbol that may seem to belong more to poetry than to the Elizabethan stage, and some recent critics have revived or reinterpreted Shakespeare the poet as against Shakespeare the practical playwright. This new romanticism has its obvious pitfalls too.

The generations of American scholars just before our own were for the most part concerned with literary sources and influences, especially in medieval literature. The finest and one of the last monuments of this kind of scholarship, *The Road to Xanadu,* was not of course medieval, and Professor Lowes's imaginative reconstruction was far above the common process of bricklaying. But even on the lower levels this kind of scholarship accomplished a great deal; the seven seas of literature were charted with a learned thoroughness that must inspire respect, if not excitement, and that at least prepared the way for informed criticism.

Purely literary and historical research, however, could be external and mechanical, and many of the younger generation desired objects and methods more fully in keeping with the high significance of literature in their own lives. One result was a new concern with the history of ideas; another was "the new criticism." To speak of the former, it would be hard to name any period that has not been illuminated by exploration of religious, philosophical, scientific, and other branches of thought; and most of the major writers, poets especially, have been reinterpreted in the new light. For instance, Spenser, Shakespeare, Donne, and Milton, indeed about

all the authors of the 16th and 17th Centuries, have been studied in relation
to the whole pattern of beliefs and ideas that goes under the name of
Christian humanism. The cultivation of other areas has yielded similarly
rich fruit. But while the history of ideas has enlightened us in all directions,
it has its liabilities. The most obvious one is a tendency to lose the work
of art in its philosophical background, to isolate its ideas and treat it as a
document, a process in which great works may be reduced to the level of
poor ones. The method in itself carries no standard of values—though its
exponents may.

In opposition to, or as supplementary to, both literary and philosophical
history arose the "new" analytical or aesthetic criticism (which began with
the Greeks). This method, inaugurated by men of letters rather than professional scholars, has attracted so many of the younger academic intelli-
gentsia that most departments of English are divided between the "Auld
Lichts" and the "New Lichts." While the new critics differ among themselves, they are united by some common principles. Their aim also is to re-
create and share the author's original experience, although, it generally
appears, within the limits of language and technique rather than in its
totality. But if the end of all scholarship and criticism is the elucidation of
works of art, the new criticism may be said to come nearest to that end. It
has done and is doing great service in teaching a slack-minded generation
how to read, and in replacing vague impressionism with rigorous, concrete
analysis. Like other methods, however, this one may seem to have its liabilities. One is a practical if not theoretical indifference to the historical
method that may result in incomplete or misleading interpretations. Another seems to be a definition of poetry that virtually excludes everything
that is not in the "metaphysical" tradition. Finally, it seems to me that
this method cannot be said, any more than other methods, to be based on
any satisfying criteria of value (apart from technical values). Critics conditioned by modern scientific scepticism, who maintain a detached scientific
objectivity, seem to assume that literature is written and read with the
aesthetic intelligence only, and to hold aloof from the elementary but central things that have always made literature a necessity of life. These objections may be ill-founded, but they can arise in the mind of an outsider who
is not, especially in regard to the last point, prepared to take so much for
granted.

The historical and analytical methods that have been touched upon, and
other methods, such as the psychological, that have not been touched, have
their evident merits and shortcomings, and one moral that emerges from
the briefest discussion is that no one approach is adequate by itself. It may
be hoped that all students of literature endorse, in theory at least, all
scholarly and critical means and methods that contribute to understanding,
from technical bibliography to aesthetic contemplation. Obviously talents
do not come in a plenary shower, and most of us can only row a skiff, not
an eight-oared shell. But it is important, for the harmonious well-being of
literary studies, that all students, whatever line they themselves follow,
should recognize the value of other methods and not condemn them out of
hand as wrong-headed and futile. In connection with the whole subject it
might be observed that criticism has of late years been elevated from the

essential but humble role of acolyte to priestly sanctity and authority, and it is always well to remember that most of the greatest writings we have were composed in periods when scholarship and criticism were either unborn or unweaned.

However, scholarship and criticism are no doubt here to stay, and the problem is the range and direction of such activity. The methods we have noticed, essential as they are, do not, it may be thought, furnish an answer to the ultimate question—why we should read literature at all. It is obviously a good thing to know the literature and culture of the past, but historical knowledge is not an end in itself. It is obviously a good thing that our aesthetic sensibilities or nervous systems should be stimulated, but that also is not an adequate end in itself. What is the ultimate end, according to my creed, is that literature is ethical, that it makes us better. It is hardly necessary to say that I do not take literature to be a branch of homiletics. And I do not mean what many educationists seem to believe, that it is a decorative appendage to Civics. That notion is only a deformed and flat-footed ghost of what I do mean, the creed that was central in Greek and Roman antiquity, in the Middle Ages, in the Renaissance, and well up into the 19th Century. To mention the men who have held this creed would be to catalogue most of the great names in literature, and not merely critics but imaginative writers. In the course of its long reign this creed operated in various ways, on various levels of sophistication, but in essence it was unchanged; and many great writers, from Aristophanes to Milton, from Pope to Tolstoi, were avowedly didactic. Unless literature is in its effect didactic (I repeat the unpleasant word), I do not know any sufficient reason for its existence, at least on the higher planes that we are here concerned with. That is not to say that all ethical writers have been conscious teachers, or that even conscious teachers have not had other and perhaps stronger motives, or that readers go to literature as they go to the doctor or the psychiatrist.

That throughout its golden ages literature has been conceived of as didactic, and that many of the greatest writers have regarded their office as priest-like, is not a naïve theory but a plain historical fact, though it is stated here with unqualified brevity. If most great literature from Homer and the Bible to, say, Conrad (to name only one especially positive modern moralist) has fortified and enriched the human spirit, why should the guardians and expositors of literature so largely remain outside the inner shrine of ethical-aesthetic experience? While it is a main part of the critic's function to display the imaginative and artistic power of literature, it is surely no less essential that he be a moralist, that he try to appraise its ethical value. It is no objection that critical moralists, from Plato to Irving Babbitt, could have their excesses and shortcomings; so do critics and scholars who pursue other interests. Most of the great critics of the past have been more or less ethical in their judgments, and the need of such criticism was never greater than it is now, when the confusion and loss of ethical values is the most familiar and paralysing of clichés, and when philosophy has abandoned its traditional ethical concerns in order to become the tail to the scientific kite. Even on the most general grounds it might seem that what was fundamental throughout the great past would be our best guide for the present and future. Without slighting either historical knowledge or aesthetic analysis, I should like to see the study of literature fired by something like the spirit with which George Chapman approached Homer's Achilles and Odysseus (if I may use again a favorite quotation):

In one, predominant perturbation; in the other, overruling wisdom: in one, the body's fervour and fashion of outward fortitude to all possible height of heroical action; in the other, the mind's inward, constant, and unconquered empire; unbroken, unaltered, with any most insolent and tyrannous infliction.

If the modern mind is confused about ethical values, it is still more so about religion—unless it rests securely in a simple naturalism that begs all the questions; and the recent symposium, "Religion and the Intellecuals," suggests that a number of the finer minds are not less befuddled than the rest of us. I have assuredly no revelation to offer. But I do think that we can achieve a partial conquest of disorder by submitting ourselves to the literature of the 16th and 17th Centuries. The classical-Christian beliefs and ideas that made up the general creed of that age may be no longer tenable in themselves, but the great and less great writers who held them possessed an ethical and religious vision of man and life that is, one may think, more comprehensive, more central, more realistic, more satisfying, than is commonly found in the great writers of later times. And a bath in that literature has a restorative power. Against its ethical sanity and religious insight, its double vision of man as both a god and a beast, may be measured those later writers who, with the decline of the old religious and ethical tradition, became more subject to individual confusions and aberrations. If the modern mind is to find the "truth," it seems to me that we are more likely to find it through the past than in a present and future increasingly cut off from the past. The process of severance, which may be said to have been begun by Descartes, is being completed by modern positivism. Since the positivist brushes aside religion and metaphysics as meaningless, he can hardly help brushing aside traditional intuitive ethics also. If the literature of the past which is ethical and religious and metaphysical is to be thrown out, and the writer of the future is to live on the husks of a "scientific morality," we are indeed entering a new Dark Age. The loss of an active consciousness of our religious, ethical, and cultural tradition is a much worse menace than atomic or hydrogen bombs; and if critics do not labor to preserve and fructify it, who will?

Another article of my creed has been implied already, that one function of criticism is to reach people outside the inner circle of initiates, to make untrue the painful saying that a liberal education ends on Commencement Day, to "make reason and the will of God prevail." (One encounters sniffs at Arnold's lack of analytical power, or his lack of historical knowledge, but he was in the great tradition of criticism.) I do not think that this or that exclusive end can be set up as a permanent absolute; needs vary from age to age. We needed more historical knowledge and more technical analysis, and both instruments will continue to be needed. But it seems to me that at the present time, when culture is threatened by barbarism within as well as without, the most urgent function of criticism is not to enlarge the learning of the learned, or to refine the perceptions of the refined, but to enlarge and refine the saving remnant. If this be damned as propagandist heresy, so be it.

As a matter of fact, I am only wishing for a fuller return to the broad and central road of criticism. If we look at the last few decades and then at the many earlier centuries, we must conclude that most of our problems are of recent origin, that it is the modern approach to literature that has become divided and complicated—a situation that is very unhappy at a time when the voice of scientists and social scientists, a voice that is not still nor small, proclaims that they have blueprints and statistics for saving a muddled world. Some symptoms have grown so familiar that we take them as normal: that the body of general readers, who were once the mainstay of literature, has dwindled into groups of self-conscious highbrows; that people genuinely interested in the literature of the past are an infinitesimal fraction of the reading public, and that few college graduates, even among those who majored in literature, read much beyond the contemporary or the ephemeral after leaving college; that scholarship and criticism have become the small preserve of academic specialists who write mainly for one another. While it may be granted that cultural disintegration is not a new phenomenon of our age, it is also notorious that it has of late been especially rapid and radical.

A glance beyond our age, however, indicates that, from the time of Sir Philip Sidney up through the 19th Century, critics wrote mainly for the general body of cultivated readers, readers whose knowledge, taste, and outlook were much the same as the writers'. There was one language, that of educated people; there was not our variety of jargons developed by various professional tribes and now partly taken over into criticism. Both writers and readers had as a rule a substantial and uniform education. There was a cultural tradition that commanded general allegiance and sustained established values. That this relatively unified and conservative tradition had its drawbacks one would not of course deny, but, looking back upon it in 1950, one may feel some envy. Moreover, such conservative solidarity did not prevent the emergence of a higher proportion of writers of genius than our enormously enlarged English-speaking world can now show.

It seems to me that we have paid much too high a price for the rapid advancement of knowledge, not merely in science but in literature as well. The extreme specialization that has made such advancement possible has impoverished us as individuals and helped to disintegrate the cultural tradition, to isolate literary students from one another and from the public. Neither scholars nor critics have given much attention to the common reader. If the common reader is now almost extinct, or devotes his time to books on Russia and atomic energy, or has delivered her soul to the book clubs, the process of reconversion will be uphill work. Most of the active forces in our civilization are against us—as they always have been against the humanities, even in more auspicious times. Moreover, if the scholar or critic does address the public (in anything except a biography), his efforts will be largely ignored by lowbrow, middlebrow, and highbrow reviews alike. None the less, I think the effort ought to be continually made. Unless modern man is hopelessly debilitated and corrupted, we must believe that he cannot live without the humanities, and that he will in time respond if scholars and critics keep the humanities alive and humane. We scholars might have in mind the fate of the ancient classics and ask ourselves if our historical projects are or ought to be of interest to even a theoretical *homo sapiens*. And the critics might ask themselves if their exegesis is or ought to be of interest to even a superior type of *homo sapiens*. And members of both parties might ask themselves if their enterprises would have the blessing, say, of Chaucer, Shakespeare, and Milton, who were not merely gentlemen of letters. I do not mean that there ought to be a law against esoteric inquiries; I only mean that the main energies of literary study should aim at a common denominator. We may remember that Sidney, Ben Jonson, Dryden, Addison, Pope, Dr. Johnson, Coleridge, Arnold, and others did not address academic scholars or academic critics but the whole body of cultivated readers. If there is now no such body, then it needs to be created by critical and pedagogical exertion.

To mention these critics is to be reminded that they—and their Continental counterparts—were all brought up on the classics, that they belonged to an unbroken tradition; and we might allow ourselves to be startled by the paradoxical fact that, while the great bulk of English and other modern literatures is closely related to Latin and Greek, an increasing majority of professional students do not read either language. (Our academic forebears, who generally knew both, were intent only upon preserving a knowledge of Gothic.) We might, as Professor Ernest Hunter Wright suggested a while ago, require Latin and Greek for the Ph.D., though the imagination falters at the reconstruction of our whole educational system that that would entail. Yet every teacher may wonder how long the great writing of the past can be understood and appreciated by readers ignorant even of Latin, and what the non-Latinist makes of the great effects of Anglo-Saxon and classical combinations in English prose and poetry—not to mention the body of classical literature, which zealous students can read "in translation." But if our "creed" is to deal only with things possible, I will not list belief in a classical education as a tenet; this is only a nostalgic footnote—and a declaration that I do not think the value of the classics has been outmoded by psychology and anthropology.

To sum up these far from novel or fashionable observations, I believe that criticism should use all helpful means and methods for the study of literature; that historical knowledge and aesthetic analysis need to work together, and preferably in the same mind, not in different minds; that, our outer and inner worlds being what they now are, the scholar or critic cannot be content with the elucidation of works of art, central as that function is; that he has the further and traditional function of actively conserving the ethical and cultural inheritance that we are in danger of losing altogether; and that he has a social or (if the word be allowed) a missionary obligation, to labor to convert the heathen. If my position is naïve, reactionary, and unrealistic, I can only say that I would rather go to hell with a Christian Platonist than to heaven with a naturalistic positivist.

*The Uses*

*Irving Babbitt*

## THE PROBLEM OF THE IMAGINATION:

### DR. JOHNSON

As is well known, the imagination was under suspicion during the neo-classical period. This suspicion extended far beyond the bounds of literature in the narrower sense and was variously grounded. Philosophers like Descartes and Spinoza objected to the imagination because it was an obstacle to truth, a truth which, as they conceived it, was to be achieved by abstract reasoning. The imagination was also attacked, especially by Pascal, in the name of religion. According to Pascal, the imagination is a "proud power," a "mistress of error," which overwhelms the reason in which the philosophers put their trust. Man can hope to escape from the deceits of imagination only by a divine succor, the illumination of grace. The imagination is at times attacked on both rationalistic and religious grounds as, for example, by Malebranche in his *Recherche de la Vérité*.

The hostility of the literary critics of the period to the imagination has somewhat different grounds. Though, like the philosophers, they oppose "reason" to imagination, by reason they mean not so much abstract reasoning as intuitive good sense. By intuitive good sense one may determine what is normal or "probable" and so achieve centrality in one's point of view. Imagination, on the other hand, tends to pull one off center. For example, false wit is, according to La Bruyère, eccentric wit; and it is eccentric, because "it has too much imagination in it." Dr. Johnson echoes many predecessors when he declares the imagination "a licentious and vagrant faculty, unsusceptible of limitations, and impatient of restraint." This distrust of the imagination can be explained historically as a recoil not only from the school of conceits but also from the extravagance of the mediaeval type of fiction, as it appears in the romances of chivalry. The neo-classicist was at times all the more hostile to this type of fiction in that he had personally experienced its perils. According to Bishop Percy, Johnson "when a boy was immoderately fond of reading romances of chivalry and he retained his fondness for them through life. . . . Yet

Reprinted from *On Being Creative and Other Essays* by Irving Babbitt, by permission of Houghton Mifflin Company, Boston, Mass., the authorized publishers. Copyright 1932 by Irving Babbitt.

I have heard him attribute to these extravagant fictions that unsettled turn of mind which prevented his ever fixing in any profession."

A movement looking to the rehabilitation of the imagination got under way in the eighteenth century and gained ground with surprising rapidity in view of the extent of the previous distrust. The important period in this movement is that which extends from the publication of Addison's papers on the imagination in *The Spectator* (1712) to Young's *Conjectures on Original Composition* (1759). It was at this time that the phrase "creative imagination" or "creative fancy" began to gain currency. If it could be shown that Dr. Johnson shared this new attitude towards the imagination there might be some justification for affirming with a recent writer that "he was an important motive force behind that tidal wave of revolt which eventually was to engulf the outworn creed (of neo-classicism)." On the contrary, Johnson displays the full neo-classic suspicion of the imagination, combined at times with a type of suspicion that reminds one of Pascal. On the other hand, he has little or nothing of the distrust of the imagination, based on an overweening faith in abstract reason, that one finds in a Descartes or a Spinoza. As a preliminary to understanding his attitude, one needs to distinguish between two main meanings of the word "imagination" in the period that preceded him. As used by the philosophers, the word refers to the various impressions of sense or else to a faculty that stores up these impressions. When Hobbes, for example, defines imagination as "decaying sense," he is still very close to the conception of fancy (*phantasia*) set forth by Aristotle in his *Psychology*. The literary critics, on the other hand, often use the word imagination in a sense that derives, not from Aristotle's *Psychology*, but from his *Poetics*. Aristotle, it will be remembered, does not employ the word "fancy" or "imagination" at all in the *Poetics*. What the neo-classic critic was later to call imagination he there describes as "fable" or "myth" or "fiction." The right relationship, according to Aristotle, between the truth that the poet can give us and fiction is of crucial importance for our whole subject. The poet, he tells us in a familiar passage of the *Poetics* (Chapter IX), is superior to the historian because the truth that he gives us is less implicated than that of the historian in the particular. Homer is the greatest of poets, he adds in Chapter XXIV, because he has the most of this general truth and his success in achieving it is due to the fact that he is the most accomplished of liars.

Critics during the neo-classic period, as well as more recently, seem to have found it singularly difficult to grasp this Aristotelian conception of representative fiction, of truth through illusion. From Robortelli, who published his commentary on the *Poetics* in 1548, to the present day, they have tended on various grounds to put their truth or reality in one compartment and their fiction or illusion in another. One may illustrate the neo-classic form of this tendency from Dr. Johnson. He never tires of telling us that poetry should aim not at the particular but at the general. He does not as a rule, however, associate his general truth with a right use of fiction or, if one prefers, with a certain quality of imagination. On the contrary, instead of dwelling on a possible coöperation between truth and fiction, he inclines to set the two in sharp opposition to one another. According to Hawkins, "he could at any time be talked into a disapprobation of all fictitious relations, of which he would frequently say they took no hold of the mind." He was especially unwilling to admit any relation between fiction and religious truth. Like Boileau he therefore rejects the Christian epic because it introduces fiction into a domain where truth alone is appropriate. "The good and evil of Eternity," he says, "are too ponderous for the wings of wit."

Though Boileau would have religious truth and fiction sharply segregated, he encouraged fiction in one of the main senses that the word had come to have in the neo-classic period—the use, namely, of the pagan myths. Johnson, though in general sympathy with Boileau, breaks with him sharply at this point. "The rejection and contempt of fiction (i.e., fiction in the sense of the classical myths) is," he says, "rational and manly." Granted that classical fiction had become intolerably trite in the hands of minor poets, one is inclined to ask whether Johnson felt sufficiently how profoundly poetical this fiction had once been, nay, how poetical it may still be, if employed imaginatively. We do not think of him as striving that he might

> Have sight of Proteus rising from the sea;
> Or hear old Triton blow his wreathéd horn.

Towards another main type of fiction Johnson was implacable—namely, the type that appears in the pastoral. He would have none of it even in a Milton. He sickened at the mere mention of lambs and shepherds' crooks and was especially angered, we are told, by any praise of the Golden Age. Here again one may grant all that Johnson says about the more factitious forms that the pastoral theme had assumed and at the same time ask whether he does justice to the poetry of which the pastoral is capable. No classicist can afford to follow Schiller in his *Essay on Simple and Sentimental Poetry,* and grant the first place to the idyllic imagination; at the same time he must recognize that man is never perhaps more spontaneously imaginative than when he yields to his Arcadian longings. "Turn where you will in mythology and literature," says Mr. P. E. More, "and you will find this pastoral ideal haunting the imagination of men. . . . Were one to attempt to display its universality by illustration, one would need to abridge the libraries of the world into a few pages."

The idyllic imagination was assuming a new importance in the time of Johnson as a result of its association by Rousseau and other primitivists with a state of nature to which men were actually invited to return. More or less innocent illusion was thus being converted into dangerous delusion. Dr. Johnson not only failed, as it seems to me, to do justice to the poetry of pastoral fiction; he also failed—though, in view of his condemnation of Rousseau, it is not possible to speak so confidently on this point—to perceive its full peril. The pastoral dream to which the princess succumbs in *Rasselas* is of the conventional rather than of the new primitivistic type.

Of the peril of fiction in general, of the ease with which illusion passes over into delusion, Johnson was only too acutely conscious. Chapter 43 of *Rasselas* on "The Dangerous Prevalence of Imagination" not only gives the key to this work, but, taken in connection with *Rambler 89* on "The Luxury of Vain Imagination," points to one of Johnson's constant preoccupations. The neo-classic distrust of the imagination is, as I have already said, reinforced in him by that of the Christian. Traditionally, however, the Christian has been more inclined than was Johnson to invite a man to enter into himself. The man who enters into himself may achieve true meditation instead of becoming the puppet and plaything of vain conceits. It is this latter possibility that Johnson seems to take too exclusively into account. He himself rather dreaded being alone. He appears to have been happier when drinking tea with Mrs. Thrale. He associated with his solitary moments the fits of "hypochondriac obnubilation" to which, as he tells us, he was subject. There is no evidence that he cultivated in a notable degree "that inward eye which is the bliss of solitude" in the sense that a Christian saint would have given to the phrase "inward eye." In the sense that Wordsworth gave to the phrase Johnson did not of course cultivate the inward eye at all. "Solitude," he says, "is a state dangerous to those who are too much accustomed to sink into themselves." In his account of the "recluse" who regales himself with "airy gratifications," who yields to "an invisible riot of mind," who is unable to distinguish between the "labor of thought" and "the sport of musing," Johnson anticipates admirably much of our modern psychology. "The dreamer," he says, "retires to his apartments, shuts out the cares and interruptions of mankind, and abandons himself to his own fancy; new worlds rise up before him, one image is followed by another, and a long succession of delights dances round him. He is at last called back to life by nature, or by custom, and enters peevish into society, because he cannot model it to his own will."

This passage, written in 1751, runs curiously parallel to the passage in the *Confessions* in which Rousseau narrates how in 1756 at the Hermitage he made of his "creative imagination" a means of escape into a "land of chimeras" and how rudely he rebuffed visitors who interrupted him at the moment when he was on the point of setting out for *"le monde enchanté."* In this particular use of the creative imagination Rousseau has had innumerable followers. The person who indulges in this quality of fiction is termed by the psycho-analyst in his own special jargon, the "introvert" or victim of "autistic" thinking. Johnson does not fall into the pseudo-scientific fallacies of psycho-analysis, especially in his dealing with the problem of the will. He does, however, remind one at least remotely of the psycho-analyst by the remedy he proposes for the maladjustment that grows out of the flight from the real into some world of fiction. He puts his emphasis on outer activity rather than on the inner activity by which Christian and Aristotelian alike would adjust themselves to a higher reality, an adjustment that Aristotle relates specifically in the *Poetics* to a right use of fiction or illusion.

One should add that though Johnson was in general very prone to see illusion passing over into delusion, he refused to admit any such passage precisely at the point where most neo-classic critics discovered it—namely, in the type of drama that conformed to the three unities. It is well known that the doctrine of the three unities arose in Italy during the sixteenth century and was imposed on the European drama in connection with the Quarrel of the Cid. In the name of pseudo-probability, the illusion of a higher reality that true tragedy requires is converted by this doctrine into literal deception. Various attacks on the unities had been made in the eighteenth century before Johnson, one of the earliest being by a French writer, La Motte-Houdard, who is in his total tendency pseudo-classical. To those familiar with these previous attacks on the unities the attack in the *Preface to Shakespeare* (1765) will not seem especially original. There is no doubt, however, that Johnson's refutation of the idea of literal deception is masterly and definitive. Toward the end of this refutation he suggests that there may be other and better reasons for observing the unities than those based on a false verisimilitude. As a matter of fact, the unities have been revived in our own day, largely through the influence of Ibsen, because they have been found to make for concentration, a prime requirement of good dramatic technique. The larger question of verisimilitude in the Aristotelian sense still remains unsolved. A melodrama may observe the unities or approximate them and in other respects display excellent dramatic technique, and yet remain wildly improbable, because its action is not motivated with reference to normal human experience. It is not enough to make a plea as Farquhar already does in his attack on the unities in his *Discourse upon Comedy* (1702) for "a free and unlimited flight of imagination." The value of the imagination that is thus free to "wander wild," that is not in other words disciplined to any norm, is precisely the problem raised by the whole modern movement. Critics contemporary of Dr. Johnson complained that, though he had shown that we are not actually deluded at a play by the observance of the unities or by any other device, he did not do justice to the degree of illusion that a play may actually produce—for example, when he says that a "play read affects the mind like a play acted." What is certain is that he did not bring together adequately the idea of fiction or illusion and the idea of verisimilitude. As I have been pointing out, he tends, like most neo-classic critics, to set imagination and reason (or judgment), illusion and verisimilitude, in sharp opposition to one another. The contrast that he establishes in *Rasselas* is between a merely deceitful fancy and "sober probability." Unfortunately, there is truth in the assertion of observers so different as Pascal and Napoleon that imagination governs mankind. Anyone who wishes, therefore, to make a right appeal to men will not be satisfied with opposing cool reason or judgment to imagination but rather one quality of imagination to another. Johnson indeed has an occasional remark of admirable perspicacity regarding the mechanical opposition between judgment and imagination that runs through the neo-classic movement. "It is ridiculous," he says, "to oppose judgment to imagination; for it does not appear that men have necessarily less of one as they have more of the other."[1] If he had developed adequately the hint he has thus thrown out, if he had done justice to the rôle of fiction or illusion in both life and art, if he had linked with a right use of the imagination, the "grandeur of generality" that he is always opposing to what seems to him every deviation from normal human experience, the romantic rebels would have been left without any legitimate grievance. As it was, these rebels simply took over the neo-classic opposition between reason and imagination and turned it upside down. Instead of sacrificing imagination to reason, they were ready to sacrifice reason to what A. W. Schlegel calls the magic of genuine illusion.

---

[1] Under the date Sept. 18, 1760, Johnson enters in his Journal the somewhat enigmatical resolve, "To reclaim imagination." See *Johnsonian Miscellanies*, edited by G. B. Hill, Vol. I, p. 25.

If there is to be any important advance in criticism at the present time a first step would seem to be to overcome the neo-classic and romantic opposition between reason and imagination and seek to recover the Aristotelian idea of a coöperation between the two. A preliminary investigation should be made of the different meanings that have been given the word "imagination," not merely by the literary critics but by the philosophers and psychologists from the Greeks down. Since the time of Johnson, one may note in passing, the task of defining imagination has been complicated by the transformation of the word attempted by Wordsworth and others at the beginning of the nineteenth century. As M. Legouis remarks acutely, "Wordsworth claimed imagination as his supreme gift, but at the same time he bestowed on the word 'imagination' a new meaning, almost entirely opposed to the ordinary one. He gave the name to his accurate, faithful, and loving observation of nature. In his loftier moods, he used 'imagination' as a synonym for 'intuition,' of seeing into, and even through, reality, but he never admitted a divorce between it and reality. The gift of feigning, or arbitrarily combining the features of a legend or story, which had long been held to be the first poetical prerogative, was almost entirely denied him, and he thanked God for its absence."

I have already suggested that the "nature" of Wordsworth and other primitivists is in no small measure a projection of the idyllic imagination and in so far is not "real" in any sense of that much-abused word. At all events, it is not yet clear that the type of imagination by which one is enabled, according to Wordsworth, to enter into communion with "nature" is more important than the type that he dismisses so disdainfully, the type that M. Legouis describes as "the gift of feigning, of arbitrarily combining the features of a legend or story." One should add that this type of imagination cannot afford to be entirely arbitrary, if it is to meet the Aristotelian requirement of probability; it must in short be disciplined to normal human experience. In proportion as it is thus disciplined it gains in reality in the humanistic and not in the current naturalistic sense. Persons are still found sufficiently naïve to suppose that the word "romantic" is specially hard to define as compared with other general terms like "real," "ideal," "nature," "imagination." As a matter of fact, a certain integrity has been maintained in the use of the word "romantic" in spite of a bewildering multiplicity of specific applications. What was called romantic in the Middle Ages is still romantic, whereas, in the case of the word "real" [2] in particular, there have been since the mediaeval period radical changes of meaning. An urgent task, if we wish to escape from our present confusion, is therefore to define above all the words real (or realism) and imagination, not only separately but in their relation to one another. If definition of the kind I have in mind is carried out with sufficient thoroughness, the way may be opened for the theory and possibly the practice of that art of representative fiction to which Johnson, in spite of his genuine humanistic wisdom, does not seem to me to have done entire justice, and to which even less justice has been done in the movements that have succeeded one another since his day.

[2] God was for the mediaeval schoolman *ens realissimum*. It is hardly necessary to comment on the contrast between this use of the word and the present one.

# 6. THE USES OF SCHOLARSHIP

## The Theory

*A. S. P. Woodhouse*

### ON HISTORICAL CRITICISM OF MILTON

As I understand the assignment given to me, it is to suggest a definition and defence of Historical Criticism as applied to Milton, while Mr. Brooks is to tell us how the New Criticism (as it is called) would deal with the poet. So short a time has elapsed since Mr. Eliot took down the sign reading "No Thoroughfare," and directing an elaborate detour around Milton, that Mr. Brooks enjoys, I imagine, a freedom from embarrassing examples, which I can only envy. Again, he has at command a growing body of theory; for the New Critics have been concerned to provide their own dialectic, whereas historical students of literature have tended to work by a silent instinct of accumulation like the bee. Obviously, no one can hope to supply in a thirty-minute paper a theory of Historical Criticism, though I shall try to set down a few points towards the formation of such a theory. Nor is it any part of my purpose to attack the New Criticism in its theory or practice. First, because I do not know enough about it, being indeed somewhat in the case of Lord Monboddo. ("Have you read my last book?" asked Lord Kames. "No, my lord," said Monboddo; "I can't read as fast as you can write.") But secondly (and seriously) because we have had enough, I think, of mutual recrimination, and it is time for each side to make plain, without polemics, what it can do for the elucidation of Milton, in the hope that students who care more for literature than for labels may find something of use to them in both schools. For criticism, of whatever

This paper was read before the Milton Group of The Modern Language Association of America on 28 December, 1950. It was followed by a paper on "Milton and Critical Reestimates" by Cleanth Brooks. Reprinted from *PMLA*, 1951, by permission of The Modern Language Association of America and the author. (The title of this essay has been changed and certain minor revisions made at the request of Professor Woodhouse.)

school, is a means, not an end; and the test to be applied to it is purely pragmatic: Does it or does it not throw new light on, or minister to an understanding of, the work or the author under examination? By that test alone it must stand or fall.

I will commence by drawing a distinction between historical criticism and historical research. The latter is concerned with the amassing and ordering of historical facts; the former, with an application of the results to the interpretation of a work or an author, which is the proper business of all criticism. In practice, of course, the two activities are often fruitfully combined, but the distinction is nevertheless valid and necessary. With historical research as such I shall not be directly concerned. But since it is clearly instrumental to historical criticism, its utility will inevitably follow from the utility of historical criticism if that is established.

Now, the common possession of all schools of criticism is the text; and where they differ is in the method which they adopt in interpreting this common possession. It is the boast of the New Criticism that it concentrates all its attention upon the text and applies to it a purely aesthetic analysis, waiving every extraneous consideration. And this we may concede to be admirable, so far as it goes. But the really difficult questions remain: What considerations are indeed extraneous, or rather, what considerations are really germane? And how far does aesthetic pattern, the object of analysis, itself involve materials which are utilized by the poetic process, but in no sense originated by it? To these questions we shall return; for they are fundamental. Meanwhile we must notice the common indictment of the Historical Critic, that he allows a consideration of sources and analogues, and of historical influences generally, to distract his attention from the text. This, in so far as it is true, is an example of human weakness, and no necessary concomitant of historical method; for the very object with which the historical data are brought forward is the elucidation of the text. But finally, under the heading of text, it is to be observed that Historical Criticism (though not every historical critic) is concerned with the text in a way in which the New Criticism is not. The establishment of the true text is the business, not merely of historical research, but of historical criticism: it demands an application of the results of historical research to this particular problem, by the critical intelligence. Of the work in progress by Professor Harris Fletcher and others, I am not competent to speak in detail. I do not know whether it has yet resulted in determinations of comparable critical importance to those reached in the very different problem of Shakespeare's text—determinations like Professor Dover Wilson's that what Hamlet really said was, "O that this too, too *sullied* flesh would melt." Whether it has or not, no one will deny that the establishment of the true text is an essential task, without which neither historical elucidation nor aesthetic analysis can proceed with safety. Here, then, is the first department of Historical Criticism, and its first claim to be regarded as indispensable. It alone can supply the text on which the New Criticism desires to focus all its attention.

With the text established, a wide field of investigation and critical decision opens out. The starting point is the text of the individual poems, but the sum of the decisions reached should yield a critical estimate of Milton the poet. So far (if I am not mistaken) the New Criticism has largely confined itself to the individual poem (and to the shorter and more purely lyric examples thereof) and has looked on, not to the character of the particular poet, but rather to the nature of poetry in general, as its larger objective. Herein it differs sharply from Historical Criticism, whose procedure is to examine all the author's poems, of whatever length and kind, and thus to advance from the individual poem (the primary concern of all criticism) to the whole body of his work. Let us compromise by taking as our starting point a poem of middle length and remind ourselves how Historical Criticism would deal—indeed has dealt—with *Samson Agonistes*.

Now, it is perfectly possible to attempt an analysis of the aesthetic pattern of *Samson Agonistes*, and to such an analysis every critic must come. The question is whether or not the analysis shall be undertaken in the light of certain historical facts. *Samson Agonistes* is Milton's deliberate effort to write a classical tragedy on a Hebrew-Christian subject (that is, an Old Testament subject as interpreted by Christianity); and to the Historical Critic this fact immediately suggests two considerations as by no means extraneous: "Milton's Debt to Greek Tragedy in *Samson Agonistes*" (to adopt the actual title of Professor W. R. Parker's book), and "Milton's Samson and the Christian Tradition" (to adopt the title of Professor F. M. Krouse's). The latter makes us aware of the various choices in interpretation and emphasis which previous commentary had placed at Milton's disposal; the former fixes our attention on his detailed imitation of the Greek tragic form. Neither seeks to lead us away from Milton's text, but at most to postpone our consideration of it till the relevant information is acquired. And both entail at the end, and indeed during the whole process, an effort of critical interpretation. It is interpretation undertaken from a particular point of view, and so can hardly even pretend to finality. But if the history of criticism demonstrates anything it is that "final interpretations" are an illusion. Criticism cannot escape from the general rhythm of human thought which prescribes its passage from thesis to antithesis to synthesis, which is itself a new thesis. Every "final interpretation" turns out to be the last but one. In certain ways the critical efforts of Parker and Krouse correct each other, simply by virtue of their different points of view. The correction of former critics is a role often assigned to Historical Criticism—particularly of course the correction of the daydreams of the Impressionist—and it is a role assumed with some degree of zest. It should not, however, be mistaken for the primary role. Historical Criticism is not merely negative in function. If it can correct errors, it can also suggest new and fruitful ways of looking at the poem under examination. Two of these are illustrated in the books to which we have referred.

There are doubtless other relevant considerations. Besides the poem, the subject, and the traditional form, there is also the poet. It was *Milton* who undertook to write a classical tragedy on the Hebrew-Christian subject of Samson, and we know a good deal about this man Milton beside the fact, never to be forgotten, that he was a poet. Upon those who would dismiss as irrelevant every consideration of Milton the man, his extra-aesthetic experience, the drama of his own life, a heavy burden of proof must rest. Now here, confessedly, we are on ground doubly debatable; for many Historical Critics draw back from the assumed presence of Milton in his works, as the "autobiographical fallacy" or the "personal heresy." The reaction against Masson's heavy-handed interpretation, and particularly his reading of *Samson Agonistes* as concealed autobiography and political allegory, is understandable enough, and no doubt salutary. But that Milton's state of mind when he undertook the tragedy had no bearing upon the work which he produced remains a proposition far more difficult to establish than is its opposite. It is interesting to notice how much Professors Hanford and Parker, in their recent writings on *Samson,* have modified their former position; and yet more significant to observe how this issue of quite fundamental importance has been brought up again for debate in connection with the effort of Professor Parker, Professor A. H. Gilbert, and others, to determine a highly controversial matter of fact, namely, the date at which *Samson Agonistes* was probably written. This is very often the way of Historical Criticism: it attacks a question of fact and finds itself confronted by a question of interpretation. The remaining problems of chronology are unlikely now to be solved by a new discovery of external evidence (that is, simply by a process of historical research). They are much more likely to demand the weighing of internal evidence (that is, an exercise of historical criticism). It would be patently absurd to consider all the evidence except that afforded by the poem itself. But to read the internal evidence aright the critic must know the whole body of his author's work. He must be able to compare the undated poem with every other, and especially with those whose dates are known; he must have formed to himself a clear notion of the probable pattern of the poet's career, and be alert to see where in that pattern the undated poem finds its most natural place; and only in relation to the poet's practice in his other poems can the critical question with which we started be answered, namely, the degree to which, not *any* poet's, but *this* poet's, extra-aesthetic experience enters into his poetry. A tentative answer to that question is essential before one can determine the nature and limits of the internal evidence with which one has to deal. In the light of Milton's practice in other poems, is it more probable that the inescapable parallels between Milton's Samson and Milton himself after the Restoration are conscious and dependent on the poet's situation and state of mind when he wrote, or that they are merely coincidental and without value as evidence?

But the answer given to this question has implications far beyond the problem of the date of *Samson Agonistes*. The question may serve therefore to conduct us to some further observations on Historical Criticism as it applies to other poems; and, first, to an observation on method. The degree to which Milton's extra-aesthetic experience enters into his poems is a question which can be approached only by means of hypothesis. That it enters in its plenitude, that it enters not at all, that it enters in certain degree and under certain conditions: each of these is an hypothesis, and to be subjected to the appropriate tests. Does the hypothesis run counter to any known evidence? Does it, then, cover all the phenomena? Is it the simplest hypothesis that will do so? The answer to these questions will dictate its acceptance, its abandonment, or its modification. Every time the hypothesis satisfactorily explains a poem, and every time it is found to have provided in advance for new evidence as this appears, the hypothesis has in effect received experimental verification. Every historical critic must form, for example, some hypothetical scheme of Milton's early development. I had the advantage (if I may be pardoned one personal reference) of forming mine with Dr. E. M. W. Tillyard's important argument on the date of *L'Allegro* and *Il Penseroso* before me, but Professor Parker's equally important argument on the date of the sonnet "How soon hath Time" came later. To find the hypothetical pattern fortified by his conclusion was to verify the hypothesis, and also, I think, to add an argument in favour of the conclusion itself. Hypothesis, then, is an indispensable instrument of Historical Criticism.

I have indicated that there is some dispute among historical critics as to the degree, and the manner, in which Milton's extra-aesthetic experience, including his thought, enters into his various poems. The results are worth examining.

Those who deny that such experience enters into his poetry at all, greatly restrict the range of Historical Criticism (as did Mr. Stoll in his treatment of Shakespeare). They reduce it to a consideration of the poems with reference to their genres and to the traditional patterns and conventions which Milton adopted, with perhaps some attention to the intellectual commonplaces of the age, but with none to Milton's more individual and distinctive ideas. That illuminating criticism may be achieved on this narrow basis need not be denied. It is illustrated, for example, in Mr. B. Rajan's admirable *Paradise Lost and the Seventeenth-century Reader*. But such criticism, by restricting itself virtually to aesthetic analysis, approaches as near as Historical Criticism well may to the concerns and methods of the New Criticism. As a device for isolating certain features of Milton's poetry this is legitimate enough. It becomes dangerous only when erected into a dogma, whose effect is to prejudge the character and the historical relations of his poetry; and when it seeks to rule out as irrelevant all those studies of Milton's life and thought, and of his religious and intellectual background,[1] which, existing in their own right, may still claim to be heard before we pass final judgment on the poet—before, indeed, we can pretend fully to understand any one of his poems.

On this, as on other subjects, Historical Criticism should, it seems, preserve an open mind, till the facts suggest an hypothesis to be tested and, in the light of this testing, to be accepted, rejected or modified. The denial of any important relation between Milton's extra-aesthetic experience and a particular poem is a perfectly possible outcome of this process. For example, it seems evident that *Arcades* neither embodies nor even finds its starting point in any important extra-aesthetic experience intellectual or emotional. It takes its rise simply from the invitation to provide the text for part of an entertainment in honour of the Dowager Countess of Derby, entailing something of the masque form and the pastoral note. *Arcades* is a pure, and a singularly effective, example of aesthetic patterning, entirely adequate to its occasion and purpose, and carrying no overtones from Milton's life unless for a moment in the exquisite "Nymphs and shepherds dance no

[1] Those of William Haller, Arthur Barker, Merritt Y. Hughes, Arnold Williams, and a host of others.

more." This view of the poem can be verified in different ways, and among others by observing the use to which Milton puts a favourite image, that of the music of the spheres. Whenever this image occurs elsewhere it bears an ethical and religious reference and becomes the vehicle of Milton's youthful idealism. The one exception is *Arcades:* there it is bent solely to the purpose of compliment and achieves a purely aesthetic effect with none of the overtones that it habitually carries.[2] So much for *Arcades.* But nothing could justify an Historical Critic in a blanket denial of relation between Milton's poetry as a whole and his extra-aesthetic experience save an examination of his work poem by poem, undertaken with a full knowledge of his life, thought, and background. Such an examination would presently entail a comparison of *Arcades* and *Comus,* and this could not fail to bring home to the critic the wide difference between them, first in general effect, and then, on more detailed perusal, in argument and image, and in the extent to which the character of the poem can be accounted for by its occasion and avowed purpose, and by the genre in which Milton has chosen to work. Whatever is not to be accounted for by these considerations must seek its explanation elsewhere, and here the hypothesis of a relation to Milton's extra-aesthetic experience presents itself. We need go no farther. For indeed the assertion that Milton's poetry in general bears no ascertainable relation to his extra-aesthetic experience is not a result of such painstaking examination at all. It is a dogma, an assumption respecting the nature of poetry, which the critic is applying or misapplying to Milton.

Now, a sense of poetry as something *sui generis* is as necessary to the Historical Critic as to any other, and if he lacks this sense he had better betake himself to some other occupation; for he will reduce poetry to a mere document and a document whose language he cannot read. But what does the proposition, that poetry is *sui generis,* mean? It certainly does not mean that all poems are alike; for that is a notion dissipated by half an hour with any anthology, or by the simple confronting of *Arcades* and *Comus.* Poems are endlessly various. But they have certain qualities in common, two of which we may specify. First, whatever the subject, the poem develops it by means of—that is, under the form of—an aesthetic pattern. And, secondly, whatever its starting point in extra-aesthetic experience, the poem is never a mere record of that experience. On the contrary, it is the realization of a new experience: or (to put it in another way) the poem *is* the experience which it records. And it is with this experience—this poem— that the critic *qua* critic is concerned, an experience of which the aesthetic pattern holds the key.

But when these common characteristics of poetry *qua* poetry are recognized, there still remains the vast difference between poem and poem, and between one poet and another. And the differentiating qualities are as much a part of the poem, or of the body of poetry, as are the common characteristics. With these differentiating qualities, the Historical Critic is likewise concerned; and he is not content merely to observe them: he wants to know why they are there. Why is *Comus* so different from *Arcades,* or *Lycidas* from

2 *Arcades,* 62–78. Contrast *Prolusion 2, Nativity Ode,* 125–32, *Comus,* 1016–20.

the *Epitaphium Damonis?* Why is *Paradise Lost* so different from the *Aeneid*, or *Samson Agonistes* from *Oedipus at Colonus?* Why do Milton's poems in their effect add up to something so different from Spenser's, or Donne's, or Dryden's, or Wordsworth's? No one, I suppose, will deny that these are important questions or that they fall legitimately within the critic's field of inquiry. For to recognize that complete and final answers are impossible is no reason for discarding such partial answers as can be found. And no one will imagine that these answers can be reached by any other method than the historical or without constant reference to Milton's text. One brief example will suffice. No doubt *Paradise Lost* differs from the *Aeneid* because one was written by Milton, the other by Virgil. But the answer in that form is unmanageable and unproductive—is, in fact, no answer at all. The question requires to be broken down into its parts, and of these some are certainly answerable. It is obvious, for example, that an important difference depends upon Milton's Christian subject-matter, and his Christian attitude, which entail marked adaptations of the traditional epic form; so that we are led back immediately from the poem's pattern to its subject-matter, and from the subject-matter to the poet's belief or thought, in order to account for differences in pattern and effect. This is the sort of question that can be dealt with by the Historical Critic, and by no one else.

Apart, however, from the comparative study, Historical Criticism has a vast field of inquiry open to it. *Paradise Lost* is not only a classical epic (and thus comparable with the *Aeneid*): it is also a Christian theodicy (whose avowed purpose is to "assert Eternal Providence And justify the ways of God to men") and a philosophical poem (with a view of man and of the cosmic order to present). In these aspects also it takes its place in history, and is fully understandable only in relation to history.

Though as an activity poetry is indeed *sui generis,* the particular view which the poet takes of the nature and end of poetry, and especially of his own poetry, has an immense effect on what he writes. But his view of poetry depends in part on his view of life. Behind every philosophy of art there lies a philosophy of life. In a poet like Milton who consistently asserts or assumes the closest relation between his art and life, every shaping experience, every idea embraced, will, or at least may, have its bearing on his poetry. For example, why was Milton able to adopt with such singular literalness the idea that the Christian poet was indeed inspired? Because he read the conventional idea of the inspired poet in the light of the Christian conviction, reinforced by the Reformation, that every believer is inspired. Why did he not proceed to the romantic conclusion, that learning, thought, and conscious artistry are, then, superfluous, are even an impediment? Because he also inherited the Renaissance tradition of learned poetry and conscious art, because (like his fellows) he incorporated the Roman ideal of the orator in his conception of the poet, and because he adopted the Platonic view of reason, which made the flash of intuitive insight the result and the reward of patient thought, not something opposed to it. By his whole conception of poetry, with its ethical and religious as well as aesthetic end, Milton is led to embody in many of his poems his most searching thoughts and his profoundest convictions. It is not by their form alone, any more than by their content alone, that these poems seek "to imbreed and cherish . . . the seeds of virtue, to allay the perturbations of the mind, and set the affections in right tune." [3] But indeed the dichotomy and the problem are of our making, not Milton's, as every historical student knows or may come to know.

Thus Milton's thought enters deeply into his poetry. The cosmology of the *De Doctrina Christiana* is (by grace of the epic tradition) embodied in *Paradise Lost* and adapted to the purpose of the poem. The doctrine of free will is central in Milton's reading of the action and in his whole effort to justify the ways of God to men, and thus is doubly essential to the poem. His view of the nature and function of Christ, argued at length in the *De Doctrina,* shapes and colours the two poems in which he is a central figure. In *Paradise Regained* this very question is the poem's secondary theme—until the end, when it becomes primary. And that this transition might be effected Milton chose the order of temptations in St. Luke. Thus the theological content conditions the pattern of the poem. And this is characteristic of Milton. Whatever may be said of some other poets, Milton's aesthetic patterns rely on a foundation, or rather perhaps a framework, of conceptual thought, and they cannot be elucidated without reference to it. This is already true in the *Nativity Ode,* and it is still true in *Paradise Regained.* Milton's thought as thought is very much "of an age," and hence susceptible only of historical elucidation. Somehow it is transmuted into poetry which is "for all time." It is for the critic to explain as best he can how this miracle is performed.

Mr. Cleanth Brooks has complained [4] that for Professor Maurice Kelley, in *This Great Argument,* "the problem of exegesis is almost amusingly simple." In the *De Doctrina* you discover what Milton's ideas were: you then explain *Paradise Lost,* that "tangled and difficult poetic document, by means of the explicit prose statement." But, Mr. Brooks continues, Mr. Kelley's argument rests on two assumptions: first, "that the Milton who wrote the *Christian Doctrine* was precisely and at all points the same man who composed *Paradise Lost*" (and this assumption Mr. Brooks surprisingly concedes); secondly, it involves "the further and much more dangerous assumption that Milton was able to say in *Paradise Lost* exactly what he intended to say, and that what he supposed he had put into the poem is actually to be found there" (and this assumption Mr. Brooks peremptorily denies).

Now, I am equally astonished at the concession of the first assumption and the denial of the second. For it seems to me that to deny to Milton a knowledge of what he was doing in *Paradise Lost* and, after it was written, a knowledge of what he had done, runs counter to all the evidence of self-possession and deliberation as distinguishing marks of Milton, which the long study of his artistry has accumulated. It appears, further, to open the way for every aberration of romantic criticism. But to me it seems equally clear that the Milton who wrote *De Doctrina* was *not* the same as the Milton who composed *Paradise Lost.* The one was Milton the thinker and controversialist; the other, Milton the thinker *and poet.* In this statement, I am

---

[3] *Reason of Church Government,* Book 2, preface.
[4] In his "Criticism and Literary History," *Sewanee Rev.,* LV (1947), 199–222.

not committing myself to that most absurd of dichotomies—the one adopted by Hilaire Belloc in what must surely be (among many strong competitors) the worst book on Milton ever written. I do not mean that the thinker and the poet bear no relation to each other. Far from it. I am simply recognizing the indubitable fact that poetry differs from prose, and thought in poetry from thought in prose. In the more controversial parts of the *De-Doctrina* Milton is arguing a case; much of his effort goes to demolishing the case of his opponents, and the animation of the work has much in common with that of Milton's other controversial prose. His concern is with theology—not with religious, and certainly not with aesthetic, experience. He fits his thought to a theological scheme, not to a vision of existence. But in the two epics argument gives place to vision, and negation to affirmation —to an affirmation, that is, of the residuum of positive faith by which Milton lived. In the *De Doctrina* Milton argues the case for monism (I will not call it materialism). In *Paradise Lost* he embodies the doctrine in his vision of creation. In the *De Doctrina* he argues the case for an Arian or semi-Arian view of Christ. In *Paradise Lost* he realizes, and makes us realize, how entirely for him this view is compatible with the impulse of worship:

> Hail, Son of God, Saviour of Men, thy Name
> Shall be the copious matter of my song
> Henceforth, and never shall my harp thy praise
> Forget, nor from thy Father's praise disjoin.[5]

*Paradise Regained* is the fulfilment of this promise, and there (as we have said) the secondary theme of Christ's divinity becomes at the end primary, when, abating nothing of his Arianism, the poet reaffirms the doctrine (and fulfils the promise) of *Paradise Lost:*

> True Image of the Father, whether throned
> In the bosom of bliss and light of light
> Conceiving, or remote from Heaven, enshrined
> In earthly tabernacle and human form—

everywhere and always, the Son is the true Image of the Father.[6] And Milton, I infer, was enabled, not to reach this position, but to realize its full implications, by the aid of poetry. For whatever his limitations, he has this indispensable mark of the religious poet: his aesthetic experience and his religious are not two things, but one. And the poem is not a record of experience: it *is* the experience. It is not a record of thought: it is compacted of those

> thoughts that voluntary move
> Harmonius numbers,[7]

and that reach full realization only in them.

Poetry, it seems clear, has two aspects, a temporal and a permanent. It is the reproach of Historical Criticism that it is sunk in the temporal and

[5] *Paradise Lost* 3, 412–15.
[6] *Paradise Regained* 4, 596–99; cf. *Paradise Lost* 3, 305–07.
[7] *Paradise Lost* 3, 37–38.

in the relativism that pertains thereto; and sometimes no doubt the charge is well founded. But one does not get rid of the temporal by ignoring it; and to pretend to do so often means no more than the introduction of a new relativism: one reads the poem in relation to one's own age instead of to the poet's. Milton has suffered and Donne has benefited by this new and usually concealed relativism. But to speak of a temporal aspect of poetry, and a permanent, is not sufficiently precise. It is the miracle of poetry that it makes of the temporal something permanent. And if one would understand how this is done, and even in some instances be sure that it is done, one must know the temporal conditions in which it is essayed.

The contemporary audience always enjoys two advantages: an intuitive and comprehensive grasp of the potentialities and limits of the genre in which the poet is working, so that it does not ask for the impossible, and an immediate recognition of the frame of reference within which his ideas move. Much of the misunderstanding of *Comus* springs from a failure to grasp the potentialities and limits of the masque form (with which confessedly Milton takes great liberties) and of Spenserian allegory. Much misunderstanding also arises from a failure to recognize the distinction and the relation of the two orders of nature and of grace, which furnish the poem's frame of reference. The sense of these things three centuries have almost completely destroyed, and they can be restored only by painful historical study. But, when restored, they do not merely serve to correct errors of interpretation or to crowd out the false assumptions which will always fill the vacuum when true assumptions are lacking: they also give us a new vantage point from which to attempt our analysis of the poem's pattern. For the function of Historical Criticism is not simply to act as a corrective: it can suggest new and productive ways of looking at the poem.

And this, as it seems to me, holds the best promise of some alliance between Historical Criticism and the New Criticism. They need each other. Certainly we historical critics have something to learn from the method of analysis employed by the New Criticism: from the method, for example, of Mr. Brooks's essay on *L'Allegro* and *Il Penseroso*.[8] Perhaps too, the New

---

[8] "The Light Symbolism in 'L'Allegro-Il Penseroso,'" in *The Well Wrought Urn* (1947), pp. 47–61. I remarked above, "Whatever may be said of other poets, Milton's aesthetic patterns rely on a foundation, or rather perhaps a framework, of conceptual thought, and they cannot be elucidated without reference to it." This suggests a reservation which must not be overlooked. The method of analysis employed by the New Criticism appears to consist in a frontal attack on the imagery of the poem, with little or no attention to its theme as presented in action or argument. Applied to imagist verse, this method, corresponding to the intention of the poet, will yield whatever is to be discovered. Applied to poetry such as Milton's, it will, by itself, yield only results which, however valuable, are secondary and supplemental. This limitation, as it seems to me, is illustrated both in Mr. Brooks's essay on *L'Allegro* and *Il Penseroso* and in the part of his paper dealing with the image of "the *fruit* of the tree of Knowledge" in *Paradise Lost*. For, Dr. Tillyard to the contrary notwithstanding, the theme of *L'Allegro* and *Il Penseroso* is not day and night, but two contrasting ways of life, or two moods, as the titles indicate; day and night enter the poems because of the temporal sequence in which Milton has found his structural pattern; the images of light and darkness do not reveal the theme, but they support and supplement it. And so with "the *fruit* of the tree of Knowledge": everything that Mr. Brooks says of it may well be true, and (if true) illuminating. (Indeed an historical critic would find confirmation in Bacon's "philosophy of fruits," with which Milton must have been familiar.) But the suggestions conveyed by this image—one among many—are sec-

Critics may sometimes gather suggestions from the findings of Historical Criticism. No doubt we shall continue to disagree, and our remarks about each other will have a certain tonic bitterness. But we are all, I assume, concerned with truth, if not with finality. And I cannot help recalling two principles which Newman invoked in another and more solemn context: "Truth cannot contradict truth"; but "truth often seems to contradict truth." And the inference surely is obvious: that we should be patient one with another.

---

ondary and supplemental to Milton's theme of the Fall and his central interpretation thereof. The role of imagery in Milton would appear to be twofold: to *support* the main theme presented in action or argument, but also to *supplement* it by other and not inconsistent suggestions, and thereby to give the poem that density and richness of suggestion which differentiates it from any mere summary of its theme, as revealed through action, argument, or structural pattern. When this relation is recognized, the technique of the New Criticism in exploring Milton's imagery seems to me of the highest value, and exemplary.

*The Uses*

Louis L. Martz

## MEDITATIONS ON DEATH:
### DONNE AND HERBERT

Among all these instruments to self-knowledge,[1] the most widely and intensely cultivated remains to be considered: the meditation upon death, which Fray Luis de Granada presents to his readers with this recommendation:

the house of earth (which is our grave) is the schoole of true wisdome, where almighty God is wont to teach those that be his. There he teacheth them how great is the vanity of this world: There he sheweth unto them the misery of our flesh, and the shortnes of this life. And above all, there he teacheth them to know themselves, which is one of the most highest points of Philosophy that may be learned.[2]

Such meditation went far beyond the single weekly exercise which Fray Luis is here advising: ideally, the devout man attempted to keep the thought of death forever in his mind, as the *Imitation of Christ* and the whole great tradition of the *Ars Moriendi* had urged: "If thou diddest well, thou shouldest so behave thy selfe in every deede, and in every thought, as thou shouldest in this instant dye." "Blessed be those persons, that ever have the houre of death before their eyes, and that everie daye dispose themselves to die." [3] And this was not just a matter for beginners in the spiritual life: it was a mode of meditation which, as Puente says, "is very profitable for all those, that walke in any of the three wayes, Purgative, Illuminative, and Unitive;

Reprinted from *The Poetry of Meditation: A Study in English Religious Literature of the Seventeenth Century* by Louis L. Martz, by permission of Yale University Press and the author. Copyright 1954 by Yale University Press, New Haven, Conn.

1 [Professor Martz has been discussing various methods of self-examination found in the religious treatises on meditation which were popular throughout England in the sixteenth and seventeenth centuries. He has pointed out the relationship of these practices of self-analysis to metaphysical poetry.]

2 Luis de Granada, *Of Prayer, and Meditation* [trans. Richard Hopkins] (Douay, 1612), pp. 203–4.

3 *Imitation of Christ*, Bk. 1, chap. 23; quoted from the version of Richard Whitford, *The Folowing of Christ* [Rouen?], 1585. For the tradition see Sister Mary Catharine O'Connor, *The Art of Dying Well; the Development of the Ars Moriendi*, New York, Columbia University Press, 1942.

wherein all men ought often to exercize themselves, though with different endes." For "Principiants," the aim is "to purge themselves of their sinnes"; for "Proficients," "to make hast to store up vertues"; for the Perfect, "to despise all things created, with a desire to unite themselves by love with their Creator." (*1, 77*)

With such incentives the sixteenth and seventeenth centuries proceeded to develop the meditation on death into a brilliantly imaginative exercise. The Jesuit "composition of place" and "application of the senses" brought their intensifying beams to bear upon the deathbed scenes and wormy circumstance which the medieval *Ars Moriendi* had simply envisioned—with the vivid results thus suggested by Robert Persons:

Imagine then (my friend,) even thou I saye, which art so fresh and froelicke at this instant, that the ten, twentie, or two yeres, (or perhaps two monethes or daies,) which thou hast yet to live, were now come to an ende, and that thou were even at this present, stretched out upon a bed; wearied and worne with dolour and paine; thy carnal friendes about the weepinge and howlinge and desiring thie goodes; the phisitions departed with their fees, as having gyven the over; and thou lyinge there alone mute and dumme in most pitiful agonie, expecting from moment to moment, the last stroke of death to be gyven unto the.[4]

Puente, Fray Luis, San Pedro de Alcántara, St. François de Sales, and dozens of others give essentially the same dramatic advice: consider the hour of death, "not as thou wouldest of thing that were to come, but as it were even now present"; "which is not difficult to perswade, for it is possible that while I am saying, or reading, or thinking upon this, I may want no more but one daye of my life: and seeing that one daye must bee the last daye, I may imagine that it is this present daye"; "imagine yourself sometime all alone in the face of the agonies of death, and consider the things that would most likely trouble you at that hour. . . . For the blow that can be struck but once should be well-rehearsed." [5]

⌣The most striking aspect of all such meditations, whether by Persons, or by Donne, or by so different a spirit as Robert Herrick,[6] is the full self-awareness of the vision: the eye of truth that cuts aside all cant, looking with a grim, satirical humor upon all the follies of the world, seeing the worst of life and death with the poise of a detached, judicious intellect: the very poise of Hamlet in the gravediggers' scene. Consider, for instance, the grim humor that plays throughout these passages from Fray Luis de Granada (which, we recall, would have been available to Shakespeare in several editions):

a time maie happen, when some buildinge maie be made neare unto thy grave, (be it never so gaie, and sumptuous,) and that they maie digge for some earthe out

---

[4] Robert Persons, *A Christian Directorie* ([Rouen], 1585), p. 437.
[5] Luis de Granada, p. 198; Luis de la Puente, *Meditations upon the Mysteries of our Holie Faith, with the Practise of Mental Prayer touching the same* [trans. John Heigham], (2 vols. St. Omer, 1619), *1*, 81; *The Spiritual Combat* [attributed to Lorenzo Scupoli] *and a Treatise on Peace of the Soul* [by Juan de Bonilla], translation revised by William Lester and Robert Mohan (Westminster, Md., Newman Bookshop, 1947), p. 187.
[6] See his "Litany."

of the same to make morter for a walle, and so shall thy seelie bodie (beinge now changed into earth) become afterwardes an earthen walle, although it be at this present the most noble bodie and most delicately cherished of all bodies in the worlde. And how manie bodies of Kinges and Emperors trowest thou have come already to this promotion. (pp. 201–2)

Then doe they make a hole in the earthe of seven or eight foote longe, (and no longer though it be for Alexander the great, whom the whole worlde coulde not holde) and with that smalle rowme onelie must his bodie be contente. There they appoint him his howse for ever. There he taketh up his perpetuall lodginge untill the last daye of generall Judgment, in companie with other dead bodies: There the wormes crawle out to geve him his interteinement: To be short, there they let him downe in a poore white sheete, his face beinge covered with a napkin, and his handes and feete fast bownde: which trewlie needeth not, for he is then sure enough for breakinge out of prison . . . . There the earthe receyveth him into her lappe: There the bones of dead men kisse, and welcome him: There the dust of his auncesters embraceth him, and invite him to that table, and howse, which is appointed for all men livinge . . . .

Then the grave maker taketh the spade, and pykeaxe into his hande, and beginneth to tumble downe bones upon bones, and to tread downe the earth verie harde upon him. Insomuch that the fairest face in all the worlde, the best trimmed, and most charily kepte from wynde, and sonne, shall lye there, and be stamped upon by the rude grave maker, who will not sticke to laie him on the face, and rappe him on the sculle, yea and to batter downe his eies and nose flatte to his face, that they maie lye well and even with the earth. And the fyne dapperde gentleman who whiles he lived might in no wise abide the wynde to blowe upon him, no nor so much as a litle haire or moote to falle upon his garmentes, but in all hast it must be brusshed of with great curiositie, here they laie and hurle upon him a donghill of filthines, and dirte. And that sweete mynion gentleman also that was wont forsooth to goe perfumed with Amber, and other odoriferous smelles, must be contented here to lye covered all over with earthe, and fowle crawlinge wormes, and maggottes. This is the ende of all the gaie braveries, and of all the pompes, and glorie of the worlde. (pp. 220–1)

### Alas, poor Yorick, poor Osric!

Yet such considerations are comparatively mild: the dissolution of the body may be accepted with a wry resignation, as Donne accepts it in his *Devotions:*

*Now* all the parts built up, and knit by a lovely *soule, now* but a *statue* of *clay,* and *now,* these limbs melted off, as if that *clay* were but *snow;* and *now,* the whole *house* is but a *handfull* of *sand,* so much *dust,* and but a *pecke* of *rubbidge,* so much *bone.* If *he,* who, as this *Bell* tells mee, is gone now, were some *excellent Artificer,* who comes to him for a *clocke,* or for a *garment* now? or for *counsaile,* if hee were a *Lawyer?* If a *Magistrate,* for *Justice?* [7]

But there are, as Fray Luis says, "two voiages" to be made in this meditation, of which this voyage of the body to the grave is the less important. The other, toward which the major effort of the meditation should be directed, is to "followe after the soule: and consider what waie it taketh through that

[7] John Donne, *Devotions upon Emergent Occasions,* ed. John Sparrow (Cambridge, University Press, 1923), p. 105.

newe region: whither it goeth: what shall everlastinglie become of it for ever, and ever, and what jugement it shall have. Imagin that thou arte now present at this iudgement." (pp. 201–2) This, says Puente, is the moment "I am to have allwaies before mine eyes." (*1*, 89)

There is the point on which three of Donne's "Holy Sonnets" are centered:

> Oh my blacke Soule! now thou art summoned
> By sicknesse . . . . (4)

> And gluttonous death, will instantly unjoynt
> My body, and soule, and I shall sleepe a space,
> But my 'ever-waking part shall see that face,
> Whose feare already shakes my every joynt . . . . (6)

> Thou hast made me, And shall thy worke decay?
> Repaire me now, for now mine end doth haste,
> I runne to death, and death meets me as fast,
> And all my pleasures are like yesterday;
> I dare not move my dimme eyes any way,
> Despaire behind, and death before doth cast
> Such terrour, and my feeble flesh doth waste
> By sinne in it, which it t'wards hell doth weigh . . . . (1)

Here is the primary horror, the grimmest terror, which Fray Luis sees besetting the soul in a mood very close, even in its wording, to this first of Donne's "Holy Sonnets":

Then is the soule in a merveilous great conflict, and agonie, not so much for her departure, as for feare of the howere of her dreadfull accompt, approaching so neare unto her. Then is the time of tremblinge, and quakinge, yea, even of such as be most stowte, and couragious . . . . he can tourne his eies on no syde, where he shall not see occasions of great terrour, and feare. If he looke upwarde, he seeth the terrible sworde of the justice of almightie God threateninge him: If he looke downwarde, he seeth the grave open ever gapinge, and tarienge for him: If he looke within himselfe, he seeth his owne conscience gnawinge, and bytinge him: If he looke about him, there be Angels, and devils, on both sides of him, watchinge and expectinge the ende of the sentence, whether of them shall have the praie . . . . if after all this he take a vewe of him selfe, and consider what he is inwardlie, he shalbe wonderfully amased, and afraide to see himselfe in such a daungerous and terrible state. . . . O how fonde and blynde are the sonnes of Adam, that will not provide in time for this terrible passage? (pp. 217–18)

And so we have John Donne carefully tying himself in his shroud, analyzing the outward and the inward conditions of the sickbed in his prose *Devotions,* and including in his *Second Anniversary* the traditional procedure for a "Contemplation of our state in our death-bed": "Thinke thy selfe labouring now with broken breath," "Thinke thee laid on thy death-bed, loose and slacke," "Thinke thy selfe parch'd with fevers violence," "Thinke that thou hear'st thy knell," "Thinke Satans Sergeants round about thee bee," "Thinke thy friends weeping round," "Thinke that they close thine eyes," "Thinke that they shroud thee up," "Thinke that thy body rots,"

Thinke thee a Prince, who of themselves create
Wormes which insensibly devoure their State.[8]

The occasion, then, may be one of actual sickness, as Holy Sonnet 4 suggests, but the ills of sin provide occasions for every moment.

Likewise we find Barnabas Oley paying tribute to George Herbert's "mortification of the body, his extemporary exercises thereof, at the sight or visit of a Charnell House . . . at the stroke of a passing bell . . . and at all occasions he could lay hold of possibly. . . ." [9] The effects of all this we may see not only in Herbert's rejected poem, "The Knell," [10] but scattered throughout *The Temple*, in "Church-monuments," "Vertue," "Life," "Mortification," "A Dialogue-Antheme," "Time," "Death." Scattered throughout —this is essential. Palmer's unfortunate attempt to provide a chronological arrangement for the poems in *The Temple* transferred four of these poems from positions earlier in the book to a special section at the very end, entitled "Death"; [11] but such a rearrangement violates the essential purpose and place of such meditations in the devout life and in its representation, *The Temple*. Death is a part of life, meditation on death only a part of man's daily meditation: four "Holy Sonnets" out of nineteen; thirty-five lines out of a whole *Anniversary*, seven songs in a whole temple of praise.

This is made especially clear in Herbert's "Church-monuments," where the "acquaintance" of the flesh with the grave is presented as a lesser, but nonetheless indispensable, discipline which accompanies the prayer of the essential "I":

> While that my soul repairs to her devotion,
> Here I intombe my flesh, that it betimes
> May take acquaintance of this heap of dust;
> To which the blast of deaths incessant motion,
> Fed with the exhalation of our crimes,
> Drives all at last. Therefore I gladly trust
> My bodie to this school, that it may learn
> To spell his elements, and finde his birth
> Written in dustie heraldrie and lines;
> Which dissolution sure doth best discern,
> Comparing dust with dust, and earth with earth.
> These laugh at Jeat and Marble put for signes,
> To sever the good fellowship of dust,
> And spoil the meeting. What shall point out them,
> When they shall bow, and kneel, and fall down flat
> To kisse those heaps, which now they have in trust?
> Deare flesh, while I do pray, learn here thy stemme

[8] See *Second Anniversary*, lines 85–120, and the marginal gloss of the first edition; cf. the meditation on death by San Pedro de Alcántara, with its repeated injunction, "piensa," "piensa," "considera": *Tratado de la Oracion Y Meditacion* (Buenos Aires, Cursos de Cultura Catolica, 1938), pp. 30–1: the words resound throughout San Pedro's meditations.
[9] Life of Herbert prefixed to *Herbert's Remains*, London, 1652.
[10] *The Works of George Herbert*, ed. F. E. Hutchinson (2d ed., Oxford, Clarendon Press, 1945), p. 204.
[11] *The English Works of George Herbert*, ed. George Herbert Palmer (3 vols., Boston and New York, Houghton Mifflin, 1905), *3*, 311–43.

And true descent; that when thou shalt grow fat,
And wanton in thy cravings, thou mayst know,
That flesh is but the glasse, which holds the dust
That measures all our time; which also shall
Be crumbled into dust. Mark here below
How tame these ashes are, how free from lust,
That thou mayst fit thy self against thy fall.

I have printed the poem here without the division into six-line stanzas which it bears in the printed versions of *The Temple;* for, as Hutchinson notes, both the early and the late manuscripts of *The Temple* present it as a unit. The stanza-divisions appear to be an editorial change prompted by the fact that the rime-scheme "implies a six-line stanza." [12] But the total effect of the poem implies a union overriding any stanzaic scheme. The movement of thought and syntax ignores stanzaic division; the key word "dust" occurs as an end-rime in three of these six-line components, while at the same time the word "dust" is used three times and the word "dustie" once within the interior of the line, to provide a subtle union of internal rime. All this, together with the steady beat of the abcabc rime, serves to reinforce the sense of "deaths incessant motion." Furthermore, the steady, onward pulsation of the poem suggests an equanimity, a calm, a measured poise that reaches its inevitable close in the balanced phrasing and alliteration of the last two lines. It is a perfectly constructed, perfectly cadenced achievement, utilizing the insistent memory of "dust" in a manner faintly reminiscent of Puente's meditations on "dust":

So that dust, and durte may serve for *Alarums* to recall to my memory myne originall, and the matter whereof I was formed, imagining, when I see them, that they crye out to mee, and say: Remember that thou are dust, humble thy selfe as dust, love, serve, and obey thy Creator that tooke thee from the dust. And when I waxe proude with the giftes that I have, I am to imagine, that they crie unto mee, repressing my vanitye, and saying unto mee: Of what art thou prowde dust, and ashes? (*1, 102*)

Here we have a prime example of the way in which Donne's influence may be overestimated: "In *Church-Monuments* the sensibility which Donne made available for poetry moulds one of Herbert's finest poems, and gives an eloquent witness to the way in which Donne modified the sensibility of his time." [13] But surely we should see here a witness to the ways in which two gifted poets developed meditative materials in which the entire age participated. It is hard to see how meditations on death could be farther apart in mood and tone than are the poetical meditations of Donne and Herbert on this subject. In all Herbert's poems on death there is no trace of fear or horror at the prospect, but a calm, mild acceptance of the inevitable, often approaching the whimsical and jesting in tone:

[12] *Works of Herbert,* ed. Hutchinson, pp. 64, 499.
[13] George Williamson, *The Donne Tradition* (Cambridge, Harvard University Press, 1930), p. 103. Merritt Hughes long ago pointed out the importance of the devotional handbooks in cultivating this preoccupation with death: see his article, "Kidnapping Donne," in *University of California Publications in English, 4* (1934), 61–89; see pp. 65–6.

> Death, thou wast once an uncouth hideous thing,
> Nothing but bones,
> The sad effect of sadder grones:
> Thy mouth was open, but thou couldst not sing.
>
> .    .    .
>
> But since our Saviours death did put some bloud
> Into thy face;
> Thou art grown fair and full of grace,
> Much in request, much sought for as a good.
>
> For we do now behold thee gay and glad,
> As at dooms-day;
> When souls shall wear their new aray,
> And all thy bones with beautie shall be clad.
>
> Therefore we can go die as sleep, and trust
> Half that we have
> Unto an honest faithfull grave;
> Making our pillows either down, or dust.

There is in Herbert no revulsion against the flesh: it is "deare flesh"—a beloved, though quite junior, partner, who may be addressed as a child who has not quite understood. But in Donne's "Holy Sonnets" we feel the depravity of the "feeble flesh"—with a consequent fear and horror of judgment, deliberately evoked: even in his "Death be not proud" there is a tone of stridency, almost of truculence—a sense of daring to stand up to the terror. The treatment of death by these two poets is, I think, typical of the way in which, whatever the topic of meditation may be, each poet develops the common tradition along lines suited to his own personality, his own spiritual needs, and also, perhaps, according to the different schools of spirituality in which each poet has been trained or in which he has found his fundamental affinity.

# 7. THE USES OF PSYCHOLOGY

## The Theory

*Herbert Read*

## PSYCHO-ANALYSIS AND CRITICISM

Any attempt to raise literary criticism above the vague level of emotional appreciation through the incorporation of scientific elements is sure to meet with opposition, not only from the great majority of critics, who depend on their emotions, but also from more serious people who imagine that the prescribed boundaries of decent critical activity are being broken down. To the former set we can only present our weapons; with the latter we must reason, and our task is all the more difficult for the lack, in England, of any scientific tradition. Our critics have, as a rule, resorted to nothing more distant from their subject than common-sense. Perhaps the only successful attempt of a more ranging kind was that of Coleridge, who did consciously strive to give literary criticism the rank of a mental science by relating it to what he called "the technical process of philosophy." Unfortunately, what this technical process amounted to in Coleridge's day was a very innate kind of metaphysical speculation, speculation rather dim across an interval of more than a hundred years. We have become more empirical, and the general effect of the growth of science has been to discredit transcendental reasoning altogether.[1] Traditional criticism, therefore, in so far as it can claim to be fundamental, is a structure whose very foundations have perished, and if we are to save it from becoming the province of emotional dictators, we must hasten to relate it to those

Reprinted from *Reason and Romanticism: Essays in Literary Criticism* by Herbert Read, by permission of Harold Ober Associates, Inc., New York, N.Y. Copyright 1926 by Herbert Read.

[1] I imply "in the general mind." That empirical science can ever dispense with all aprioristic processes is a vulgar error to which the general tenour of this book is opposed.

systems of knowledge which have to a great extent replaced transcendental philosophy. Physics, demanding as it does such impressive modifications of aspect and attitude, provides the most general background for all subsidiary efforts, but for the literary critic psychology gains an intimate importance because it is so directly concerned with the material origins of art.

The critic, in approaching psychology, will not be altogether disinterested: he will merely raid it in the interests of what he conceives to be another science, literary criticism. This science—if it is permissible to call it a science—really covers a very wide field indeed. It is the valuation, by some standard, of the worth of literature. You may say that the standard is always a very definitely aesthetic one, but I find it impossible to define aesthetics without bringing in questions of value which are, when you have seen all their implications, social or ethical in nature. There is no danger, therefore (or very little danger), in the direction of a too inclusive conception of the critic's function: danger, and death, is rather to be found in the narrow drift of technical research, the analysis of the means of expression and so on. But it is a proper complaint against literary criticism in general that it has reached no agreed definition of its boundaries, and until it does it has no serious claim to be considered as a science. It is only because I want to distinguish one kind of literary criticism from another, even as you distinguish astronomy from astrology, or chemistry from alchemy, that I resort to a pretence of science. That distinction established, there is no need to carry the pretence any further: it is not necessary, I mean, to simulate the vocabularies of science.

Another consideration meets us at the outset of this inquiry, and the more one realizes it the more it appears to put the whole utility of our discussion in doubt. I mean the very obvious difference in the subject-matter of our two sciences: psychology is concerned with the processes of mental activity, literary criticism with the product. The psychologist only analyses the product to arrive at the process: art is, from this point of view, as significant as any other expression of mentality. But of no more significance: its significance does not correspond to its value as literature. The psychologist is indifferent to literary values (too often, alas, even in his own work), and may even definitely deplore them, especially when they represent the trimming of subjective phantasies under the influence of some objective standard or tradition. But in any case the psychologist has found and will always find a large body of material in the imaginative literature of all epochs: that side of the question is so obvious that I shall pay no more attention to it. But whether in the nature of things it is possible for such psychology to add anything positive to the principles of literary criticism is more in doubt. Analysis involves the reduction of the symbol to its origins, and once the symbol is in this way dissolved, it is of no aesthetic significance: art is art as symbol, not as sign. Alfred Adler, whom I have found, for my purpose, one of the most suggestive of the psycho-analytical school, has recognized this, pointing out that *"the attraction of a work of art arises from its synthesis,* and that the analysis of science profanes and destroys this synthesis."[2] This is perhaps *too* respectful an attitude; there is no need

2 *Individual Psychology*, English edition, 1924, p. 268.

to make a mystery of art. But it is an easy and an unprofitable task to translate into crude terms of sexual phantasy a poem like William Blake's "I saw a Chapel all of Gold." One might as well confess that the impossibility of avoiding such a translation is a serious defect in the psychological critic; for him the naïve acceptance of such a poem is impossible; here at least there is no beauty without mystery. Luckily for the critic, few poets are so artless as Blake, and meaning and intelligence tend to be remote in the degree that they are profound.[3]

I have perhaps laid sufficient emphasis on the general limitations of the psychological method in criticism. Before I begin with my main task, which is to explore the uses of psycho-analysis to literary criticism, let me deal with one of its misuses. It perhaps concerns literature rather than criticism, but we must all realize by now that no good artist exists who is not, at every point of his career, firstly a good critic. The work of art emerges within a radiation of critical perceptions. But, criticism apart, the author who imagines that he can start from psycho-analysis and arrive at art is making a complete mistake. No literature, not even a novel, can arise out of a schematic understanding of the phenomena of life. Art has only one origin—experience. Art is itself a schematic construction; an order imposed on the chaos of life. As such it has its own delicate and individual laws. But to conceive art as the illustration of science, or even as the embodiment in tangible fiction of aprioristic views of the universe, is surely a final sort of degradation, a use of the imagination more finally discredited than any it is possible to think of.

That is not to say that the study of psycho-analysis is entirely without object for the would-be novelist or poet. It might at least help him to realize, more quickly and more reasonably than the normal man would realize from his own experience, such facts as the subjectivity of love,[4] and the general law of determinism in which all our emotions and ideals are bound. Again, the novelist cannot in his plot ignore with impunity what we might now call the psycho-analytical probabilities. Then surely, it might be said, the examination of such probabilities is an opportunity for the critic well versed in psycho-analysis. But it does not follow. Here, admittedly, is the opportunity of the psycho-analyst, straying from his strict domain, eager to show what fools these artists be. But the literary critic will ignore this obvious use of psycho-analysis, if only for the sufficient reason that to a critic of any worth these psychological defects in a work of the imagination will appear as literary defects. You cannot write well—you cannot, as we say, "create" your atmosphere—without a "germ of the real." Any psycho-

---

[3] When this remoteness occurs, as in the case of Shakespeare's *Hamlet,* then I think it inevitably follows that any explanation that psychology can offer for the complicated strands of poetic creation tends to quicken our general sensibility. Reasoning and mechanism do not lose their value because we follow step by step the process of their operation; and I think a poetic process is exactly analogous. It is where you have, not a dynamic process, but a static symbol, that analysis is without any critical significance, and may be positively destructive of the aesthetic effect. I shall return to this point in dealing with Dr. Ernest Jones's study of *Hamlet.*

[4] *Cf.* Jacques Rivière, "Notes on a Possible Generalisation of the Theories of Freud" (*The Criterion,* Vol. i, no. iv, pp. 344–5).

logical unreality will, in the end, be apparent in some insincerity of style or method.

In the endeavour to discover the critical utility of psycho-analysis I will, merely for dialectical reasons, formulate three questions.

I. What general function does psycho-analysis give to literature?

II. How does psycho-analysis explain the process of poetic creation or inspiration?

III. Does psycho-analysis cause us to extend in any way the functions of criticism?

I ask the first question, apart from its intrinsic interest, to make sure from both points of view—that of psycho-analysis and that of criticism—that we have the same subject-matter in mind. I ask the second question—again apart from its intrinsic interest—to make sure that we have a common conception of what "creative" literature is. We can then, without fear of misconstruction, deal with the third question—which is the question I have all the time been leading up to.

To most questions in psycho-analysis there are three answers—those respectively of Freud, Jung, and Adler—and as a mere expropriator in this territory I take the liberty to lift my material from whichever quarter suits me best. Perhaps in this matter of the general function of literature Jung is the only one of the three to work out a theory in any detail. Freud and Adler do not seem to press the question beyond its individual aspect, to which I shall come in my second question. Jung's theory springs from that general principle of contrasted attitudes which is really the characteristic method of his psychology—the contrasted attitudes which he calls introversion and extraversion, a fundamental division of the self which may be traced in every activity and which we may variously paraphrase as the opposition between subject and object, between thought and feeling, between idea and thing. Now Jung's theory is that living reality is never the exclusive product of one or the other of these contrasted attitudes, but only of a specific vital activity which unites them, bridges the gulf between them, giving intensity to sense-perception and effective force to the idea. This specific activity he calls *phantasy,* and he describes it as a perpetually creative act. "It is the creative activity whence issue the solutions to all unanswerable questions; it is the mother of all possibilities, in which, too, the inner and the outer worlds, like all psychological antitheses, are joined in living union." [5] Jung further differentiates *active* and *passive* phantasy—the latter a morbid state which we need not stop to consider here. Active phantasy he describes as owing its existence "to the propensity of the conscious attitude for taking up the indications or fragments of relatively lightly-toned unconscious associations, and developing them into complete plasticity by association with parallel elements." [6] Now although Jung remarks that this active phantasy is "the principal attribute of the artistic mentality," he nowhere seems to have pressed home the conclusions which are surely latent in his theory, namely, that the poetic function is nothing else but this active phantasy in its more-than-individual aspect. The poet, in

[5] *Psychological Types,* English edition. London, 1923, p. 69.
[6] *Ibid.,* p. 574.

fact, is one who is capable of creating phantasies of more than individual use—phantasies, as we should say, of universal appeal. Thus art has for psycho-analysis the general function of resolving into one uniform flow of life all that springs from the inner well of primordial images and instinctive feelings, and all that springs from the outer mechanism of actuality—doing this, not only for the artist himself, from whose own need the phantasy is born, but also, by suggestion and by symbol, for all who come to participate in his imaginative work.

And here at last the processes of psycho-analysis and literary criticism run together. "Whether the actual social validity of the symbol," says Jung, "is more general or more restricted depends upon the quality or vital capacity of the creative individuality. The more abnormal the individual, *i.e.*, the less his general fitness for life, the more limited will be the common social value of the symbols he produces, although their value may be absolute for the individuality in question." [7] Now "the social validity of the symbol" is a phrase which I confess I would willingly annex for literary criticism, for it is to some such concept that any thorough critical activity leads us, and though I think the "symbol" in literature (we should never call it that) is something more precise, more deliberate, something more intelligent than the normal unconscious symbol of psychology, yet, if psycho-analysis can help us to test its social validity, then it can in this respect be of some use to literary criticism.

I come to the individual aspect: do we gain any further light from the psycho-analysis of the creative mind? How does the modern psychologist define inspiration, and does his definition bear any correspondence to our critical concepts? It is the general problem of the psychology of genius and far too big a field to explore in any detail here. But it will, I think, be worth while to examine one or two relevant aspects of the question. I think that in the mind of every artist (though I think particularly of the literary artist) there are two contrary tendencies. In one direction he is impelled to shuffle off conscious control and to sink back into his primitive mind, where he knows he can find a fresh elemental imagery, a rich though incoherent phantasy. It is the disjointed fortuitous world of dreams—day-dreams. In the other direction he is impelled to establish strong affective tendencies—ideals of moral beauty, of plastic form, of order and architecture. These resolve themselves into some kind of unity and form the goal towards which, consciously or unconsciously, the artist's life is formed. You get the harmony of perfect art when the two forces achieve a balance. I think this is all a matter of psychological observation, but it has a direct bearing on what we may call the central problem of literary criticism—I mean the question of  romanticism and classicism. There is, therefore, a peculiar echo of reality in these words of André Gide, written from a purely literary standpoint, in reply to an inquiry on Classicism:

It is important to remember that the struggle between classicism and romanticism also exists inside each mind. And it is from this very struggle that the work is born; the classic work of art relates the triumph of order and measure over an inner

[7] *Op. cit.*, p. 380.

romanticism. And the wilder the riot to be tamed the more beautiful your work will be. If the thing is orderly in its inception, the work will be cold and without interest.[8]

It is this riot within that we ordinarily call inspiration, and a good deal of attention has been devoted to its description by modern psychologists. By some it is assumed to be a function of the unconscious mind, which is credited with autonomous activity, with powers of incubation and elaboration. Most people will be familiar with Poincaré's account of his own experiences in mathematical discovery (Science et méthode, chap. iii), where he describes how some sudden illumination would come to him after a period during which conscious application to the problem had been abandoned. Poincaré attributed these sudden illuminations to the unconscious workings of the mind, but he did not really advance any proof of his hypothesis, and I do not think the idea is any longer entertained by psychologists. Modern psychologists explain sudden illumination or inspiration rather as due solely to a fortuitous entry into activity of ideas which are immediately associated and seized upon in their happy combination,[9] and this theory is, I think, entirely satisfactory as an explanation of poetic inspiration. It will not, perhaps, satisfy the poets themselves, who all, like Blake, imagine that they take down from the dictation of angels. But we are none of us very exact in the description of our own emotional states. What really happens may perhaps be described in the following way: you have in the first place the prevailing affectivity, the latent ideal of form or thought; what forms this ideal, what brings it into being, I shall explain in a moment. You have, next, the bringing into activity fortuitously of some image or memory which until the moment of inspiration had lain latent in the unconscious mind; this fortuitous image is as it were criticized by the excited interest; it is selected or rejected; and if selected it is developed and transformed by the ever prevalent affectivity. If the affective tendency is suddenly and strongly roused, then you get a state of emotion, bringing with it an intensity of awareness to all the images and ideas that follow in the wake of the first fortuitous image. This is the state of ecstasy. Images seem to leap from their hiding-places all fully equipped for the service of the ideal or affective tendency. But even in this state of animation or ecstasy I believe that a good deal of selection and rejection of images still goes on. However, normally a creative act occurs when the exact word or image is found. And the full creative process is but a summation of many of these primary creative moments.

If this be a correct description of the process of poetic creation—and it is based both on my reading of psychology and on the analysis of my own putative experiences—then the part that may be played by suggestion or self-

[8] "Il importe de considérer que la lutte entre classicisme et romantisme existe aussi bien à l'intérieur de chaque esprit. Et c'est de cette lutte même que doit naître l'oeuvre; l'oeuvre d'art classique raconte le triomphe de l'ordre et de la mesure sur le romantisme intérieur. L'oeuvre est d'autant plus belle que la chose soumise était d'abord plus révoltée. Si la matière est soumise par avance, l'oeuvre est froide et sans intérêt."—Réponse à une enquête de la Renaissance sur le classicisme, 8 Janvier 1921 (Morceaux Choisis, p. 453).

[9] Cf. E. Rignano, The Psychology of Reasoning. London, 1923, p. 129.

hypnosis in the encouragement of such states is obviously considerable, and I think that in time a complete technique of inspiration may be evolved. That this will result in a vast increase in the number of poets need not be feared, for nothing ever comes out of the unconscious mind that has not previously been consciously elaborated or sensibly felt: the product of the unconscious mind will always strictly correspond with the quality of the conscious mind, and dull intellects will find as ever that there is no short cut to genius.

It will be observed that there is nothing essential or peculiar in this description of the creative process: it is just what occurs in any man's mind when he is suddenly endowed with a "bright idea." Where then must we seek for an explanation of the abnormality of the artist? Obviously, I think, in the nature of the ideal or affective tendency to which his whole creative life is subservient. And for an explanation of this I return to the psychoanalysts.

Freud and his disciples would trace back the formation of the abnormal mentality of the artist to the period of infancy. "Analysis of this aspiration" (for ideal beauty), says Dr. Ernest Jones, "reveals that the chief source of its stimuli is not so much a primary impulse as a reaction, a rebellion against the coarser and more repellent aspects of material existence, one which psychogenetically arises from the reaction of the young child against its original excremental interests." [10] The repression of such tabooed interests may indeed contribute to the details of aesthetic activity, but this particular hypothesis seems far too limited in conception, and far too poorly supported by facts to account for the variety and profundity of aesthetic expression in general. The less specialized theory of Adler seems to offer a clearer explanation. According to the principles of "individual psychology," "every neurosis can be understood as an attempt to free oneself from a feeling of inferiority in order to gain a feeling of superiority." [11] The feeling of inferiority usually arises in the family circle, and the compensatory feeling of superiority is usually a phantasy so absurd in its high-set goal of godlikeness that it remains in the unconscious; it is repressed by the communal standards of logic, sympathy, and co-operation. This buried sense of superiority is present in most of us, but the artist takes the goal of godlikeness seriously and is compelled to flee from real life and compromise to seek a life within life; [12] and he is an artist in virtue of the form and ideal perfection which he can give to this inner life. The neurotic fails to create a formal phantasy, and lapses into some degree of chaos. Now it is worth observing, as a confirmation of the general truth of this theory, that the most general period for the formation of the superiority-complex coincides with the most general period for the outburst of the poetic impulse. I mean the time of the awakening of the adolescent sexual instincts, the time of the withdrawal of parental protection, the period of intense conflict between instinctive desires and social control. I think there can be no doubt that the artist is born of this conflict. Freud himself lends support to this view. He

10 *Essays in Applied Psycho-Analysis*, 1923, p. 262.
11 Alfred Adler, *The Practice and Theory of Individual Psychology*, English edition. London, 1924, p. 23.
12 *Cf.* Adler, *op. cit.*, p. 8.

says: The artist "is one who is urged on by instinctive needs which are too clamorous; he longs to attain to honour, power, riches, fame, and the love of woman; but he lacks the means of achieving these gratifications. So, like any other with an unsatisfied longing, he turns away from reality, and transfers all his interest, and all his libido too, on to the creation of his wishes in the life of phantasy." And Freud goes on to explain how the artist can, by the expression and elaboration of his phantasies, give them the impersonality and universality of art and make them communicable and desirable to others—"and then he has won—through his phantasy—what before he could only win in phantasy: honour, power, and the love of woman." [13]

The essential point to notice is that psycho-analysis seems to show that the artist is initially by tendency a neurotic, but that in becoming an artist he as it were escapes the ultimate fate of his tendency and through art finds his way back to reality. I think it will be seen now where psycho-analysis can be of some assistance to the critic—namely, in the verification of the reality of the sublimation of any given neurotic tendency. The psycho-analyst should be able to divide sharply for us, in any given artistic or pseudo-artistic expression, the real and the neurotic. There is much in literature that is on the border-line of reality: it would be useful for the critic to be able to determine by some scientific process the exact course of this border-line. But again I would suggest that in all probability the critic could determine this border-line by general critical principles; but psycho-analysis might be a shorter path to the test; and in any case it would supply collateral evidence of a very satisfactory kind. Psycho-analysis finds in art a system of symbols, representing a hidden reality, and by analysis it can testify to the purposive genuineness of the symbols; it can also testify to the faithfulness, the richness, and the range of the mind behind the symbol.

There still remains the third question that I propounded: Does psycho-analysis modify in any way our conception of the critic's function? The clear difference in subject-matter, already defined, makes it unlikely that we shall find any fundamental influence. It is merely a question of what kind of attitude, among the many possible to the critic within the strict limits of his function, psycho-analysis will stress. It does not, so far as I can see, amount to anything very definite—anything more precise than a general admonition to tolerance. Human activities are shown to be so inter-related, so productive of unrealized compensations, that any narrowly confined application of energy and intelligence results in a distortion of reality. Hence the futility of a purely categorical criticism—which may be illustrated by reference to "the Hamlet problem." During the past two hundred years an extensive body of criticism has accumulated around Shakespeare's cryptic masterpiece. The difficulty, for the critics, is to account within the canons of art for Hamlet's hesitancy in seeking to revenge his father's murder. Dr. Ernest Jones has given a fairly complete summary,[14] which I will summarize still further, of all the various theories advanced at different times. There

---

[13] Sigm. Freud, *Introductory Lectures on Psycho-Analysis*, English edition. London, 1922, pp. 314–15.

[14] *Essays in Applied Psycho-Analysis*, 1923, pp. 1–98, "The Problem of Hamlet."

are two main points of view: one, that of Goethe and Coleridge, finds a
sufficient explanation of the inconsistencies of the play in the temperament
of Hamlet, whom they regard as a noble nature, but one incapable of decisive
action of any kind—"without that energy of the soul which constitutes the
hero," as Goethe expresses it. The second point of view sees a sufficient explanation in the difficulty of the task that Hamlet is called upon to perform.
Both these theories have been decisively refuted, time and time again, from
the very facts of the play, and finally criticism has manoeuvred itself into a
paradoxical position, boldly asserting that the tragedy is in its essence "in-
explicable, incoherent, and incongruous." This is the position taken up
with so much force by Mr. J. M. Robertson. "Robertson's thesis" (I quote
from Dr. Jones's summary) "is that Shakespeare, finding in the old play 'an
action that to his time discounting sense was one of unexplained delay,
elaborated that aspect of the hero as he did every other,' 'finally missing
artistic consistency simply because consistency was absolutely excluded by
the material'; he concludes that Hamlet is 'not finally an intelligible drama
as it stands,' that 'the play cannot be explained from within' and that 'no
jugglery can do away with the fact that the construction is incoherent, and
the hero perforce an enigma, the snare of idolatrous criticism.' " All this
can be said, and said intelligently, and with a convincing absence of emotional prejudice. But it leaves us curiously dissatisfied. We cannot dismiss
so easily the personal intensity of expression throughout the play, and such
intensity, such *consistent* intensity, gives the play a unity which the old
academic criticism has failed to perceive. It seems that here is a case of an
instrument not large enough, or not exact enough, to measure the material
in hand.

And where literary criticism fails to account for its problem, what can
psycho-analysis do? Dr. Jones has shown that it will claim to do a great deal,
and he has elaborated in his study of Hamlet a psychological explanation
of the peculiar problems of the play. He sees in Hamlet's vacillation the
workings of a typical "complex"—the Oedipus complex, as it is called by the
psycho-analysts. That is to say, the mental peculiarities of Hamlet, expressed
throughout the play with such vividness and actuality, can be explained as
the consequences of "repressed" infantile incestuous wishes, stirred into
activity by the death of the father and the appearance of a rival, Claudius.
With the use of this hypothesis Dr. Jones can explain, and explain very
plausibly, all the difficulties and incoherences of the action; and he finds
in the play such an exact delineation and such a rich wealth of detail that
he cannot but conclude that in writing *Hamlet* Shakespeare was giving
expression to a conflict passing through his own mind. There is a certain
amount of biographical confirmation of this further hypothesis in the circumstances of the composition of the play, but not facts enough, alas, to
be of much use to any solution of the problem.

It would be interesting to follow this application of psycho-analysis to
literary criticism into further detail, but perhaps I have indicated enough
of Dr. Jones's theory and method to show the possibilities of this new approach to the problems of literature. Whether Dr. Jones's explanation is
tenable or not, it does provide what is at present the only way out of a
critical impasse, and for that reason alone it merits serious consideration.

At the very least it points to a defect in our critical methods, for the failure of literary criticism to deal with *Hamlet* is largely due to its approach to the problem along too narrow a front: we must always be prepared for literature refusing to fit into our critical categories. Criticism is a process of crystallization, of the discovery and elaboration of general concepts; but we must be prepared for the voyage of discovery leading us into strange and unfamiliar tracts of the human mind.

That is one way in which psycho-analysis supplies a corrective to the narrowness of criticism. I find still another, tending to the same end. I have referred before to the eternal opposition of the classic and the romantic: to this blind difference under the influence of which even the best of critics race into untenable dogmatisms. Can psycho-analysis resolve this difficult conflict and supply us with a common standpoint?

I think it can—particularly the psycho-analysis associated with the name of Jung. Jung has devoted his best work to the analysis of psychological types. As I have mentioned before, he distinguishes between two fundamental types, the extraverted and the introverted, determined according to whether the general mental energy of the individual is directed outwards to the visible, actual world, or inward to the world of thought and imagery. These two fundamental types are further subdivided into types determined by the functions of thinking, feeling, sensation, and intuition, but the psychological types so determined do not form hard-and-fast categories into which the whole of humanity can be classified: they are merely indications of extensive divisions which merge one into another. But in our particular sphere they do supply a scientific basis for the description of literary types. You will find, for example, that the romantic artist always expresses some function of the extraverted attitude, whilst the classic artist always expresses some function of the introverted attitude. Now this suggests that the critic, like the psychologist, should take up a position above the conflict, and although his own psychological state may lead him to sympathize with one school or the other, yet as a scientific critic he must no longer be content with a dog-in-the-manger attitude. Again, he must broaden the basis of his criticism: he must see the romantic and classic elements in literature as the natural expression of a biological opposition in human nature. It is not sufficient to treat the matter one way or the other as a question of intellectual fallacy; it is a question, for the individual, of natural necessity; and criticism must finally, for its general basis, resort to some criterion above the individual.

I would like to indicate, in conclusion, what I think might be a fruitful direction for further work in the application of psycho-analysis to literature. Recent theories explain memory, and indeed most of the characteristics of mind, on a basis of physiological "traces" left by experience. Experience may be individual or collective, and what happens individually must also happen collectively, and those instincts and experiences incidental to the struggle for adaptation and existence leave their traces on the mind when, and in so far as, it functions collectively. The accretion of innumerable traces ensures a set response to environment. A given physical structure of the brain results in certain inevitable forms of thought, and these Jung, following Burckhardt, calls primordial images. Such images eventually crystallize as myths and religions,[15] and psychology has already devoted a good deal of attention to the relation of such myths and religions to the unconscious processes of which they are the expression. Sometimes these collective ideas or primordial images find expression in literature, which, from an evolutionary point of view, has been regarded as a rational mythology.[16] Jung quotes from a letter of Burckhardt's these very suggestive sentences:

> What you are destined to find in *Faust,* that you will find by intuition. *Faust* is nothing else than pure and legitimate myth, a great primitive conception, so to speak, in which everyone can divine in his own way his own nature and destiny. Allow me to make a comparison: What would the ancient Greeks have said had a commentator interposed himself between them and the Oedipus legend? There was a chord of the Oedipus legend in every Greek which longed to be touched directly and respond in its own way. And thus it is with the German nation and *Faust.*[17]

This train of thought, allied to what we know of the possibilities of psycho-analysis in dealing with myths, seems to suggest the further possibility of relating the types actualized by the poetic imagination to their origin in the root-images of the community. In this way criticism would possess still another basic reality on which it could ground the imaginative hypotheses of art. Whether criticism, under the guidance of psycho-analysis, could go still further and indicate the needs of the collective mind, is perhaps too venturesome a suggestion to make. But with the advance of reason we have lost the main historic content of the collective mind: the symbols of religion are no longer effective because they are no longer unconscious. We still, however, retain structural features of the mind that cry for definite satisfaction. The modern world is uneasy because it is the expression of an unappeased hunger. We need some unanimity to focus the vague desires that exist in the collective mind. Will the psychologist unite with the critic to define and to solve this problem?

[15] This process, however, should not be held to exclude the possibility of the specific origin of myths. The opposition recently created between psycho-analysts and ethnologists of the Manchester school is largely fictitious. The origin of the myth may be a plain event devoid of psychological significance: the elaboration of this event into a mythical structure, often over a period of many years, even centuries, may all the same be a process for which we should seek an explanation in psychology.

[16] *Cf.* Th. Ribot, *Essai sur l'Imagination Créatrice,* Paris, 1900, p. 114: "La Littérature est une mythologie déchue et rationalisée."

[17] C. G. Jung, *Psychology of the Unconscious,* English edition, 1918, p. 490.

# The Uses

*Ernst Kris*

## PRINCE HAL'S CONFLICT

For well over a century some of Shakespeare's critics have pointed to inconsistencies in the character of Henry, Prince of Wales (later King Henry V), occasionally explained by the poet's lack of interest, whose attention, it is said, was concentrated mainly on the alternate but "true" hero, Falstaff. This seemed the more plausible since most of the puzzling passages or incidents occur in *King Henry IV*, Parts I and II of the trilogy; however, closer examination of three inconsistencies, to which critics are wont to refer as typical of others, seems to throw new light on the psychological conflict with which Shakespeare has invested the hero of the trilogy.[1]

Prince Hal's first appearance on the stage as Falstaff's friend and Poins's companion is concluded by the soliloquy in which he reveals his secret intentions. While he has just made plans to riot with the gang and to rob the robbers, his mind turns to the future.

> I know you all, and will awhile uphold
> The unyok'd humour of your idleness:
> Yet herein will I imitate the sun,
> Who doth permit the base contagious clouds
> To smother up his beauty from the world,
> That, when he please again to be himself,
> Being wanted, he may be more wonder'd at,
> By breaking through the foul and ugly mists
> Of vapours that did seem to strangle him.
> If all the year were playing holidays,
> To sport would be as tedious as to work;

[1] It is generally assumed that Part I of *King Henry IV* was written in 1596 or 1597, immediately or soon after the completion of *King Richard II*, and Part II in 1597 or 1598. *King Henry V* must have been completed shortly before or some time during 1599. *Cf.* Spencer, Hazelton: *The Art and Life of William Shakespeare*. New York: Harcourt, Brace & Co., 1940.

But when they seldom come, they wish'd-for come,
And nothing pleaseth but rare accidents.
So, when this loose behaviour I throw off,
And pay the debt I never promised,
By how much better than my word I am,
By so much shall I falsify men's hopes,
And, like bright metal on a sullen ground,
My reformation, glittering o'er my fault,
Shall show more goodly and attract more eyes
Than that which hath no foil to set it off.
I'll so offend, to make offence a skill;
Redeeming time when men think least I will.[2]

Some critics feel that this announcement deprives the play of part of its dramatic effect: the change in the Prince's behavior should surprise the audience as it does the personages on the stage. The anticipation, we are told, was forced on the poet as a concession to the public. Henry V appeared to the Elizabethans as the incarnation of royal dignity and knightly valor. His early debauches had therefore to be made part of a morally oriented plan; but some critics find the price of justification too high, since it leaves a suspicion of hypocrisy on the Prince's character.

The second inconsistency is seen in the course of the Prince's reformation which proceeds in two stages. In Part I, Prince Hal returns to his duties when the realm is endangered by rebels; at Shrewsbury, he saves the King's life and defeats Percy Hotspur in combat; but while the war against other rebels continues, we find him back in Eastcheap feasting with his companions. His final reformation takes place at the King's deathbed. Critics usually account for this protracted and repeated reformation by assuming that the success of the Falstaff episodes in Part I suggested their continuation in Part II, an argument supported by the widely accepted tradition that Falstaff's revival in *The Merry Wives of Windsor,* after the completion of the trilogy, was at the special request of Queen Elizabeth. It has nevertheless been emphasized that the concluding scenes of Part II follow in all essential details existing tradition.

The third and most frequently discussed inconsistency is King Henry V's treatment of his former companions with merciless severity. Falstaff, who waits to cheer the new King, is temporarily arrested and, while he hopes that Henry will revoke in private his public pronouncement, we later hear that he has hoped in vain. The King's harshness has broken his heart. In the "rejection of Falstaff," [3] who has won the audience's heart, the dramatist has "overshot his mark"; the King's reformation could have been illustrated by gentler means, and some critics suggest how this could have been achieved without offending the Old Knight. The formula of banishment, however, is only partly Shakespeare's invention since it paraphrases traditional accounts.

This tradition originated soon after Henry V suddenly died in Paris, at

2 *King Henry IV, Part I,* Act I, Sc. 2.
3 *Cf.* Bradley, A. C.: "The Rejection of Falstaff," in *Oxford Lectures on Poetry.* London: Macmillan & Co., 1934. Bradley's censure of Shakespeare is moderate compared to that of Hazlitt, William: *Characters of Shakespeare's Plays.* 4th Ed., London: C. Templeman, 1848.

the age of thirty-five, crowned King of England and France (1421). The tradition grew in chronicles and popular accounts, hesitantly at first, more rapidly later, when Henry's striving for European leadership and hegemony in the Channel appeared as an anticipation of the political goals of Tudor England. In Shakespeare's time, fact and legend had become firmly interwoven.[4]

Prince Henry (of Monmouth, born 1387) was early introduced to affairs of state. He was twelve years old when, in 1399, his father succeeded Richard II. At fifteen he took personal control of the administration of Wales and of the war against the Welsh rebels. He had shared in this task since 1400, initially guided by Henry Percy, Hotspur, who at that time was thirty-nine, three years older than the Prince's father. In 1405 Hotspur led the rebellion of the Percies and attacked the Prince's forces at Shrewsbury. Supported by the King and his army, Henry of Monmouth carried the day. The rebellion and the pacification of Wales kept the Prince busy until 1408 or 1409. He then entered politics as leader of the parliamentary opposition against the King's council. Repeated illnesses complicated Henry IV's negotiations with Parliament that at the time of his uprising against Richard II had vested royal power in him. Since 1406 rumors concerning his abdication had been spreading. In 1408 he was thought to have died in an attack of seizures "but after some hours the vital spirits returned to him." From January, 1410 to November, 1411 the Prince governed England through the council, supported by the King's half brothers, Henry and Thomas Beaufort. In November, 1411 Henry IV took over again and dismissed the Prince from the council. One of the reasons for the Prince's dismissal was his desire for an active policy in France. It seems that, initially without the King's consent, he had arranged for a small expeditionary force to be sent to the continent in support of Burgundy against the Royal House of France; later the King agreed to the expedition but the Prince had to renounce his intention to lead the forces.

The circumstances that led to Henry of Monmouth's removal from the council are not entirely clear. It seems that Henry IV was motivated by the suspicion that the Prince intended to depose him. The Prince issued public statements denying such intention, and demanded the punishment of those who had slandered him. He finally forced an interview on the King, during which a reconciliation took place. The struggle between father and son was terminated by Henry IV's death in 1413.

According to the chronicles of the fifteenth and sixteenth centuries, Henry of Monmouth's character changed after his accession to the throne. The early chronicles do not state in detail wherein the conversion consisted. They familiarize us, however, with two areas in which the Prince's attitude was different from that of the later King. The first of these areas is less

[4] For the legend of Prince Hal see especially Kabel, P.: *Die Sage von Heinrich V, bis zur Zeit Shakespeares*, Palaestra, LXIX, Berlin, 1908; and Bowling, W. G.: "The Wild Prince Hal in Legend and Literature," *Washington Studies*, Humanist Ser., XIII, 1925–1926, pp. 305–334. For summaries of historical facts see mainly Kingsford, C. L.: *Henry V, The Typical Medieval Hero*. New York: G. P. Putnam Sons, 1901; and McFarlane, K. B.: "The Lancastrian Kings," in *The Cambridge Medieval History*. Cambridge, England: Cambridge University Press, VIII, 1936, pp. 363–416.

well defined than the second: during the conflict with his father, the Prince appeared twice at court "with much peoples of lords and gentles." This show of strength was meant to exercise pressure on King and council. During his reign Henry V never used similar methods; no appeal to forces outside "government" is attributed to him, neither in his dealings with Parliament nor with the baronage. Within the framework of his age he was a rigorously constitutional monarch. Somewhat better defined is the change of the Prince's attitude to the Church. The noble leader of the Lollards, Sir John Oldcastle, was the Prince's personal friend, and at least by tolerance, the Prince seems vaguely to have favored the cause for which he stood. Shortly after Henry V's accession to the throne the persecution of the Lollards was intensified. Sir John was arrested and asked to abandon his error. He refused any compromise, succeeded twice in escaping, but he was finally, in 1417, executed after Parliament had determined on the extirpation of Lollardry as heresy.

The legendary versions of the Prince's reformation elaborated these incidents later on; in their earliest formulation they simply stated: "that the Prince was an assiduous center of lasciviousness and addicted exceedingly to instruments of music. Passing the bounds of modesty he was the fervent soldier of Venus as well as of Mars; youthlike, he was tired with her torches and in the midst of the worthy works of war found leisure for excess common to ungoverned age." [5] Later sources place the Prince's reformation in relation to the conflict with his father: the baronage that had adopted the Prince as leader becomes a group of irresponsible delinquents. Amongst this group the name of Sir John Oldcastle appears. The fanatic leader of a religious sect thus underwent the transformation into Sir John Falstaff, whose name was substituted by Shakespeare only after Oldcastle's descendants had complained of what seemed a vilification of their ancestor; but various traces of the original name are extant in Shakespeare's text. The banishment of Falstaff then may be considered as an elaboration of Henry V's persecution of the Lollards whom he once had favored. Other elements of the legendary tradition are inserted with clearly moralistic intentions: the Prince's reformation is used to exemplify the nature of royal responsibility. Thus Sir Thomas Elyot in his treatise, *The Book Named the Governor* (1531), introduced the tale of Prince and Chief-justice according to which the King confirms that Chiefjustice in office who, in the royal name, had once arrested the riotous Prince. The image of Henry V was thus idealized into that of the perfect Renaissance ruler.[6]

Shakespeare borrowed these and similar incidents of his trilogy from a variety of sources, but mainly from the second edition of Raphael Holinshed's *Chronicles of England, Scotland and Ireland* (1587).[7] In addition to historical sources he relied upon a popular play produced a few years earlier. So closely does he follow *The Famous Victories of Henry V* that it seems as if he had set himself the task to retain as many as possible of the

[5] Kingsford, C. L.: *Op. cit.* p. 12.

[6] *Cf.* Spencer, Theodore: *Shakespeare and the Nature of Man.* New York: Macmillan & Co., 1942.

[7] *Cf.* Ax, Herman: *The Relation of Shakespeare's King Henry IV to Holinshed's Chronicle.* Freiburg I. Breisgau: D. Lauber, 1912.

incidents familiar to his audience in spite of the total transformation of the context. Without commenting in detail upon this transformation—though such a comparison would permit one to support the hypothesis here to be proposed—it suffices to point to its general direction. The historical facts concerning the conflict between Henry IV and his son and "heir apparent," Henry of Monmouth, had been blurred by legend. The conversion of the Prince became the dominant theme, a conversion modeled after that of the life of the saints. Shakespeare returns to the core of this tradition, or rather rediscovers that core, in the sources accessible to him. He centers his attention on the conflict between father and son which is made to account for both the Prince's debauchery and his reformation.

The conflict between father and son appears in Part I of *Henry IV* in three versions, each time enacted by one central and two related characters.[8] The theme is manifestly stated by the King in the introductory scene of the trilogy, when he compares Henry of Monmouth to Henry Percy.

> Yea, there thou makest me sad and makest me sin
> In envy that my Lord Northumberland
> Should be the father to so blest a son,
> A son who is the theme of honour's tongue;
> Amongst a grove, the very straightest plant;
> Who is sweet fortune's minion and her pride:
> Whilst I, by looking on the praise of him,
> See riot and dishonour stain the brow
> Of my young Harry. O! that it could be prov'd
> That some night-tripping fairy had exchang'd
> In cradle-clothes our children where they lay,
> And called mine Percy, his Plantagenet!
> Then would I have his Harry, and he mine.[9]

The position of the Prince between Falstaff and the King is almost as explicitly stated; he has two fathers, as the King has two sons. When he enacts with Falstaff his forthcoming interview with his father, the theme is brought into the open.[10] It is not limited to court and tavern, the centers of the "double plot," as W. Empson calls it,[11] but extends to the rebel camp. Henry Percy stands between a weak father, Northumberland, who is prevented by illness from participating in the decisive battle, and a scheming uncle, Worcester, who plans the rebellion, conceals from Percy that the King offers reconciliation and drives him thus to battle and to death.

The three versions of the father-son conflict compelled Shakespeare to deviate from his sources and thereby to enrich the stage: he sharpened the report of the chronicles on the rebellion of the Percies in order to create

---

[8] That the repetition of one theme in various configurations indicates its central position was pointed out by Jekels, Ludwig: "Das Problem der doppelten Motivgestaltung," *Imago*, XIX, 1933, pp. 15–26.

[9] *King Henry IV, Part I*, Act I, Sc. 1.

[10] The idea of the travestied interview itself is borrowed from *The Famous Victories of Henry the Fifth*. London: Thomas Creede, 1898. There the Prince and his companion enact the Prince's subsequent interview with the Chiefjustice.

[11] Empson, W.: *Some Versions of Pastoral*. London: Chatto & Windus, 1935, pp. 43–46.

the contrast of Worcester and Northumberland; he reduced Henry Percy's age from a slightly older contemporary of Henry IV to a somewhat older contemporary of the Prince—and he invented Falstaff.

The triangular relationships are not only similar to each other, since they all contain variations of the theme of good and bad fathers and sons, but within each triangle the parallel figures are closely interconnected; thus the two Harrys, whom Henry IV compares, form a unit; Hotspur's rebellion represents also Prince Hal's unconscious parricidal impulses.[12] Hotspur is the Prince's double. Impulses pertaining to one situation have thus been divided between two personages; [13] but though in the triangles the characters are paired and contrasted, each of the play's personages transcends the bondage to his function in this thematic configuration. They have all outgrown the symmetry which they serve, into the fullness of life.

To appraise Falstaff as a depreciated father figure is to grasp the superficial aspect of a character who, more than any other of Shakespeare, has enchanted readers and audiences since his creation. Franz Alexander finds two principal psychoanalytic explanations for this universal enchantment: Falstaff's hedonism, he says, represents the uninhibited gratification of an infantile and narcissistic quest for pleasure, a craving alive to some extent in everyone of us; this hedonism, moreover, is made acceptable by contrast: one turns with relief from the court or the rebel camp to the tavern.[14] In accordance with the last is the traditional antithesis of "tragic King and comic people" (Empson) used by Shakespeare to emphasize a moral antithesis. From Prince Hal's point of view, Falstaff is a contrast to the King, who represents another version of the unsatisfactory paternal image. Henry IV succeeded his cousin Richard II by rebellion and regicide. The feeling of guilt that overshadowed his life becomes manifest when on his deathbed, in addressing the Prince, he reviews the sorrows that the unlawfully acquired crown inflicted on him.

> How I came by the crown, O God forgive;
> And grant it may with thee in true peace live! [15]

In this great scene Prince Henry's mood accords with his father's; he too is burdened with guilt. In the preceding scene he finds his father sleeping, and believes him to be dead. Shakespeare, adapting this scene from the chronicle play, has added a prop device: the crown which lies next to the King's bed.[16] The crown inspires the Prince with awe and apprehension. He longs to possess it, but "the best of gold" is "the worst of gold"; it endangers the bearer. He wages "the quarrel of a true inheritor," controls his

[12] This point was made by Alexander, Franz: "A Note on Falstaff," *Psychoanalytic Quarterly*, II, 1933, pp. 592–606; and by Empson, W.: *Op. cit.*, p. 43.

[13] Ernest Jones speaks in a similar connection of decomposition; see "A Psychoanalytic Study of Hamlet," in *Essays in Applied Psycho-Analysis*. London: Int. Psa. Library, No. 5, 1923.

[14] Alexander, Franz: *Op. cit.*

[15] *King Henry IV, Part II*, Act IV, Sc. 5.

[16] The very crown that literally he had taken from Richard II. *Cf. Richard II*, Act IV, Sc. 1.

desire and, in a mood of contemplation, concludes that royal responsibility is a heavy burden. He has overcome the hostile impulse against the dying King and can now reply to his father:

> You won it, wore it, kept it, gave it me;
> Then plain and right must my possession be; [17]

It is an attempt to reassure: "Since I have come guiltless into the possession of the crown, since I refrained from regicide and parricide, I shall rightfully be King"; yet in the greatest crisis of his life, the Prince, now King Henry V, reveals that his apprehension has not been vanquished. The night before the battle of Agincourt, when his outnumbered army is weakened by disease, and confidence is more than ever required, he turns to prayer to avert divine retaliation for his father's crime that, with the crown, seems to have moved to his shoulders.

> O God of battles! steel my soldiers' hearts;
> Possess them not with fear; take from them now
> The sense of reckoning, if the opposed numbers
> Pluck their hearts from them! Not to-day, O Lord!
> O, not to-day, think not upon the fault
> My father made in compassing the crown!
> I Richard's body have interred anew;
> And on it have bestow'd more contrite tears
> Than from it issu'd forced drops of blood:
> Five hundred poor I have in yearly pay,
> Who twice a day their wither'd hands hold up
> Toward heaven, to pardon blood; and I have built
> Two chantries, where the sad and solemn priests
> Sing still for Richard's soul. More will I do;
> Though all that I can do is nothing worth,
> Since that my penitence comes after all,
> Imploring pardon.[18]

The essential passages of this prayer follow Holinshed's *Chronicles* wherein it is reported that after his succession to the throne Henry V had King Richard's body ceremoniously interred in Westminster Abbey and made specified donations in commemoration. Reference to this incident and the place in which it is made invite comment. By reintroducing the theme of the tragic guilt attached to the House of Lancaster, Shakespeare establishes a link between *Henry V* and his older plays that dramatize the downfall of the Lancastrian Kings (*Henry VI, Richard III*). The victory of Agincourt and the life of Henry V are thus made to appear as a glorious interlude in a tragic tale of crime and doom; however, the King's prayer before the battle reveals the structure of the conflict which Shakespeare embodied in his character: the desire to avoid guilt and to keep himself pure of crime is paramount in Henry V. In one passage of the prayer the King recalls the tears he shed on Richard's coffin, a detail not recorded by Holinshed, and yet obviously suggested by other passages of the *Chronicles*.

---

[17] *King Henry IV, Part II,* Act IV, Sc. 5.
[18] *King Henry V,* Act IV, Sc. 1.

It may well be considered a hint—the only one we find in the trilogy—
that there ever existed a personal relationship between Richard II and the
son of his banished cousin Henry of Lancaster—Henry of Monmouth. During the last months of his rule King Richard II sailed for Ireland to quell
a local rebellion and he took Henry of Monmouth with him. The young
Prince seems to have attracted the King's attention. The Prince was knighted
by King Richard, Holinshed records, "for some valiant act that he did or
some other favourable respect." Shakespeare was undoubtedly familiar with
this account and very probably familiar with reports of the Prince's reaction
to the news of his father's rebellion. Young Henry of Monmouth is said to
have replied to a question of Richard's that he could not be held responsible for his father's deed.

In Shakespeare's *King Richard II* no direct reference is made to the relationship between Prince Hal and Richard,[19] but the theme to which we
refer is present and clearly emphasized: one entire scene is devoted to it, the
first in which the Prince is mentioned. Henry IV, newly enthroned, meets
with his Lords—but his son is absent.

> Can no man tell of my unthrifty son?
> 'Tis full three months since I did see him last:
> If any plague hang over us, 'tis he.
> I would to God, my lords, he might be found:
> Inquire at London, 'mongst the taverns there,
> For there, they say, he daily doth frequent,
> With unrestrained loose companions,
> Even such, they say, as stand in narrow lanes,
> And beat our watch, and rob our passengers; [20]

The Prince has dissociated himself from the court that his father won by
treason. In silent protest he has turned to the tavern rather than to participate in regicide.[21] Regicide dominates the scene that starts with Henry IV's
quest for his absent son. The last of Richard's followers and the new King's
cousin, the Duke of Aumerle, confesses to Henry IV that he has plotted
against his life. Before Aumerle can complete his confession, the Duke of
York, his father and the uncle of Henry IV, forces his way into their presence. He doubts whether the purpose of Aumerle's audience be murder or
repentance and is prepared to surrender his son.[22] This is the environment

---

[19] One might conjecture that Shakespeare preferred not to refer to the personal relationship between Prince Hal and King Richard since he needed a more mature Prince, not a
boy of twelve.

[20] *King Richard II*, Act V, Sc. 3.

[21] Only once Henry V states openly his disapproval of his father's actions, and then in a
highly restrained fashion. When wooing, somewhat abruptly, Katharine of France he
says

> . . . I dare not swear thou lovest me; yet my blood begins to flatter me that
> thou dost, notwithstanding the poor and untempering effect of my visage. *Now
> beshrew my father's ambition! He was thinking of civil wars when he got
> me.* . . . (Italics added.)

[22] York himself had plotted against Richard II and seeks his son's punishment out of a
displaced feeling of guilt. Some of the complexities of this relationship were elucidated
by Taylor, M. P.: "A Father Pleads for the Death of His Son," *Int. J. of Psa.*, VIII, 1927,
pp. 53–55.

from which the Prince withdraws, to which he prefers the vices of Eastcheap and the freedom of Falstaff's company.

In *King Henry IV, Part II*, the contrast between court and tavern is re-emphasized in a scene in which Falstaff's carefree vice is juxtaposed with John of Lancaster's virtuous villainy. This younger brother of Prince Hal is in command of the campaign against the still surviving rebels. Falstaff serves in his inglorious army. Lancaster promises the rebels pardon; they accept his offer and he breaks his word to send them to the gallows. We have just witnessed this monstrous performance—taken directly from Holinshed's *Chronicles*—when Lancaster and Falstaff meet. The "sober blooded youth" provokes Falstaff's soliloquy in praise of Sherristack and of Prince Hal, whose valor has not made him addicted to "thin potations."

Falstaff's loving praise of the Prince, and what others say when they refer to the Prince in the latter part of Part II of *Henry IV* remind us once more of how well he has succeeded in deceiving the world. His conversion upon his accession to the throne comes as a surprise to the court and to the tavern. Only the audience, having been in his confidence from his first soliloquy, are enabled to understand the contradictions in his behavior as being a part of his paramount conflict.

When Shakespeare familiarized himself with the youth of Henry V this conflict must have imposed itself upon his mind as one that would unify the various traits and incidents reported. The tendentious accounts in the *Chronicles* had not fully obliterated the traces of antagonism in the relationship between the Prince and the King. This antagonism, the legends of the Prince's debauchery and conversion, and other elements that the dramatist found in his sources, he wove into a plausible character. The Prince tries to dissociate himself from the crime his father had committed; he avoids contamination with regicide because the impulse to regicide (parricide) is alive in his unconscious. When the King's life is threatened he saves the King and kills the adversary, who is his alter ego. In shunning the court for the tavern he expresses his hostility to his father and escapes the temptation to parricide. He can permit himself to share Falstaff's vices because he does not condone the King's crime; but hostility to the father is only temporarily repressed. When finally he is in possession of the crown, he turns against the father substitute; hence the pointed cruelty of Falstaff's rejection. Both paternal figures between which the Prince oscillates have less meaning to him than appears at first. What he opposes to them is different and of an exalted nature: his ideals of kingship, royal duty and chivalry. These ideals are with him when he first appears on the stage; they grow in and with him throughout the tragedy, and they dominate throughout the five acts of *King Henry V*.

These ideals, one might speculate, may have been modeled on an idealization of Richard II, the murdered King, whom Prince Hal as a boy had accompanied to Ireland and whose favor he had won. Richard, however, was hardly fit to serve as model of a great king. Shakespeare has drawn him as a weak and irresponsible man, who depended presumptuously on the trappings of royalty for his kingship, on that ceremony that meant so little to Henry V and for which he substituted royal duty. One may conjecture this to have been a further reason why Shakespeare did not explicitly refer to the existence of a personal relationship between Prince Henry and King

Richard. But all this is speculative. Opposed to it is solid evidence of the importance of moral conflicts in the personality of Henry V; it would be easy to demonstrate from metaphors and puns alone, with which the poet speaks through the hero, his proclivity to such conflicts. His major actions and interests all indicate too the Prince's search for moral justification.

While living the roistering life of the tavern, his thirst for glory won in battle—but only battle with a moral purpose—and chivalry was great; hence the Prince's bitter caricature of Hotspur.

. . . I am not yet of Percy's mind, the Hotspur of the North; he that kills me some six or seven dozen of Scots at a breakfast, washes his hands, and says to his wife, "Fie upon this quiet life! I want work." "O my sweet Harry," says she; "how many hast thou killed to-day?" "Give my roan horse a drench," says he; and answers, "Some fourteen" an hour after; "a trifle, a trifle." [23]

There is jubilant relief when Percy turns to rebellion and the Prince can finally fight an envied rival, and in the service of a just cause liberate and use his own aggressive impulses; hence also, before the invasion of France, the preoccupation with legal points; and finally, on the night before Agincourt, the protracted debate with Williams, the soldier. Assuming that his partner in discussion is "Harry le Roy" an English commoner, the soldier argues

. . . There are few die well that die in a battle; for how can they charitably dispose of anything, when blood is the argument? Now, if those men do not die well, it will be a black matter for the king that led them to it. . . .[24]

Henry goes to great lengths to refute this thesis. He contends that the King is answerable only for the justice of his cause and cannot be answerable for "the particular endings of his soldiers," since "every subject is the King's, but every subject's soul is his own." The moving subtleties of this theological discourse [25] lead to the King's soliloquy on ceremony and royal destiny:

> Upon the king! let us our lives, our souls,
> Our debts, our careful wives,
> Our children, and our sins lay on the king!
> We must bear all. O hard condition,
> Twin-born with greatness, subject to the breath
> Of every fool, whose sense no more can feel
> But his own wringing! What infinite heart's-ease
> Must kings neglect that private men enjoy!
> And what have kings that privates have not too,
> Save ceremony,—save general ceremony?
> And what art thou, thou idol ceremony? [26]

[23] *King Henry IV, Part I*, Act II, Sc. 4.
[24] *King Henry V*, Act IV, Sc. 1.
[25] Canterbury says of the newly enthroned Henry V (Act I, Sc. 1.):
> Hear him but reason in divinity
> And, all admiring, with an inward wish
> You would desire the King were made a prelate.
[26] *King Henry V*, Act IV, Sc. 1.

Summoned to battle, the King kneels in prayer in which he disclaims any complicity in his father's crime; thus prepared, the hero can conquer.

Henry V's preoccupation with morals is not glorified by Shakespeare nor presented as the dominant virtue of "a Christian soldier"; it is shown in its dynamic interplay with opposite tendencies, and occasionally—with a slightly ironical smile—exposed as a pretense. While the King is urging the clergy to establish his claim to the throne of France, the audience knows that he has forced the support of the Church by political pressure. The bishops, who have accepted the deal and supplied the garbled justification, are well aware of the King's burning desire for conquest. We are left in doubt as to whether it is political shrewdness or self-deception which prompts the King to pose the question: [27]

> May I with right and conscience make this claim? [28]

Ambiguities and schisms of motivation are characteristic of the King. He flees to the tavern to escape from the evils of the court—but he becomes a past master of licentious living. He strives for humane warfare, and protects the citizens of conquered Harfleur; [29] but when the French break the laws of warfare in attacking the English encampment and killing the boys, Henry has every French prisoner's throat cut. The "friction between flesh and spirit" (Traversi), between impulse and inhibition, is fully resolved only when from moral scrutiny Henry proceeds to heroic venture, when as leader of men who are determined to fight with a clear conscience against overwhelming odds, he feels himself one among peers:

> We few, we happy few, we band of brothers.[30]

The inconsistencies in Prince Hal's character that some of Shakespeare's critics thought to have detected are not inconsistencies but attempts to resolve a conflict which is in some of its elements similar to Hamlet's. In Hamlet the Oedipus [complex] is fully developed, centering around the Queen. In Shakespeare's historical dramas women are absent or insignificant. Prince Hal's struggle against his father appears therefore in isolation, enacted in male society. Hamlet stands between a murdered father and a murderous uncle. Prince Hal's father murdered his second cousin—and predecessor— to whom the Prince had an attachment. Thus the crime is in both cases carried out by the father or by his substitute—the King in *Hamlet*—while both heroes are battling against the murderous impulse in their own hearts.

The psychological plausibility of Prince Hal as a dramatic character is not inferior to that of Hamlet, whatever the difference in depth and dramatic significance of the two plays may be. While only one part of the

---

[27] A somewhat similar analysis of this passage has been given by Traversi, D. A.: "Henry V," *Scrutiny,* IX, No. 4, March, 1941, pp. 352–374, who in a remarkable essay stresses the importance of "cool reasoning" and "self-domination" in the King's character.
[28] *King Henry V,* Act I, Sc. 2.
[29] Traversi notes that when the King presents his ultimatum to Harfleur his passion rises, and that in accepting the surrender he regains self-control. *Op. cit.*
[30] *King Henry V,* Act IV, Sc. 3.

Oedipal conflict is presented, the defenses which Prince Hal mobilizes in order to escape from his internal predicament are well known from the clinical study of male youths. In our analysis of the Prince's character we have implicitly referred mainly to two mechanisms: first, to the formation of the superego; second, the displacement of filial attachment onto a father substitute.

The Prince, in his thoughts, compares the King, his father, with an ideal of royal dignity far superior to the father himself. This ideal, derived from paternal figures but exalted and heightened, is his protection in the struggle against his parricidal impulses and against submission to the King. This mechanism operates in some form or other in every boy's development at the time of the resolution of the Oedipal conflict. During this process the superego acquires part of its severity and some of its autonomy. It is a process subject to many vicissitudes, as illustrated by a clinical example.

A boy of eight approached his father, a distinguished judge, with a request for advice. He held two one dollar bills and wanted to know whether he might keep them. They had been acquired by the sale to neighbors of pencils which a mail order house had sent him on his request. Upon the receipt of the two dollars he was to be sent a premium to which he now preferred the money. The judge asked to see the advertisement to which the boy had responded and the letter of the mail order house. After reading both he ruled: "You may keep the money; they have no right to make such contracts with minors."

When thirty-five years later the incident was recalled in analysis it appeared that he had not only lost confidence in all authority since that time, but also that when he had asked his father's advice he was testing him. He had grown suspicious that the father did not live up to the principles—sexual and moral—he advocated, and when in his own conflict he sought the father's advice, he had hoped that the father would support his own hesitant moral views. When this expectation was disappointed, he acquired a cynical independence. The compulsion to live up to his ideal became part of a complex neurotic symptomatology.

In one detail only did this patient resemble Prince Hal: his own moral standards assured his independence from all paternal figures and were used as aggressive reproach in every contact with them. Prince Hal uses not only his ideal of moral integrity as reproachful contrast against his father, but also his own playful depravity. The second mechanism of defense the Prince mobilizes is no less common than the first. He adopts an extrafamilial substitute who, true to a pattern frequently observed, is the antithesis of the father. Falstaff is closer to the Prince's heart than the King; he satisfies the libidinal demands in the father-son relation through his warmth and freedom. Yet the Prince proves superior to Falstaff in wit and royal reveling: he triumphs over both father and father substitute.[31] He is paramount in licence as he will be paramount in royal dignity.

Literary critics seem of late weary of the intrusion of psychoanalysis.

[31] The son's superiority over the father occurs also in other connections in the trilogy. Hotspur is superior to both Worcester and Northumberland and Aumerle is superior to his father, York, who first betrays King Richard before he betrays his own son.

However politely, they assert—and rightly so—their independence.[32] This essay is a psychological analysis which attempts only to underline a few universal, unconscious mechanisms, and is not intended as literary criticism. It suggests that Shakespeare had puzzled about the nature of Henry V's personality, and that already, while writing the last act of Richard II, was aware of the conflict on which he intended to center the character development of the King. Shakespeare's plan, suggested in this case by the nature of the tradition about the subject, must have been one of the trends of thought that, on various levels of awareness, directed him in writing the trilogy. It is not suggested that the plan was complete from the beginning; it might have manifested itself to the poet during his work, i.e., it might have been preconscious before. Moreover, some elements we here consider part of this plan probably never reached consciousness. What answer Shakespeare might have given if asked why Henry V kills Falstaff by his harshness is comparatively irrelevant. What counts is that he had the King do so, and he surely must have known that this could hardly be popular with an audience. Such internal consistency, the final parricide, can only have been conceived by one who in creating had access to his own unconscious impulses.

If investigations similar to the one here attempted, but more complete and authoritative, were carried out systematically, if they were to comprehend all of Shakespeare's work and, at least for purposes of comparison, the works of other Elizabethans; if conflicts and their varied or preferred solutions, and those omitted by one author, one group of authors, one period, or one cultural area were collated, such an application of psychoanalysis might be integrated with the work of the literary historian or critic.

Plot and character are clearly not the only, and not always the most important, tools of the dramatic poet. Psychoanalysis suggests other approaches for the study of poetic language, its metaphors and hidden meanings.[33] Systematic investigation in this area may lead to other types of integration than the study of plot or character. The combination of various sequences of such systematic studies might finally lead to a topic in which critics and psychoanalysts are equally interested and about which they are both, each in his own field, almost equally ignorant: the nature of the artist's personality, a question that must be studied in its cultural variations before generalizations can be made.

Psychoanalysis has frequently attempted short cuts, mostly by correlating one of the artist's works with an occurrence noted by his biographers,[34] assumptions that can rarely be verified.

Clinical analysis of creative artists suggests that the life experience of

[32] Cf. Trilling's excellent essay, "Freud and Literature," Horizon, XVI, No. 92, 1947, pp. 182–200; or Knights, L. C.: Explorations. London: Chatto & Windus, 1946, especially the essay, "Prince Hamlet," pp. 66–77.

[33] Cf. Sharpe, Ella Freeman: "From King Lear to The Tempest," Int. J. Psa., XXVII, 1946, pp. 19–30. Cf. also Kaplan, Abraham and Kris, Ernst: "Aesthetic Ambiguity," Philosophy and Phenomenological Research, VIII, No. 3, March, 1948, pp. 415–435.

[34] This procedure was initiated in 1900 by a remark of Freud who envisaged the possibility that Shakespeare's choice of Hamlet as a topic and the treatment of the conflict might have to do with the death of Shakespeare's son Hamnet.

the artist is sometimes only in a limited sense the source of his vision; that his power to imagine conflicts may by far transcend the range of his own experience; or, to put it more accurately, that at least some artists possess the particular gift to generalize from whatever their own experience has been. One is always tempted to look for a cue that would link this or that character to its creator's personality. Falstaff, it has been said, is clearly Shakespeare himself. Why not Percy or Richard II? Are they not equally alive, equally consistent? Could not for each of these characters that very same psychological plausibility be claimed, that we here claim for Prince Hal? Such a quest seems futile and contrary to what clinical experience with artists as psychoanalytic subjects seems to indicate.[35] Some great artists seem to be equally close to several of their characters, and may feel many of them as parts of themselves. The artist has created a world and not indulged in a daydream.

This writer is not exempt from the temptation to detect a neat connection between the artist and one of his characters. I therefore record my own venture in this direction, with appropriate reservations. At the time Shakespeare was working on *Richard II,* and studying the life of Prince Hal, he re-established the prestige of the Shakespeare family (which had been lost through his father's bankruptcy) by purchasing a coat of arms. The motto chosen is one that might well have been used to characterize Prince Hal's striving for the crown: "Non sanz droict."

[35] *Cf.* Kris, Ernst: "Probleme der Aesthetik," *Int. Ztschr. f. Psa., u. Imago,* XXVI, 1941, pp. 142–178; for clinical aspects *cf.* Bergler, Edmund: "Psychoanalysis of Writers and of Literary Production." In *Psychoanalysis and the Social Sciences.* I. Edited by Géza Róheim. New York: International Universities Press, 1947, pp. 247–296.

*Maud Bodkin*

# A STUDY OF "THE ANCIENT MARINER"

AND OF THE REBIRTH ARCHETYPE

**II**

. . . I would propose first the question: What is the significance, within the experience communicated by *The Ancient Mariner,* of the becalming and the renewed motion of the ship, or of the falling and rising of the wind? I would ask the reader who is familiar with the whole poem to take opportunity to feel the effect, in relation to the whole, of the group of verses, from Part the Second:

> Down dropt the breeze, the sails dropt down,
> 'Twas sad as sad could be;
> And we did speak only to break
> The silence of the sea!

·   ·   ·

Reprinted from *Archetypal Patterns in Poetry: Psychological Studies of Imagination,* 1934, by Maud Bodkin, by permission of Oxford University Press, New York, N.Y., and the author. (Sections I and VII of this chapter are not here reprinted.)

> Day after day, day after day,
> We stuck, nor breath nor motion:
> As idle as a painted ship
> Upon a painted ocean.
>
> .    .    .

and from Part the Sixth:

> But soon there breathed a wind on me,
> Nor sound nor motion made:
> Its path was not upon the sea,
> In ripple or in shade.
>
> It raised my hair, it fanned my cheek
> Like a meadow-gale of spring—
> It mingled strangely with my fears,
> Yet it felt like a welcoming.
>
> Swiftly, swiftly flew the ship,
> Yet she sailed softly too:
> Sweetly, sweetly blew the breeze—
> On me alone it blew.
>
> Oh! dream of joy! is this indeed
> The lighthouse top I see?
> Is this the hill? is this the kirk?
> Is this mine own countree?
>
> We drifted o'er the harbour-bar,
> And I with sobs did pray—
> O let me be awake, my God!
> Or let me sleep alway.

I ask him, before attempting any answer to the question regarding the general significance of the stanzas, to turn upon the experience aroused by them in his mind and see what can be discerned there. If fragments of reminiscence appear, let him follow them far enough for identification, and see if they throw any light upon the value of the lines to himself personally.

I would refer at this point to the experiments upon himself recorded by Francis Galton, in his *Inquiries into Human Faculty*. Wishing to observe the flow of ideas in his own mind without hindrance from self-consciousness, he adopted the following method. He allowed his mind to play freely, for a very brief period—from the starting-point, in his first experiments, of different objects seen during a walk; later, from single words shown on cards. Then the plan was, while "the traces or echoes" of the ideas aroused still lingered, "to turn the attention upon them with a sudden and complete awakening: to arrest, to scrutinize them, and to record their exact appearance."[1] He observes that in this exercise he did not permit himself to indulge in reverie. By this he means not that the ideas he recognized were all of the simple kind required when one is told to say or write down the first word that occurs—they might consist in mental attitudes, or modes of feeling, or in "a glance down a familiar line of associations"—but that he

[1] *Inquiries into Human Faculty and its Development* (Macmillan, 1883), "Psychometric Experiments," p. 185.

never followed them so far as to allow them wholly to displace the object that formed the starting-point (p. 184).

The results of his experiments—both at first, when he simply reviewed them in retrospect, and later, when he managed to keep a methodical record —gave him, he says, a new insight into the obscure background of his own mental process. He found that "many bygone incidents, which I never suspected to have formed part of my stock of thoughts, had been glanced at as objects too familiar to awaken the attention" (p. 187). He was amazed, he says, at the number of events referred to, "about which I had never consciously occupied myself of late years." Yet there was less variety in the stock of ideas thus revealed than he had expected; and his general conclusion was "that the mind is perpetually travelling over familiar ways without our memory retaining any impression of its excursions. Its footsteps are so light and fleeting that it is only by such experiments as I have described that we can learn anything about them" (p. 192).

It was as a result of moments of introspection, conducted by the present writer somewhat in the manner described by Galton, that she conceived the idea that a somewhat similar method might be applied to the study of the experience communicated by poetry. In her own case it happened frequently that in turning round upon the free play of the mind, either in times of idleness, or in momentary pauses amidst other activities, she discovered fragments of verse drifting in marginal consciousness with other fainter imagery—verse familiar enough, perhaps, from childhood, which she was yet surprised to find present, since she had not, as Galton says, been consciously occupied with it of late years. The discovery suggested that, at any rate in her own case, certain poems had, without any activity of conscious attention, become closely interwoven with the emotional life. This conclusion further observation confirmed, revealing a tissue of interrelations established between certain passages of prose or verse and characteristic emotional states of mind.

Amongst such passages occurred the stanzas quoted above, concerning the swift homeward flight of the ship. These seemed to be linked with moments of eager successful mental activity coming after periods of futile effort and strain. In a time of mental inertia and painful oppression there was found to occur, not actually the lines quoted from Coleridge describing the calm, but others interrelated with these. When the line, "Down dropt the breeze, the sails dropt down," was used as a starting-point for associations, there came, as immediately linked with it, the lines of Rossetti, from *The Woodspurge*, with its brief characterization of the blankness of "perfect grief":

> The wind flapped loose, the wind was still,
> Shaken out dead from tree and hill:
> I had walked on at the wind's will,—
> I sat now, for the wind was still.

This stanza, when thus first recalled in experimenting with *The Ancient Mariner*, appeared to the writer not to have received conscious attention since the distant time when, as girls, she and her sisters were fascinated by Rossetti's poetry. Faint memories were recalled, from nearly the same period, of certain experiences in a little sailing-boat whose response to changes of the wind seemed strangely to magnify one's own awareness of them; also a memory of a remark offered, at that same period of youthful awakening to poetry, by a sister little given to literary confidences, who had also noted how vividly the words of Rossetti described what one felt when sails, or other live-seeming things, relapsed to stillness at the falling of the wind. Other lines in the same passage from Coleridge's poem recalled images of similar character accruing from the reading of later years. "As idle as a painted ship," for example, suggested the ship pictured upon a dust cover of Conrad's novel, *The Shadow Line*, linked with all the experience communicated by that tale of the sufferings of the becalmed.

These associations are mentioned here, certainly not because there is anything particularly striking about them, but because, if it is true for other readers also that complexes of interwoven personal and literary reminiscence are formed, and vibrate unrecognized in the background of the mind, contributing again and again emotional significance to words or happenings that make connexion with them—this would be a truth from which certain results might follow of interest for literary psychology.

Mr. Hugh I'Anson Fausset in his study of Coleridge has pronounced the poem of *The Ancient Mariner* "an involuntary but inevitable projection into imagery of his own inner discord." [2] Of the images of the stagnant calm and of the subsequent effortless movement of the ship, Fausset says they were "symbols of his own spiritual experience, of his sense of the lethargy that smothered his creative powers and his belief that only by some miracle of ecstasy which transcended all personal volition, he could elude a temperamental impotence" (p. 163). If we pass from considering our own response to the poem to consider with Fausset the more speculative question, what were the emotional associations in the mind of Coleridge with the imagery he used, there seems to be a good deal that confirms Fausset's interpretation.

Coleridge has told us how poignantly he felt an obscure symbolism in natural objects. "In looking at objects of Nature," he writes, "I seem rather to be seeking, as it were *asking* for, a symbolical language for something within me that already and for ever exists, than observing anything new." [3] This is a typical expression of that attitude which Abercrombie describes as characteristic of the romantic poet—the projection of the inner experience outward upon actuality. There seems little doubt that, possessing this tendency to find in natural objects an expression of the inner life, Coleridge felt in wind and in stagnant calm symbols of the contrasted states he knew so poignantly, of ecstasy and of dull inertia.

He has told us of the times when he felt "forsaken by all the *forms* and *colourings* of existence, as if the *organs* of life had been dried up; as if only simple Being remained, blind and stagnant"; and again, of his longing for the swelling gust, and "slant night-shower driving loud and fast" which, "whilst they awed"—

> Might now perhaps their wonted impulse give,
> Might startle this dull pain, and make it move and live!

[2] *Samuel Taylor Coleridge* (Cape, 1926), p. 166.
[3] *Anima Poetae*, p. 136.

So, also, the image of a ship driving before the wind is used by him as a conscious metaphor to express happy surrender to the creative impulse. "Now he sails right onward" he says of Wordsworth engaged upon *The Prelude,* "it is all open ocean and a steady breeze, and he drives before it." [4] In *The Ancient Mariner* the magic breeze, and the miraculous motion of the ship, or its becalming, are not, of course, like the metaphor, symbolic in conscious intention. They are symbolic only in the sense that, by the poet as by some at least of his readers, the images are valued because they give—even though this function remain unrecognized—expression to feelings that were seeking a language to relieve their inner urgency.

In the case of this symbolism of wind and calm we have a basis of evidence so wide that we hardly need go for proof to introspective reports of reader or poet—interesting as it is to see the confirmatory relation between evidence from the different sources. We find graven in the substance of language testimony to the kinship, or even identity, of the felt experience of the rising of the wind and the quickening of the human spirit.

"Come from the four winds, O breath, and breathe upon these slain, that they may live." Behind the translated words, in the vision of Ezekiel, we can feel the older meaning, strange to our present-day thought, in which the physical wind, and the breath in man's nostrils, and the power of the Divine Spirit, were aspects hardly differentiated. So again, in the passage from St. John's Gospel concerning the new birth by the spirit that bloweth where it listeth; or where the writer of Acts tells how, when the Holy Spirit descended, there came a sound from Heaven as of a rushing mighty wind; or where, in the inscription upon his coffin, Akhnaton prays to Aton: "I breathe the sweet breath which comes forth from thy mouth. . . . It is my desire that I may hear thy sweet voice, the wind, that my limbs may be rejuvenated with life through love of thee" [5]—in all these sayings we discern a nearer influence of that older undivided meaning which the feeling-prompted speech of the modern poet can reveal only across a gulf made by age-long labours of abstracting thought.

The poet, in his metaphorical speech, says Barfield, restores, conceptually, a unity which has now "been lost from perception." [6] His imaginative thought recreates as poetry what was once experienced intuitively, but with no sense of poetic achievement, such as now pertains to it.[7] In the older, unwitting fashion the images of our dreams seem to combine aspects which, when our waking thought divides them, startle us as imaginative and poetic; similarly, as we read the straightforward language of Coleridge's ballad, it is the contrast of our waking thought, running alongside our dream-like acceptance of the tale, that gives us the sense of it as a thing of poetic witchery, made to minister to some imaginative need.

To the mind of the present writer the magic of Coleridge's poem is enhanced, not dissipated, by the play of thought around it, explaining the connexions of ideas that seem to contribute to the felt significance. For some

---

[4] *Ibid.,* p. 30.
[5] *Life and Times of Akhnaton,* by Arthur Weigall, new and revised ed. (Thornton Butterworth, 1923), p. 249.
[6] *Poetic Diction,* by Owen Barfield (Faber & Gwyer, 1928), p. 73.
[7] *Ibid.,* pp. 96–7.

minds, it appears, this is not the case. Analytic thought is regarded as an intruder that breaks the dream and mars the beauty, and can have little of value to contribute even to understanding.

The reader who has accompanied me so far in this investigation has probably some sympathy with the assumption that underlies it, namely, that there is present in such a poem as *The Ancient Mariner,* an obscure emotional significance which seems to invite inquiry—provokes us to fathom its symbolism. At the same time, there is so much confusion surrounding the idea of symbolic speech and imagery, so much opportunity for the play of subjective caprice, that I cannot expect the reader to feel other than doubtful concerning the attempt to explore the poem's symbolism in further detail.

I shall hope to return later, with more illustrative material before us, to the question what exactly we should understand by the "emotional symbolism" of poetry [section vii]. In the meantime I would ask the reader to grant to the suggestions and results I lay before him only so much sympathy as shall be necessary for testing them in the light of his own experience.

### III

In this section some study is to be made of the group of stanzas that constitute the climax of the poem's action—the stanzas of the fourth Part that lead up to the blessing of the water snakes, and those of the fifth Part that describe the immediate consequences of that impulse of love.

As before, I would invite the reader to examine his own response to this central passage, which I will not quote at length here, since the poem is so readily accessible. Certain further considerations may be put forward in regard to the attempt to study one's own response to poetry.

When a reader has succeeded in turning the flashlight of attention back upon a moment of vivid emotional apprehension of poetry, inquiring as to its content, the answer to that inquiry is often that nothing is to be discerned there but the words of the poem. Professor Valentine, in his experimental study of "The Function of Images in the Appreciation of Poetry," [8] found that some of his students, who were quite capable of vivid imagery and accustomed to recognize it, reported that they understood and appreciated various poems, even some of descriptive character, with practically no imagery, other than of the words, present. One such observer noted that certain striking phrases made images "stir in the depths," but for the most part appreciation took place "as if by unconscious reference to experience." [9] Several observers found that the attempt to observe imagery interfered with the enjoyment of the poem, through breaking "the continuity of poetic experience." [10] When attention is directed to imagery it seems that something more important is "displaced."

My own experience in regard to Coleridge's poem is that at the moment of completest appreciation no imagery, other than the words, is present. I

---

[8] *Brit. J. of Psychol.* xiv, part 2.
[9] *Ibid.,* p. 181.
[10] *Ibid.,* pp. 183–4.

am in some manner aware of a whole of far-reaching significance, concentrated like a force behind any particular stanza or line. It is as the tension of the apprehensive act slackens that I become aware of images, or references to particular past experiences. In speaking of a tissue of interrelated personal and literary reminiscence as found in connexion with certain lines of poetry, I was describing what comes into awareness as the grasp of poetic apprehension loosens. Yet when thus discriminated, this material seems to be recognized as having contributed something to the preceding unified experience of meaning—as having operated in the manner of a "fused" association.[11] The apprehension of the line "Down dropt the wind . . ." would have been different for me if some other memory-complex had entered into it than just that one whose constituents I can partly identify as I suffer free associations to arise.

"I cannot think it a personal peculiarity," writes James Russell Lowell,[12] "but a matter of universal experience, that more bits of Coleridge have imbedded themselves in my memory than of any other poet who delighted my youth—unless I should except the sonnets of Shakespeare." This rather naïve confession may illustrate the point that unless we attempt, by the help of comparative psychological study, to measure and allow for our own "personal equation" in criticism, we are all apt to feel as though our own personal responses were "matters of universal experience." It seems as though every one must experience the grip upon emotion, the sense of penetrating significance, that certain poems or particular passages have for ourselves. Actually, diversity of temperament and of nurture bring it about that very different memory-complexes exert their selective influence in the case of different individuals. We learn that the lines that carry such haunting overtones for ourselves sound quite flatly to another, through the difference, or the lack, of the associations, "imbedded in the memory" and fused with those particular phrases, images, and rhythms, which give them for us their special significance. Yet amidst the diversity, certain associations may still be reckoned upon as holding good for individuals of widely different nurture and temperament. Those just considered, for instance, of the ship becalmed, and of its homeward flight, would seem to have a universal, "archetypal" character, amidst whatever minor difference temperament and experience may impose upon the individual response to the lines describing the dropt wind and sails, or the sweet blowing of the breeze.

I will begin the consideration of the stanzas to be examined in this section by some reference to the extremely interesting study which Professor Livingston Lowes has made of *The Ancient Mariner* and its sources, as revealing "the imaginative energy . . . at work." Professor Lowes shows the relation of certain lines and phrases in the poem to passages in books that Coleridge had read, and thus gives us glimpses of the content of the poet's mind—"the surging chaos of the unexpressed," he terms it, "that suffuses and colours everything which flashes and struggles into utterance." [13]

[11] *Cf.* the use of this term by Professor Valentine and Mr. Bullough [E. Bullough, "Distance as an aesthetic principle," *Brit. J. of Psychol.* v. part 2], as referring to associations "intimate, unavoidable, permanent." *Op. cit.,* p. 177.
[12] *Complete Writings of James Russell Lowell,* vol. vii, p. 88.
[13] *The Road to Xanadu,* by John Livingston Lowes (Constable, 1927), p. 13.

Lowes's work presents a striking contrast to that of Fausset, referred to in the last section, in that Lowes, in his detailed study of this suffusing background, makes hardly any reference to emotional forces. He is anxious to keep to evidence which can "be weighed and tested"; and, on that account perhaps, ventures to call upon the resources of psychology for little but, first, a machinery of associative links—in Coleridge's own phrase "hooks and eyes of the memory"—equipping the images derived from books he had read; and, secondly, marshalling the flow of these "hooked atoms," "a controlling conscious energy" of "imagination," "directing intelligence," and "driving will." [14] An insight into more than this is implied in certain observations, but in his general theory Lowes seems to take no account of emotional forces as determining either the selection or the fashioning of the material of the poem. Such forces he appears to regard as necessarily personal, not to be discovered, as he says, after the lapse of a hundred and more years. In a note (p. 400) he emphatically repudiates any intention of dealing with the "possible symbolism of wish-fulfilment or conflict or what not" that might be suspected to underlie the poem. He does not, apparently, conceive the possibility of conflicts or wish-fulfilments of a character so universal as to echo through poetry from age to age, and to leave in language traces that may, in some sense, "be weighed and tested."

If, then, we turn to Lowes's study for some suggestion as to what kind of memory-complex in the mind of Coleridge lay behind the lines in which he described the Mariner's despairing vigil on the stagnant tropic seas, we may learn where Coleridge, who at this time had never been to sea, became familiar with such things as he describes.

> The very deep did rot: O Christ!
> That ever this should be!
> Yea, slimy things did crawl with legs
> Upon the slimy sea.
>
> .　　.　　.
>
> The many men, so beautiful!
> And they all dead did lie:
> And a thousand thousand slimy things
> Lived on; and so did I.

and again:

> Beyond the shadow of the ship,
> I watched the water-snakes:
> They moved in tracks of shining white,
> And when they reared, the elfish light
> Fell off in hoary flakes.
>
> Within the shadow of the ship
> I watched their rich attire:
> Blue, glossy green, and velvet black,
> They coiled and swam; and every track
> Was a flash of golden fire.

[14] *Op. cit.* See especially pp. 44, 304–5.

What "surging chaos of the unexpressed" lay behind these slimy things, and rotting seas, and shining water-snakes?

Lowes tells us of descriptions Coleridge had read of many kinds of "slime-fish"; of a description, in one of his "best-loved folios," of "partie-coloured snakes" seen by Hawkins when he was "at the Asores many months becalmed" and his men "could hardly draw a Bucket of Water, cleare of some corruption withall"; [15] and again, of a description by Captain Cook of small sea animals swimming during a calm, when "parts of the sea seemed covered with a kind of slime"—animals that "emitted the brightest colours of the most precious gems," blue, or red, or green "with a burnished gloss," and, in the dark, "a faint appearance of glowing fire." [16]

Lowes notes the "hooks," or "almost chemical affinities of common elements"—here of "colour and calm and a corrupted sea"—which brought about fusion of the snakes of Hawkins and the animalculae of Cook, and other such memory-fragments—"fortuitously blending images"—in "the deep well of unconscious cerebration." [17] He notes, further, the vision and controlling will that imposes form upon the chaos. He has in view such form as appears, for example, in "the exquisite structural balance" of the two stanzas quoted above, describing the snakes beyond and within the shadow—"stanzas which answer to each other, phrase upon phrase, like an antiphon" (p. 64).

In all this we have no explicit reference to that need for emotional expression which to Fausset, and to the present writer also, appears the supreme shaping force within the poem—and, as I would add, the force also in the mind of the reader, through which the poem is appreciated.

"Few passages," says Lowes, "which Coleridge ever read seem to have fecundated his imagination so amazingly as that 257th page of Cook's second volume, which described the 'small sea animals swimming about' in 'a kind of slime,' with 'a faint appearance of glowing fire'" (p. 90). Can we at all divine the reason for this powerful influence? Lowes helps us to see the reason—and discerns it himself, one fancies, more clearly—when he is thinking not in terms of psychology but of literary insight. He tells us that Coleridge when reading these descriptions was vigilantly seeking material for those Hymns to the Sun, Moon, and the Elements, which he planned but never executed. His mind was directed "upon every accident of light, shade and colour through which the very expression on the face of sea, sky, earth, and their fiery exhalations might be seized and held" (p. 76). Lowes quotes the passage from Coleridge's earlier poem, *The Destiny of Nations,* which likens the "glad noise" of Love's wings fluttering to the fresh breeze breaking up the—

> long and pestful calms
> With slimy shapes and miscreated life
> Poisoning the vast Pacific, . . .

We begin to see what kind of symbolic value the imagination of Coleridge, ever seeking a language for something within, would feel in those shapes,

---

[15] Quoted *op. cit.,* p. 49.
[16] Quoted *ibid.,* p. 46.
[17] *Op. cit.,* pp. 56, 58, 65.

slimy and miscreate in the stagnant water, that yet glowed with gemlike colour and strange fire. Lowes asks, concerning Cook's description:

Would that strong suggestion of a windless sea glowing red in the night be likely to leave his imagination quite unstirred? [and continues:] In the great stanza which leads from the soft ascent of "the moving Moon" to the luminous shapes whose blue and glossy green derived from those same animalculae, the redness of the protozoa burns ominous in the very sea which before had burnt with their green, and blue, and white:

> Her beams bemocked the sultry main,
> Like April hoar-frost spread;
> But where the ship's huge shadow lay,
> The charmed water burnt alway
> *A still and awful red.*

There is, I suspect, no magic in the poem more potent than this blending of images through which the glowing redness of animalculae once seen in the Pacific has imbued with sombre mystery that still and boding sea (p. 89).

The reader, looking back from this stanza to the suggestion in Cook's page of a windless sea glowing red in the night, may guess from his own response to Coleridge's line what was the emotional symbolism of Cook's description for the imagination of the poet. Here, as always, it is through our sense of the emotional forces stirring in the experience communicated to ourselves that we can discern something of what the forces were that first gripped the significant aspects in the material to the poet's hand, and then held and fashioned this into perfect expressiveness.

I will now attempt, focusing upon that "great stanza" with its contrast of white moonlight and red shadow, to give something of what I find to be the experience communicated.

In following the description of the Mariner's vigil upon the stagnant sea, it is not till I come to this stanza that I recognize an image detaching itself spontaneously and strongly from the synthetic grasp of the poem's meaning. I live in the Mariner's anguish of repulsion—from the rotting deck where lay the dead, and rotting sea and slimy creatures—with no discernible image at all, other than the voice speaking with inflexions of despair, and the faint organic changes that go with such inflexions—unless, of course, I demand an image. When I did that on one occasion, there appeared an image of a crowd of people struggling for a bus at a particular London street corner. For a moment I thought the numerical suggestion in the "thousand thousand slimy things" had broken right away from its context; but then, catching the atmosphere of my street-corner image, I recognized the mood of shrinking disgust that had operated in calling up the picture.

With the transition from the Mariner's utter despair to his yearning vision of the moon in its soft journeying through the sky, there comes a stirring of images which, however, do not emerge spontaneously from out the magic of the charged verse; but when I come to the lines that lead from the white moonlight to the "huge shadow" of the ship where the water burns red, the emotional stress upon that colour-word has become so intense that an image breaks out from it of a red that burns downward through shadow, as into an abyss. Words, Maupassant has said, have a soul as well as a sense—a soul that a poet may reveal in the word by his placing of it. "Il faut trouver cette âme qui apparaît au contact d'autres mots. . . ." [18] The word "red" has a soul of terror that has come to it through the history of the race. Dante helped to fashion that soul in the terrible lines that, for one who meets them, even in translation, at the right moment of his youth, leave the word "red" never again quite the same as before Dante touched it:

> . . . the city that is named of Dis draws nigh, . . .
> . . . "Master, already I discern its mosques, distinctly there within the valley, red as if they had come out of fire."
> And to me he said: "The eternal fire, which causes them to glow within, shows them red, as thou seest, in this low Hell."

It is—for me, at least—the same soul that is evoked from the word "red" in Coleridge's stanza and in Dante's lines; and thus—to my feeling—it is as though the Mariner, his deliverance just begun through the power of the moon's beauty, for the moment falls again to Hell in the red shadow of the ship.

I am not sure how far such an influence as this I recognize of Dante upon the word and image of red, in the stanza of Coleridge, would be accepted by Mr. T. S. Eliot as an illustration of what he says concerning a racial or traditional mind, a "mind of Europe" which to the poet is more important than his private mind. This larger mind, he says, changes, but "this change is a development which abandons nothing *en route,* which does not super-annuate either Shakespeare, or Homer, or the rock drawings of the Mag-dalenian draughtsman." [19] One aspect of his "impersonal theory of poetry is the relation of the poem" to the "living whole of all the poetry that has ever been written." Such a relation can clearly not be realized in any indi-vidual mind. The "mind of Europe" is a conception that has meaning only in reference to something approached and realized in different degrees in different minds of individuals, especially through their communication one with another. Through the mystery of communication—operating between the minds of Dante, and Coleridge, and their readers—I, in some degree, realize the presence of a mind in myself beyond my private mind, and it is through this mind that the image of red colour, that had already, we sur-mise, symbolic value to the artist of the Magdalenian rock drawings, has transmitted its ever-growing significance to Dante and to Coleridge, and on to readers at the present moment. [20]

18 Quoted by Barfield, who discusses this latent "soul" in words, *Poetic Diction,* p. 113.
19 *Selected Essays, 1917–32* (Faber & Faber), p. 16.
20 My argument implies an influence of Dante upon Coleridge for which evidence cannot be given—though Lowes, examining the evidence for Dante's influence upon another passage, surmises that, even at the time of writing *The Ancient Mariner,* Coleridge knew Dante, not only in Boyd's translation, but penetrating, perhaps through the help of the Wordsworths, to the true sense of the Italian. By whatever channels it may have passed I think the influence of such lines as those quoted from the *Inferno* would have reached a poet who so far approached the ideal of the European mind as did Coleridge.
In regard to the question of the significance of red, as "a surrogate for blood," to the artists of the Stone Age, I would refer to the writings of Elliot Smith and others.

Let us pass now to the storm—the roaring wind and streaming rain and lightning, by which the stagnant calm and drought is broken, when the Mariner's impulse of love has undone the curse that held both him and Nature transfixed.

> The upper air burst into life!
> And a hundred fire-flags sheen,
> To and fro they were hurried about!
> And to and fro, and in and out,
> The wan stars danced between.
>
> And the coming wind did roar more loud
> And the sails did sigh like sedge;
> And the rain poured down from one black cloud;
> The Moon was at its edge.
>
> The thick black cloud was cleft, and still
> The Moon was at its side:
> Like waters shot from some high crag,
> The lightning fell with never a jag,
> A river steep and wide.

Lowes has traced passages in the Voyages known to have been studied by Coleridge, which describe tropical or subtropical storms—for instance, a description from Bartram, of torrential rain that obscured every object, "excepting the continuous streams or rivers of lightning pouring from the clouds." [21] Such lightning, he remarks, Coleridge had pretty certainly never seen in Devon or Somerset, but he had seen it "in those ocular spectra of his which kept pace with his reading."

Lowes traces to passages read by Coleridge not only the lightning, but the more obscure references to "fire-flags" and the "wan stars" seen through the auroral lights; and we may gratefully acknowledge the interest of the glimpses his researches give of the transmutation into poetry of scattered fragments of traveller's tales. Yet here again, it seems to me we must add to what he tells us insight from our own experience into the emotional forces that are the agents of the transmutation. I would ask the reader who has dwelt upon these storm stanzas of Coleridge, and felt that in his mind they take, as it were, a place shaped and prepared for them, how would he account for such sense of familiarity. In my own mind the streaming rain and lightning of the poem is interrelated with storms felt and seen in dreams. Fading impressions of such rain and lightning recalled on waking have clothed themselves in the flowing words of the poem and become fused with these.

Is it again the racial mind or inheritance, active within the individual sensibility, whether of Coleridge or of his reader, that both assimilates the descriptions of tropical storms, and sees in a heightened pattern those storms of our own country that "startle," and overpower, and "send the soul abroad"? It was, I think, of a Sussex storm, "marching in a dark breastplate and in skirts of rain, with thunders about it," that Belloc wrote:

21 Quoted *op. cit.*, p. 186.

No man seeing this creature as it moved solemn and panoplied could have mistaken the memory or the knowledge that stirred within him at the sight. This was that great master, that great friend, that great enemy, that great idol (for it has been all of these things), which, since we have tilled the earth, we have watched, we have welcomed, we have combated, we have unfortunately worshipped.[22]

The thought of the storm image, and the place it has held in the mind, not of Europe only but of a wider, older culture, takes us back to that order of conception, illustrated already in reference to wind and spirit, wherein the two aspects we now distinguish, of outer sense impression and inly felt process, appear undifferentiated. Dr. Jung [23] cites from the Vedic Hymns lines where prayers, or ritual fire-boring, are said to lead forth, or release, the flowing streams of Rita; and shows that the ancient idea of Rita represented, in undifferentiated fashion, at once the cycle of nature of which rain and fire are offspring, and also the ritually ordered processes of the inner life, in which pent-up energy can be discharged by fitting ceremonial.

The storm which for the experiencing mind appears not as differentiated physical object but as a phase of its own life, is naturally thought of as let loose by prayer, when prayer transforms the whole current and atmosphere of the inner life. In Coleridge's poem the relief of rain follows the relaxing of the inner tension by the act of love and prayer, as naturally and inevitably as do sleep and healing dreams.

> The silly buckets on the deck
> That had so long remained,
> I dreamt that they were filled with dew;
> And when I awoke, it rained.
>
> My lips were wet, my throat was cold,
> My garments all were dank;
> Sure I had drunken in my dreams,
> And still my body drank.

We accept the sequence with such feeling as that with which we accept the narration in terms of recognized metaphor, of a psychical sequence of emotional energy—tension and release—as when, for example, we are told by St. Augustine in his *Confessions* of the long anxiety and suspense that preceded his conversion, and how, when reflection had "gathered up and heaped together all my misery in the sight of my heart, a mighty storm arose, bringing a mighty shower of tears."

Another such psychical sequence, corresponding to that in the story of the Ancient Mariner, may be found set forth in a wealth of detail in the poetry of Emile Verhaeren, as analysed by Charles Baudouin. In Verhaeren's poems the intention of giving expression to states of soul-sickness and recovery, experienced by the poet, is present as it is not in Coleridge's poem. We have metaphor, as against latent emotional symbolism; but a sequence of similar character finds expression, in part through the same imagery.

22 "The Storm" from *This and That*, Hilaire Belloc.
23 See his discussion of "the reconciling symbol as the principle of dynamic regulation." *Psychological Types* (Kegan Paul, 1923), pp. 257 *et seq*.

Thus Baudouin notes that in the poems expressing the "tortured and tragical phase" of Verhaeren's life there is an obsession by images of reflection in water, especially in foul and stagnant water—the water of meres and marshes. He quotes as an example the lines from *Les rues* in *Les soirs:*

> Une lune souffrante et pâle s'entrevoit
> Et se mire aux égouts, où des clartés pourrissent.
>
> [A suffering and wan moon is glimpsed,
> And is mirrored in the foul ditches wherein radiances rot.] [24]

And again:

> La lune et tout le grand ciel d'or
> Tombent et roulent vers leur mort . . . .
> Elle le fausse et le salit,
> L'attire à elle au fond du lit
> D'algues et de goëmons flasques.[25]
>
> [The moon and all the great golden firmament
> Fall, and roll towards their death . . . .
> Death violates it and defiles it,
> Drags it to her right down into the bed
> Of algae and of flaccid seaweed.]

The common element in the imagery—of stagnation and corruption, where even radiance is foul—appears in these passages, but with the contrast that in Verhaeren's lines the moon image is caught into the downward movement toward decay and death; while, in the stanzas of the crisis in *The Ancient Mariner,* the movement toward deliverance begins with the vision of the moon's beauty, pure and aloof from the despair of the watcher below.

The shrinking, before the turning-point was reached, in horror and disgust from every surrounding object—the eyelids closed till the balls like pulses beat—in Coleridge's poem, are paralleled by images which Baudouin quotes from the writings of Verhaeren in the crisis of his "introverted" suffering: for example, the phantasy of self-inflicted blindness, "the extirpation of the eyes in front of the mirror," in a prose fragment of this period. "Kindred ideas," says Baudouin " (a failure of the impetus towards the real world, debility, and withdrawal into the self) are expressed by images of 'broken' and 'flaccid' things:

> Cassés les mâtes d'orgueil, flasques les grandes voiles.[26]
> [Broken the masts of pride, flaccid the great sails.]"

And after the crisis, when Verhaeren has turned once more towards the world of men and human interests, the same images stand to him for the sufferings he has left behind:

[24] *Psycho-analysis and Aesthetics* by C. Baudouin, trans. by Eden and Cedar Paul (Allen & Unwin, 1924), p. 115.
[25] From *La baie,* in *Les vignes de ma muraille,* quoted *ibid.,* pp. 115–16.
[26] From *Les malades,* in *Les soirs,* quoted *op. cit.,* p. 119.

Je suis celui des pourritures grandioses
Qui s'en revient du pays mou des morts.[27]

[I am the one who comes back from the land of widespread corruption,
The one who comes back from the flaccid realm of the dead.]

In speaking of Verhaeren's deliverance from the state of morbid introversion, Baudouin quotes the saying of Goethe: "I said to myself that to deliver my mind from this state of gloom in which it was torturing itself, the essential was to turn my attention towards nature, and to share unreservedly in the life of the outer world." Verhaeren's later poems express vehemently the need to share in the life of the outer world. Baudouin notes how Verhaeren has placed the words "Admire one another" as an epigraph at the beginning of *La multiple splendeur;* and how he "carries out his own precept," writing:

Pour vivre clair, ferme et juste,
Avec mon coeur, j'admire tout
Ce qui vibre, travaille et bout
Dans la tendresse humaine et sur la terre auguste.[28]

[In order to live serenely and firmly and justly
With my heart, I admire everything
Which vibrates and ferments and boils
In human tenderness and on the august earth.]

and again:

Si nous nous admirons vraiment les uns les autres . . .

Nous apportons, *ivres du monde et de nous-mêmes,*
Des coeurs d'hommes nouveaux dans le vieil univers.[29]

[If we really admire one another . . .

We bring, *drunken with the world and with ourselves,*
The hearts of new men into the ancient universe.]

Thus the sequence of Verhaeren's poems presents the same movement of the spirit that is communicated by Coleridge's story of the paralysing spell undone by the impulse of admiration and love, and of the reawakening of energies within and without.

The wind, that roars in the distance, or breathes magically upon the Mariner as the ship flies homeward, is celebrated in Verhaeren's later verse, with its emotional symbolism made explicit.

Si j'aime, admire et chante avec folie,
Le vent, . . .
C'est qu'il grandit mon être entier et c'est qu'avant
De s'infiltrer, par mes poumons et par mes pores
Jusques au sang dont vit mon corps,
Avec sa force rude ou sa douceur profonde,

---

[27] From *Celui du rien,* in *Les apparus dans mes chemins,* quoted *ibid.,* p. 162.
[28] From *Autour de ma maison,* in *La multiple splendeur,* quoted *ibid.,* p. 258.
[29] From *La ferveur,* in *La multiple splendeur,* quoted *op. cit.,* p. 285.

Immensément, il a étreint le monde.[30]

[If I love, admire, and fervently sing the praises
Of the wind, . . .
It is because the wind enlarges my whole being, and because,
Before permeating, through my lungs and through my pores,
The very blood, which is the life of my body,
It has with its rugged strength or its consummate tenderness,
Clasped the world in its titanic embrace.]

From the symbolism made explicit in Verhaeren's poems with the help of Baudouin's commentary, it is but a further step to the generalized exposition of the same psychological sequence by Dr. Jung—still in the metaphorical language so inevitable when one speaks of the inner life. In his discussion of Progression and Regression, as "fundamental concepts of the libido-theory," Jung describes progression as "the daily advance of the process of psychological adaptation," [31] which, at certain times, fails. Then "the vital feeling" disappears; there is a damming up of energy—of libido. At such times, in the patients he has studied, neurotic symptoms are observed, and repressed contents appear, of inferior and unadapted character. "Slime out of the depths" he calls such contents—using the symbolism we have just been studying—but slime that contains not only "objectionable animal tendencies, but also germs of new possibilities of life." [32]

Such an ambivalent character in the slimy things, glowing and miscreate, Coleridge seems to have felt through the travellers' tales, and wrought into expressiveness in his magical picture of the creatures of the calm, which the Mariner first despised and then accepted with love, to his own salvation. Before "a renewal of life" can come about, Jung urges, there must be an acceptance of the possibilities that lie in the unconscious contents "activated through regression . . . and disfigured by the slime of the deep." [33]

The principle which he thus expounds Jung recognizes as reflected in the myth of "the night journey under the sea" [34]—the myth of the entrance of the hero into the body of a whale or dragon, and his journey therein towards the East. It is not my intention to examine here in any detail the theory of Dr. Jung. I do not wish to venture beyond the range of experience open to the student of literature. But, within that domain, I would select, for comparison with *The Ancient Mariner*, the most familiar example of the night-journey myth—that in the second chapter of the Book of Jonah.

What is perhaps most interesting here is to note the coming together, from different levels of thought, of the wonder-tale and the psalm of spiritual confession, and to observe how easily their rather incongruous coalescence has been accepted by readers content to feel rather than reflect:

The waters compassed me about, even to the soul: the depth closed me round about, the weeds were wrapped about my head.
I went down to the bottoms of the mountains: the earth with her bars was about me for ever: yet hast thou brought up my life from corruption, O Lord my God.

[30] From *A la gloire du vent*, in *La multiple splendeur*, quoted *ibid.*, p. 166.
[31] *Contributions to Analytical Psychology*, p. 34.
[32] *Ibid.*, pp. 39–40.
[33] *Ibid.*, p. 38.
[34] *Ibid.*, p. 40.

Here again is the imagery of corruption associated with the descent; imagery too of one transfixed, held motionless as was the Mariner. The weedy bed at the roots of the mountains is little compatible with any literal entry into, and casting forth from, a monster's belly, but the sensibility that seizes the expressive value of the myth is not disturbed by discrepancies discoverable in an attempted matter-of-fact rendering. The earth with her bars, the engulfing seas—like a monster's jaws yawning to receive the victim —or the breathless calm when sea and sky lie like a load on eye and heart, can all alike be made the language of the emotional forces that crave sensuous form for their expression; and, in relation to each symbol, the pattern of deliverance is wrought out in appropriate detail, more or less elaborated, and, as it were, more or less opaque, according as imagination plunges, more or less deeply, and more blindly or with more conscious insight, into its plastic material.

## IV

I have so far attempted, with the help of comparisons of parallel sequences of imagery, to discover the emotional forces which find expression in the experience communicated by the central stanzas of Coleridge's poem.

I have urged, in opposition to the view of Professor Lowes, that it is not a complete account of the poem, as an imaginative achievement, to trace the literary sources of its imagery and to refer to the effort of conscious thought and will ordering, in accordance with a lucidly conceived design, the chaos of "fortuitously blending" elements. The design itself, I urge, is determined by forces that do not lie open directly to thought, nor to the control of the will, but of which we may learn something through the comparative study of literary material, and its psychological analysis.

Attempting such comparison, I have taken advantage of the work of a psychologist who has already undertaken the analysis of a sequence of poems. I have compared, also, myth and the metaphor of religious confession and of psychological exposition, selecting material in accordance with similarity of imagery, especially of form or pattern. Particular words and images, such as those of wind, of storm-cloud, of slime, of red colour, have been examined for their emotional symbolism, but mainly with reference to their capacity to enter into an emotional sequence. Within the image-sequences examined the pattern appears of a movement, downward, or inward toward the earth's centre, or a cessation of movement—a physical change which, as we urge metaphor closer to the impalpable forces of life and soul, appears also as a transition toward severed relation with the outer world, and, it may be, toward disintegration and death. This element in the pattern is balanced by a movement upward and outward—an expansion or outburst af activity, a transition toward reintegration and life-renewal.

To the pattern thus indicated in extreme generality we may give the name of the Rebirth archetype. Any further attempt to characterize it may be postponed until we have carried somewhat farther our study of the pattern as it appears in *The Ancient Mariner,* for which purpose we must take account of certain salient passages in the earlier and later parts of the poem.

Once more I would invite the reader to co-operate, examining his own experience of particular stanzas.

> "God save thee, ancient Mariner!
> From the fiends, that plague thee thus!—
> Why look'st thou so?"—with my cross-bow
> I shot the Albatross.

What images or memory reference, if any, arise in connexion with the experience communicated by the telling of this deed, in its context in the poem; and again, with that communicated by the stanzas near the end, telling of the penance brought by his deed upon the Mariner?

> Forthwith this frame of mine was wrenched
> With a woeful agony,
> Which forced me to begin my tale;
> And then it left me free.
>
> Since then, at an uncertain hour,
> That agony returns:
> And till my ghastly tale is told,
> This heart within me burns.
>
> I pass, like night, from land to land;
> I have strange power of speech;
> That moment that his face I see,
> I know the man that must hear me:
> To him my tale I teach.

Professor Lowes in his examination of the figure of the Mariner reaches conclusions from his material which are of interest for the purpose of this study. He shows, by comparison of the phrases used in the poem with the language of descriptions either written by Coleridge or familiar to him, that the figure of the Mariner in the mind of Coleridge merged or interpenetrated with that of the Wandering Jew, Cain, and perhaps also a sea wanderer, Falkenberg—a variant of the Flying Dutchman. "Guilt-haunted wanderers," says Lowes, "were the theme which for the moment was magnetic in his brain," [35] so that when, during the memorable walk on which the poem was planned, Wordsworth proposed that the shooting of an albatross should call down upon the offender the vengeance of tutelary spirits, the suggestion awakened in Coleridge's mind "throngs of dormant memories." [36]

In regard to the figure of the Mariner, Lowes recognizes in the reader's response also the activity of something like an archetype, answering to that present in the mind of the poet. Demons, spectre-barks, and eternal wanderers alike belong, he says—and the sentence goes far toward the admission of the hypothesis here maintained—to that "misty midregion of our racial as well as literary inheritance, toward which we harbour, when the imagination moves through haunted chambers, the primal instinctive will to

[35] *Op. cit.*, p. 278.
[36] *Op. cit.*, p. 224.

believe." Such images, he continues, are "the immemorial projections of elemental human questionings and intuitions." [37] Of what elemental intuition, then, is the figure of the Mariner—as a guilt-haunted wanderer, akin to Cain, the Wandering Jew, and the Flying Dutchman—an immemorial projection?

I think that one can hardly begin to answer this question without some reference to the analysis of dreams. The writer, in examining the ideas marginally aroused by the stanzas considered in this section, found, as noticeably active, memories of certain dreams in which she herself had killed some animal, and experienced a vague and overwhelming sense of guilt.[38] The crime of Cain and of the Wandering Jew, however, was not the killing of an animal. That of Cain was a crime against human relationship, that of the Wandering Jew the rejection of God in man, of a divine opportunity, a crime against the soul. Such crimes as these seem plainly fitting as a symbol for that haunting and inexpiable guilt which may terrify the mind in dreams:

> Deeds to be hid which were not hid,
> Which all confused I could not know
> Whether I suffered, or I did:
> For all seem'd guilt, remorse or woe,
> My own or others still the same
> Life-stifling fear, soul-stifling shame.[39]

Why is it that the slaying of a bird, or some other animal, is also an acceptable symbol for such guilt?

If we imagine, says Lowes, the substitution of a human being, as the victim, for a bird, we realize the artistic rightness of this particular act in the place it occupies. For the impression of illusive, dream-like reality which the poem communicates "the very triviality of the act" is essential.[40] But is the act trivial? From the prosaic, common-sense standpoint no doubt it is; but within the experience communicated by the poem it is far otherwise.

A friend who, at my request, examined the associations awakened in her mind by the poem, found that with the shooting of the albatross she associated most vividly the memory of an experience upon a recent voyage, when amidst the seeming emptiness of sky and ocean a pigeon appeared, and, though fearful of being approached, tried timidly to settle, as if seeking to rest upon the ship. The strong feeling-tone of the memory—of compassion for the bird, and sympathy with it as a form of kindred life amidst the alien waste—mingled with and enhanced the communicated horror at the crime against life perpetrated by the Mariner, upon the creature that had claimed and received hospitality amidst the desolate Antarctic seas. The Mariner's crime, though not against a human being, has the nature of a

---

[37] *Ibid.*, p. 240.
[38] An analysis of certain of these dreams is attempted in an article "The Representation in Dream and Fantasy of Instinctive and Repressing Forces," by A. M. Bodkin, in the *Brit. J. of Med. Psychol.* vii, part 3.
[39] From *The Pains of Sleep*, by Coleridge.
[40] *Op. cit.*, p. 303.

crime against the sanctity of a guest—the sin which, according to ancient feeling, incurred the special wrath of Heaven and called out the Erinys upon the track of the offender.

It seems that an act by common-sense standards trivial serves best as a symbol to focus the deep haunting emotions of the inner life. Thus Clutton Brock tells of an incident of his childhood "that still makes me feel guilty, far more guilty than many evil things I have done since." The incident was an ungracious, shy refusal of some small leafy branches once offered him by cottage children. He explains the sense of guilt as the sense of a weakness, of snobbery or fear, that the offer surprised in him—a mean fear by which he was shut out from fellowship, led to refuse "the Kingdom of Heaven." [41] Such a refusal, or violation, of fellowship—of the Kingdom of Heaven—seems to be the crime alike of the Mariner, of Cain, and of the Wandering Jew—or of the archetypal figure that, behind and beneath all these, haunts the imagination.

In deference to the force of collective assertion of the well-organized school of Freud, one finds oneself thinking of a more specialized offence— repressed childish lust in regard to one parent and hostility to the other— as the crime which analysis should discover beneath the haunting dream-sense of guilt. The insistence of Freudians upon conclusions established no doubt in certain cases, should not, however, lead us to prejudge evidence, from other cases, for conflicts of somewhat different character underlying the guilt feeling. No doubt some form of failure in the relation to the parents merges its influence in whatever maladaption of attitude underlies the dream-sense of guilt; but other factors are also to be considered.

The writer would be glad at this point to give some account of certain emotional ideas which she has found connected in her own mind with the stanzas describing the wanderings of the Mariner and the compulsive telling of his tale. These ideas have come to centre about the memory of a dream which is connected also with the passage from *Hamlet* examined in the pre-ceding essay [Chapter I]; so that the dream may serve to illustrate what appears to her a common factor in the emotional patterns underlying the ballad and the play.

The dream was of a man condemned to death—as I gathered, for treason— to whom it was permitted to speak some last words to the people who stood about the scaffold. It was my duty to take notes of what he said. He seemed to speak with intense effort, and I knew that he was trying to give something of the history and meaning of his life and its failure. I took scribbled notes—just as I scrawl the first draft of my own writings, hardly legibly in pencil. He stopped to entreat me: could I not make better, fuller, more intelligible notes? I tried eagerly to reassure him: I understood his meaning so well, I could reproduce it apart from the notes. Yet at the same time I felt: what did it matter? No one would care or understand what he said.

The dream was so emotionally vivid, and to me so significant, that since it occurred, some years ago, it seems to have become for me one of those

[41] *What is the Kingdom of Heaven?* (Methuen, 1919), pp. 118–19.

memories which, as Galton says, flit through the mind unfocused, merely "glanced at as objects too familiar to awaken the attention." Such memories are not commonly put into words; they form no part of our ordinary social currency. They keep their place, it seems, in the undercurrents of the mind's activity, through their function as a barely conscious means of reference to some determining tendency or recurring attitude.

The memory of this dream has become connected in my mind both with the passage from *Hamlet* in which the dying prince charges Horatio with the telling of his story; and with the figure of the Mariner, wandering like a ghost charged with a single message, wrenched by a recurring agony of need that his story should be told.

Fausset says of the stanza "I pass, like night . . ." that it is an allegory of Coleridge's own longing to escape from the solitude of an abnormal consciousness. The Mariner is Coleridge himself, "seeking relief throughout his life in endless monologues." [42] This may well be; but the critic who discerns it probably arrives at his intuition because the figure of the Mariner, in the communicated experience, affords an expressive symbol for the longing he himself feels to escape from solitude and find relief, in sharing with others the intimately felt discoveries of his life. The consciousness of Coleridge may have been abnormal in some special degree; but the need to escape from a sense of frustration and solitude by means of some form of communication more adequately expressive than our ordinary intercourse with others can hardly, I think, be abnormal, in the sense of rare, among those who find value in literature.

In the preceding essay the hypothesis was put forward that the form of tragedy—the character of its essential theme—reflects the conflict within the nature of any self-conscious individual between his assertion of his separate individuality and his craving for oneness with the group—family or community—of which he is a part. The sense of guilt which haunts the child whose emerging self-will drives him into collision with his parents echoes that guilt that shadowed the early individuals who broke the bonds of tribal feeling and custom; and the personal and racial memories combine in our participation in the tragic hero's arrogance and fall. But with the emotionally pre-determined fall of the hero goes a pre-determined resurrection. The life-force which, in one manifestation, perishes, renews itself in another. So the tragic lament passes into exultation. The ingrained pattern of tragedy, as it vibrates in the deeper recesses of our minds, lends force to that forward leap of Hamlet's dying thought to the vision of his story, his life's meaning, living on in the minds and hearts of others.

Similarly, the immortality that belongs to the figure of the Mariner is that of a story—an almost disembodied voice compelling its destined hearer —a tale that remains, as the outcome, and the atonement, of the suffering that went before. How should it fail to serve as a symbol, and to find echo in the emotional life of the individual whose consciousness of lonely frustration and personal mortality wars with his impersonal vision of a vast inheritance and far-reaching destiny? Such, at all events, is the emotional

---

42 *Op. cit.*, p. 165.

meaning that the writer's examination of these stanzas has led her to believe underlies their wide and deep appeal.

## V

Our study has so far been focused upon a particular poem. The conclusions arrived at may now be taken up into a further study of that emotional pattern which we have termed the Rebirth archetype. We may consider first an example of a dream which appears to illustrate this archetype, and so examine the general question concerning the relation between dreams and poetry.

In an article on "The Idea of Rebirth in Dreams" Dr. Maurice Nicoll gives the following dream as one of the simplest examples which his material supplied showing this pattern.

A man in the early thirties, an officer, *dreamt that he was on a steamer with a crowd of people. He suddenly dived over the side of the steamer and plunged into the sea. As he went down the water became warmer and warmer. At length he turned and began to come up. He reached the surface, almost bumping his head against a little empty boat. There was now no steamer, but only a little boat.* He had no idea why he should have such a dream. In his associations he said that the water was about blood-heat at the depth at which he turned.[43]

This dream, recorded at a first interview, was interpreted by the analyst, in accordance no doubt with other indications in the patient's account of himself, as the expression of an unconscious need to "leave collective values, which are represented by the crowd on the steamer, and go through a process of rebirth whereby he comes to the little boat; that is, to something individual." Accepting hypothetically the interpretation given of this dream, we may use it as an example to illustrate a comparison between the manner of appearance of an archetype in dream and in poetry.

We may note first the resemblance, emphasized by Lowes, between the dream and the romantic poem. In the passage already referred to,[44] where he urges the rightness, in *The Ancient Mariner,* of the "trivial" character of the crime which precipitates so astounding a train of effects, he maintains that in the inconsequence of the poem, as in that of a dream, we feel "an intimate logic, consecutive and irresistible and more real than reality." "Logic" may not be the best term for the compulsion experienced, but of the existence of the compulsion, in the case of such a poem as *The Ancient Mariner,* we can have little doubt—and Lowes offers "proof," referring to the words of Lamb, writing to Wordsworth: "For me, I was never so affected with any human Tale. After first reading it, I was totally possessed with it for many days—I dislike all the miraculous part of it, but the feelings of the man under the operation of such scenery dragged me along like Tom Piper's magic whistle." "Lamb's attestation," Lowes observes, "anticipates the experience of thousands since." Similarly, there are certain dreams which, in spite of strangeness and inconsequence that his reason may dislike,

[43] *Brit. J. of Med. Psychol.* i, part 2, p. 130.
[44] *Op. cit.,* p. 303.

possess the dreamer's mind for days afterwards, and may remain imprinted upon his memory for life.

The compulsion, or magic, of the poem is for thousands; that of the arresting dream is for one alone. This is the great difference which strikes us at once between the poem and the dream bluntly recorded, as it is in our example. Its magic is not communicated.

This would seem to be one of the differences making up the contrast emphasized by Signor Leone Vivante, in an article on "The Misleading Comparison between Art and Dreams." [45] He considers the comparison misleading because the originality and spontaneity together with independence of the arbitrary will, that is sometimes said to characterize dreams and art productions alike, is characteristic, he holds, of all genuine thought, and of dreams only in a slight degree. In dreams the underlying thoughts, or values, appear to express themselves only "through a kind of mask." The texture of the dream is not, as is that of poetry, *"formed* by the dominating thought, not intimately penetrated by it"; its "mental pictures are relatively inert." [46]

Thus, in our example, if the dominating thought, or value, is that of a process of rebirth leading from a collective to an individual standpoint, certainly the thought has not intimately penetrated the dream's imagery. The image of sudden transition from life on a crowded steamer to solitude "under the whelming tide" is full of potential poetry, or expressive power. We may recall how the story of the man washed overboard came upon the mind of Cowper, almost at the end of his distressful life, as an eloquent image of his own despair:

> Obscurest night involved the sky
>    Th'Atlantic billows roar'd
> When such a destin'd wretch as I,
>    Wash'd headlong from on board,
> Of friends, of hope, of all bereft,
> His floating home for ever left.
>
>          .  .  .
>
> Nor soon he felt his strength decline,
>    Or courage die away;
> But wag'd with death a lasting strife,
> Supported by despair of life.

We recognize these lines as poetry so far as we feel that the medium has become a transparent vehicle of the emotional meaning, which is communicated in its full intensity. So again, when Conrad, in his novel, *Lord Jim,* makes us feel the terrible moral isolation of the little group of men who had abandoned their ship to save themselves in a boat on the open sea, and Marlowe muses how, when your ship fails you, the whole world seems to fail you, the world that made and sustained and cared for you—again we find the medium of word and image moulded and penetrated by the thought. Whereas in the dream, as recorded, the image of the man, under the water or bumping his head against the little boat, remains enigmatic and inert.

---

45 *The New Criterion*, vol. iv, no. 3.
46 *Loc. cit.,* p. 438.

It may be suggested, however, that in the mind of a literary artist the dream images would not remain thus inert. If, without being an artist, one is in some degree sensitive to the shades of meaning of words and the expressive possibilities of images, one realizes, on waking with a dream still vivid but fading in the mind, the difficulty of choosing swiftly enough words that shall retain for oneself the true character of those obscure yet impressive, sensuous intimations that are left of the dream experience. So swiftly they fade that, usually, only so much survives as one can succeed in telling over to oneself in the first moments of waking. Thus failure in the process of adequate translation into words may in part account for the lifelessness of the dream as communicated.

In dreams I have known, of sinking down and down, solitary amid darkness, there seemed, as I recalled the experience upon waking, to be present within it, something of that emotion which made the Psalmist cry both "The waters compassed me about even to the soul," and "I went down to the bottoms of the mountains: the earth with her bars was about me for ever." It was not material fact of definite character, but feeling in itself fluid and formless, that constituted the burden conveyed by the imagery both of the dream and of the verses from Jonah. The emotion of the dream, however, remained obscure and formless, while that of the Psalmist found form in rhythmic memorable words.

If a part of the poverty and inertness of the recorded dream belongs, then, more to its expression than to its character as experienced, there is another peculiarity we may notice as illustrated by our example, which seems to characterize the nature of the dream itself.

The dreamer recalls that as he went down the water became warmer, till it was about blood heat. "This," says Nicoll, "is a mythological expression used by the unconscious to indicate the idea of returning to the maternal depths"—to the womb. Such direct relation to a physiological source seems characteristic of much dream imagery. If it strikes our waking consciousness strangely, hindering rather than helping the communication of feeling, shall we account for this simply by reference to repression? Is it the case that a regressive craving for the warm shelter of the mother's womb persists unmodified in the mind of the adult, and that it is only as a result of repression that we fail to feel response to the expression of such a craving in the dream?

I would ask the reader to compare with this recorded dream any example which may come to his mind of poetry in which the image of the sea seems to be fused with that of the mother. In Swinburne's poetry many examples are to be found; though perhaps at the present time not many readers experience vivid response to these. One may cite two fragments from those stanzas of *The Triumph of Time* which express the longing to find oblivion within the sea as in the body of a mother:

> O fair green-girdled mother of mine,
>   Sea, that art clothed with the sun and the rain,
> Thy sweet hard kisses are strong like wine,
>   Thy large embraces are keen like pain.
> Save me and hide me with all thy waves,

.   .   .

> Clear of the whole world, hidden at home,
> Clothed with the green and crowned with the foam,
> A pulse of the life of thy straits and bays,
> A vein in the heart of the streams of the sea.

With these lines I would ask the reader to compare those from the conclusion of Matthew Arnold's *Sohrab and Rustum,* which express, I think, a similar impulse in language of greater poetic power. The description is familiar of the river that flowed

> Right for the Polar Star, past Orgunjè,
> Brimming, and bright, and large: then sands begin
> To hem his watery march, and dam his streams,
> And split his currents; that for many a league
> The shorn and parcell'd Oxus strains along
> Through beds of sand and matted rushy isles—
> Oxus, forgetting the bright speed he had
> In his high mountain cradle in Pamere,
> A foil'd circuitous wanderer:—till at last
> The long'd-for dash of waves is heard, and wide
> His luminous home of waters opens, bright
> And tranquil, from whose floor the new-bath'd stars
> Emerge, and shine upon the Aral Sea.

In poetic vision, says Vivante, "our whole being is stirred, every fibre of it"; "crude instincts and remote experiences" are present; but these are "approached and made intelligible by actual values and forms (*actual,* that is, present and active, realizing themselves anew)." [47] It is this view which, as it seems to me, is verified by the psychological student of literature, against the view of those psychologists who believe that crude instincts and remote experiences maintain, even in highly conscious and developed minds, a subterranean existence, repressed but unchanged.

Within the poetic vision opened to the reader by Matthew Arnold's lines we can, I think, identify, as a single element, that death-craving, expressed also in Swinburne's stanzas, which appears to be a primary tendency of the organism. By the neurotic, medical psychologists tell us, death is envisaged, not objectively, as "normal people" are expected to view it—as the end of life, an event with social, moral, and legal implications—but as "a quiescent resolution of affective excitement"; "the tendency to it is an effort of the organism to restore the quiescent equilibrium," [48] realized once (it is supposed) at the beginning of life, within the mother's womb. Like the neurotic, the poet or his reader, dreaming on the river that breaks at last into the free ocean, sees in this image his own life and death, not at all in their social and legal implications, but in accordance with a deep organic need for release from conflict and tension. Within the poetic vision, however, this death-craving is not a mere crude, repressed impulse; it is, as

---

[47] *Op. cit.,* p. 441.
[48] "Significance of the Idea of Death in the Neurotic Mind," by A. Carver, *Brit. J. of Psychol.* iv, part 2, p. 121. *Cf.* also the work of Otto Rank, who has gone so far as to interpret all life and experience in terms of this particular craving.

Vivante says, an impulse actively realizing itself anew in consciousness, attaining a new character in synthesis with other tendencies.

In Swinburne's poem I feel that the synthesis is not complete. The childish craving for the mother's embrace seems, to my feeling, to mix somewhat incongruously with the adult's sense of the sea's glory. But in Arnold's lines there is no mixing of metaphor. The great image of the river flowing to the sea shines clear; though the words that convey that image bear also a meaning they have won through our continual struggle to express in imagery the felt changes of our inner life. We know from within what it is to be "a foiled circuitous wanderer," our own life-currents hemmed and split. This great image, however, stands not alone but as the close of a poem in which we have read of the father who, unawares, slays his son, and in the agony of a great fulfilment of nature suddenly destroyed, craves death; but by the words of the dying youth is restrained and led to await the due time:

> And Rustum gazed on Sohrab's face, and said:
> "Soon be that day, my Son, and deep that sea!
> Till then, if Fate so wills, let me endure."

Seeing in the image of the river the vision of man's life and death as the whole poem has communicated it, we experience a death-craving akin to that of infant or neurotic for the mother, but in synthesis with the sentiment of a man's endurance.

It is through such syntheses that crude instincts realize themselves anew in poetic vision; while within the dream the persistence of physiological imagery appears to indicate a much lower degree of synthetic activity. Thus, the result of our comparison seems to confirm Vivante's judgment that a relative inertness characterizes the dream imagery, not only through defective expression but in its own nature.

I think, however, that we cannot on account of these differences dismiss, as Vivante seems to do, the comparison between poetry and dream as mainly misleading. That the forces of our sensibility find expression, in a manner somewhat parallel, within the imagery of dream and of poetry gives us a twofold method of approach, which may be of considerable value in the study of these forces. Moreover, in poetic thought we find, as has been already illustrated, many different degrees of conscious insight, ranging from an almost dream-like opaqueness to philosophic lucidity and analytic self-consciousness; so that from this point of view the dream may serve as a limiting term in a scale of imaginative values.

Of the Rebirth pattern appearing in the dream one element has so far been used to illustrate the comparison between dream and poetry—the element of sinking down toward quiescence, as in the womb of the mother. The pattern includes also a return from that state, renewed and changed. Before, however, considering the complete pattern in its wider relations, we may recur to *The Ancient Mariner*, to compare the poem with our dream example. We may put the question: does the Rebirth archetype as it appears in Coleridge's poem show an element which may be identified with the primary impulse of return to the mother, transformed within a new synthesis?

One friend who recorded for me her experience in regard to the stanzas from the fourth and fifth parts of *The Ancient Mariner* noted that "the turning-point" of the experience comes always for her at the stanza beginning "The moving moon went up the sky." A change occurs both in the inner voice always heard by her when reading poetry, and also in the accompanying organic sensations. There is "sudden lightening and removal of weight from head and chest, a freeing of the breathing, and relaxing of the strain of listening and watching."

This subject had noted that in realizing the stanza beginning "Down dropt the breeze," she experienced an organic sensation of "loss of life and energy, as if these were suddenly drained from me"; but the experience communicated by the Mariner's vigil—and this point was emphasized even more strongly by another subject—was by no means one of quiescence: it was full of strain and tension.

In attempting to indicate in the most general terms the elements constituting the Rebirth pattern, as it appeared in *The Ancient Mariner* and certain other examples studied, I spoke of a represented downward movement, which might be felt as toward quiescence or toward disintegration and death. As a movement toward quiescence, this element of the image pattern can be accepted by that impulse of primary feeling which Freud has called the death instinct, or Nirvana principle. Such acceptance has been illustrated in the present section. Balancing the Nirvana principle, however, our nature includes the more easily recognized familiar tendency towards life-activity and self-preservation; and, so far as tendencies of this nature operate, the represented death-trend is a source of conflict—of resistance and painful tension. This accounts for the fact that the emotional effect of the imagery of fixity and stagnation in the poem is an experience of effort and tension.

After that experience has been fully developed, however, before the description of the outburst of activity in the elements, there comes a moment of true and blissful quiescence:

> Oh sleep! it is a gentle thing,
> Beloved from pole to pole!
> To Mary Queen the praise be given!
> She sent the gentle sleep from Heaven,
> That slid into my soul.

It is from this sleep, sent by Mary, queen and mother, that the Mariner wakes renewed, as though by death:

> I was so light—almost
> I thought that I had died in sleep,
> And was a blessed ghost.

Not only is the sleep sent by Mary, but, as just noted, the moment which the sensitive reader feels as bringing the first relaxation of tension is the moment when the Mariner yearns towards the moon and stars as they move, like adored presences, through their native domain. It is, as Coleridge's marginal gloss reminds us, by the light of the moon that the beauty and happiness of the creatures of the calm is so revealed that in place of loathing the Mariner's impulse of love flows forth. Beneath the words in which Coleridge describes the moon lie haunting associations through which the moon's name and image have become those of goddess, queen of Heaven, and mother, in the imagination of men. It is, then, as through a mother's power that the renewed childlike vision, reaching outward in love and delight, has come to the man in his despair.

In view of all this we can perhaps discern something of the manner in which the impulse of yearning towards the mother—crudely expressed in the dream through the image of organic warmth—is present, transformed, within the pattern of feeling that responds to the subtle and complex imagery of the poem.

## VI

We have observed that the patterns we are studying can be regarded in two ways—as recurring themes or image-sequences in poetry, and as configurations of forces or tendencies within the responding mind. We have identified the main theme in the poem of *The Ancient Mariner* as similar to that in the Book of Jonah—the theme of "the night journey," or of rebirth. Some further study, it was suggested, should be undertaken of this theme on its psychological side, viewed as an interplay of mental forces.

In examining the relation between poetry and dream we referred to Freud's theory of a pair of opposite tendencies, termed by him life and death instincts. Considering a little more closely the nature of these tendencies, with reference to the Rebirth pattern, we may note the point made by Miss Helen Wodehouse in examining Freud's view.[49] A determining influence in Freud's thought, Miss Wodehouse has pointed out, seems to be the "picture" which he uses to make his meaning clear, of a protoplasmic mass such as an amoeba, elongating and retracting itself, putting out pseudopodia and drawing them back. In this manner, he says, the libido destined for objects flows outward and flows back from those objects; the reservoir from and into which it flows being named at first the ego.[50] Afterwards, when from the ego Freud had distinguished the "id"—as a wider undifferentiated whole from which the organized self-conscious ego emerges—he recognized [51] that it was this undifferentiated whole from which energy flows forth to objects and into which, in sleep and other withdrawn states, it again returns. In the condition of sleep, says Freud, we see the likeness conjured up, both in its physical and mental aspects, of "the blissful isolation of the intra-uterine existence" [52]—that prototype of the state of peace and freedom from tension, to which, in accordance with the Nirvana principle, or death instinct, it seems to be the aim of the organism to return. But while life

[49] "Natural Selfishness and its Position in the Doctrine of Freud," *Brit. J. of Med. Psychol.* ix, part 1, p. 46.
[50] *Collected Papers,* vol. iv, p. 350.
[51] *The Ego and the Id,* 1927, p. 38, note.
[52] *Introductory Lectures,* p. 348.

lasts, Freud notes: "for complete health it is essential that the libido should not lose this full mobility" [53]—the readiness for the outward and inward movement described.

This remark corresponds to Jung's insistence that extraversion and introversion—the outward and inward turning of the libido—are both, as attitudes exclusively maintained, dangerous to mental health, while both are necessary as alternations within a vital rhythm—a rhythm which "repeats itself almost continually, but of which we are only relatively conscious in its most extensive fluctuations." [54]

Of such an extensive fluctuation of vital rhythm, compelling some degree of conscious recognition, Jung has given an account in the passage to which reference was made in the third section of this essay. The description was there considered as one way of representing metaphorically the same kind of psychical sequence which poetry might depict in terms of a symbolism at once more opaque and more appealing. In regard to such sequences, the philosopher or psychologist, as Jung says,[55] cannot escape metaphor. He can only attempt to create symbols in some respects of more exact correspondence and greater practical utility.

We may at this point examine a little more closely Jung's formulation of the vital process that appears as mental or spiritual rebirth. According to his view the regression, or backward flow of the libido, that takes place when conscious or habitual adaptation fails and frustration is experienced, may be regarded as a recurring phase in development. It may be felt by the sufferer as a state of compulsion without hope or aim, as though he were enclosed in the mother's womb, or in a grave—and if the condition continues it means degeneration and death. But if the contents which during the introverted state arise in fantasy are examined for the hints, or "germs," they contain "of new possibilities of life," a new attitude may be attained by which the former attitude, and the frustrate condition which its inadequacy brought about, are "transcended." [56]

We may take, I think, these two terms, "frustration" and "transcendence," as happily expressing the stages of the Rebirth process. As conceived by Jung, the process is no mere backward and forward swing of the libido— such rhythm of sleeping and waking, resting and moving on, as appears to be all Freud has in view when he speaks of the necessary mobility of the libido. It is a process of growth, or "creative evolution," in the course of which the constituent factors are transformed.

Freud and his school are also aware, naturally, of the fact of growth and readjustment of attitude. In a published discussion of the differing standpoints of Freud and Jung, between Dr. John Rickman and Dr. H. G. Baynes, Dr. Rickman, representing Freud's view,[57] says that the integrating or synthetic power—which is conceived as pertaining to the conscious ego,

---

[53] *Collected Papers,* vol. iv, p. 350.
[54] *Psychological Types,* by C. G. Jung, 1923, p. 313.
[55] *Ibid.,* p. 314.
[56] See the account of Progression and Regression in *Contributions to Analytical Psychology,* pp. 34–44. *Cf.* the account of transcendence in *Psychological Types,* especially p. 313.
[57] *Brit. J. of Med. Psychol.* viii, part 1, pp. 46–7.

not at all to the unconscious id—is not in psycho-analytic practice found susceptible of direct influence. The most that can be done is to remove hindrances by making the patient aware of himself; he must then be left to achieve his own adaptation to life. Jung would agree that the analyst's task is to help the patient to self-awareness, and that he himself must achieve re-adaptation. The difference between the two schools lies in Jung's belief that a synthetic or creative function does pertain to the unconscious— that within the fantasies arising in sleep or waking life there are present indications of new directions or modes of adaptation, which the reflective self, when it discerns them, may adopt, and follow with some assurance that along these lines it has the backing of unconscious energies.

Jung has noted that a state of introversion and regression, preceding a kind of rebirth into a new way of life, has been recognized and organized by religions of all times, so long as such religions retained vitality.[58] The same point has been discussed by Dr. R. R. Marett in a lecture entitled "The Birth of Humility." [59] In this lecture he tentatively outlines a theory of the psychological needs which appear to explain and justify the organization by many religions of periods of retreat, or times when an individual is *tabu*.

Dr. Marett considers that the psycho-physical study of the individual shows periods of inertia or brooding, normally occurring while latent energies gather strength for activity on a fresh plane. He suggests that religious ritual has socialized and, in a manner, spiritualized, the psycho-physical crises occurring in the course of organic growth and change—crises of which puberty is the most typical, though marriage, motherhood, and the assumption of priestly office, are also examples. For such crises the representatives of tribal religion prescribe rest, abstinence, and isolation—holding "by sheer force of that vital experience which is always experiment" that "to mope, as it were, and be cast down" is a means toward arising afterwards "a stronger and better man." [60]

A somewhat similar view is presented by Dr. Cyril Flower [61] who suggests as typical of religion a psychological sequence, of frustration, withdrawal, or suspended response, followed by new orientation through liberation of fantasies and their projection upon the situation that led to the withdrawal.

An example of such a sequence, in a highly developed mind, has been considered in the case of the poet Verhaeren, as analysed by Baudouin. Baudouin has shown how forces of sensibility linked with the religious symbols of Verhaeren's childhood appear to have been held frustrate when those symbols were rejected by his more mature thought; until from the depth of the distressful introverted state fresh symbols arose, and the very objects —the factory, the railway, the busy town—from which, even while partly fascinated, he had turned in loathing, became, like the creatures of the calm for the Mariner, the objects of an outrush of love and wonder.

Comparison of these examples and analogies may give some idea of the

58 *Psychological Types*, p. 316. *Cf. Contributions to Analytical Psychology*, p. 395.
59 Included in *The Threshold of Religion*, 2nd ed. (Methuen, 1914).
60 *The Threshold of Religion*, p. 200.
61 *An Approach to the Psychology of Religion* (Kegan Paul, 1927).

nature of the tendencies whose continual interplay within us finds expression in the image-pattern analysed under the name of Rebirth, or the Night Journey. In its simplest form this interplay may be recognized as a rhythm characterizing all conscious and organic life. In the more complex form that generates the need for expression, there is tension and conflict. A sense of pain and guilt attends persistence in that particular mode of adaptation, or self-assertion, whose abandonment in the condition of surrender and quiescence gives opportunity for the arising impulse of some new form of life.[62]

.    .    .

[62] It is interesting to note how in the analysis of the intellectual life a similar pattern appears. Professor Graham Wallas has introduced his account of the stages of the formation of a new thought by quoting the description given by Helmholz, the great German physicist, of the way in which the solutions of his theoretic problems were commonly attained. There was a stage of "Preparation," or deliberate exploration of the problem in all directions; then a stage of abstention from conscious thought—rest and recovery from fatigue—which Graham Wallas calls the stage of Incubation. Then, in Helmholz's words, "unexpectedly, without effort, like an inspiration"—often in the morning on waking, or out of doors—the "happy ideas" came. This Graham Wallas calls the stage of Illumination. (*The Art of Thought* [Cape, 1926], pp. 79–80.) In his *Autobiographical Sketch* Helmholz gives a vivid picture of his condition when his intellectual problem absorbed him, but when "the redeeming ideas did not come. For weeks or months I was gnawing at such a question until in my mind I was

> Like to a beast upon a barren heath
> Dragged in a circle by an evil spirit,
> While all around are pleasant pastures green."

Here in the intellectual sphere is something akin to "The Night Journey" before the spiritual Rebirth.

With this description we might compare, as an example of similar working of sub-human intelligence, Köhler's account of the behaviour of his apes when faced with the problems he arranged for them. Köhler emphasizes, in the case of the more intelligent animals, the occurrence, after failure of habitual adaptations, of "an interval of hesitation and doubt," the baffled creature gazing about him till, suddenly, the impulse arises which carries him to success. (*The Mentality of Apes*, p. 181.)

# 8. THE USES OF MYTH

## The Theory

*Philip Wheelwright*

## POETRY, MYTH, AND REALITY

Poetry suffers today from at once too high and too low an appraisal. We burden Shakespeare with flatteries which his contemporaries would have reserved for royalty or for the ancients, but there is reason to believe that modern theater audiences are insensitive to much in his plays that the rowdier but more perceptive frequenters of the Globe Theater took in as an expected part of the entertainment. Charged language, language of associative complexity, is a rarity on the stage or in the cinema today, and when it occurs it is likely to embarrass by its artiness, its rather too evident snob appeal. We read poetry as a special discipline, becoming scholarly about it or ecstatic about it according to our profession, temperament and mood, but we deprecate its intrusion into the sober business of everyday living. Poetry seems to most of us something to be set upon a pedestal and left there, like one of those chaste heroines of medieval romance, high and dry.

Why is there this impoverishment of response toward poetry in present-day society? The question may be one of the most important we can ask, for it concerns not poetry and poetic response alone, but by implication the general sickness of our contemporary world. The symptoms, though diverse, are connected; and I suspect we shall not understand why great poetry is no longer written in an age which endows innumerable lecturers to talk about poetry, unless we also understand why it is that we must let our fellow-countrymen starve in an era of productive plenty, and why as Ameri-

Reprinted from *The Language of Poetry* edited by Allen Tate, by permission of Princeton University Press. Copyright 1942 by Princeton University Press, Princeton, N. J.

cans we spent twenty years professing our love of peace and democracy while helping to finance dictatorships and throttle democracies on three continents, and why as Christians we think it proper to build imposing churches while treating God as something out of last year's Sunday supplement. The question of poetry's status in the present-day world is interrelated with such questions as these, and it seems to me that we cannot adequately understand any one of the questions except in a perspective that catches at least the outlines of the others. The needed perspective is to my mind a mythoreligious one, without any of the claptrap sometimes associated with either word; for it involves a rediscovery of the original and essentially unchangeable conditions of human insight and human blessedness. The aim of this lecture is to indicate the nature of that perspective and to discover its latent presence in some of the great poetry of past times.

Suppose we represent the dimensions of human experience, very tentatively, by means of a diagram,—where the horizontal line E-P represents the dimension of secular experience, *empirical* experience as I think we may call it without redundancy; of that trafficking with things, relations and ideas that makes up our everyday commonsense world. It has two poles: outwardly there are the phenomena (P) that constitute our physical universe; these are space-like, are interrelated by causal laws, and are the

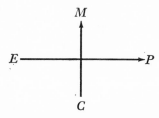

proper object of scientific inquiry. At the other pole of this horizontal axis stands the ego (E) which knows the phenomena—partly as a spectator and partly no doubt as a contributor to their connection and significance. The major philosophical movements of the past three centuries owe their character and their limitations to the stress, I think the undue stress, which they have put upon the horizontal axis. Descartes made the additional mistake of hypostatizing E and P, establishing the thinking self and the extended world of things over against each other as distinct substances; he "cut the universe in two with a hatchet," as Hegel said, separating it into two absolutely alien spheres, thought without extension and extension without thought: thereby settling the direction, perhaps the doom, of modern philosophy. Granted that the Cartesian bifurcation was immensely fruitful for the subsequent development of natural science, the benefit was purely one of conceptual efficiency, not of interpretive fulness. The general result was to alienate nature from man by denuding it of human significance, and thereby deprive man of his natural sense of continuity with the environing world, leaving him to face the Absolute alone. To this stark confrontation the Cartesian man brings a single talisman—pure reason, which, rightly used, can answer all questions, solve all mysteries, illumine every dark cranny in the universal scheme. All truth becomes to the unobstructed reason as clear and indubitable as the truth of an arithmetical sum. A child who performs an arithmetical sum correctly—so Descartes declares—knows the utmost, with respect to that sum, that the human mind, and by implication God's mind, can ever discover. Analogously a physicist, by confining himself to clear and distinct ideas, may come to know the utmost, with respect to any given problem, that can possibly be known; and this would be true, on Cartesian principles, even of a psychologist or a theologian or a student of any field whatever who adhered to properly rational methods. Athene springs full-born from the head of Zeus; or to use a more modern simile, wisdom consists in a sort of klieg-light brilliance rather than in adjusting one's eyes to the chiaroscuro of the familiar world. For the familiar world—here is its essential defect to a rationalist like Descartes—has a past, it develops, is time-burdened, and draws much of its meaning from shared tradition; while to Descartes' view tradition, except so far as reason can justify it, is superstition, loyalties to the past are servile, and the philosopher should be like an architect who tears down the lovable old houses and crooked streets of a medieval town in order to erect a symmetrical city where no one can lose his way. Thus in this rationalistic philosophy of Descartes we have, close to its modern source, the deadliest of all heresies. It is the sin, or, if you prefer, the delusion, of intellectual pride, a reënactment of Adam's fall and of the building of Bab-el, and it leads in our time to the fallacy of hoping for a future without organically remembering a past, the imbecility of trying to build history out of an unhistorical present.

The influence of Descartes' dualistic rationalism has been far-flung. In subsequent philosophy, although various parts of his doctrine became modified or rejected, the Cartesian way of conceiving human experience, as an individual ego able by its own powers to know the world of phenomena confronting it, played a decisive rôle. British empiricists and positivists in particular, from Locke through Hume and Mill right down to Bertrand Russell and a majority of professional philosophers in our own day, have differed from one another not in any doubt as to the self-sufficiency of the horizontal axis of experience but in their particular ways of distinguishing or connecting or distributing the emphasis between the ego and its objects. Today the horizontal philosophy has reached its clearest and most intractable expression in the related doctrines of behaviorism, instrumentalism, and semantic positivism: behaviorism, which reduces the human mind to what can be experimentally observed of its bodily behavior; instrumentalism, which reduces the meaning of any concept to that set of experimental operations by which the denotation of the concept could be objectively shown; and semantic positivism, which aims at a one-to-one correspondence between units of language and the sets or types of objects and events which such language-units denote. These three doctrines, which may be grouped under the general name of positivistic materialism, have acquired great prestige in our time. Every honest and sane intellectual must, I believe, come to grips with them: must recognize both that they are the logically inescapable outcome and expression of our secular way of life, and that they are utterly disastrous. The only truth on this basis is experimental truth, structures built out of the common denominators of human experience; religious truth and poetic truth are dismissed as fictions, as misnomers.

Religion ceases to have more than a tentative and subjective validity: it expresses the yearnings and fears and awe-struck impotence of human minds with respect to events and sequences in the external world which up to a given stage of human development have eluded scientific explanation and experimental control. Poetry, likewise, has no truth-value that is distinctive to it as poetry. It contains, on the one hand, a "subject" (in Matthew Arnold's sense), a "scenario," a literal meaning, which could be expressed without essential loss in the language of science; and beyond this there is only the pleasurable decoration and emotional heightening which the form and evocative language of the poem bestows. The poet is not in any sense a seer or a prophet; he is simply, in the jargon of advertising, an effective layout man. Science has thus become the Great Dictator, to whom the spiritual republics of religion and poetry are yielding up their autonomy in bloodless defeat. There is no help for it within the purely horizontal perspective of human experience: if we see the world only as patterns of phenomena, our wisdom will be confined to such truths as phenomena can furnish. And this situation is very barren and very unpromising, not only for religion and for poetry, but for expanding love and the sense of *radical significance* which are at the root of both.

Now my belief is that the problem as posited exclusively in terms of the horizontal consciousness is an unnatural problem, an intellectual monstrosity which leads away from, rather than toward, the greater and more enduring truths. No genuine religious teacher, and with the lone exception of Lucretius no great poet, has ever sought truth in exclusively empirical terms; and I must say I find deeper truths, richer and more relevant truths, in the mysticism of Lao-tse and Jesus, in the dramatic suggestiveness of Aeschylus and Shakespeare, than in the impersonal experiments of scientists or the voluminous literalism of scholars. How then are we to validate, and in what terms are we to discuss, the transempirical factor in truth which is presupposed in all religion and in all the profounder sort of poetry?

The thing required of us, I believe, if we are to escape the blind alley of empirical positivism, is a proper understanding of myth, and of mythical consciousness. It is the habit of secular thought to dismiss myth either as pure fiction, a set of fairy-tales with which the human race in childhood frittered away its time; or else as allegory—that is, as a roundabout and inexact way of expressing truths about physical and human nature which could be expressed just as pertinently and much more accurately by the language of science. On either interpretation myth becomes regarded as an archaism, a barren survival, with no function of its own which cannot be served more efficiently by more up-to-date language and methods; a kind of fiction that should be renounced as completely as possible by the serious truth-seeker. What I want to stress is that this secular, positivistic attitude toward myth appears to me quite inadequate to explain the facts—I mean, of course, the salient, the really interesting aspect of the facts. It ignores or deprecates that haunting awareness of transcendental forces peering through the cracks of the visible universe, that is the very essence of myth. It blandly overlooks the possibility, which to Aeschylus, Dante, Shakespeare and many others was an axiom of assured faith, that myth may have a non-exchangeable semantic function of its own—that myth may express visions of truth to which the procedures of the scientists are grossly irrelevant; that the mythical consciousness, in short, (to exploit a convenient mathematical metaphor) may be a dimension of experience cutting across the empirical dimension as an independent variable.

In the foregoing diagram I have represented the mythico-religious dimension of human experience by a vertical line *C-M* cutting across the horizontal axis *E-P*.

*C* represents the community mind, which is to myth more or less what the individual mind is to science; and the upper pole *M* represents Mystery, of which the community mind is darkly aware. Thus the semantic arrow points from *C* to *M*, as it points from *E* to *P*. This double relation should not be conceived too rigidly: scientific truth is admittedly established by some degree of social cooperation, and mythical truth is apprehended and given form by individuals. Nevertheless the distinction is basically sound. Myth is the expression of a profound sense of togetherness—a togetherness not merely upon the plane of intellect, as is primarily the case among fellow-scientists, but a togetherness of feeling and of action and of wholeness of living. Such togetherness must have, moreover, a history. Community mind is nothing so sporadic as the mass mind of a modern lynching party or a wave of war hysteria, nor even is it found to any considerable degree in a trade union. In such manifestations as these the collective mind possesses little or no significant pattern, for it has had no time to mature. It creates not myths but merely ideologies—an ideology being a sort of parvenu myth which expresses not the interests of the group as a cooperative organism but the interests of each member of the group reflected and repeated in each other member: to this extent it lacks also a transcendental reference. A mass cannot create myths, for it has had no real history. Myths are the expression of a community mind which has enjoyed long natural growth, so that the sense of togetherness becomes patterned and semantically significant. A patterned sense of togetherness develops its proper rhythms in ceremony and prayer, dance and song; and just as the micro-rhythms of the eye project themselves as a visible world of trees and stones, and as the micro-rhythms of the ear project themselves as an audible world of outer sounds, so the larger rhythms of community life project themselves as a sense of enveloping Mystery. In cultures where the mythico-religious consciousness has developed freely, this sense of mystery tinges all cognition: whether called *mana* as by the Melanesians, or *wakonda* as by the Sioux Indians, or *brahma* as by the early Aryan invaders of India, there is felt to be a mysterious Other, a spirit or breath in the world, which is more real, more awful, and in the higher religions more reverenceable than the visible and obvious particulars of experience, while at the same time it may manifest or embody itself in persons, things, words and acts in unforeseeable ways. Sometimes this basic Mystery becomes dispersed and personified into a polytheism of gods and daemons, sometimes concentrated and exalted into a single majestic God. Whatever its eventual form, it appears to express on the one hand man's primordial way of knowing, before the individual has separated himself with clear critical awareness from the group; and on the other hand an indispensable element in the cognitive activity of every vital culture, primitive or civilized. What I am arguing, in short, is not merely that the consciousness which arises from group-life and group-memories is the original matrix of individual consciousness—that much is a sociological truism—but that when the consciousness of individuals separates itself too utterly from the sustaining warmth of the common myth-consciousness, the dissociated consciousness becomes in time unoriented and sterile, fit for neither great poetry nor great wisdom nor great deeds.

What concerns the student of poetry most directly is the relation of myth to speech, the characteristic forms in which the mythical consciousness finds utterance. Shelley declared truly that "in the infancy of society every author is a poet, because language itself is poetry"; and, we may add, the reason why primitive language is poetry lies in the fact that it is the spontaneous expression of a consciousness so largely, in our sense, mythical. There are two outstanding respects in which primitive language, and especially spoken language, tends to be poetic, or at any rate to have a natural kinship with poetry: first, in its manner of utterance, its rhythms and euphonies; second, in its manner of reference, in the delicacy and associative fulness with which it refers to various aspects of the all-encompassing Mystery. In short, primitive speech—for I am dealing here with language that is meant to be spoken—employs both rhythm and metaphor. The reasons for the possession of these characteristics by primitive speech are doubtless clear from the foregoing description of the mythical consciousness. Primitive speech is a more direct expression of the community mind than speech that has grown sophisticated, and rhythm is the vehicle by which the sense of community is projected and carried through time. Rhythm has furthermore a magical function: for since the primitive community mind is not limited to a society of actual living persons but embraces also the ghosts of ancestors and the souls of things in the environing world, the rhythms of gesture and speech are felt to include and to exert a binding effect not only upon men but, when conducted under auspicious conditions, upon ghosts, gods, and nature; which is the essence of magic. Such language thus possesses a naturally evocative quality: it is felt as having a tendency to endow the world with the qualities which it declares to be there. The metaphorical character of primitive language, on the other hand, consists in its tendency to be rather manifoldly allusive: it can be so, because of the varied associations with which communication within a closed society has gradually become charged; and it has a semantic necessity of being so, because only in language having multiple reference can the full, manifold, and paradoxical character of the primordial Mystery find fit expression. Owing to such referential plenitude the language of primitives tends to employ paradox freely: it makes use of statements contradicting each other and of statements contradicting an experientially accepted situation; for the Mystery which it tries to express cannot be narrowed down to logical categories.

The island of Fiji furnishes a particularly interesting illustration of uses to which primitive poetry can be put. When a Fijian dies, the legend is that his ghost spends three days traversing the fifty-mile path that leads from the principal Fijian city to the sacred mountain Naukavadra, situated on the western coast of the isle. This mountain has a ledge overlooking the sea, called Nai-thombo-thombo, "the jumping-off place," from which the departing ghost hurls itself down and swims to a distant paradise beyond the sunset, where it rejoins its ancestors. Before the final immersion, however, the ghost on arriving at the sacred mountain is received hospitably in a cave by the ghosts of ancient hero-ancestors, guardians of the tribe's morality and well-being. After a feast, partly cannibal, has been eaten in common and ancient tribal lays have been sung, the newcomer finds his spiritual eyes awakened, and realizing for the first time that death has befallen him he is overwhelmed with grief. To the accompaniment of native instruments, addressing the ancestors he chants these words:

> My Lords! In evil fashion are we buried,
> Buried staring up into heaven,
> We see the scud flying over the sky,
> We are worn out with the feet tramping on us.
>
> Our ribs, the rafters of our house, are torn asunder,
> The eyes with which we gazed on one another are destroyed,
> The nose with which we kissed has fallen in,
> The breast with which we embraced is ruined,
> The mouth with which we laughed at one another has decayed,
> The teeth with which we bit have showered down.
> Gone is the hand that threw the tinka stick.
> The testes have rolled away.
>
> Hark to the lament of the mosquito!
> It is well that *he* should die and pass onward.
> But alas for my ear that he has devoured.
>
> Hark to the lament of the fly!
> It is well that *he* should die and pass onward.
> But alas! he has stolen the eye from which I drank.
>
> Hark to the lament of the black ant!
> It is well that *he* should die and pass onward.
> But alas for my whale's-tooth [1] that he has devoured.

The dead man's meeting with the ancestors takes place on the third day after death, and is followed by the leap into the sea and the passage over into the afterworld. Thus far we are in the realm of myth. Parallel to the myth-pattern is a behavior-pattern which is traditional with the survivors. On the third day they bury the now putrefying corpse, and while doing so they chant ceremonially the same songs that the dead man hears and sings in the cave at Mt. Naukavadra. Evidently the cause-effect relation involved is complex. Sociological analysis will regard the belief as a fictional projection which has the function of explaining and justifying the tribal burial processes; while to the survivors, on the other hand, the matter appears in reverse, their ceremonies being designed to annotate, and by imitative magic to assist, the dead one's situation. In any case the dirge I have just quoted serves by its strongly marked rhythms, inescapable even in translation, to establish a sense of widened community, whereby, for the duration of the ceremony at least, the chanting survivors, the recently deceased, and

---

[1] Whale's-tooth: the phallus; also used (in its literal sense) as a symbol of wealth and medium of exchange.

the ancient ancestor-gods are brought into a strongly felt and tersely articulated togetherness. Such expressions of a widened community-sense, paced in the tribal calendar according to the occurrence of emotionally significant events like births and deaths, puberty, marriage, and war, are the most vitalizing forces in tribal cultural life.

In ancient Egypt a similar phenomenon was current, although in Egyptian death chants the magical element is more explicit. The Pyramid Texts —those ancient inscriptions dating from the fourth millennium B.C. which are found on the inner walls of the pyramid tombs—are records of the royal chants by which bands of faithful subjects, led ceremonially by the high priests, helped the Pharaoh whom they were burying there to secure immortal divinity. Here, in part, is one of the noblest of these texts:

> The flier flies from earth to sky.
> Upward he soars like a heron,
> Upward he leaps like a grasshopper,
> Kissing the sky like a hawk.
>
> Crowned with the headdress of the sun-god,
> Wearing the hawk's plumage,
> Upward he flies to join his brothers the gods.
> Joyously we behold him.
>
> Now we give back your heart, Osiris.
> Now we give back your feet, Osiris.
> Now we give back your arms, Osiris.
>
> Flying aloft like a bird,
> He settles down like a beetle
> On a seat in the ship of the sun-god.
> Now he rows your ship across the sky, O Glowing One!
>
> Now he brings your ship to land, O Glowing One!
> And when again you ascend out of the horizon,
> He will be there with staff in hand,
> The navigator of your ship, O Glowing One!
>
> The primordial gods, the ancient nine, are dazzled,
> The Lords of Forms are shaken with terror
> As he breaks the metallic sky asunder.
> Older than the Great One, he issues commands.
> Eternity is set before him,
> Discernment is placed at his feet,
> The horizon is given to his keeping.
>
> The sky is darkened, the stars rain down,
> The bones of the earth-god tremble
> When this one steps forth as a god
> Devouring his fathers and mothers,
> With the sacred serpents on his forehead.
>
> Men and gods he devours.
> His sky-dwelling servants prepare the cooking-pots,
> Wiping them out with the legs of their women.
> The gods are cooked for him piece by piece
> In the cooking-pots of the sky at evening.

Cracking the backbones he eats the spinal marrow,
He swallows the hearts and lungs of the Wise Ones.
Their wisdom and their strength has passed into his belly.
Their godhood is within him.

The community-sense expressed in this hymn has a definite but again complex pattern. On the plane of earthly actuality the celebrants feel their union in a shared joy at the heavenly prowess of their dead king. On the transcendental plane, the plane of myth, there is another sort of union—an identification of the dead king with Osiris, god of periodic and perpetual rebirth, and with Ra the sun god. Although a reverent distinction is observed between the worshippers and the "Osirified One," the exalted king-god whose deification they celebrate, nevertheless the surviving community enjoys a vicarious participation in godhood, since the Pharaoh is felt to be still the worshippers' representative and the symbol of their communal solidarity as he had been on earth. That sense of mystical community, in Egypt as elsewhere, found its natural expression in a type of poetry characterized by marked rhythms and transcendental imagery, which are the esthetic correlates of the lower and upper poles of myth-consciousness.

Thus the logic of myth proceeds on different assumptions from the logic of science and of secular realism, and moves by different laws. Attempts to deal with myth by the methods of science fall inevitably short of the mark. While objective methods of inquiry can trace the occasions of myth, the conditions under which it may flourish, they are quite incapable of understanding the mythical consciousness itself. For science and myth are basically incommensurate ways of experiencing, and science cannot "explain" myth without explaining it away. Its explanations are not interpretative but pragmatically reductive. The questions which science poses about myth are never quite relevant, for the questions essential to myth are patterned on a different syntax. Always in scientific thinking there is the implicit assumption of an "either-or" situation. Is the Pharaoh identical with Osiris after death or is he not? If so, and if all the Pharaohs who ruled before him share the identity, it follows (by the logic of science) that they must be identical with each other; and in that case why are they buried and worshipped individually? Moreover, if identification with Osiris is the soul's final attainment, as the Pyramid Texts indicate, why is the corpse mummified as if to preserve symbolically, and perhaps magically, just this individual to whom the body had once belonged? Such questions as these do not admit of any logically clear answer, and it is important for the understanding both of myth and of poetry to see why they do not. Science seeks clarity of an outward, publicly recognizable kind; it can regard mysteries as but materials for its particular techniques of clarification. By scientific logic a thing is either *A* or *B* and not both; or, if both, its double character must mean either that the thing is complex and can be dissociated into *A* and *B* as its elements, or else that *A* and *B* share a common quality *K* which with sufficient care is susceptible of exact description. The tendency of science is always to think in terms of mechanical models—structures analyzable into parts which, added up, remake the originals. Mechanical operations do work in that way, but wholeness of experience does not, and myth is an expression of whole experiences that whole men have known and felt.

Passing from primitive poetry to the poetry of more civilized eras, we find that while a greater proportion of the poem is contributed by the genius of some individual poet, yet in those poems which carry the signature of greatness, myth still plays a prominent and usually a more deliberate rôle. Myth is invaluable to the poet, furnishing as it does a background of familiar reference by which the sensibilities of the poet and his readers are oriented and so brought into profounder communication than would otherwise have been possible. The ways in which myth is poetically employed, and the effects gained by its employment, depend not only upon the artistry of the individual poet but also upon the general attitude toward myth in the age in which he has the good or bad luck to be born. He may be born, like Aeschylus or Dante, in a period when a substantial body of myths enjoys wide acceptance as literally true: his greatest poems in such a case will be poetic intensifications and elaborations of some of those myths. He may be born, like Virgil or Shakespeare, at a time when a more sophisticated attitude toward myths is beginning to set in but before it has made such headway as to drain the myths of all vitality: the poet will then employ his myths thematically, breaking them up and redistributing their elements as may best suit his esthetic purpose. Or he may be born, finally, in an age like our own, in the late afternoon of a culture, when the myths that once moved men to great deeds now survive as antiquarian curiosities: such a poet will feel himself to be living in a cultural wasteland, his materials will be fragmentary and unpromising, and while he may prove an ingenious renovator of ruined monuments or a resourceful practitioner of metajournalism, his contribution as a poet—the contribution of a whole man who speaks powerfully to whole men—will be small.

Aeschylus, the first great dramatic poet of the West, exemplifies the early condition of civilized poetry in its relation to myth. In his time the chorus of dancing priests, which probably stemmed from ancient religious rituals associated with Dionysus and the grain-goddess Demeter, had become partly secularized, until, although the religious background was still a vital part of the whole show and amply familiar to the playgoing Greeks, the predominant purpose of the great dramatic festivals had insensibly slipped from worship to entertainment. The spectators, who in an earlier age had no doubt participated in the ritualistic dance, were now become relatively immunized: their function is to sit still and at proper times to applaud and perhaps even to chant in unison some of the choric refrains—a practice apparently indicated by the closing exhortation of *The Eumenides*. But atavistically they are still religious celebrants, being led in their observances by the band of rhythmically chanting priests, which has now become the tragic chorus; their emotions pulsate synchronically with those which the chorus expresses by word and gesture, and their acceptance of the dramatic situations which unfold themselves is largely governed by this dramatic communion.

The characteristic problem of Aeschylean drama is human guilt and its consequences. In the Greek mind two conceptions of destiny and of guilt

interplayed: the Olympian and the chthonic. According to the former conception man's cardinal guilt was *hybris,* pride, which consisted in trying
to overstep the boundary that separated man's ordained lot from that of
the blessed and deathless gods, while virtue consisted in observing due measure, remaining loyal to one's destined station in life, and especially to one's
condition of earthbound mortal manhood. The Olympian conception was
thus at bottom *spacelike,* a matter of observing boundaries, limits and
middle paths: indeed, in Hesiod's *Works and Days* it is particularized, in
what may have been its original form, as an admonition to till one's own
soil and not trespass on one's neighbor's. The chthonic conception, on
the other hand, related guilt to the earth *(chthôn),* which became infec-
tiously polluted when innocent blood was spilled, and to the vengeful ancestor ghosts who, living within the earth, were offended by actions that weakened the power and prestige, or violated the moral code, of the tribe or
nation to which they still in a manner belonged. Thus the ghost of King
Darius, in *The Persians,* returns from the underworld to berate his royal
son for leading the Persian host into a disastrous war; and thus too the three
Furies (originally snakes and still wearing snaky locks at the beginning of
*The Eumenides*) haunt Orestes for his crime of matricide; and thus again
in Sophocles' *Oedipus Rex* a plague has fallen on the land and cannot be
removed until the unwitting murder and incest have been brought to light
and expiated. In all these cases the dominant motif is the rhythmic succession of guilt and expiation, which at once expresses the ingrained Greek
sense of a rhythmically pulsating nature in which moral qualities like physical ones undergo seasonal alteration, while at the same time it provides a
forceful and intelligible form into which tragic drama can be moulded.
There is a clear sense, therefore, in which the chthonic conception of guilt
tends to be *timelike,* a matter of working out the patterned destiny of an
individual or family or city or nation.

Clearly the chthonic conception of destiny lends itself to representation
most readily through the time-charged medium of tragic drama, the Olympian conception through the relatively static medium of the epic. The distinction is a shifting one, however: in the sculpturally conceived *Prometheus
Bound* the Olympian conception appears to predominate, while in that one
great surviving trilogy, the *Oresteia* the chthonic theme of guilt and retribution is intertwined with Olympian imagery, until in the end both elements
are sublimated in a magnificent patriotic finale, by which the dramatic
community-sense is explicitly secularized. Nevertheless it is worth noting
that in the *Oresteia,* which without much dispute may stand as his greatest
work, Aeschylus is more respectful and attaches greater dramatic and moral
importance to chthonic than to Olympian ideas. He dismisses gravely the
Olympian myth that the gods envy human prosperity, while the chthonic
myth of the inheritance of guilt haunts him right through to the end, and
motivates the long tortured struggle that constitutes the three dramas. Again,
in the final play of the trilogy, although Apollo is strangely ridiculed, the
Furies are treated with exaggerated respect, as powers who must be placated
and even reverenced since they are the life-germ of Athenian moral and
political life. All in all, the time-myth, as Nietzsche's *The Birth of Tragedy*

explosively demonstrates, is at the core of Greek as of every other vital culture, and when its rhythms become weakened or vulgarized the culture grows senile.

Magic, which has played so large and so explicit a rôle in primitive poetry, appears in Aeschylean drama in sublimated form. For what is magic but operation through a direct emotional congruence established between the operator and his object? The dramatist no longer operates like the primitive magician upon gods and daemons and unnamed mysterious forces of the outer world. His magic is turned, at least to a very large degree, upon the responsive feelings of his audience. We still speak today of a dramatist's "magic," but the compliment is usually vapid. In Greek tragedy the word was applicable more literally, as through the medium of rhythmic chants with musical and choreographic accompaniment, behind which lay the common heritage of mythological background that found stylized expression in plot and imagery, the vast throng that packed the City Dionysia was brought for a few hours into significant emotional unity. Aristotle has noted the katharsis of pity and terror which takes place on such occasions, but they do not exhaust the emotional effect. Deeper than they and deeper than any conscious recognition is the communally felt, ceremonially induced emotion of religious awe, by which the Greek spectators in a miraculous bubble of time are caught up and momentarily identified with the transcendental forces that envelop them and impregnate their culture.

Shakespeare was of course a more eclectic mythologer. As a masterdramatist he could adapt expertly to poetic and dramatic uses the myths that colored the popular consciousness of his time. And yet there is in Shakespeare's mythical consciousness a deep-lying unity, which becomes gradually visible as we trace in their varied expressions what I suggest are the two Shakespearean key-myths—the myth of love and the myth of divine and earthly governance. Every play that Shakespeare wrote shows a large concern with one or the other and usually both of these themes—if not in plot, at least in imagery and allusion.

The love myth enjoys a varied and imagistically colored career in its earlier expressions—*Venus and Adonis,* the Sonnets, such comedies as *Love's Labour's Lost,* and culminating in *Romeo and Juliet.* Love, as represented here, although often strikingly realistic—

> He wrings her nose, he strikes her on the cheeks,
> He bends her fingers, holds her pulses hard, . . .

is much more than a transient phenomenon of human experience. Unlike the anarchy of lust, love is a harmony, a sweet concord, a transcendently heard music; and Venus' consuming passion for Adonis strikes the reader as sufficiently redeemed and justified by its harmonization with the universal passion that throbs through nature. Venus' desire, allied by pedigree with the high concerns of the gods, becomes merged in the poem with such natural manifestations as the strong-necked stallion who breaks rein on espying a young breeding mare:

> Imperiously he leaps, he neighs, he bounds,
> And now his woven girths he breaks asunder;
> The bearing earth with his hard hoof he wounds,
> Whose hollow womb resounds like heaven's thunder;
>   The iron bit he crusheth 'tween his teeth,
>   Controlling what he was controlled with.
>
> His ears up-prick'd; his braided hanging mane
> Upon his compass'd crest now stand on end;
> His nostrils drink the air, and forth again,
> As from a furnace, vapors doth he send;
>   His eye, which scornfully glisters like fire,
>   Shows his hot courage and his high desire.

The sexual and procreative imagery of these stanzas needs no underlining. But the important thing is that love and procreation are joined—here by imagery as later, in the Sonnets, by explicit statement:

> And nothing 'gainst Time's scythe can make defence
> Save breed, to brave him when he takes thee hence.

This couplet introduces the villain of the love-myth: Time, who devours like a cormorant all of this present breath's endeavors. Or rather, all save one. For through the medium of art man can rise above his mortal existence, and making himself the heir of all eternity can bate the scythe's keen edge.

> Yet do thy worst, old Time; despite thy wrong,
> My love shall in my verse ever live young.

Poetry and music uphold the immortality of love in all Shakespeare's plays; love's frailty or perversion is announced by jangling discordant rhythms, with the frequent imagistic accompaniment of tempests as indicative of discord in nature.

The myth of universal governance, divine and earthly, has its double source in Christianity and in Elizabethan patriotic consciousness; like the love-myth it expresses a harmony that joins mankind with divinity and with ordered nature.

> The heavens themselves, the planets, and this center
> Observe degree, priority, and place.
>                     . . . But when the planets
> In evil mixture to disorder wander,
> What plagues and what portents! what mutiny!
> What raging of the sea! shaking of earth!
> Commo.ion in the winds! Frights, changes, horrors,
> Divert and crack, rend and deracinate
> The unity and married calm of states
> Quite from their fixture.

These plagues and portents, tempests and deracinations, symbolize the inverse side of the governance-myth: they accompany—at first in verbal imagery, then later in actual stage-presentation—not only the regicide of a Caesar and a Duncan, but the insurrections of man's inner state which are always the most crucial motivation of Shakespearean tragedy. The myth of governance affirms "degree, priority and place" at once in the political order, in nature, in the soul of man, and in the divine government of the world; now one, now another of these aspects is given foremost emphasis, and at times the last of them is denied, according to the contextual requirements of the individual drama. But in the king-god imagery of *Richard II,* in the allegorical overtones of *Measure for Measure* and *The Tempest,* in the demonology of *Macbeth,* and most subtly of all in the tragic katharsis of *King Lear,* the unity is reaffirmed: earthly and divine government, the order of nature, and the nobility of man are brought again and again into symbolic and always somewhat incomplete identification.

Running through and giving form to the other mythical material, there is, in the greater achievements of Shakespeare, the myth of tragedy itself. This myth, which attains increasingly full realization in Shakespeare's successive experiments with tragedy up to and including *Lear,* finally receives brief explicit utterance in Edmund's cry:

> The wheel is come full circle; I am here.

We today have lost this sense of cyclical fulness and therewith of transcendental significance in human affairs; accordingly we no longer produce great tragedy, because we no longer believe in the tragic myth. In its place we have substituted the shabbier myth of comedy, which Shakespeare utilized for a time and then, when it had lost its power to move him dramatically, unleashed his contempt by expressing it as the title of one of his worst and weakest plays, "All's Well That Ends Well." This wretched quarter-truth is exploited in most of the novels and nearly all of the movies of our day—no longer as healthy comedy merely, but decked out with false sentimentality in the trappings that once belonged to tragedy. Our failure in tragic intuition, our substitution for it of bathos and business practicality in loose-wedded conjunction, is not least among the disastrous factors of the contemporary world.

These considerations of the rôle of myth in great poetry of the past may throw some light upon the predicament of the poet and the unpromising estate of poetry in our non-mythological present. The poet of today—and by that I mean the poetic impetus in all of us today—is profoundly inhibited by the dearth of shared consciousness of myth. Our current motivating ideas are not myths but ideologies, lacking transcendental significance. This loss of myth-conciousness I believe to be the most devastating loss that humanity can suffer; for as I have argued, myth-consciousness is the bond that unites men both with one another and with the unplumbed Mystery from which mankind is sprung and without reference to which the radical significance of things goes to pot. Now a world bereft of radical significance is not long tolerated; it leaves men radically unstable, so that they will seize at any myth or pseudo-myth that is offered. There have been ages of scepticism in the past, and they have always succumbed in time to new periods of belief, sometimes of violent fanaticism. It appears to me historically probable that whether we like it or not, our own present philosophy of liberal democratic scepticism will be succeeded within the next generation, perhaps sooner, by a recrudescence of myth-consciousness in America, although we can only dimly foresee what form that consciousness will take. Probably it will include a strong consciousness of America and the American destiny, but the important question is whether it will include something more—whether America will become a genuine symbol or merely a dogma. The myth of the nation must be shot through with a larger, transcendent mythological consciousness, or it lacks sanctity and in the long run will not satisfy the deeper human cravings. But we have to reckon with the possibility that this development will not take place at once. History does serve human needs, but not on the table d'hôte plan; the preparations are slow and we have to expect a certain amount of bungling in the kitchen. Perhaps our immediate prospect is one of darkness, and waiting, and wholesale liquidation of much that has seemed indispensable to us, spiritual as well as material. We do not know what is to come; we can only try to learn what we must do. I suspect we must be like starving men who keep a little from their meager store to plant it in the ground for a future crop. The poetry of our time doesn't matter much, it is a last echo of something important that was alive long ago. What matters is the myth-consciousness of the next generations, the spiritual seed that we plant in our children; their loves and insights and incubating sense of significant community. On that depend the possibilities of future greatness—in poetry and in everything else.

# The Uses

*I bless his story, The Good Being hung and gone to glory.*—Herman Melville [1]

R. W. B. Lewis

## MELVILLE: THE APOTHEOSIS OF ADAM

### I

*The Marble Faun* completed a cycle of adventures carrying a representative American fictional hero from his ritual birth (in Cooper) through a "fall" which can be claimed as fortunate because of the growth in perception and moral intelligence granted the hero as a result of it. If we abstract an anecdote, in this hazardous way, from a series of novels taken in sequence, we find something dealt with so often and so variously by American writers after Hawthorne that it may be regarded as the major (if not the only) "matter" by which they have sought to advance their craft. We can call it "the matter of Adam," since for those who have recognized it—Hawthorne, Melville, James, and Faulkner at the least—it was as usable as "the matter of France" or "the matter of Troy" once was for poets in the medieval world. It has been the primary stuff by which the American novelist has managed to articulate his sense of the form and pressure of experience and by which he has extended the possibilities of the art of fiction. In this chapter we consider how the one novelist in nineteenth-century America gifted with a genuinely myth-making imagination was able to elevate the anecdote to the status of myth, and so give it a permanent place among the resources of our literature.

The matter of Adam: the ritualistic trials of the young innocent, liberated from family and social history or bereft of them; advancing hopefully into a complex world he knows not of; radically affecting that world and radically affected by it; defeated, perhaps even destroyed—in various versions

Reprinted from *The American Adam: Innocence, Tragedy and Tradition in the Nineteenth Century* by R. W. B. Lewis, by permission of The University of Chicago Press. Copyright 1955 by The University of Chicago, Chicago, Ill.

[1] From a fragment contained in the so-called "Daniel Orme manuscript," i.e., an unfinished anecdote, intended to be part of *Billy Budd* and presumably dealing with the life of the old Dansker in that *novella*. The fragment seems a variation on the ballad, "Billy in the Darbies," which closes *Billy Budd* (*Melville's Billy Budd*, ed. F. Baron Freeman [Cambridge, Mass., 1948], p. 282).

of the recurring anecdote hanged, beaten, shot, betrayed, abandoned—but leaving his mark upon the world, and a sign in which conquest may later become possible for the survivors. *In hoc signo vince:* the analogy is inescapable, and it was Herman Melville who first made it manifest.

The Adamic hero is the equivalent, in American fiction, of the prince or king in the long tradition of classical drama. The telling distinction is one of strategic distance: the distance at the outset between the hero and the world he must cope with. For the traditional hero is at the center of that world, the glass of its fashion, the symbol of its power, the legatee of its history. But the American hero as Adam takes his start outside the world, remote or on the verges; its power, its fashions, and its history are precisely the forces he must learn, must master or be mastered by. Oedipus, approaching the strange city-world of Thebes, was in fact coming home; the hero of the new world has no home to begin with, but he seeks one to come.

The Adamic hero is an "outsider," but he is "outside" in a curiously staunch and artistically demanding manner. He is to be distinguished from the kind of outsider—the dispossessed, the superfluous, the alienated, the exiled—who began to enter European fiction in the nineteenth century and who crowds its almost every page in the twentieth. A distinguished critic of Conrad, Morton Zabel, has listed the major causes of "alone-ness" for Conrad's heroes, and the list will serve, I think, for many another European writer obsessed with the same theme: "A man may be alone because he is a banished wastrel who has made life a law unto himself . . . because he is young and irresponsible . . . because fate has estranged him from the ties of normal life . . . because he has become disgraced in the eyes of society or betrayed by a false confidence or idealism . . . because he has betrayed a trust . . . because he fosters the intolerance and arrogance of self-willed pride . . . or because . . . a fatal vein of skepticism in his nature has induced a nihilism of all values." [2] Most of the outsiders in European fiction of the past century may be catalogued under one or another of those heads, from Turgenev's superfluous men to Gide's bastards and Mann's artists, to the hero of the existentialists and the restless spiritual prowlers of Kafka and Greene (especially if we allow a theological flavor to words like "fate" and "society" in the quotation). But there is no satisfactory category there for Donatello or Redburn, Pierre or Billy Budd, for Huck Finn or Daisy Miller, Isabel Archer or even Jay Gatsby. These are, by some magic of art, morally *prior* to the world which nonetheless awaits them; as between them and the world, it can be questioned who is outside of whom. It is not, as with the European characters, that the realities of social experience and action catch up with them; but it is they who approach and enter into those realities, with alternative comic, disastrous, or triumphant consequences. Their creators seem ready to proffer their private dignity and their very amount of being as worthy to compare with the dignity and being of the public world—something demanding a special gift of artistic duplicity. And even if Mr. Zabel's *loci* can contain Hester Prynne, Captain

---

2 Morton D. Zabel, Introduction to the Viking Portable *Conrad* (New York, 1947).

Ahab, and Faulkner's Joe Christmas, it cannot contain the whole of them; for they are tormented extensions and distortions of their Adamic prototypes.

What is perhaps surprising is the regular recurrence of the hero as Adam, long after his story had been brought to its logical conclusion by Hawthorne and Melville. Two possible but opposite explanations for the endurance of the hero and the story suggest themselves. We may suppose that there has been a kind of resistance in America to the painful process of growing up, something mirrored and perhaps buttressed by our writers, expressing itself in repeated efforts to revert to a lost childhood and a vanished Eden, and issuing repeatedly in a series of outcries at the freshly discovered capacity of the world to injure.

On the other hand, when the narrative account of the hero as Adam is lit by the author's awareness of the American habit of resistance to maturity, then the continuing life both of the hero and of his story are evidence rather of cultural manhood. It has been said that America is always coming of age; but it might be more fairly maintained that America has come of age in sections, here and there—whenever its implicit myth of the American Adam has been a defining part of the writer's consciousness. When this has happened, the emergent mythology of the new world has been recognized and exploited as a stable resource; the writer has found means, at hand and at home, for a fresh definition of experience and a fresh contribution to the culture. This is what is meant, I take it, by cultural maturity.

Melville is our most revealing example of both the contradictory inferences here suggested. He may or may not, as Professor Thompson has argued,[3] have engaged in a lifelong quarrel with God; but he certainly engaged in a long quarrel with himself—the kind of quarrel which, as Yeats said, makes poetry. For Melville took the loss of innocence and the world's betrayal of hope as the supreme challenge to understanding and to art. He wanted not to accept that betrayal; and for a while he kept going back over the ground of the experience as if to prove the betrayal untrue or avoidable. That illusory effort is part of the meaning of *Redburn* and most of the meaning of *Pierre* and *Clarel*. But in the course of his deeply vexed odyssey, Melville found the resources for coming to terms with his losses: terms of extraordinarily creative tension in *Moby-Dick* and terms of luminous resolution in *Billy Budd*. His resources were moral and intellectual ones, but they were available to him only as he discovered the artistic resources. Experience fulfilled and explained itself for Melville only and finally in language. He was the writer above all others who could have asked Forster's question: "How do I know what I think till I see what I say?"

What Melville thought at the end, when he saw everything he had said, was, curiously enough, a dialectically heightened value in something he had supposed irretrievably destroyed. He found a new conviction about the saving strength of the Adamic personality. When this conviction became articulate in *Billy Budd*, the American hero as Adam became the hero as Christ and entered, once and for all, into the dimension of myth.

3 Lawrance Thompson, *Melville's Quarrel with God* (Princeton, 1952).

## II

Only so much of Melville and his writing is relevant here as bears upon the history of the American Adam: as symbol of a possible individual condition, as type of hero for fiction. But it is in the nature of Melville's achievement that any fragment of his writing, or all of it together, can seem to respond directly to any serious question we ask of it. Any set of symbols, as Mark Van Doren gracefully remarked about *The Tempest,* "lights up as in an electric field" when moved close to a novel or *novella* of Herman Melville. The best of him corresponds to the "substances" mentioned in *White-Jacket,* which "without undergoing any mutations in themselves, utterly change their colour, according to the light thrown upon them." Critical light, pumped out all too dazzlingly these latter years, has thus been able to disclose a multitude of Melvilles: the God-hating Melville, the father-seeking and castration-fearing Melville, the traditionalist-and-quasi-Catholic Melville; Melville the cabalistic grubber in obscure philosophies, Melville the liberal democrat and defender of the vital center, and Melville the jaunty journalist of the adventures of boys at sea. Such proliferating multisidedness is an evidence of genius, but not, in my opinion, of the very highest genius; and if there are already more Melvilles than there have ever been Dantes, it is partly because Dante's poetry is firm in an inner coherence and is not totally plastic to the critic. But a certain lack of finish was a deliberate element in Melville's aesthetic as well as his metaphysic; and criticism can always finish the story according to its private enthusiasms. With this *caveat,* we may consider Melville the myth-maker at work upon the matter of Adam.

We may begin with a passage from chapter 96 in *Moby-Dick,* "The Try-Works"—taking the passage as a summary of Melville's attitude to innocence and evil; as an example of Melville's way with the material (attitudes, tropes, language) available to him; and as a guide for the rest of this chapter.

The incident of "The Try-Works" will be recalled. Ishmael falls asleep at the tiller one midnight, as the "Pequod" is passing through the Java seas heading northward toward the haunts of the great sperm whales. Waking up, but not yet aware that he has been asleep, Ishmael finds himself staring into the mouth of hell: "a jet gloom, now and then made ghastly by flashes of redness," an infernal scene through which giant shadow-shapes like devils are moving about some dreadful work. He is "horribly conscious of something fatally wrong"; "a stark bewildered feeling as of death" comes over him. Then he realizes—just in time to swing about, grasp the tiller, and save the ship from capsizing—that he has turned in his sleep and is facing the two furnaces, or "try-pots," amidships, and the three black harpooners stoking the masses of whale blubber from which the oil is extracted ("tryed-out"). The moral follows, the felt analogy between the natural event and the soul of man, offered by the Ishmael who tells the story after the whole of it has been completed:

[1.] Look not too long in the face of fire, O man! Turn not thy back to the compass; accept the first hint of the hitching tiller; believe not the artificial fire, when its redness makes all things look ghastly. Tomorrow, in the natural sun, the skies will be bright; those who glared like devils in the forking flames, the morn will show in far other, at least gentler relief; the glorious, golden, glad sun, the only true lamp—all others but liars.

[2.] Nevertheless, the sun hides not Virginia's Dismal Swamp, nor Rome's accursed Campagna, nor wide Sahara, nor all the millions of miles of deserts and of griefs beneath the moon. The sun hides not the ocean, which is the dark side of the earth, and which is two-thirds of this earth. So, therefore, that mortal man who hath more of joy than sorrow in him, that mortal man cannot be true—not true, or undeveloped. With books the same. The truest of all men was the Man of Sorrows, and the truest of all books is Solomon's, and Ecclesiastes in the fine-hammered steel of woe. "All is vanity." ALL. This wilful world hath not got hold of unchristian Solomon's wisdom yet. But he who dodges hospitals and jails, and walks fast crossing graveyards, and would rather talk of operas than hell; calls Cowper, Young, Pascal, Rousseau, poor devils of sick men; and throughout a carefree lifetime swears by Rabelais as passing wise, and therefore jolly;—not that man is fitted to sit down on tombstones, and break the green damp mould with unfathomably wondrous Solomon.

[3.] But even Solomon, he says, "the man that wandereth out of the way of understanding shall remain" (i.e., even while living) "in the congregation of the dead." Give not thyself up then to fire, lest it invert thee, deaden thee; as for the time it did me. There is a wisdom that is woe; but there is a woe that is madness. And there is a Catskill eagle in some souls that can alike dive down into the blackest gorges, and soar out of them again and become invisible in the sunny spaces. And even if he forever flies within the gorge, that gorge is in the mountains; so that even in his lowest swoop, the mountain eagle is still higher than the other birds upon the plain, even though they soar.

The passage divides into three paragraphs which are more nearly three stanzas, and I have marked them accordingly. The subject of this, one of the richest meditations in all of Melville, is the different degrees of moral alertness—with variations on the realities present in the world and man, on the quality of moral illumination for the perceiver, on the states of being accompanying the various perceptions.

There occur (as Ishmael sees it) two dangerous alternative conditions. On the one hand: an empty innocence, a tenacious ignorance of evil, which, granted the tough nature of reality, must be either immaturity or spiritual cowardice. On the other: a sense of evil so inflexible, so adamant in its refusal to admit the not less reducible fact of existent good that it is perilously close to a love of evil, a queer pact with the devil. Each alternative is a path toward destruction; the second is the very embrace of the destroying power.

Now these two conditions have affinities with the contemporary moral visions of the party of Hope and the party of Memory. They could be grasped and expounded only by someone who had already by an effort of will and intelligence transcended them both. By the time he wrote *Moby-Dick*, Melville had dissociated himself in scorn from what he now regarded as the moral childishness of the hopeful.[4] But he was not blind to that

---

4 *Cf.* Melville's annotations of his copies of Emerson's *Essays* (now in Houghton Library, Harvard). Checking one passage in *Spiritual Laws*, Melville added in the margin: "A perfectly good being, therefore, would see no evil—But what did Christ see?—He saw what

hypnosis by evil which a bankrupt Calvinism had visited upon the nostalgic.
He was beginning to share the good sense of Dante's Virgil, chiding Dante
(in *Inferno,* XXX) for allowing himself to be momentarily transfixed by the
spectacle of evil: "Il voler cio udir é una bassa voglia" (it is vulgar to linger
in the fire-lit darkness, for the end of our journey is the center of light).

Melville, that is to say, had penetrated beyond both innocence and despair
to some glimmering of a moral order which might explain and order them
both, though his vision remained slender, as of that moment, and the center
of light not yet known, but only believed in—and still ambiguously, at
that. But, like the elder Henry James, Melville had moved toward moral
insight as far as he had just because he had begun to look at experience
dramatically. He had begun to discover its plot; and Melville understood
the nature of plot, plot in general, better than anyone else in his generation. (For Melville was a poet.)

So "alternative" is a misleading word, in speaking of any characteristic
passage in Melville. Indeed, one way to grasp this passage and Melville's
achievement in general is to notice that Melville is *not* posing static alternatives but tracing a rhythmic progression in experience and matching the
rhythm as best he can in language. This is the way of a Platonist, and not
of a polemicist; much more, it is the way of a poet. We still tend, for all
the good criticism of our time, to read a poem the way we watch a tennis-
match: turning our heads and minds back and forth between what we
presume to be unchanging opponents, as though a poem moved between
fixed choices of attitude before plumping conclusively for one of them as
the unequivocal winner. (The best kind of poem is a process of generation—
in which one attitude or metaphor, subjected to intense pressure, gives symbolic birth to the next, which reveals the color of its origin even as it gives
way in turn by "dying into" its successor. Such a poem does not deal in
dichotomies but in live sequences.

Here, then, in "The Try-Works," we have a series of displacements.
Artificial light gives way to natural light, darkness to morning, and the
imperative to the indicative. Then dawn and sunlight yield to darkness,
to the moon and "the dark side of the earth"—to hell, to sickness, and to
death. But hell and death are the source at last of a new and loftier life,
new "sunny spaces" and new imperatives. Those sunny spaces are not the
same bright skies of the opening stanza. The moral imagination which
contemplates the sunny spaces in stanza 3 has been radically affected by the
vision of hell and death at mid-point. The sunny spaces (tragic optimism)
relate to the earlier morning skies (empty-headed cheerfulness) as does the
Catskill eagle to "the other birds upon the plain"; it is the sky, as the eagle
is a bird—but bird and sky have been raised to a higher power.

---

made him weep." Checking Emerson's remark, "Trust men and they will be true to you,"
Melville commented: "God help the poor fellow who squares his life according to this."
Emerson (in *The Poet*): "The evils of the world are such only to the evil eye"; and Melville: "What does the man mean? If Mr. Emerson travelling in Egypt should find a plague-
spot come out on him—would he consider that an evil sight or not? And if evil, would
his eye be evil because it seemed evil to his eye . . . ?" "Still," Melville added characteristically, in another place (opposite a passage in *Heroism*), "these essays are noble."

What Melville has done here is to accomplish what, in an ugly phrase translated from Nietzsche, has been called "the transvaluation of values": something which Melville had to do in his poet's way, by what we perhaps can call the "transfiguration of figures." The figures are drawn from Melville's own cultural environment; their transfiguration here is a *précis* of Melville's development—and of this chapter.

The passage may be cited as Melville's guess about the design of experience. Like Hawthorne, Melville testified to a spiritual journey from sunlight through the fires of hell to a final serenity. But Hawthorne's guess was present to his mind before he started writing; the writing merely tested it. It was what remained to him of a shredding religious tradition, and it was a guess rather than a creed just because the tradition was in shreds. But for Melville the business of writing was not so much a test as a consummation. His guess was what he came out with only after his experience had drawn significance out of his account of it in language.

He had to come far, in order, by December, 1850, to make even the tentative guess contained in chapter 96 of *Moby-Dick*. We can follow him on his way by looking briefly at some of his experiences and a couple of his books prior to *Moby-Dick: Typee* and *Redburn*. With the "Try-Works" passage as a guide, we find *Typee* corresponding in mood to the morning spirit of stanza 1; and *Redburn* to the sense of sickness in stanza 2. During his apprentice years, Melville had lacked the well-rounded sense of life's potential that Hawthorne had had from the outset. He tended to hang on to each successive discovery with exaggerated intensity, as though it were the whole of the truth; and he released his grasp and clutched at the fresh perception only when he had acquired the means of a fresh articulation. The measure of achievement in *Moby-Dick* is the measure of great new resources greatly possessed.

### III

Melville, who came of age in 1840 during the years when hopefulness was all the fashion, began his career as an unstable but energetic member of the forward-looking party. When he got around to reflecting on the American writer, he added his more robust accent to the hopeful program for literature: "This Vermont morning dew is as wet to my feet as Eden's dew to Adam's. . . . We want no American Goldsmiths; nay we want no American Miltons. . . . Let us boldly condemn all imitation." The accent was the product of personal experience; for Melville had long since contributed his robust symbolic gesture to that series of gestures by which the hopeful had signalized the driving motion from memory to hope. For Emerson, who could make so much out of so little, it had been enough to leave his Concord study and go tramping in mud puddles; Thoreau went farther, a few miles into the near-by woods to little Walden Pond. Melville's gesture was more sweeping and extravagant—he "jumped off" by crossing the Pacific and jumping ship to plunge into the interior of a primitive island. His action characterized a man whose imagination could expand into the mythic just because it was steadily nourished by the roughness of the actual. But as an act and as a kind of act, it assured the sequel: for in so all-engaging an assault upon life, Melville could scarcely avoid bumping into that part of it which was bitter, ugly, and destructive.

Melville and his friend Toby jumped ship in July, 1844. According to his account of the event two years later in *Typee,* the escape was made during a tremendous storm, and the first night was passed in a violence of wind and rain which left the narrator with "cold shiverings and a burning fever"—before the morning revealed "the beautiful scene" of the sunlit "Happy Valley." This suggests the transition accomplished more or less consciously in the book, even if only partially during the actual experience—a transition from the alarming night which begins "The Try-Works" meditation to the "natural sun" and the bright skies of "tomorrow," when "the morn will show in . . . gentler relief." The mood of *Typee* is pretty well warmed by "the golden, glorious, glad sun." Amid the wholly natural, preconventional life of the island paradise and during his Adam-and-Eve relation with Fayaway, Melville found a "continual happiness" and a surface beauty without blemish. "There seemed to be no cares, griefs, troubles, or vexation in all Typee." By contrast, civilization looked to Melville, from Typee, the way it would look to Thoreau, from his hut at Walden: a fantastic scene of self-imposed torments—"a thousand self-inflicted discomforts," as Melville said, with "a hundred evils in reserve."

Yet it was the very absence of cares and griefs and troubles that turned out to be unendurable. Melville stayed in fact less than a month in the Happy Valley; in *Typee,* he stayed over four months, for he was always able to invade and then enlarge ordinary units of time, he saw so much in any one moment; but he did depart at last, both in fact and in the book. In neither case was he altogether clear why such continual happiness was unacceptable. There was, to be sure, the occasional danger of being cooked and eaten; but Melville realized later that there had been a much greater danger of permanently arrested development. "That mortal man," Ishmael would say for him, "who hath more of joy than sorrow in him, that mortal man cannot be true—not true or undeveloped." All he could say at the time was that Polynesian life never advanced into the realm of spirit; its buoyancy, though extreme, came entirely from a "sense of mere physical existence." Melville's response was comparable to Thoreau's complaint that his neighbor, the French-Canadian backwoodsman, was an animal, a child. Life, in the Typee valley, was restricted to the visible spheres of love; it was Melville's restless ambition to penetrate to the invisible spheres, and it was his lot to find out that those were the spheres which were formed in fright.

So Melville returned to America. He never stopped "jumping off"; but after his return in 1844, the act was more purely symbolic and was co-extensive with Melville's effort to become a writer. The act now consisted in dispatching hero after hero, Adam after Adam, in novel after novel— sending them forth like Whitman's child, full of hopeful expectancy, only to tell how, in every case, they fell among cannibals: Wellingborough Redburn, the lad called "White-Jacket," Pierre Glendinning, and Billy Budd.

In *Redburn* (1849), the Adamic coloration of the experience which most interested Melville became explicit. This has been remarked by Melville's best commentator, Newton Arvin, who observes that the boy-hero of the novel "sets out from his mother's house in a state of innocence like that before the fall"; and the voyage to Liverpool and back comprises for young Redburn "the initiation of innocence into evil." Here we are at the second stage of Ishmael's soliloquy: the exploration of the degree of sickness in the world, of hospitals and jails and graveyards, of deserts and griefs and "Virginia's Dismal Swamp." For Melville and Redburn the swamp is not a comforting assurance of nature's variety, as it was for Thoreau. Much of the physical and spiritual disease the young lad discovers is packed symbolically into the demonic figure of the sailor Jackson; and Jackson is introduced eating a bowl of mush that "looked for all the world like . . . the Dismal Swamp of Virginia." With the appearance of Jackson, the consciousness alive in the story passes from the opening mood of elementary cheerfulness to the injured tone at the novel's center.

But the emphasis in *Redburn* is perhaps less upon what happens to the boy himself than upon the wretchedness and depravity that are uncovered as existing independently of him in the world; Redburn emerges with, at most, a sort of jocular but puzzled ruefulness, like that of Major Molineux's disillusioned cousin in Hawthorne's story. The Liverpool through which Redburn wanders, growing ever more appalled at its stench of corruption, may well remind us of the plague- and crime-ridden Philadelphia of *Arthur Mervyn;* but Redburn is more the passive spectator than the ludicrous reformer. What Redburn beholds in Launcelot's-Hey, along the dock walls, and in "the booble alleys" of Liverpool merely adds to the cluster of scabrous impressions that began with the deceitful pawnshop-keeper in New York and continued with the drunken sailor who jumps overboard on Redburn's first nightwatch and the plague which breaks out among the passengers. All these impressions become concentrated and intensified for Redburn, in the "foul lees and dregs of a man" which were all that remained of the dying Jackson. It is Jackson who reveals to Redburn the power of the scabrous, the terrible power of mental superiority when it possesses a nerve of the diabolic. "He was the weakest man, bodily, of the crew"; but he was the crew's bully. His power operated through and not in spite of his wasted appearance; and the strength of his fascination for Redburn (who is aware, though only very dimly indeed, that Jackson in turn is covertly fascinated by him) suggests something not yet articulated about disease in the world at large. Yet, while Jackson is a wicked man, as Redburn tells himself in his Sunday-school language; there is a still deeper possibility— that "his wickedness seemed to spring from his woe."

This conjunction of sickness and power and wickedness and sorrow is the substance of *Redburn:* these and the impression they make upon the lad's character. But if there is something more astir in the novel, it derives from another dead figure: Redburn's father—not from his presence but from the acknowledgment of his absence. In Liverpool, taking with him a guidebook which his father had used to explore that very city "years and years ago," Redburn sets forth to follow his father through the town, "performing a filial pilgrimage." The sense of his father becomes so vivid that Redburn feels that, if he hurries, he will "overtak[e] him around the Town

Hall . . . at the head of Castle Street." Both the hope and the guidebook are cheats; the guidebook is half a century out of date, and his father is not just around that corner or any other: "He had gone whither no son's search could find him in this world." This is the moment when Melville's hero realizes that he is an orphan; but since the realization comes together with the discovery of the amount of destructive unhealthiness in the world and in human nature, it has little of the hopeful joy of a liberation from family and history. It partakes rather of the tragic feeling of the lost son, or even, perhaps, of the son betrayed.

We ought to locate the moment chronologically not in 1839, when young Herman Melville actually did visit Liverpool, but ten years later, when he was investing that visit with meaning in the writing of *Redburn*. For in that book, two perceptions which would be the making of Melville as an artist hovered on the verge of fusion—the betrayal by the father and the corruption in nature. These were the elements which decisively shaped Melville's treatment of the hopeful legend: what we may cautiously call the "objective"—the knot of hostility in the very structure of created things; and the "subjective"—the bubbling-up of whatever Melville had suffered during those dreadful weeks in 1831 when his bankrupt father went mad and died, leaving behind (abandoning, deserting, as it must have seemed to the bewildered child) a lost, helpless, poverty-stricken family. These were the elements and the perceptions which took the form of a growing resentment in Melville: something which only just begins to get into the writing of *Redburn,* but which had, as Auden puts it, to "blow itself quite out" in the books that followed.

*Moby-Dick* begins where *Redburn* leaves off. The hero, all too absorbed in his contemplation of that "hopper of misfortune" to which Redburn alludes in his closing pages, is now "growing grim about the mouth." He has a "damp, drizzly November" in his soul; he pauses before coffin warehouses and falls into line in funeral processions. He wants to knock people's hats off and speculates about suicide. He has come so far from the saluting of the glad sun of morning that he feels most at home seated on a tombstone. No one should miss the fine, firm, knowing humor of these sentences in the first chapter of *Moby-Dick*. It is the firmest humor in the world: the humor which results from tragedy, and specifically from the "tragedy of mind" symbolically re-enacted in the story of *Moby-Dick*. But *Moby-Dick,* for all its humor, is, of course, a novel ablaze with anger. Yet it is the humor, or what the humor represents, that makes us fully aware of the scope of the anger.

What had been a mere rustle of resentment over a world false to the promises of hope had grown, by 1851, into a fury of disenchantment: Adam gone mad with disillusion. *Moby-Dick* manages to give very clear voice to that fury. If Melville could not yet overcome his anger, he was able to do something which a number of his critics would regard as better. He was able to hold his anger in balance, which may have been the only way to bring it alive and make it clear. Melville had discovered how to establish an attitude toward his own sense of outrage or, inversely, how to establish his outrage in relation to a comprehensive and in some ways traditional attitude. The relation expresses itself in *Moby-Dick* in the actual dramatic relation between frenzied Ahab and farseeing Ishmael; and psychologizing critics might tell us that what happens in the novel is the "splitting-off" of a personality first introduced as Ishmael into fragments of itself—one still called Ishmael, others called Ahab and Starbuck and Pip and so on. But we can regard the achievement in terms of the materials of narrative. From this viewpoint, it may be argued that the success of *Moby-Dick* and the clarity of its anger are due to Melville's peculiar, yet skilful, exploitation of the legacy of European literature—and "the tradition" which that literature has made manifest.

The legacy was the greatest of Melville's resources as, in his own way and according to his own needs, he gradually came into possession of it. The anger in *Moby-Dick* becomes resonant in the tension it creates with the legacy and the tradition. And, conversely, it is the tradition which—in the choral voice of Ishmael and for what it is worth within the ironic frame of the novel—transvaluates the values implicit in the anger.

## IV

For the author of *Moby-Dick,* the central strain in the European tradition was tragic. The tragic sensibility defined in the long quotation from the "Try-Works" is attributed to books as well as to men: "That mortal man who hath more of joy than sorrow in him, that mortal man cannot be true— not true or undeveloped. With books the same." There, plainly enough, is an antihopeful judgment, and almost the reverse of it can be read on many pages of Emerson and Thoreau. But there is a point beyond that, which has to do with the creative process itself; and we should recall the actual  experience out of which Ishmael's meditation rises, for the enterprise of trying-out was an explicit trope for Melville of the act of creativity. He wrote Dana, while at work on *Moby-Dick,* that the novel would be "a strange sort of book . . . blubber is blubber you know; though you might get oil out of it, the poetry runs as hard as sap from a frozen maple-tree." And since trying-out was associated in the story with so hellish a scene and nightmarish an experience, it is hard to resist the inference that creativity for Melville was closely, dangerously, associated with the monstrous vision of evil. You have to go through hell, he suggests, either to get the oil or to write the book.

Melville, that is to say, belongs to the company of gifted romantics from Blake and Baudelaire to Thomas Mann, who have supposed that art is somehow the flower of evil and that the power through which the shaping imagination is raised to greatness may also be a power which destroys the artist; for it is the strength derived from the knowledge of evil—not the detached study, but perhaps a very descent into the abyss. At some stage or other, Melville felt, art had to keep an appointment with wickedness. He believed with Hawthorne that, in order to achieve moral maturity, the individual had to engage evil and suffer the consequences; and he added the conviction that, in order to compose a mature work of literature, the artist had to enter without flinching into the "spheres of fright." For Melville, the two experiences happened not to be separable.

But how, having looked into the fire, was the artist to articulate his vision of evil in language? Still another clue is provided by the "Try-Works." It can scarcely be a coincidence that, after the slices of blubber (the source of oil) have been pointedly referred to as "Bible leaves," the insight gained from the spectacle is conveyed by Ishmael in a cluster of biblical references. The "Bible leaves" are passed through the furnaces, and oil is the result; similarly, Melville hints, the formed and incrusted language of the past must be "tried-out" in the transforming heat of the imagination, and the result is the shaped perception which can light up the work of art.

The transforming process was crucial, for Melville never simply echoed the words of the great books of the past; he subjected them to tremendous pressure and forced them to yield remarkable new revelations. His characterizing "relation to tradition" was extremely ambiguous: it was no more the willing enslavement exemplified by the nostalgic than it was the blithe patriotic indifference manifested by the hopeful. I take his reading and his treatment of the *Odyssey* of Homer as a major illustration of Melville's "trying-out" of a traditional poem.

Melville's Homer, like Keats's, was the Homer of George Chapman. He acquired the Chapman translations in 1858 and preferred them at once to the translations by Pope, which he probably read (and read carefully) as early as 1848.[5] What impresses us at once as we follow his check-marks, underlinings, and marginal comments through the poems is this: that Melville was a creative reader; he was the poet as reader who became the reader as poet. His markings, rarely casual or isolated, fall usually upon essential threads and force the poems to yield the figure within them. But it is Melville's figure, and not always the figure we are accustomed to discover ourselves.

His responsive reader's effect upon the *Iliad* is, to be sure, less conspicuous than its effect upon the *Odyssey*. The *Iliad*, under Melville's inspection, emerges as the somber portrait of a world at war, of sorrowing men caught up in vast forces and moving without hope to the violent death which awaits them, under the rule of implacable divinities. This is perhaps the *Iliad* we too are disposed to see; though it was not the *Iliad* of Melville's contemporary, Emerson, whose hopeful reading showed him only the "firm and cheerful temper" of a Homer who lay in the sunshine. But Melville read the *Odyssey* on a more symbolic level; his markings lead it to take the form of a tragic *Bildungsroman,* with the relation between the characters and the sequence of events standing for growth of insight into the heart of reality. There is evidence of Melville's immense enjoyment of the adventures themselves; but he was primarily interested in meaning.

The meaning Melville found borrows force from the unusual emphasis his markings laid upon the griefs and hardships of Odysseus and the

---

[5] *Cf.* Merton M. Sealts, Jr., "Melville's Reading: A Check-List of Books Owned and Borrowed," *Harvard Library Bulletin,* Vol. III, No. 2 (spring, 1949), pp. 268 ff. I quote from a letter Mr. Sealts kindly wrote to me, February 21, 1949: "On 19 March 1848 HM was charged with '1 Classical Library, 37 v. 12.23.' . . . Pope's Homer constitutes three of the volumes." Melville purchased the complete works of Pope at some time after 1856. Mr. Sealts concludes: "He may have known [Pope's Homer] before *Moby-Dick* or even as early as his days at the Albany Academy, though that last is pure speculation. He *almost* bought a Chapman's Homer in London" in 1849.

generalizations about the evil lot of mankind, to the point where a rich and spacious poem looks surprisingly gloomier than we remembered it. Melville seized upon the recurring descriptions of Odysseus and his dwindling crew sailing on, stricken at heart after some frightful encounter; and he made much of the hero's artful lament to Nausicäa that he was the victim of "a cruel habit of calamity" (vi, 257). He marked the disclaimer of Telemachus:

> Not by any means
> If Hope should prompt me or *blind confidence*
> (*The God of fools*) or ever deity
> Should will it, for 'tis past my destiny.
> [iii. 309—Melville's italics.]

And the reaction of Telemachus to the dishonor shown his father:

> Never more let any sceptre-bearing man
> Benevolent, or mild, or human be,
> Nor in his mind form acts of piety,
> But ever feed on blood [ii. 348].

The gods are no more benevolent than they had been in Melville's *Iliad*. There they had comprised a remote and hostile race, indifferent to man and interfering in his affairs only to blast his tenuous hopes; here Melville obtrudes Nestor's observation that "I know God studied misery to hurl against us" (iii). By focusing attention on these lines and many more like them, Melville forced the *Odyssey* to move perceptibly, to shift and re-form; he exposed within it a vision of terror and evil which casts a deep shadow over the beauty and steady assurance the poem could otherwise be seen to reflect.

That vision is the frame for the educational process Melville traces for us. The process begins with the departure of Telemachus for sandy Pylos and the admonitions of his nurse and his mother, both of which are strongly checked:

> It fits not you so young
> To suffer so much by the aged seas
> And err in such a wayless wilderness [ii. 545].

> Why left my son his mother? Why refused
> His wit the solid shore to try the seas
> And put in ships the trust of his distress
> That are at sea to man unbridled horse,
> And run past rule? [iv. 492.]

The echoes of Redburn and of Melville's personal life and relation to his mother are clear. Going to sea, both in deed and in symbol, was always Melville's way of fronting what Thoreau called "the essential facts of life"; and what must be stressed is that the venture was so much the more harrowing for Melville because malice and evil were central among the facts to be fronted. As he read on in the *Odyssey*, Melville ran a line alongside Proteus' warning to Menelaus, indicative of the dangerous nature of the venture:

> Cease
> To ask so far. It fits not to be
> So cunning in thine own calamity.
> Nor seek to learn what learned thou shouldst forget.
> Men's knowledges have proper limits set
> And should not prease into the mind of God [iv. 657].

Melville's conviction about the peril did not prevent his own heroes from making the plunge nevertheless and "preasing" with all their might into the mind of God: into whatever it was which lay behind the appearances of things; and so they all "suffered so much by the aged seas." It is with the suffering and the lies and the silence of the much-buffeted Odysseus that Melville's pencilings of the *Odyssey* come to an end.

Having noticed Homer's observation (vi. 198) that "the hard pass [Odysseus] had at sea stuck by him," and, having digested the obvious fabrications with which Odysseus regaled the court of Antinöus, Melville greeted the wanderer's decision, upon arriving at last in Ithaca, with one of his heaviest markings, three emphatic lines in the margin:

> He bestowed
> A veil on truth; for evermore did wind
> About his bosom a most crafty mind [xiii. 370].

That scene, in which the slippery explanations of Odysseus are affectionately shown up by Athena, can be read as high comedy. If Melville did not read it so, and if this moment is one of the last he would underscore in the poem, it was not only because he felt as Lear's Fool felt (in a passage he checked elsewhere) that "Truth's a dog must to kennel." To suppose so would be to remember the markings while forgetting the poem. And I want to suggest that the markings and the poem together make a curious tension which is representative both of Melville's relation to tradition and of the operation of that relation in the best of his fiction.

Melville had perhaps the most strenuous doubts of his generation about the possibility of uttering the truth, and in his later years he was greatly taken by Arnold's allusion to the "power and beauty in the well-kept secret of one's self and one's thoughts." Here we find him, perhaps, attributing such beauty to the secretive Odysseus in Ithaca. But these doubts were embraced by a larger doubt which had to do with the nature of the truth to be uttered; and Melville was increasingly sure that truth was double—that it was dialectical and contained, so far as any poet could utter it, in a tension. In his reading of the *Odyssey*, Melville inserted a tension into the poem: the tension between his own tragic and truncated design—the departure, the journey of inquiry, the suffering, the secretiveness—and the grand pattern which the poem nonetheless maintains of homecoming, reunion, and resounding victory.

Melville's reading reinforces the sense we have of how any formal and formulated myth functions in *Moby-Dick* and afterward. What I have said about the *Odyssey* myth can be matched by his response to the Christian myth (if that is the right phrase for it), or to the tragedies of Aeschylus or Shakespeare. Bits and pieces or the whole of these myths are introduced into the narrative. But they are not precisely the model echoed in the central

action, re-enacted by the main event. They are the known elements by a
sort of bold breaching of which the incident or the character or the phrase
or the whole action must be understood. Yet the mythic elements are not
negated either. They serve to comment contrapuntally on the action and
the hero, which, of course, comment in turn upon them: and this is how the
figures on both sides become transfigured.

The process is not always radiant in Melville, for the traditional materials
appear raggedly, they are lumpy and not altogether digested; there is
hardly a doctrinaire theory behind their treatment. A much clearer example
in recent fiction is the functioning of *The Divine Comedy* in Thomas
Mann's *The Magic Mountain*. When, for instance, Hans Castorp's second
"guide," Naphta, challenges the young man's first "guide," Settembrini,
to a duel and then kills himself, we are meant to hear the almost endless
discordant vibrations set up by the contrast between this event and the
relation, in the *Comedy,* of Dante's guides—Virgil (whom Settembrini
cherishes and resembles) and Beatrice (like Naphta, a theologian). The
relation between Virgil and Beatrice is perfectly harmonious; it enacts,
indeed, the process toward perfection; it dramatizes the formula of St.
Thomas that grace does not destroy nature but perfects it. The harmonious
hum of the *Comedy* behind the pistol-shots of *The Magic Mountain* establishes the tension: a tension of symbolic relationships, which is a tension
of worlds; and the world of Mann's novel announces itself in its ironic
contrast to Dante's.

Nothing so crafty or so conscious may be found in the fiction of Melville; yet the achievement is comparable. And even the lumpiness of the
traditional elements included is significant: significant, anyhow, that his
relation to the tradition was American. For the American writer has never
(if he is honest and American) been able to pretend an authentic initial
communion with the European past; and especially not if he begins, as
Melville did, imbued with the antitraditional principles of the party of Hope.
He can know a great deal, even everything, about that past; he can go
after it, which is just the demonstration that he is not in communion with it.
And if he establishes a communion, it is one of a quite different order from
that which most European writers—until 1939, at least—possessed as their
birthright. The American kind of communion will usually be a sort of
tussle, and the best of our writers (like Melville) can convert the tussle into
drama. At the same time, since the American writer is outside the organic
world of European literature to start with, there is no limit to how much
of the world he can draw upon. He has the Protestant's contempt for the
long line of commentary and influence; he can go directly to the source
and find it anywhere. Nothing is his by right; and so nothing constrains
him; and nothing, ultimately, is denied him. Such has been and such must
continue to be the actual relation between the American writer and the
European tradition: a queer and vigilant relation, at once hospitable and
hostile, at once unlimited and uneasy.[6]

6 *Cf.* the discussion of "communion" in chap. 9, and especially in the closing pages of that
chapter. "Communion"—or the attempt to achieve it—is, I suggest there, a link between
the various members of what I call "the third party": the elder James, Bushnell, Hawthorne, Melville, Parkman, etc. *Cf.* also the mention [in chap. 8] of the American loss of
"communion with history."

## V

A comparison between the description of Jackson in *Redburn* and our first glimpse of Ahab in *Moby-Dick* may further illustrate Melville's practice. Here is Jackson: "Nothing was left of this Jackson but the foul lees and dregs of a man; he was thin as a shadow; nothing but skin and bones; and sometimes used to complain that it hurt him to sit on the hard chests." A man who could write a sentence like that might not be thought to need any further resources. There had been no sentence in previous American fiction to match its deceptive cadence, its linking of perfectly common language with the shock of almost literally felt visual detail. These words *stick* to their subject. But then here is Ahab:

He looked like a man cut away from the stake, when the fire has overrunningly wasted all the limbs without consuming them, or taking away one particle from their compacted aged robustness. . . . His bone-leg steadied in that hole; one arm elevated, and holding by a shroud; Captain Ahab stood erect, looking straight out beyond the ship's ever-pitching prow. There was an infinity of firmest fortitude, a determinate, unsurrenderable wilfulness, in the fixed and fearless, forward dedication of that glance. Not a word he spoke; nor did his officers say aught to him; though by all their minutest gestures and expressions, they plainly showed the uneasy, if not painful consciousness, of being under a troubled master-eye. And not only that, but moody stricken Ahab stood before them with a crucifixion in his face; in all the nameless regal overbearing dignity of some mighty woe.

The visual image is not less sharp; but it is incomparably larger, indeed it is almost outsize—and chiefly because Ahab is animated within a density of suggestive and echoing language that carries us into the outsize world of heroic legend, without wholly detaching us from the hard wood of the quarter-deck. But the substance of that heroic dimension is a fusion of violently contradictory "visions"—the vision vitalized by anger and vengeance and pride and wilfulness, on the one hand, and the vision of Christian-cum-Greek tragic acceptance, on the other.
It is in the interplay, the so to speak open-ended dialectic, of the visions that Melville's "relation to tradition" is to be found and where his expanded resources reveal themselves. Ahab's heroic pride, his wilfulness, his defiance of God and his destruction of the world make sense within our imaginative recollection (constantly prodded throughout the novel) of Christian heroism —meekness, submission, obedience, and the salvation of mankind. Annihilation at sea makes sense within our stimulated recollection of the homecoming myth, the *Odyssey*. *Moby-Dick*'s sustained mood of impending disaster sharpens itself against the Homeric echo of impending triumph. The cosmic anger of Ahab at betrayal, by God, by the father, is correlative to Melville's anger at the devastating betrayal by experience of the promises of hope. All this rage assumes its full dimension because it is established in opposition to the traditionally comprehensive acceptance voiced by Father Mapple and by Ishmael.
*Moby-Dick* is an elaborate pattern of countercommentaries, the supreme instance of the dialectical novel—a novel of tension without resolution.

Ishmael's meditation, which transfigures the anger and sees beyond the sickness and the evil, is only one major voice in the dramatic conversation; and not until *Billy Budd* does this voice become transcendent and vic- torious. In *Moby-Dick*, Melville adopted a unique and off-beat tradition- alism—a steadily ambiguous re-rendering of the old forms and fables once unequivocally rejected by the hopeful—in order to recount the total blast- ing of the vision of innocence. He went beyond a spurious artistic originality to give narrative birth to the conflict with evil: that evil against which a spurious and illusory innocence must shatter itself. In doing so, he not only achieved a sounder originality but moved a great step toward perceiving a more durable innocence. In *Pierre,* the following year, Melville faltered and went back once more over the old dreary ground of disillusion; but in *Billy Budd,* he was to come home.

## VI

The new Adam . . . is the Lord from heaven [ST. PAUL, I Cor. 45–47].

At least one of Melville's critics has found Homer's *Odyssey* a broad metaphor useful not only for gauging Melville's novels but also for de- scribing his life. Toward the end of that life, W. H. Auden says in his poem "Herman Melville":

> he sailed into an extraordinary mildness,
> And anchored in his home and reached his wife
> And rode within the harbour of her hand,
> And went across each morning to an office
> As though his occupation were another island.

> Goodness existed: that was the new knowledge
> His terror had to blow itself quite out
> To let him see it; but it was the gale had blown him
> Past the Cape Horn of sensible success
> Which cries: "This rock is Eden. Shipwreck here."

Mr. Auden's poem, which outlines Melville's life perhaps a shade too tidily by means of the Homeric allusions, has to do with the final tranquillity and the firm concluding Christian acquiescence out of which—according to Mr. Auden—Melville composed *Billy Budd.*

> . . . now he cried in exultation and surrender
> "The Godhead is broken like bread. We are the pieces."
> And sat down at his desk and wrote a story.

Melville's cry about "the Godhead" was in fact uttered in 1851, in the letter responding to Hawthorne's praise of *Moby-Dick,* some forty years before Melville sat down at his desk in New York and wrote Billy's story. But *Billy Budd* is, of course, unmistakably the product of aged serenity; its author has unmistakably got beyond his anger or discovered the key to it; and it would be pointless to deny that it is a testament of acceptance, as Mr. Watson has said, or a "Nunc Dimittis," as Mr. Arvin proposes. It is woeful, but wisely, no longer madly. Its hero is sacrificially hanged at sea, but its author has come home, like Odysseus.

In Melville's last work, the New World's representative hero and his representative adventure receive a kind of sanctification. Mr. R. P. Blackmur has said of the last three novels of Henry James that they approach the condition of poetry, which Mr. Blackmur explains as the exemplification in language of the soul in action—"the inner life of the soul at the height of its struggle, for good or evil, with the outer world which it must deny, or renounce, or accept." This, precisely, is what *Billy Budd* asks us to say about it; *Billy Budd* helps us to see that the action so described is one grounded in the pressures and counterpressures not of any world but of the New World. It is the action of the soul in general as shaped under a New World perspective. Melville's achievement was double: he brought myth into contemporary life, and he elevated that life into myth—at once transcending and reaffirming the sense of life indicated by the party of Hope.

Compare, for example, the personality and the career of the Handsome Sailor with the analysis of historic American Adamism offered by Horace Bushnell in 1858. Billy is innocence personified—"To be nothing more than innocent!" Claggart exclaims, in malice and tears. He can neither read nor write, though he can sing like an angel. He springs from nowhere; he returns a cheerful "No, sir," to the officer's question, "Do you know anything about your beginning?" "His entire family was practically invested in himself." He fulfils every hopeful requirement; no historic process or influence intrudes between him and the very dawn of time; his defining qualities seem to be "exceptionally transmitted from a period prior to Cain's city and citified man."

So it can be said of him that he "was little more than an upright barbarian, much such as Adam presumably might have been ere the urbane Serpent wriggled himself into his company," and that "in the nude [he] might have posed for a statue of Adam before the Fall." This is just the personality that Bushnell saw his culture fostering and which he deplored. Even Billy's stammer and his illiteracy are integral to the portrait: they are the evidence of that "condition privative," they constitute that "necessary defect of knowledge and consequent weakness" which Bushnell assigned to any "free person or . . . power considered as having just begun to be." The defect and the weakness, under Claggart's goading, precipitate the disaster; and Billy falls, as the mythological Adam had fallen, and as Bushnell foresaw that any Adamic American would fall. The myth enters into the life and re-enacts itself: *but not at the expense of the life.* Bushnell invoked the myth in order to chastise the tendencies of life in his day. But if Melville celebrates the fall, he also celebrates the one who fell; and the qualities and attitudes which insure the tragedy are reaffirmed in their indestructible worth even in the moment of defeat. Melville exposed anew the danger of innocence and its inevitable tragedy; but in the tragedy he rediscovered a heightened value in the innocence.

Melville's achievement, as in *Moby-Dick,* was an artistic achievement, and it may be measured by the failure of *Pierre,* more than three decades earlier. For the action fumbled with in *Pierre* is essentially the same as that of *Billy Budd.* From the moment on the novel's first page when we are introduced to a "green and golden World" and see young Pierre on a "morning in June . . . issuing from the embowr'd . . . home of his fathers . . . dewily refreshed and spiritualized by sleep," we know where we are and what and whom we have to deal with. The very language contains strong verbal echoes of Whitman's most explicit Adamic verse:

> As Adam, early in the morning,
> Walking forth from the bower refresh'd with sleep . . .

The story of Pierre Glendinning consists in the explosion of what Dr. Murray has called "this myth of paradise"—an explosion resulting from an unpreparedness for the subsequent myth of the Fall; and in the explosion both the book and its hero are blown to pieces. It is not the hero who is at fault; he is not obliged to be prepared, his condition forbids it. But we have the impression that the hero's inventor was unprepared: he is not less shocked than Pierre when he sees what he says. The symbolic distance accomplished in *Moby-Dick* narrows fatally in *Pierre;* and if ever there was a case of symbolic suicide in literature, it is Melville's in the indiscriminate destruction in the concluding pages of *Pierre.* The myth which had been an ambiguous source of strength in *Moby-Dick* has now overwhelmed the life. And so in *Clarel,* Melville's next extensive piece of writing, we are not surprised to find an imagination winding its way through a maze of waste-land imagery, quite explicitly lamenting the bewildering and painful loss of Eden.

The recovery in *Billy Budd* is astonishing. The entire story moves firmly in the direction of a transcendent cheerfulness: transcendent, and so neither bumptious nor noisy; a serene and radiant gladness. The climax is prepared with considerable artistry by a series of devices which, though handled somewhat stiffly by a rusty creative talent, do their work nonetheless. The intent of all of them is to bring into being and to identify the hero and his role and then to institute the magical process of transfiguration. Billy appears as another Adam: thrust (like Redburn and Pierre) into a world for which his purity altogether unfits him. His one ally, the Danish sailor who is the prophetic figure in the story, eyes Billy with "an expression of speculative query as to what might eventually befall a nature like that, dropped into a world not without some mantraps and against whose subtleties simple courage lacking experience and address and without any touch of defensive ugliness is of little avail; and where such innocence as man is capable of does yet in a moral emergency not always sharpen the faculties or enlighten the will." [7]

The Dansker carries the burden of awareness within the *novella*—awareness that "the matter of Adam" is being tested again; and the atmosphere grows thick with echoes of *Paradise Lost.* But all the time, other energies are linguistically at work. Melville sets swirling around his hero other allusions which relate Billy by inference to other beings: splendid animals,

[7] *Melville's Billy Budd,* p. 177. Mr. Freeman, the editor, observes in a footnote that Melville wrote "an expression of speculative *foresight,*" then changed the final word to "query." It is instructive to watch, with Mr. Freeman's scholarly aid, as Melville subdues his more explicitly ritualistic language to the more realistic and dramatic.

Catholic priests, royalty, the gods—Apollo, Hercules, Hyperion. It is the
destiny of these figures to suffer transfiguration, to die into their sacrificial
counterparts—the sacrificial bull, the "condemned Vestal priestesses," the
slain monarch, and the dying god. This is the process by which Adam
changes into the "new Adam" of St. Paul—"the Lord from heaven." The
value of the American Adam is thereby, at last, transvalued.

   The process is both complicated and enhanced by the ironically entitled
"digression" on Lord Nelson. The story of the common sailor is suddenly
stretched into great drama by a glimpse of the "heroic personality" of "the
greatest sailor since the world began." Nelson, too, is killed at sea; and
Melville anticipates the quality of Billy's death by investing Nelson, at the
moment of *his* "most glorious death," with "a priestly motive," which led
him to adorn himself as "for the altar and the sacrifice." The classical
drama of the heroic nobleman points up the little adventure of the stam-
mering and illiterate orphan; and Melville gets back to that adventure by
remarking that profoundest passion does not need "a palatial stage" but may
be enacted "down among the groundlings."

   Accused by Claggart of mutiny and thereupon striking and killing his
accuser, Billy Budd falls like Adam, tempted (through Eve) by the serpent; it is observed that the lifeless sergeant-at-arms resembles "a dead snake."
In the court-martial and conviction of Billy which follow, the institution-
alized world has its familiar way with the defenseless hero. But where the
Hawthorne version came to its end in the imprisonment of Donatello, a
new dimension of meaning and emotion is introduced in *Billy Budd,* and
the story moves toward ecstasy. The sense of divine commandment is indicated in a linking of Billy with Isaac; and the ship's deck—where Billy lies
handcuffed and at peace through the vigil of his death—is associated with
a cathedral. The pitch of exaltation is reached at the instant of the hanging.

   The last signal . . . was given. At the same moment it chanced that the vapory
   fleece hanging low in the East, was shot through with a soft glory as of the fleece
   of the Lamb of God seen in mystical vision, and simultaneously therewith, watched
   by the wedged masses of upturned faces, Billy ascended; and, ascending, took the
   full rose of the dawn.

   After such a sentence, which is wholly saved from sentimentality by the
breath-taking detail of the "wedged masses," it must be regretted that Melville thought it necessary to tell us that, for the sailors who witness the
sacrificial death, a chip of the spar from which Billy was hanged "was as a
piece of the Cross." It is enough that Captain Vere, dying himself a little
time later, murmurs "Billy Budd, Billy Budd" at the last—in agony of spirit,
but also in a kind of prayer. And it is enough that the manner of Billy's
death transforms the sailors' mutinous anger into acceptance and understanding and that, for them, Billy is the subject of song and fable thereafter.

   Billy is the type of scapegoat hero, by whose sacrifice the sins of his world
are taken away: in this case, the world of the H.M.S. "Indomitable" and
the British navy, a world threatened by a mutiny which could destroy it.
Melville brought to bear upon such a hero and his traditional fate an
imagination of mythic capabilities: I mean an imagination able to detect

the intersection of divine, supernatural power and human experience; an imagination which could suggest the theology of life without betraying the limits of literature. Hawthorne, for example, had only very faint traces of such an imagination; his fiction never (unless in *The Scarlet Letter*) rose beyond the unequivocally humanistic level of insight and expression. He realized that the "pristine virtues" would inevitably encompass their possessor's destruction; and for him the proper denouement was the acquisition through suffering of different and tougher virtues. His version of the fortunate fall found the fortune in the faller; and it suggested an acceptance of the world and its authority. In the doctrine of *felix culpa,* the Fall was regarded as fortunate not because of its effect upon Adam the sinner but because of its effect upon God the redeemer; and the world was to be transformed thereafter. Melville's achievement was to recover the higher plane of insight, without intruding God on a machine: by making the culprit himself the redeemer.

It is this, I suggest, which accounts for something that might otherwise bother us in the *novella:* the apparent absence of impressive change—not in the world but in the character of Billy Budd. We expect our tragic heroes to change and to reveal (like Donatello) a dimensionally increased understanding of man's ways or of God's ways to man. Billy is as innocent, as guileless, as trusting, as *loving,* when he hangs from the yardarm as when he is taken off the "Rights of Man." What seems like failure, in this respect and on Melville's part, is exactly the heart of the accomplishment. For the change effected in the story has to do with the *reader,* as representative of the onlooking world: with the perception forced on him of the indestructible and in some sense the absolute value of "the pristine virtues." The perception is aroused by exposing the Christlike nature of innocence and love, which is to raise those qualities to a higher power—to their highest power. Humanly speaking, those qualities are fatal; but they alone can save the world.

So, in *Billy Budd,* Melville's own cycle of experience and commitment, which began with the hopeful dawn and "the glorious, glad, golden sun," returns again to the dawn—but a dawn transfigured, "seen in mystical vision." Melville salvaged the legend of hope both for life and for literature: by repudiating it in order to restore it in an apotheosis of its hero. There will be salvation yet, the story hints, from that treacherous dream.

# APPENDIX

## DIVERSE ESSAYS ON INDIVIDUAL WORKS

The essays below represent examples of the various critical methods included in this book as they apply to single important works in English and American literature. An asterisk indicates that the item noted appears in this collection.

### Shakespeare: KING LEAR

Donnelly, John, "Incest, Ingratitude and Insanity: Aspects of the Psychopathology of King Lear," *Psychoanalytic Review*, XL (1953), 149–155.

Empson, William, *The Structure of Complex Words* (London, 1951), pp. 125–157.

Freud, Sigmund, "The Theme of the Three Caskets," *Complete Psychological Works of Sigmund Freud,* ed. James Strachey, Vol. XII (London, 1958), pp. 291–301.

*Heilman, Robert, *This Great Stage: Image and Structure in "King Lear"* (Baton Rouge, 1948), pp. 67–87.

Jaffa, Harry V., "The Limits of Politics: An Interpretation of *King Lear,* Act I, Scene I," *American Political Science Review,* LI (1957), 405–427.

Knight, G. Wilson, *The Wheel of Fire* (London, 1949), pp. 177–206.

Pearson, Hesketh, *A Life of Shakespeare* (New York, 1961), pp. 139–145.

Rinehart, Keith, "The Moral Background of *King Lear,*" *University of Kansas City Review,* XX (Summer, 1954), 223–228.

Smirnov, A. A., *Shakespeare* (New York, 1936), pp. 68–71.

Spurgeon, Caroline, *Shakespeare's Imagery and What It Tells Us* (Cambridge, 1936), pp. 338–343.

## *Milton:* LYCIDAS

Adams, Richard P., "Archetypal Patterns of Death and Rebirth in Milton's *Lycidas*," *PMLA,* LXIV (1949), 183–188.

Battestin, Martin C., "John Crowe Ransom and *Lycidas:* A Reappraisal," *College English,* XVII (1956), 223–228.

Brooks, Cleanth and John E. Hardy, *Poems of Mr. John Milton* (New York, 1951), pp. 169–186.

Daiches, David, *Milton* (London, 1957), pp. 85–92.

Frye, Northrop, "Literature as Context: Milton's *Lycidas*," *University of North Carolina Studies in Comparative Literature,* XXIII (1959), 44–55.

Hanford, James Holly, "The Pastoral Elegy and Milton's *Lycidas*," *PMLA,* XXV (1910), 403–447.

More, Paul Elmer, *On Being Human* (Princeton, 1936), pp. 184–202.

Prince, F. T., *The Italian Element in Milton's Verse* (Oxford, 1954), pp. 71–88.

Ransom, John Crowe, *The World's Body* (New York, 1938), pp. 1–28.

Tillyard, E. M. W., *Milton* (London, 1930), pp. 76–85.

Tuve, Rosemond, *Images and Themes in Five Poems by Milton* (Cambridge, Mass., 1957), pp. 73–111.

## *Coleridge:* THE ANCIENT MARINER

Babbitt, Irving, *On Being Creative and Other Essays* (Boston, 1932), pp. 97–133.

Beres, David, "A Dream, A Vision, and a Poem: A Psycho-Analytic Study of the Origins of the *Rime of the Ancient Mariner*," *International Journal of Psycho-Analysis,* XXXII (1951), 97–116.

*Bodkin, Maud, *Archetypal Patterns in Poetry: Psychological Studies of Imagination* (London, 1934), pp. 26–89.

Bowra, C. M., *The Romantic Imagination* (Cambridge, Mass., 1949), pp. 67–75.

Buckley, Vincent, "Coleridge: Vision and Actuality," *The Melbourne Critical Review,* I (1961), 3–17.

Fausset, Hugh I'Anson, *Samuel Taylor Coleridge* (New York, 1926), pp. 160–169.

Harding, D. W., "The Theme of 'The Ancient Mariner,'" *Scrutiny,* VIII (1940), 406–411.

Lowes, John Livingston, *The Road to Xanadu: A Study in the Ways of the Imagination* (Boston, 1927), pp. 125–134.

Tillyard, E. M. W., *Five Poems 1470–1870* (London, 1948), pp. 74–86.

Warren, Robert Penn, "A Poem of Pure Imagination," *Kenyon Review,* VIII (Summer, 1946), 402–418.

## *Melville:* MOBY-DICK

Baird, James, *Ishmael* (Baltimore, 1956), pp. 317–337.

Bezanson, Walter E., "*Moby-Dick:* Work of Art," *Moby-Dick Centennial Essays,* eds. Tyrus Hillway and Luther S. Mansfield (Dallas, 1953), pp. 30–58.

Blackmur, R. P., "The Craft of Herman Melville," *The Virginia Quarterly Review,* XIV (Spring, 1938), 266–282.

Feidelson, Charles, Jr., *Symbolism and American Literature* (Chicago, 1953), pp. 27–35.

Hutchinson, William H., "A Definitive Edition of *Moby-Dick,*" *American Literature,* XXV (1954), 472–478.

Murray, Henry A., "In Nomine Diaboli," *Moby-Dick Centennial Essays,* eds. Tyrus Hillway and Luther S. Mansfield (Dallas, 1953), pp. 3–21.

Rourke, Constance, *American Humor: A Study of the National Character* (New York, 1931), pp. 191–200.

Slochower, Harry, "Freudian Motifs in *Moby-Dick,*" *Complex,* III (Fall, 1950), 16–25.

Smith, Henry Nash, "The Image of Society in *Moby-Dick,*" *Moby-Dick Centennial Essays,* eds. Tyrus Hillway and Luther S. Mansfield (Dallas, 1953), pp. 59–75.

Vincent, Howard P., *The Trying-Out of Moby-Dick* (Cambridge, Mass., 1949), pp. 55–117.

Winters, Yvor, *In Defense of Reason* (Denver, 1960), pp. 200–221.

## *Faulkner:* THE SOUND AND THE FURY

Burgum, Edwin Berry, *The Novel and the World's Dilemma* (New York, 1947), pp. 205–215.

Campbell, Harry Modean and Ruel E. Foster, *William Faulkner: A Critical Appraisal* (Norman, 1951), pp. 125–130.

Collins, Carvel, "The Interior Monologues of *The Sound and the Fury,*" *English Institute Essays 1952,* ed. Alan S. Downer (New York, 1954), pp. 29–56.

Edel, Leon, *The Psychological Novel 1900–1950* (New York, 1955), pp. 149–153.

Humphrey, Robert, "The Form and Function of Stream of Consciousness in William Faulkner's *The Sound and the Fury,*" *University of Kansas City Review,* XIX (Fall, 1952), 34–40.

Ryan, Marjorie, "The Shakespearean Symbolism in *The Sound and the Fury,*" *Faulkner Studies,* II (Fall, 1953), 40–44.

Thompson, Lawrance, "Mirror Analogues in *The Sound and the Fury,*" *English Institute Essays 1952,* ed. Alan S. Downer (New York, 1954), pp. 83–106.

Vickery, Olga W., *"The Sound and the Fury:* A Study in Perspective," *PMLA,* LXIX (1954), 1017–1037.

Waggoner, Hyatt H., *William Faulkner: From Jefferson to the World* (Lexington, 1959), pp. 34–43.

Wilder, Amos N., *Theology and Modern Literature* (Cambridge, Mass., 1958), pp. 119–131.